FORTRESS EUROPE

The Big Shiny Prison Vol. II c/o Ryan Bartek

Copyright © 2012 Ryan Bartek
"Fortress Europe (The Big Shiny Prison Vol. II)"
First Edition 2016 // All Rights Reserved.

ISBN/SKU: 9780692628430
ISBN Complete: 978-0-692-62843-0

Please ask your local book store to carry books by Anomie Press. **Anomie Press is a D.I.Y. Publisher -----------> www.BigShinyPrison.com

1// **FORTRESS EUROPE**: *a military propaganda term from WWII, referring to areas of Continental Europe occupied by Nazi Germany. In British phraseology, Fortress Europe was a Battle Honor accredited to Royal Air Force & Allied Squadrons for operations made against AXIS targets from the British Isles.*

2// **FORTRESS EUROPE**: *modern slang used to describe the state of immigration into the European Union (EU). This can be in reference to antagonistic attitudes toward immigration, or to the system of border patrols/detention centers used to make illegal immigration difficult. Since would-be immigrants are often of non-European ethnicity, the phrase "Fortress Europe" is frequently used in a derogative context to reference the extreme nationalism within European politics.*

-- PROLOGUE --

PORTLANDIA

(– march twenty sixth // two thousand eleven –)

And thus it begins – once again, all over again – hung-over & with a brutal case of the shits outside a Starbucks in Portland, Oregon…

I'm about to wheel across town & hang with Rotting Christ from Greece, one of the most preeminent black metal bands from their respective country, as well as a brutal no-nonsense death metal band from Poland called HATE. Melechesh will be there as well, the first real-deal extreme metal band from Jerusalem. Abigail Williams & Lecherous Nocturne, it is rumored, will be mulling around as well...

I've been in PDX nearly a year – the Northwest for three, give or take – an experience summed up as an unspeakable roller-coaster of false starts & dramatic anticlimaxes. Like all the other ragged transplants that have escaped to this "Green DC," I'm but another one of the vague, tragic lemmings blindly seeking the superficial dream of the 90's…

If you've never lived here, none of this will make sense… Once upon a time, in 1999, another Detroit refugee returned to our native land. Having inhabited Seattle for a year, she explained best she knew how – still, nothing resonated. She pleaded with me to leave at once – I was the only one from our old reality that could make "The Cut" – an ominous reality all transplants know too well, bitterly or joyously… Alas, I was young – 18 years old – and needed to dismember the plot-lines of my youth… 7 gruesome, long years passed before I actually made The Emerald City. Then I *understood*…

I had a taste of Seattle & its boundless promise – but only the very last gasp, that mechanical jerk before total suffocation. Summer 2008 I rode high on the final roar of that elusive & widely misunderstood "Grunge Inertia" (a term used only for vaguely perceiving minds – and one that is instantly laughable to every Seattleite). In reality, the Seattleverse has zilch to do with Nirvana & everything to do with an ingrained cultural resistance & the ever-continual counterculture exodus there. That last summer, in 2008, before the dam finally broke – the city was on fire. Seattle was among the few territories poised to ransack the entire United

States on every level – musically, artistically, politically. It was a glorious beacon of purist example...

Then AIG exploded, shrapnel-slicing the planetary economic sphere. Wall Street fell, and within days I was unemployed. Within two months, I was homeless & every magazine I ever wrote for withered into nothingness like the extinction of the dinosaurs...

And as the cold froze to record temps & mortgages foreclose & the Union's were defeated & the budgets were crashing & unemployment was running out the Seattleites acted as all Americans did in sensing the budding catastrophe. While they pretended everything was peachy keen they moved in a flanking conspiracy of self-denial, silently cannibalizing each other, growing greedier, more fearful, more desperate. Thousands began pouring onto the streets, transplants bailing for hometown ground. It was trickling away, but the screws hadn't totally come undone...

***Jump to now. Portland is Seattle with missing teeth & a bad case of the shakes. If Seattle represents the end of something, then this is where the mutated backwash flows – dirtier, dingier & harder-edged. Portland is a veritable nation-state within the perimeters of a city: *"The People's Republic of Cascadia"* – or *"Cascadia"* for short, the oft ubiquitous term among the fringe. Whereas Seattle is more the New York of this "Northwest Axis," Portland is a neighborhood-centric cocktail – something between Ann Arbor & Berkeley (at least in SE PDX). Downtown, however, is a freakish collision of Detroit & Manhattan.

The naked bicycle races stretching for miles of flesh, the endless film festivals with full bar service, a culture divorced from automobile slavery & the greatest public transportation system in the nation. Hundreds of house venues, info-shops, street-vendors & street performers, DIY health care, legal household pot crops & urban farms with cawing roosters, public outreach programs so well organized it makes a tragic joke of any other shit-hole in the US of A...

...but the cold has arrived; the sickness is in. The great promise has devolved into an empty hog-pen of intoxication. As the doomed lurch the shadows, the young ones light up the neon stretch. The rich ones, the beautiful ones press on – 50 square miles of drunk people being drunk, falling over themselves – and so many nut-hugging jeans & Borat 'staches it burns out the irises...

Freak Mecca has crumbled substantially, rendering itself a near impenetrable clique of omnipresent, nihilistic flakiness. For every attempted transplant showing up with nothing but $100 life savings, there are 5 more hipsters already planted that stroll right on by, ignoring them completely: *Tough shit buddy, go back to Kansas.*

In one year I've seen at least 2,000 soul-seeking travelers repelled. And not just Kerouac-brained explorers – I'm talking entire families of the freshly homeless; people that worked full-time factory jobs & mortgages, marriages, children in places like Arkansas, Iowa, Connecticut. By official figures, the market is now experiencing 60,000 home foreclosures per month.

Some refuse to leave & starve on the streets. Others give in & shuffle off to who knows where. Some fall apart and turn to massive junkies. And some, like me, get lucky. By "lucky" I mean a minimum wage job at 20 hours per week. And that was only after 700 resumes & walking every inch of this city, block by block, for 3 months straight. Being a famous metal journalist guy means nothing in the USA.

Well, I'm done. After 12 solid months of living like a dog, I'm ready to leave this place for the sake of doing something phenomenally insane. In two months I'll be taking the cheapest one-way plane ticket to Europe and getting dumped off smack-dab in the middle of The Old World with nothing more then a backpack of survivalist doom. I will then, as before, use every hustler trick in the book to make my way across the continent – all while unearthing the deepest fringe undercurrents in the European counterculture…

And maybe, just maybe, I won't have to come back. Maybe some gorgeous Scandinavian honey with flowing blonde locks & a Triple D will marry me for a green card. Maybe I'll ditch out & dodge that lethal FUCK-U-SHIMA creeping towards the coast. Maybe I'll be absent when the billion gallons of Corexit-laced Neurotoxic oil sludge thaws & rises from the Gulf Floor. Maybe I'll be stretched out on an Italian mountainside when the Tea Party descends on Washington DC Cairo-style to demand the reinstatement of pre-existing medical conditions…

* * *

It's Saturday March 26th, 2011 – "The Future" – and still there is a lunatic on the street ranting gibberish about hellfire, blasphemy, totalitarian Christ. This one – this pot-bellied trailer hick – is sporting a hoodie & white hat that reads "FEAR GOD." He's got Westboro-style protest signs about damnation, real tacky & shameless. And he's shouting face to face with an enraged Moloch (of Melechesh) who's reiterating: *"Fuck you! Fuck you! I'm from Jerusalem!"*

I'm dodging traffic in drizzling rain, hustling towards the crowd of metalheads surrounding the buffoon. They're egging him on, laughing hard; every band from the tour has at least one member watching. I walk into the chaos, this heated debate. Moloch darts off exasperated like he's really, really trying hard not to knock this guy unconscious – but *you* know that *he* knows that he is a better human & cannot do so as to set an example for said douche to later comprehend.

After a futile attempt to de-escalate the preacher, I make it to the tour bus where I meet the fellows. Adam Sinner from HATE & Sakis Tolis from Rotting Christ are on one side, other band members & crew are everywhere. It's like a clown-car of metal. Vikki, the tour managers asks my response to the street maniac: *"I think it's a perfect example… of why we do what we do…"*

* * * * *

The interior of the Hawthorne Theater is dimly lit – high ceiling, red curtains draping down the lengthy stage – & Sakis Tolis, the mastermind of Rotting Christ, is grinning at me with mad energy, a high-octane aura that could only be cultivated in the perimeters of Europe. Rotting Christ are a big deal in Greece & an even bigger deal on the international stage. 11 albums in, they've toured relentlessly for years on end. Starting as a grindcore act in 1987, they soon launched into the emerging black metal wave of the early 90's. They nearly signed to Euronymous' Deathlike Silence label, but Mr. Aarseth found his tragic fate in the rampage of Varg Vikernes & the rest is dread history.

By 1996 Rotting Christ signed to the burgeoning roster of Century Media, becoming one of the main bands on the label. 10 years of heavy promotion later they wound up on Season of Mist, having solidified an international touring history with monster names in extreme metal like My Dying Bride, Tiamat, Finntroll, Agathodaimon, Malevolent Creation, Vader, Krisiun, Deicide, Old Man's Child, Behemoth & Nile…

They've also enraged a host of Christian groups & conservative personalities. In November '99 during the USA Presidential Primaries for

Republican nomination, candidate Gary Bauer accused the band of a litany of heinous articles. And in May 2005 Dave Mustaine actually had Rotting Christ kicked off a concert bill that Megadeth was playing because their name was offensive to his newly Born Again sensibilities – something that was a massive shock to the worldwide metal community, and which Mustaine never recovered from in terms of respect...

Nearly 25 years in, Rotting Christ are one of the longest running bands in black metal – and they've never grown stale. AEALO, the band's latest album, was released on February 15, 2010 – easily the groups most symphonic & atmospheric ...

"Well is this your first time here in Portland?"

"Is my third time here, but this is the first we saw something like this."

"I don't know if the street preacher is coming directly at you, or just heavy metal in general..."

Yes, yes... try to correct my English, ok?"

"No problem... Well you're the first interview in this new book – I guess start off by telling me about this new tour..."

"It's doing very well. In the first week we were a little bit hectic, but no, things are getting better – more & more come to the show. We are about 15 shows into this tour. It's a very small tour, but everyone is satisfied – except for some people out here on the street. We just saw the first protest against our name. But that's good, ok..."

"What's the strangest thing you've seen in America?"

"Actually this is our fourth time in America. It's not that strange because everyone watches American movies back in Europe so we know more or less what's going on. But the strange thing here is that everyone is about the money. That maybe scares me a little bit -- everyone is about the money. No one does it for free or good purpose, for the hell of it. That's really what scares me here."

"Do you think 'no money mentality' is bigger in Europe?"

"Yup, ok, everyone needs money. But here in the USA, it's very strict and everyone's doing it for money. That does not mean someone is a bad person or good person, but that means, how can I say... It's what you are taught in the school, you know? But I really enjoy America – I love America – because the mentality of the people."

"Well the band started as grindcore back in 1987 – I was wondering if you'd ever revert to grind on a future album."

"No, no – I like grindcore, but everything took off at the right point. Back then I was feeling more into grindcore so I did play this music.

Right now I feel more heavy metal, more atmospheric music. It all depends on the period of time."

"People here don't have a clear conception about Greece…"

"We have a big scene – people are really into metal music. I think in general the Europe scene is very strong, metal is very strong. It's even stronger than here. When European bands play here, they don't pull a lot of people. In Europe we pull much more people – metal is an everyday life. You see a lot of metal kids on the streets, blah blah blah, so I think it's quite strong and we are very glad to be representing the Greek scene."

"Tell me about your new record"

"We just had a new album come out, this just happened last year – this is album number 11. Its still metal with a well established rotting Christ sound, but on the other hand we put some ethnic elements. We put some ancient Greek inspired music on our last album, so this is a different thing. And I think people react very positive. Some people think that this is by far our best album so it makes me really happy, really proud as a composer."

"Lyrically and thematically, what topics do you discuss?"

"The whole concept is about battle. About the feelings a warrior has during the battle. This is a feeling that everyone has in their every day life."

"I've been watching news about Greece -- economic turmoil, massive protests. I'm just curious your comment on the situation…"

"…We messed up. Greece, we messed up, you know. I think everyone is very dissatisfied, this economical system destroyed the country. And everyone is very aggressive about this. We have protests every day, we have bombs. Now Greece is like a battlefield. You might wake up tomorrow and see our money gone. That's the thing about this, you know. There is no insurance now – things are very difficult back there. But of course that does not mean that Greece will disappear, because as a nation we've been existing more then 3000 years…"

"Have you read 'The Colossus of Maroussi' by Miller?"

"No, but Maroussi is the area which I live. It's a suburb…"

"If I come to Greece what are the main cities to visit?"

"You should definitely go to the south, to see all the ancient monuments, you should go to the north to see all the Macedonian monuments. And you must have some days off in the ?? isolated islands just to enjoy the sun & nice beaches. The sea there is very smooth, very calm unlike the ocean here. You can stay on the island doing nothing, it's a very nice area. Greece is very nice to go.

"Here's a random one. I read a lot of history – is General Metaxas considered a war hero by the Grecian people?"

"I don't know if its hero – some people consider him a hero, but some as a dictator. But he's a hero by saying no to these Nazi's battles in 1940. Always Greece is like this – we never surrender…"

"What is the overall message of Rotting Christ?"

"Keeping the underground spirit alive. That's the most important message that we wish to spread to the people. We are metal, we play dark music, but the most important thing for me is just to be yourself. I'm a fan, I go to shows, I buy albums. This is the message we like to pass to people – there is no difference between the musicians & the people that come to the show."

"I'm looking for a weird story now, something strange that happened to you & when you tell people they think you're a pathological liar – it can be about anything – UFO's, ghosts, bizarre rituals…"

"One time after touring for two years in a row, I start to have illusions. I don't know why. I used to take some drugs ok, but a little bit. When I was in Mexico, for instance, I thought I was seeing UFO's, stuff like that. I don't know why. But I was very tired, I did some medical treatment and now I'm ok. Because sometimes when you're one year on the road, you get tired a lot, really tired, playing shows every day. Sometimes, you know, you drink a lot. But now I quit everything. I don't drink, I don't take any drugs, I don't smoke anything in order to be strong for the self."

"What do you think of Manowar?"

"I love them. They are one of my favorite bands because this is metal and I am a metal fan. Sometimes I don't like their attitude but I love Manowar, come on. I put it in my MP3 player and listen to this every night before I go to bed man…"

* * *

Adam Sinner is comfortably relaxed in one of the black quasi-fold out chairs in the venue, while varied metal plays over the loudspeakers now that doors are 20 minutes away. This individual is the vocalist/guitarist of HATE, one of the most lethal death metal bands in Poland today & complete w/ corpse-paint, warrior gear, Satanic overtones & industrialized undertones wrapped in a caustic slab of death metal…

Formed in Warsaw in 1990, it was only after 3 self-released efforts before signing to Novum Vox Mortiis & later the famed Polish label Metal Mind Productions. The subsequent years would find HATE dropping a new album on a new label every few years, including Mercenary Musik (in the States), Dwell Records, Blackened Records, & finally Listenable Records where they are currently. HATE's new record *Erebos* is the one they now tour for, a monstrous slab of leviathan girth…

"So is this your first tour in the United States?"

"No, no, the second time actually. There's a nice, friendly atmosphere on the bus with Rotting Christ and Melechesh. The shows are really, really good. We have seen a growing interest in the band definitely, compared to the first tour we did with Hypocrisy last year. So there's a progress for sure and this time we are in America to promote our new album *Erebos*…"

"The first time I heard HATE was Cain's Way back in 2002, that was in the Mercenary Musik days. You're on Listenable now. Tell me about your new album, how it differs from your past works & what you're progressing towards…

"Talking about the music, how it's evolved – we started from traditional death metal, brutal death metal; a mixture of American influenced death with some European roots, thrash bands like Kreator or Destruction. But in 2005 there was a big change in the bands style – we started using industrial influences, samples. Also the music was enriched with some black metal, thrash metal. The industrial & ambient stuff in our music is very important. It makes us different from the rest of the Polish death metal scene, also it gives our music some dirty character on live shows. On the American version of *Erebos* there are some bonus track that go even further in this direction – remixed in dark ambient form by a French artist called Melecta – quite well known in Europe for his industrial attempts. I think it's something experimental, something fresh when it comes to extreme metal."

"Obviously you have a thread of Satanism…"

"When it comes to the lyrics, in ideology – yeah we were very, might I say, 'declared satanic band' in the beginning. It hasn't changed that much. We're still into Satanism, or mysticism, but we don't express it in so much of a blatant way. I mean, it's more, you know… We are grown ups now. So we look at these things from a more grown up perspective. So those topics, that ideology, it's still an important part of the contents of the lyrics, but its not expressed in this open way. We've been more into mysticism, say Luciferian stuff, then plain Satanism. That's why we don't use inverted crosses or pentagrams, which are too obvious – and very often misinterpreted & used by everybody around. That's why we're trying to put it in some other way & to show other aspects of these ideologies."

"Tell me about the Polish scene – what am I walking into?

"The Polish metal scene is present in many different cities – it's all over the country, lots of extreme metal bands. The scene is really, really strong; there are hundreds of bands. Some will call it the 'Polish death metal phenomenon.' I don't believe that there's just one polish death metal style… On the other hand there might be something in common for all those bands, but it's more the sound then the riffs. All of us use the same studios, the same sound engineers – sometimes even the same equipment in the studio… If you want to know more about the Polish scene, you should interview all the main bands – especially VADER, because it all started from them, back in the 80's even, when they started to make their name internationally. All the other bands, mine also, are following VADER's footsteps. They were the first band from the other side of The Iron Curtain, and they were a great success at the time. They were proof that we could do something." *"Coming from Europe, how do you feel about cultural absurdity – I mean in America, specifically, the odd things you've seen that would never happen elsewhere…* "Today we had a great example of absurdity, those guys protesting outside the club, protesting against satanic bands. It's a kind of protest that's full of contradictions. If they are soldiers of Christ they shouldn't be so angry, they shouldn't hate other people. But they openly hate us. It's just stupid – it's something you wouldn't see in Europe anywhere. It's a surprise that in Portland we have such a protest. It should be in the South States rather, Texas or… It shows that America is built on capitalism and bible. I understood it today seeing this. Those people were really serious, they were really angry – they didn't act. So they must've been brainwashed to the point when they really believe in this shit & they speak openly in the street in such a dynamic manner about it… America – people are really open here. Here in America I can see many people willing to speak openly about love of things. In Europe, most countries, especially in the North, people are more to themselves. Not straight-forward, not outgoing… It's a different culture, in this way, that people are more kind here in America. Also, the way that metal community is organized here is something completely different from Europe, because here you can meet young people & also people that are elderly, you know, like 50 years old. It's something unheard of in Europe – there the crowd is 20-something-year-olds. But here it's a metal culture. In Europe, people who are 25 are taking up some serious stuff for life – they don't go to the concert. 30 is the breaking year – you cannot really meet people over 30 at metal shows. So it's a kind of lifestyle & it ends at about 30. That's it. "

"So are you a total rarity? You're about 32 right?"

"35. Most my friends, former metal fans, crazy metal fans, these people are now business men sitting in offices. Sometimes they look with some envy, they're all a bit jealous of my career because they are stuck. They don't go to the venue for metal shows because they don't belong there anymore. They would feel strange, they'd feel awkward, jumping around with all those youngsters there."

"You grew up in Poland when it was still Iron Curtain. Now that that's all done with, do the older population in Poland still embrace the ideals of communism or do they feel it was a bad thing altogether? Do they even want to think about it?"

"You know there are still people in Poland who long for communism, long for that period. And it's because capitalism is difficult. You need to get to work, you need to learn something. I remember life in the 70's and 80's in Poland and I remember that people were perfectly happy, even though there was nothing in the shops, people were in a way one big community. There weren't big differences, everybody had almost the same. Of course there were privileged guys connected to the Communist Party, but all the other people were like equal. It really worked this way. And people lived with sport, maybe some Polish TV, films, stuff like that – they were one community living the same things. It ended quite abruptly, violently I mean, and the new situation was a shock for many people... It's changing now for the better. More & more people have become accepting of the situation, being perfectly benefited after all. But I remember the first 10 years after the transition, it was a great shock. And from a perspective of a metal musician, it changed in a good way. You could travel freely – no Iron Curtain, no divisions. No borders, you know. I can go shopping in Germany.

"What is the message of HATE?"

"HATE is a symbolic name – it means reaction, lets say opposition, against all captivating systems that suppress human powers. Religion is the first thing that comes to mind, but also politics, civilization. So it means freedom from all this, all this shit, and what we do is try to get across a message that is full of metaphors. It's not so obvious – the lyrics are metaphors on the condition of the human in general. It's not based on any mythology anymore. Even though we use the word Erebos from Greek mythology, it's just a metaphor. Erebos here means the evil side of human being, these evil aspects that exist in each of us. What is important is to make this chaos, this evil part, be beneficial – make it work for you, make the most of it in a creative way because it's a great power. If it works for you, you can do anything. It's not about killing people. It's rather about being, I wouldn't like to say '*superhuman*' because that has some connotations, but to become a better personality. Become a person that can realize his or her goals in life. And at the same time be free, totally free in mind."

"You've been all over Europe playing with all sorts of these hardcore Satanic bands, these guys into mysticism & the occult. In your opinion, who are the 'real deal' living this stuff 100% all the time? Who are the total freaks?"

"You know, there are different ways of perceiving this magical side… We've been touring with lots of bands – Norwegian bands like Carpathian Forest, we've had meetings with Gorgoroth. Played that famous show actually – we supported them while recording our DVD *Litanies of Satan*. We've had lots of experiences with other bands you may call 'satanic' or 'magical', using this ideology… We lead quite normal lives & this is the way that keeps us sane. But those guys, for example, those black metal crazy bands from Norway, were living in chaos in their normal lives. What we saw touring with them was really strange because they were up to everything, you know. Those guys seem to be completely lost. And this is the way they 'worship Satan,' they say this, at least, you know, by being in chaos all the time – by destroying themselves also, if necessary. So there are very different perceptions of what Satanism is, what magic is; how to open to it, how to use it. It's a long story… If you ask other bands this question, you will see how different it is. The band Shining for example, you know Mayhem – those bands are completely different from us…"

The guys in Melechesh are hanging in the back, All night they've been these mysterious shadow people, silently floating the venue & emanating this intense, secret vibe. It sounds corny, but I can only think of ancient Pharaohs – the ones with the lotus flower vials filled with DMT. The Melechesh people are their own mystery, & though I'd like to chat with them, they are obviously in their own world & preparing to hammer the audience. Besides, they are in the first book, & if you want to read about them you know where to look…

I sneak out the back door, bypassing security, and make it to Hohenstein from Lecherous Nocturne. We smoke a little grass hidden between the tour busses & banter the usual. This is their first national tour, the making of their *Myth Manifest* (as the new record is entitled). They hail from South Carolina & like most American bands, Lecherous Nocturne exudes the prevailing attitude amongst my fellow countrymen – do or die & DIY: *"[The band message] is question everything, reject everything that's fed to you, be it religion or politics – anything that's being shoved down your throats. Totally reject it – & not only that but lash out against it, rant about it…"*

Hohenstein raps the usual formalities then gives a great soliloquy regarding their recent Detroit excursion: *"A few nights ago in Detroit, we stopped at a gas station – my guitar player & I, we went to get pizza – the guy ran & locked the door. So we saw a McDonalds across the street & walked through the drive thru. Two minutes later 3 cops swarmed in, got out – 'The Domino's guy said you guys were jerking on the door, trying to get in.' We're like, 'No dude, we didn't even get 20 foot to the door.' So they're like, 'Oh, you guys in a band?' One of the guys was an ex-NARC & a metalhead with all sorts of tattoos. So he told his cop buddies to give us a ride to the store where our van was parked. We were in the back of the squad car, so he pulled in & blocked the van off like he was gonna fucking bust us & shit. The guy got out and said, 'You know these guys? It's gonna cost you $500 to get them out the car!' Then he busted out laughing, got a cd and…"*

* * * * *

***We alone now? Ok, ok… If you are just now stepping into the maelstrom, then this book probably won't make much sense. If you are oblivious to the underground, then nothing will make sense. Which is fine, quite frankly, because "FORTRESS EUROPE" disregards such courtesy. Foreshadowing is overdone & retreads are a drag, but it's important to comprehend that this book is a sequel…

Some time ago, I was desperately unhappy. 25 years of Detroit was enough. One night, not thinking the matter over too clearly, I dispatched a press release declaring a "living book" entitled "THE BIG SHINY PRISON." I hopped on a Greyhound for California, determined to make my way through every territory possible – to cover all aspects of the American Underground & regurgitate the journey through my own twisted aesthetics…

293 days, 30,000 miles, 35 states, 2 national tours, 50 hours of interviews & 606+ hours on Greyhounds later, I somehow completed this objective. It took 8 months to finish the book, and another year of rejection before I dropped it online Free. The biggest news services in the underground picked it up, RSS Feeds shot all over the planet & the

download count kept going... and the emails, the mad offers & karmic craziness – the resonance continual...

So here we are again – *one man, one vision, no budget* – ready to lunge headfirst into an array of dicey situations, bad noise, street freaks & total uncertainty... Whereas "PRISON" set out to educate, "FORTRESS EUROPE" is for the real trolls. It is therefore expected that the reader already possesses a considerable knowledge (*or basic understanding*) of the slang & tribes of the counterculture.

Secondly, "FORTRESS EUROPE" is a book of action. Unlike its predecessor which shot deep into personal narrative, philosophy, sociology, politics, etc – I'm generally going to keep my big mouth shut & let it flow. Everything major I wanted to say about America & the underground at large I already did – & *what's the point of forced rhetoric anyway?*

1 month left & the confirmations are in. Just a waiting game until Deutschland, Belgium, Netherlands, UK, Finland, Sweden, Norway, Poland, Italy, Denmark, Slovenia, Czech... *the only trouble left is actually getting to them...*

[– R. Bartek // 4.30.11]

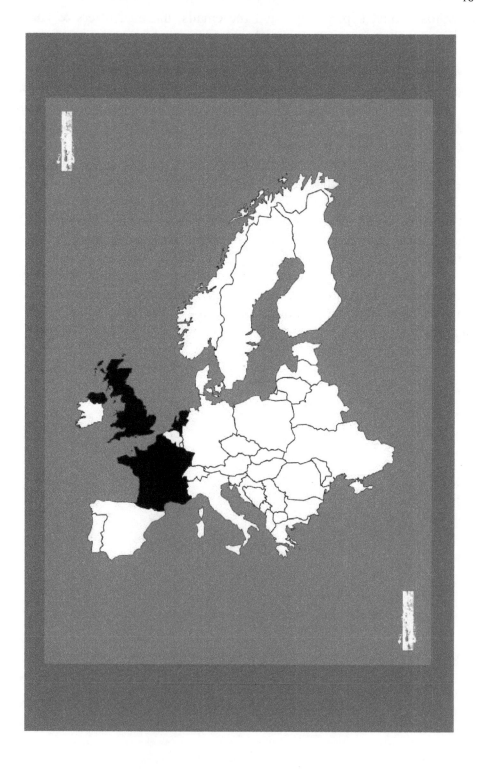

 LONDON

6.1.11   6.8.11

I. *"CCTV et mon Droit"*

In the mind of the foreigner, there is a substantial gulf between tangible impression & vague reality. One can theorize about alien culture until the sun bursts, but no amount of raw-dog experience hammers the senses like high-voltage transoceanic vagabondage...

Take for instance the Kiwi's – no one bothered to inform me that those Zealanders have a penchant for Richard Simmons the way the Kraut's have a boner for Hasselhoff. Frizz-hair Richie is sweatin' for the newbies on the airplane monitor, hosting the safety video & gymnastically leaping through the aisles. Flight attendants copy-cat his motions, slipping on life jackets & oxygen masks...

If the Air New Zealand plane spirals towards irreversible doom, it's not the buzz from huffed oxygen that will pacify everyone's fears – it's the lingering image of Richard Simmons in his tiny blue shorts, that 80's leg slit flashing pasty white thighs bright as the belly of an Orca...

The plane elevates from American soil. All in-flight purchases are Kiwi cash only –complimentary wine, lunch & dinner; monitors dug into the hind-side of every chair offering free movies, tourist intel & 8-bit Tetris. *At 20,000 feet, I soar above The Big Shiny Prison; the terra-vortex spittoon of casino immolation...*

What I know, <u>*what I think I know*</u>, is that Europeans do not actually detest Americans – they loathe FOX America, which is a separate race altogether. The Europeans have learned the historical lessons & have ingrained bullshit detectors like Geiger Counters. They withstand the American advance, shrugging off naivety as a hangman's morality contorts the pleas of the condemned...

I'm clearly not one of them & I have absolutely no issue with spitting venom at my homeland in return for a nightly squat. Indeed, my hatred towards the greediness of my country is ice cold. So profound, in fact – so extreme – that I hope to utilize such volcanic rhetorical eruptions as an omnipresent party favor...

Writing about America makes me want to napalm America. Yet in this vein of insult, it is cautionary to mention that it's really not all that difficult to repeatedly kick a mongoloid in the face. This is the case with America – a target so rancid you can't help but to assault it while it's down. The stars & stripes bleed as profusely as a dog with broken legs, shot to pieces by the B.B. guns of white trash children in a back road dirt-alley of Arkansas…

Just keep moving forward at all costs & abandon the beast its own self-calculated degradation – *just make sure to wipe your feet before you stroll back inside…*

(Day I): "الخنازير الأمريكية"

There is but a mammal blockading total freedom; a lone female clasping that final *"ker-chunk"* of the visa stamp. I've everything in order, theoretically – *fresh passport, proof of return ticket, $5,000 in the bank, no felonies…*

But irony, destitute irony – she is a Muslim draped in ḥijāb, and has already sent 5 people into the authoritarian scrutiny limbo line. She locks eyes with me & I read it all too clear: *"That's right Americano – I know the stereotypes you possess. Even as you write this now, the audience will from one thousand directions scoff at your political incorrectness. Your stupid nation & foolish assumptions, you all fear us. Your warped paranoia justifications regarding us all bloodthirsty terrorists…"*

"It's tough enough dealing with this bullshit on the street – at the grocers, on The Tube, but you – ignorant Americano – I will prove to you & to the Orwellian apparatus that employs me & that aims its hideous electric eye at my brow every ticking second of every paycheck – I will <u>*DESTROY*</u> *this stereotype of my great people. Fuck you Americano & prepare to be grilled – prepare to be made an example of myself making an example out of you…"*

Or maybe I'm just overreacting. Maybe it's just the American in me fearing the other Americans that normally surround me but accumulated into one entity that is in turn projected into her: *"Hi there, I'm just coming in as a tourist. I've never been to Europe before. As you can see I have my return ticket information right here. I plan to stay in London for a week and then head on into France and then Italy."*

"Well, where are you staying?"

Damn. I hadn't even thought of that. Like almost everything my life has become, the absurdity of what I'm doing fails to register as even a moderate truth & the actual truth would be suicide.

Yeah, ok, so I have no idea where I'm going apart from a loose itinerary & a landslide of contacts which involve a number of potentially shady people whom I all met online in a non-transparent manner. All of these telephone numbers you see scribbled here on this computer print-out include an array of internationally renown Satanists, Anarchists, drug beasts & dissidents who all surely have lengthy criminal backgrounds in the Interpol data bank…

Furthermore, I don't have a dime saved for a hotel or hostel nor would I pay for one, as I've specifically come to be homeless & regularly eat out of your fine Euro-trash receptacles. You see Ma'am, I intensely crave those rare feats of disillusion when one is helplessly isolated & anonymous in a foreign gutter, dropped back to the absolute zero. I have no phone, no maps, no traveling partner – I don't even know how to get out of this airport, nor do I technically have anywhere to go once I measure that one all out.

Yes, I've places to stay all over Europe – but the truth is I never even bothered to look at a map. Sure, I know where France is, the UK, but I'm totally lost on the majority. Say *"Romania"* and I'll respond: *"Somewhere over there, probably by Slovenia,"* because I have this notion that Slovenia borders everything in Europe. Or maybe it's the notion of LAIBACH bordering everything, since you can't contain a global state like NSK & their occupation is omnipresent, eternal...

So I give her a line I think will fly: *"To be honest my plan was to head downtown and find a cheap hostel or hotel. I figured it would probably be cheaper to do this in person."*

FIRES OF NAPALM: ***"You mean you don't have anything booked in advance? Why would you come to a country and not have any arrangements?"***

Damn, she's got me again. My eyes are vacant & obvious – I have the air of a man totally aloof with no clear idea why he is even there. *"Well I like to be a bit spontaneous, you know. It's always been a dream of mine to visit here & see all the tourist attractions, meet some authentic British folks in their natural environment."*

"Well then, what tourist attractions will you visit?"

Double damn. I can't name a single thing except Big Ben, Hyde Park & Buckingham Palace which I promptly declare. If it weren't for those name-dropping airplane monitors, I'd be fucked…

But she's still not buying it, demanding names & intel. She says she needs an address where I'll be staying or I can't be let into the country. I tell her again that it will be figured out once I get into town and not to worry, because I've plenty of money in the bank & if I get low on cash my parents are well-off financially and promised to assist whilst I give this Norman Rockwell gee-whiz purist Americana vibe & empathetically explain how I saved for a whole year to make this happen.

She half-buys it, so I cut the bullshit & go in for the kill: *"Look, I also write for some tiny online zines doing band interviews. I have contacts that will be meeting up & giving me a place to stay. I'm planning to go to some concerts."*

Danger Will Robinson, *Danger!* **"Well what are the names of these magazines? Are you getting paid? If you're getting paid why don't you have a work visa lined up? If you're going to all these concerts where are your tickets for these concerts?"** I try to explain how I do this for free as a hobby & no money is involved, and that these concerts are bar shows: *"You know, like punk rock – you just show up & pay at the door."* The punk rock concept is unsurprisingly lost on her – she demands proof that I've purchased entry to these gigs well in advance.

"Where do you work? Where do you live? You're just leaving you're apartment and job and you tell me that it's just there when you show back up?" I explain that I'm a cook at a small family owned non-corporate restaurant, that they approve of my adventure, and that I'll be staying with friends upon return.

Not buying any of it, she demands I go to the ATM and get a bank statement. Nervous, shaky & obvious – with her molten eyes dissolving my skull – the rotten machine won't take my card. SKYNET is flipping me the bird. When I re-approach the customs desk & tell her this, actually incorporating the word SKYNET into my description of the problem, she tells me to sit in the line of possible dope dealers, con artists & economic refugees.

<u>Is it already over?</u> <u>Are they really going to deport me?</u> I think of all the press outlets that promoted this lunatic experiment & my characteristic fear of humiliating defeat. I cannot lose this one – I'll jump out the fucking plane screaming *"Vive Gay PARIS!!!"*

She gives the head nod to the other Arabic security officer & I'm double-teamed by example setters… *He grills me. I'm sweating. I'm fucked…*

But then he asks what my parents do. *"Well, my step dad, he's a retired cop and…"* The guard lights up, smiling: *"Good enough for me – let him through."* Muslim lady drops her hard-edged persona – but she still knows whatever I'm hiding is larger then that avalanche of horse manure I dropped on her desk…

"Look," she says, **"We've got this bad problem with illegal immigration. We have them pouring over our borders looking for work. You're story sounded like it could be…"** And, like a Boy Scout, I reply: *"No Ma'am, I love living in the United States; I wouldn't leave it for* *anything. Let me be honest with you – I'm a lil' homesick already…"* And just like that, *I was in…*

* * *

6pm; the descending nova casts crooked lengths of shadow architecture. One Man vs. FORTRESS EUROPE, entrapped by the dimensions of time & the unorganized spatial limits of *one thousand eight-hundred* hours. Every millisecond is spontaneous origami & menacing as the ominous, black obelisk. Snake Plissken was granted 24 hours; I've got *75 days* to kill…

I collect from my long nap at the park; the sidelines of a football field midst a sprawling complex of gardens, brooks, asphalt pathways & open grass plateaus somewhere beyond the limits of Camden Town. An idyllic scene with clear blue skies, little humidity; babies, bicycles & ice cream vendors…

I caught quick glimpses of Camden & Piccadilly Circus; cobblestone streets, a twisting maze of buildings. The modern world has had its way, but the Victorian frame remained intact yet coated with corporate neon logos. Tiny Brit cars zoomed about as I played *Frogger*, continually stumbling into wrong lanes of traffic…

Shuffling through it with 15 hours of jet-lag, I caught glimpses of San Francisco. The city was brimming with life, hope & promise. The buzz in the air, in terms of humanity – you could feel the depressurized aura of a healthy people not quite living in fear. You could feel the absence of psychological weight…

But the staggering economics drove me into a frustrated cat-nap. It was, after all, 5am PDX time & whenever the shit hits the fan, just slip under for some slumber & maybe when you wake up it'll all really be some turgid dream. At least you're brain gets a manual restart. In any case, it's quite daunting when a widespread American concept like a fast food 'value menu' is foreign to the foreign Burger King. In the USA every McDonald's, KFC, etc has a $1 menu with 20 or so items. This is why, my dear European readership, that Americans are raging with obesity statistics. We are poor & therefore live off this genetically modified, heart-clogging filth.

But not in the UK. Here, a $1 hamburger in the USA comes out to like $7.00 in conversion. And black coffee – *the juice of the American bloodline* – the smallest to-go cup clocked in around $6.00. Even bottled water clocks in around $3.00 USD – unless, of course, you want to chug this cheap & awful carbonated fizz water the Brit's are seemingly hooked on… Then again, I am in one of the most expensive cities in the world, and should've seen this coming. Still, when experienced first person, the reality whaps you harder then the enraged fist of Joe Louis…

Dayal Patterson cordially shakes my hand, dispersing the fog of nervousness. Patterson – a long-haired, long-time metal journalist & photographer – has just swooped me up from the entrance of The World's End; a pub so adequately named I've decided to make it my HQ for the duration of this UK campaign.

We're in the heart of Camden Town, the freak village of London. In every direction the streets are clogged with mobs of ravers, punks, metal-heads, artists, the deftly unclassified. It doesn't take much to realize this is the New York of Europe, insofar as music/art goes. Just like LA, every luminary & hack flocks here that's trying to '*make it*,' wheeling & dealing until they scurry back from whence they came. Most will come & go within a few years, if not a few months. Dayal estimates that the vast majority of those on these streets are immigrants.

Patterson is the Q to my 007 whom will fill me in on everything I need to know about the civilization here. Tonight he is taking me to a metal press junket filled with journalists, photographers & whatever local musicians felt like stumbling in for the free booze & political schmooze.

We're headed to a listening party for the new In Flames & Arch Enemy records, hosted by Century Media & Nuclear Blast [**record labels*] whom are providing an open bar & faux-money gambling. You can win prizes with the fake cash, but I'm way more into the infinite Guinness tap…

We turn down a cobbled alley & reach a back entrance, climb a steep staircase into the party area which is a confined sweat-box of a miniature tavern. In Flames posters coat the walls; a silkscreen flag of Arch Enemy. No one seems much interested in either of the promo records being jammed by the stereo – its all background noise to the loud crowd of Englishmen gambling with Monopoly money.

20 minutes with Dayal & he's already nudged me in front of the Earache Records upper echelon, *Metal Hammer* staff, management from Century Media/Nuclear Blast. The guitarist from Evile, a Spanish photographer that did Burzum's *Belus* photo shoot & the former editor of *Terrorizer*, Jonathan Selzer, who is now one of the main writers at *Metal Hammer*.

I waste no time & when I introduce myself to Selzer, I was surprised to find out that he actually knew who I was. That he's had *The*

Big Shiny Prison for sometime now & was more then happy to participate. So we head back down the long staircase & into the alley, drinks in hand...

Mr. Selzer spares no time in unleashing the well-scripted rant of a journalist who has conducted 8 million heavy metal interviews: "Well I'm the editor of 'Subterranean' in *Metal Hammer*, the extreme metal section where they channel all the filth. Before that, I was editor of *Terrorizer* magazine. As you know there's kind of a big debate at the moment about the fate of metal – I'm actually quite a purist in this way. The reason metal's still existing after all these years is because metal, more then anything else, has this continuity that if you're really into metal, where it came from, you know all the basic elements. Metal as a whole, there is continuity."

"Now, the whole indie scene, they seem to be based on everything that's happened in the last 2 or 3 months. And there's no collective memory anymore – there's no development, no avant garde. To have avant garde you have to know about the whole span of things. What I'm trying to do is... If you care about metal, you have to know where it comes from, you have to care for the continuity. I'm a bit worried that some of that's getting lost in the flavor of the month. Now you get 2nd or 3rd generation bands playing At The Gates stuff. And I think once you lose that sense of continuity, everything starts becoming 3rd tier."

I quickly jump in: ***"I'm sure you've interviewed hundreds of bands – what were some of the strangest encounters you had?"***

"To be fair I don't rate interviews if they're really weird or not, just if you make a connection with people. I've spoken to WATAIN quite a few times, in their sort of blood dripping studios... So you're wearing blood, but you actually have a sort of beautiful rationale for this. Most interviews, they're set environments. I've never had anyone do something really fuckin' weird during an interview – I just try to get eye contact, get into their world, and then you find a narrative that makes this band make sense."

"How do you feel about the evolution of metal journalism? What's the next step?"

"Looking at all the metal journalism around, I find its really dry. Very *'what this sounds like/what that sounds like,'* drum sound, this n' that. And you never know what the spirit of the album was... Now you have this kind of black metal theory of things in America. I like some of the context, but I find most of it pretty nasty & its not really communicating what the spirit of black metal is, or even the spirit of metal. I think you've a lot of imaginative writers doing a sort of forced personality to get across the spirit of being ritualistic."

"What were some interesting personalities you've met?"

"Without a doubt, WATAIN. I've done lots of interviews with some pretty crazy people – one was Pete Steele, when *Origin of the Feces* came out I was in Queens & we argued about an hour. He's basically 3 times the size of me & really into the whole social Darwinism thing, so I was arguing the whole time with him about that – it was brilliant & really great. In the end he was telling me about his stock car and was like '*you need a ride?*' and Pete Steele, he drove me to the airport in his evil fucking car. Pete Steel was for real cause everyone said as mad as it is, he had a complete coherence & logic to him. And those are the people that I really trust. And it's usually the people that have the most coherent logic that do the craziest shit. I love the chaos & the rationale at the same time."

"So in terms of contemporary black metal, you'd trump WATAIN?"

"I think WATAIN have that totally, I think Gaahl – in a real kind of way, in a weird postmodern way, he's very genuine. I think a lot of what he says about himself is made up. But at the same time, there's a kind of truthfulness in everything he says that makes sense... I think Adam Namethenga from Primordial is totally genuine. Aaron Weaver from Wolves In The Throne Room, he totally has a world. In black metal you have to create a world – that's the most important thing, to create a rationale."

"Do you ever have a weird sense of jigsaw pieces in doing this, like when the right people just appear at odd times & any other time would be an incomplete meeting for whatever reason?"

"I believe in connections, and when you're on the right track things connect. Things kind of happen at the right time & for the right reason. I was at college doing my first piece of journalism, and I was obsessed with Alan Moore. All I wanted to do was get an interview, but I'd no idea how to get a hold of [him]. He's a man that odd coincidences happen to a lot. And this one Saturday I went to the comic shop & then to the coffee shop, a ritual of mine – and the first time ever I couldn't find a seat. So I went to the coffee shop across the road, sat down & 5 minutes later who walks in? Alan Moore. It's like FUCK – and I'm a shy 16 year old. So I do the "*Um, you don't know me, I have this project for my class.*" He gave me his home phone number... The basic moral of that story is, if you really know why you want to do something, and you have a mission, that attracts things to happen around it, I'm very lucky that I am where I am & I never take that for granted. But I had one mission in mind – I wanted to write for these magazines that have amazing writers & I want to be as good as them. I think that's why I like black metal so much, because black metal has a mission."

"What do you think of Aliester Crowley"

"The trouble I have with the a Crowley stuff – at least The Golden Dawn – is it's a kind of quasi-religion in the sense that there's something out there that you have to accept like Qabalic or Egyptian. I'm agnostic with The Golden Dawn – especially in England, it kind of gets mixed in with a slightly camp, Hammer horror thing, without people actually really getting to grips with what Thelema was really about. I think that takes a massive amount of work & knowledge to come to grips with Crowley's cosmology. You know, magick is all about systems. Its about – as long as you have a system, it doesn't really matter what it is. The most important thing is to create a correlation between things & to really have a connection to animals. That's when magick occurs. I think whichever system you go with is pretty arbitrary. I believe in magick, but I believe it takes work – and it doesn't matter which system you go for…"

The guitarist from Evile has had a little too much barley & hops distillation & has apparently bolted. But the Burzum photographer – a Spanish woman named Ester Segarra – is glad to jump into the fray. She's from Barcelona and has been covering extreme metal for just over 10 years now: "I'm a photographer first of all – that's my medium of expression. One of the first magazines I started working for was *Terrorizer*. My first passion is horror film; my second is metal. I work for *Metal Hammer*, *Decibel*, *Rock Hard* in France…

"What's the Burzum thing all about?"

"Last year I was asked to photograph Varg Vikernes – how could you say no? He's such a character, such a legend. I was going to be the only photographer to be allowed to take pictures of him *[**post-prison release]*. I landed in Norway & his manager took me to his place. Personally it was very interesting talking to him; it was amazing to see how much he's misunderstood by people. Actually he's a very charming man & has a wicked sense of humor, and he doesn't take himself as seriously as people assume he does. It was to the point where we joked about killing each other. At the time I didn't really think to much about it, but after I'd left, I was like, '*Hold on a second – I've been with Varg Vikernes who just came out of prison for 17 years over stabbing someone & in a small room of his house with him holding a knife & him joking about killing me.*' We got along very well…

"What do you have to say about Barcelona?"

"Barcelona is very anarchic. After the war & before the war, it was the only city where the anarchists took over the government. There's still a strong left-wing movement there, there is a very strong squatting scene… My generation grew up hating Franco, and Franco's been blamed for a lot of things. I think the civil war that happened, it happened for a reason. In a sense, Spain is very violent. You have a strong sort of right wing mentality and left wing mentality. After the war, people wouldn't talk about politics because it had been so painful – the way the country was divided. And it was a military state, the police presence was very strong. People were just quiet, get along with their lives. As time went by & democracy came along – you still have a lot of people who support Franco ideas, and you have the usual resistance. So it depends who you ask.

"What sort of government is in place today? I heard a lot of unrest has been brewing with student & activist demonstrations?"

"We have a left wing party in government – before that the party that was rooted out after the terrorist attack in Madrid was the right wing party. It was founded during Franco times, so a lot of the politicians from that party were working in Franco's government – and people still voted for that. All the politicians in Spain, even though they work in democracy, were born into a dictatorship. We had a dictatorship for 40 years, so that's a whole generation & you have all these people in power meant to work according to the rules of democracy, but they actually have no ideas. I think that explains a bit of the problem in Spain…"

Dan Tobin is next on the list. He's worked at Earache for 17 years and before that Peaceville as well. Tobin grew up in London & has been involved in the scene here since he was 14 years old. 20 odd years later, he's still doing *"the same old shit."*

"What am I excited about in music? Everything that sounds different & new. I love death metal, brutal music, but everything's been done… People think [*working at Earache is*] more exciting then it is. Meeting random people, of course – I've hung out with Darkthrone, Pentagram, Morbid Angel, Napalm Death. The bottom line? They all just love the music & what they do. Essentially were all there for the same reason. I've tried to analyze it a number of times, why the hell I'd turn up for Napalm Death gigs when I've seen them 300 times before. I mean, why the hell do they even turn up? Because they fuckin' love it, don't you? When you hear Napalm kick in & the blast-beats & all that – god knows what those guys feel on stage; something must swell up inside them."

"Still, you've probably accumulated a ton of crazy stories during your tenure..."

"Crazy stories? Yeah. But the point is sadly – and somewhat disappointingly – its just according to the music, and that's... You came all the way from America, right? Detroit or whatever you were saying, so you're sitting there in your bedroom listening to fucking Terrorizer or Morbid Angel & you felt the same thing I did but you were 6000 miles away. That's what counts. All the bullshit like *'we played in front of 3000 people or we sold this many t-shirts or fucked this many chicks'* or whatever – yeah that's all awesome too, but deep down – when we all get back home – you still turn on the Terrorizer album... I don't have any gospel to give to anybody – all I know is if you love music go for it, support it, promote it, do anything you can to get involved with it. Enjoy it. Its music & none of us are going to be millionaires..."

**(Day II): *"tele-mutation through the lens of BBC"*

I wake up in a jolt somewhere on the south side of London, on Patterson's apartment floor. The living space is just as cramped as his tiny Euro-shower, which I had to crouch in with a little spray nozzle hoping it wouldn't shoot all over the tiling. No matter which position I tossed & turned in all night, some part of my body was rubbing up against stacks of CD's or guitar equipment. So I head off for a brief walk...

I realize then how impossible it will be to describe London without mentioning BBC programming or Monty Python, because as a Yankee my only glimpses come from the media. The apartment complex is like one polygon inside another & tightly compacted. Brick chimneys hit the skyline like the backdrop of one too many Pink Floyd videos. The alien habitat etches itself onto my brain...

Some hours later, Patterson & I have headed up to the local diner. Pork & Beans come as a side dish on all UK food, the same ways we'd get hash browns in The States. Eggs sunny side up, sausage, breakfast potatoes; complimentary OJ thrown in the mix & some black coffee to liven the mood...

Patterson is a Cornish guy from the not-quite autonomous South. He has traveled abroad in Europe but finds himself quite content within the perimeters of London. I hit record & let the MP3 player do it's magic. Such a huge step up from the last book, might I say, where it was all cassette tapes & excess weight: "...as I was saying earlier, it's good to be in London because a lot of stuff comes here before it goes elsewhere – like press trips, that kind of stuff. I've thought about moving to Berlin, somewhere else in the UK, but you always ending up here. About 50% of my work is writing & photography, music related stuff – the other 50% is design, photo-shop touch-ups… Music's always been my passion – photography I do for *Terrorizer, Metal Hammer* – but I just fell into writing. I started doing *Crypt Fanzine* in 2003. In London, in England ,you used to have so many print zines in metal – in the late 90's there were maybe 15, and that's what I grew up with. By 2004 you could see that was disappearing & webzines were taking over, so *Crypt* was a tribute to that – one final print zine…"

"How did you end up in the big leagues, per se?"

"I never had the intention to write professionally – its only because I sent a copy [of *Crypt Fanzine*] to *Metal Hammer* for review. And that was just the hope that maybe a review could sell 10 more copies & I could get some money back... I'm always interested in meeting musicians but I was never into that 'fan thing' – you know, where you're looking up to somebody & idolizing them. I was never the guy waiting outside the gig trying to meet somebody or get their signatures… The Gorgorth interview I did, that was what got me the gig at *Metal Hammer*. That was with Infernus – it was very intense. They were all in the room – Gaahl, King, Infernus – they're all quite intense people in their own ways. Infernus, I've been to his place & I get on with him pretty well, but I guess that day he was in a fairly intense mood. A lot of these people tend to be very… I've never had an interview that was unreasonably difficult. I've seen others doing interviews & you can see that their putting them on a pedestal already, so that changes the whole dynamic. And then maybe it seems more intense or strange, because they're playing up on it a little. But I think if you just treat someone like an equal, like a human, people tend to be fairly straight with you – you can cut through a lot of the bullshit. Even though a lot of the black metal people have this image on stage & are quite strange people, still they are human. It's like Gaahl, you see him on that *Headbanger's Journey*, and he's nothing like that. I don't think there's anyone I've interviewed who laughs as much..."

"Gaahl recently came out of the closet. It's no stereotype that black mettalers in The States are pretty homophobic. Is there an equal variable of crude opinions towards queer lifestyles in European metal, or do you think the Europeans are a little more over it by now?"

"I think if it had been anyone else, it might have been a bit more extreme. The thing is nobody in their right mind would say anything to his face. I think if it had been a member of Cradle of Filth or Anorexia Nervosa, or a band already seen as slightly effeminate or not true black metal, or maybe if it was like the guy from Creed – then it would've been a bit more extreme. People would have turned on him a bit more… I think the fact that he was so unapologetic about it all – also its Gaahl, you know, who's going to say anything to him? I know there was an incident at Wacken [**the festival] – that's the first time I saw Gaahl with his boyfriend, and somebody said something to him, and you know, it didn't end well for him. You know, you see all these NSBM people with Blasphemy patches. I interviewed Blasphemy once, and I said, 'Do you ever get any problems for having a black member?' And the guy said, 'Well you ever seen the size of his arms?' So I think its about the same as that. Rob Halford is still loved by everyone, even homophobic people. And also Gaahl is friends with Faust, which is a another strange twist…"

"Did Faust disavow what he did?"

"Now he does… I think the problem with black metal – the good thing and the bad thing – is that everything becomes drama. Importance is placed on stuff in a way I appreciate cause it gives things significance & weight. And it tends to place a deeper emphasis on events. It tends to be very dramatic – here's the power of nature, or here's the power of Satan or murder. And that's great in many ways, but the problem is that fans tend to glorify everything that happens so they glorify the murders or when Dead died – when he committed suicide – Euronymous built a legend. It kind of removes the human aspect, that these guys were quite young. I've spoken to Necrobutcher a number of times, and he hates all that cause he was really good friends with Dead. He was very upset about dehumanizing – just turning someone into a myth or a legend. I think it's the same with Faust – a lot of people want to glorify, you know, he killed, no remorse, and all this sort of stuff. But he was a young guy & he's trying to get over what he's done…"

"Have you ever made it up to Norway?"

"I've been to Norway about 10 times now, but I would never want to live in Scandinavia. It's great to visit – I love the clean air, the clean water, but its so depressing. The darkness, the cold – I'm too old for that now. I used to think that was great when I was a teenager, but now I'd rather live in Istanbul. The only thing that stops me is making a living."

"What about Finland?"

"I really like Tampere [Finland]. That's the most alternative place I've ever been to. Honestly, I got out the train station – I walked downtown & within 30 seconds I saw a guy wearing a Vlad Tepes shirt. 50% of the people under the age of 45 were wearing punk stuff, metal stuff. I remember one Sunday evening at midnight there were 3 bars still playing metal. In London, on a Saturday night, you'd have trouble even finding 3. So Tampere is the place man, and Finland in general. Metal is really entrenched in the culture – you can by Lordi Cola at the supermarket. You know Reverend Bizarre? They got to number one in the normal charts, with a 15 minute demo track. You know, in radio play. So I would say it's the most metal country it the world – I think Finland is the metal success story of the decade…"

* * *

Back in March, buried deep in odd correspondence, was one random email that stood out with a subject heading I couldn't ignore. It read, quite simply, "**HAIL SATAN**." *"Greetings from Chicago… I am contacting you to inquire about your upcoming odyssey into the geopolitical epicenter of the culture of death. I am also writing to volunteer my services. To be brief, I have reached a place in my life where my inborn curiosity combined with a festering wanderlust has overcome my common sense. I feel the need to escape because the prospect of a continued downtown grind grows increasingly untenable by the day…"*

"Bike messenger, 23, Polish-American, metalhead, weirdo longhair extraordinaire. Been done with college for a little while now, miraculously debt free, and now I gaze down the barrel of a working class life. I'm eminently aware of the fact that my situation could easily be worse. Maybe I've read too many books, maybe I've seen 'Fight Club' too many times, or maybe I'm far less mature than I think myself to be, but I feel trapped. To be blunt: I'm willing to forsake the meager possessions I've accumulated and put my energies into assisting you in blazing a trail of across Europe…"

"I'm near certain we would get along on a personal front, and I might actually be of assistance: I have experience with media (involved in radio since high school), and I'm good with bikes. I imagine you've received emails like this. I imagine you could construct quite an entourage, if you haven't already. I'm open to the idea that there might not be a place for me in this, but I don't want you to get the idea that I'm pining for this for the wrong reasons. I'm not volunteering myself out of fandom. I would prefer you think of me as an aspiring co-conspirator. I want to contribute somehow, and I am not without ideas of how I might do such a thing... I'm asking for your serious consideration. What would it take?"

So I give the gentlemen a ring at something like 3am his time, since his message clearly read *'wired insomniac.'* His name was Matt Rozycki; said he found *The Big Shiny Prison* on a random message board

& read nearly the entire thing in one burst. Said he wanted adventure & I was the guy to make it happen...

To asphyxiate the element of surprise, I was upfront about my peculiarities. In terms of traveling, I'm a lone wolf. There is only one guy that I'll hit the road with as a duo, and his name is Dr. Jeremy Sullivan [**of the Free Therapy Brigade]. But Doc, that old scalawag – you can't get him off the rails, let alone the North American continent. Fucker is a train-hopping junkie & I've never been a fan of that hobo jazz. Too many obnoxious oogles want to flex their street cred & the choo-choo ain't my jive, nor is dodging railway conductors & yard dogs, salt-guns & trespassing citations. I'm more into rubber tramping, or the cheap bus-line or ride-share – *plus I'd rather just Flakfizer some Oglethorpe then deal with an extremist roach squat of dogmatic crusties far too punk rock for their own good.* But that's just me & if you didn't understand a lick of what I just said, you weren't really supposed to anyway...

So I told Matt that I was inconsequential & what he really needed was the correct lunatic to kick him in the ass & get him on the move. That my hustle is a perpetually doomed ship & I was going solo at all costs. But I was OK to hang with him in London, get him up to speed & then possibly meet back up down the line.

I encouraged him to do his own book on the underground, or at least a siege of radio interviews for his show, & promised to export him to contacts/countries of the FORTRESS EUROPE experiment that I wouldn't be able to make in person. Said a Free Agent Surrogate was what I could offer, but at least it was something. He thought it a negotiation: *"Well then, I guess I'll sell all of my shit & see you in London..."*

Time goes by & I hear nothing. Write him a few times but never get a response. I fairly much gave up on Matt & his crazy mission – until I checked my Facebook after breakfast...

Matt & I are in a section of London called Tottenham, which is equivalent to a Brit ghetto. Whereas any raw section of The States would have shady characters congregating in dark alleyways, Tottenham keeps them at bay due to CCTV, the Big Brother system of government installed cameras that are in every nook & cranny, light post & traffic stop, shopping mall & street corner of the UK...

Tony Blair is the culprit behind this. His cabinet created this Department of Homeland Security styled security apparatus which now employs hundreds of thousands of snitches. 24 hours a day the British government records all reality & savors it in a massive, continual database of stock footage. CCTV is used by the law enforcement in any case they see fit. No crimes pass unnoticed, unless you live with a ski mask glued to your face.

We're following Keef Thomas to his flat down cobblestone streets of a seemingly ancient Victorian neighborhood – this stretch of grimy houses & businesses built upon the what you'd consider the hunting grounds of Jack The Ripper. Keef is the vocalist from hardcore punk band FLOWERS OF FLESH & BLOOD. Initially tonight's interview was to be Black Ram/National Anarchism founder & spokesman Troy Southgate, but he bailed out of the project at the last second. It would have been an epic mega-rant with the progenitor of "Anarcho-Fascism" [*as it's been dubbed by Southgate's opposition*] but Keef – this blonde dreaded block of a Scotsman – is quite epic in his own right.

Matt, on the other hand, is fearless. For a newcomer to the traveling game, he remarkably hit the bull's-eye in finding us a communal squat on Chalk Farm, an area within walking distance of Camden Town itself. There are at least 20 people in & out of the place – a 4 story flat currently fighting eviction but will last, at least, until the end of the UK mission. More on that later…

As for Matt, being new to this whole game, he's rusty as the Titanic on the Arctic floor. He's a skinny & tall metal freak that literally sold everything he had & took a plane into Manchester arriving with little more then eight grand, a tape recorder & high-speed bike which he plans to cycle through most of Europe with this summer. He's got this rough plan of cruising his own *Tour De France* & then popping up in Poland to attempt duel citizenship due to his Grandparents immigrant lineage…

Our walk to Keef's pad is marked by a frank discussion over the ever-growing Pan-European police state & the general rise of right wing politics abroad. We agree that the exercise of force is never a jolly thing, but at least in the UK, the cops don't carry guns but rather billy-clubs. Which is far more noble, because at the bare minimum they actually have to fight you like men to take you down. Fisticuffs is still a samurai-like code of honor in England, unlike the USA where they'll just brutally tazer you to death like cowards…

"I've lived in London for 12 years; I came down [*from Scotland*] with the idea to spend as much of my life doing music. First I did a band called The Mirrormen, which lasted about three years. That band dissolved and became FLOWERS OF FLESH & BLOOD. In 2006 I hooked up with Matt Jarman & Wagner, our drummer, & formed LamRatLazIt1st which was inspired by Washington DC hardcore, something a bit less like the full-on hardcore of FLOWERS. We did that band for 9 months, went to

Brazil, put a record out... Wagner's [*the sole Brazilian member*] visa actually elapsed & had to go back, but then we met another Brazilian guy named Santiago who's been our drummer ever since."

"What's the message?"

"Things that make me angry, but articulated in a reasonably intelligent way – my frustration with the general public's' apathy. The sense of disenfranchisement you have when you see stupid fucking rules & laws coming in that restrict peoples freedoms to do things they shouldn't have a problem doing. I guess kind of standard anarchist, anti-governmental lyrics..."

"When I look at the UK, the parliament – it seems there is much more of an authentic democracy then a lot of other countries. At least in The States. Do you feel that it is hopeless in any mainstream sense? But again, I'm coming from America..."

"I think what's happened in my lifetime is that we've actually gone from a situation where there was a genuine alternative to right wing government. When I was a kid, the Labor Party had genuine aspirations to be socialist, but Tony Blair kicked that all into oblivion. Now its like something you have in The States where its two parties with little actual difference. That is a great source of frustration to me & other intelligent people who believe you can't have a functional democracy unless you have two parties who are fundamentally different from one another."

"Does the general population detest Tony Blair?"

"Tony Blair is not a popular guy because of the Iraq war & the lies that were told. A lot of people were really upset about that, but did you not think there is a professional politician that rises to the top of his profession who doesn't fuckin' lie to you? I guess not everyone is as cynical as me."

"Tell me about the crusty, anarcho hardcore scene..."

"I think that squatting should be much better protected by law. There's a lot of movements around Europe to ban squatting. In Holland, they've virtually banned it. In the UK, the government we've got now – they're definitely making moves to try & end the squatting movement which I think will be a great cultural loss. There's still a lot of prejudice against squatters that is fanned by the media & politicians, people who feel that everybody's got to pay for a home whether or not they can reasonably afford it. I think that's pretty ridiculous. If there's empty buildings, people have the right to take them. A lot of people just cant get their feet on the ladders. Not only do they sort of look after a building which would otherwise go to ruin, but they also add vitality. Saint Agnus was the last holy squatted street in London – that was an amazing place, these enormous Victorian town houses – five-story houses, terraces, community centers, people sharing skills, bike workshops. They would have reggae festivals, street festivals – an awful lot of artistic cultural events. When that got evicted it happened almost completely overnight – they literally were dragging people, pregnant women out the houses. In one night they got everybody out & bulldozed it in 20 minutes."

"What does anarchism meant to you?"

"Well, I don't think its realistic to expect that it would mean overthrowing the government. I think anarchism is about looking at what you can do in the circumstances of your own life & contributing positively to your community in that direction. To meet like-minded people who want to put themselves out a little bit for what they actually believe in & do things which are positive and make a real difference. Think lively/act locally is how I see it."

"What are some of the best bands in this scene here?"

"Armed Response Unit, who you'll meet later tonight – definitely one of the most interesting bands in the London scene. Very original approach to doing some very aggressive music, but also they've got influences from the Mike Patton side of things, the fucked up noise, jazz kind of stuff but also crust. Hello Bastards who are a full-on straightedge sort of band. They're a very multi-national band – one of their guys is Israeli. Don't quote me on this, but I think he was in some trouble because he refused to go back to be a part of the Israeli Army because they're a very pro-Palestine band. They've actually been on tour in the Gaza Strip, which is fucking impressive. Cavity Search is another one…"

"That's a great band name."

"They're sort of London's 2011 answer to GG Allin."

"Do you think the UK is becoming a police state?"

"The assault on peoples liberties & public sector pay in The States is more advanced – but I'm also very scared that the UK is heading down that road. Blair's government passed something like 3000 pieces of legislation in 10 years, which was about 20 times as much as had been done in any 10 year period of parliament. Most of it was aimed at restricting people's personal freedoms. Before they came in, we had the Criminal Justice Bill. It basically made it illegal to have parties outside. Before that we had a really healthy scene of people though would just turn up in a field with a sound system, or a forest, & it would maybe last for a week. These were some of the most glorious events I'd ever been to. After Blair got in, they built on this platform of reducing what people were actually able to do. There's been a specific series of changes aimed at preventing protesters from effectively being able to protest – it's now impossible to protest anywhere within a mile of parliament. I've honestly given up in terms of marching in the streets because its so limited now that its got no chance of actually affecting anything…"

6 blocks from Keef's flat we've found ourselves with a manic Italian woman & her husband, a refugee from the San Diego area. He's got that gleam of victory, that dream-like stasis of having forever escaped the United States by randomly hooking up with a Venice punk rock goddess while on vacation. He & I swap stories of sweltering El Cajon madness in this cramped flat covered with black sheets over the walls & dominatrix gear & leather whips & cuffs & chains & all you can imagine dangling on nails like casual decorations. You'd think someone popped *The Lament Configuration*…

Kiara Banuet is animated, ranting, talking with her hands like spastic Jiu Jitsu. She's the bassist of Armed Response Unit, this weirdo hardcore punk act that crosses innumerable genre boundaries. They've been around for 6 years, put out a bunch of vinyl & LP's. They are very multi-national with members that also include an Irishmen, a born-in-Brazil Brit & a mixed member of Spanish/Slovakian background: "I come from a squatting background – this is my first flat in some time. Cause I got married & everything & blah blah blah. The thing about the London scene is there is this split between the north & south, – the south is like the crust, the north is more the drunk punks. Armed Response Unit, we've never been one or the other…

"What's your background, in terms of Italy?"

"I left Italy in '94, mainly because that's when Berlusconi got elected prime minister & I realized it was going to be really tough shit for musicians & artists & that's exactly what happened. Years later they are still in the same political situation – its become a fucking circus. It's too much, it's surreal – it's completely ridiculous. I just cannot believe they let him slowly change the law to make it entirely convenient for himself. The man could kill a man & not be prosecuted. I personally believe that he is bribing everybody – he managed to get 5 television channels & now he's got his hands into the actual state channel. He's managed to brainwash the whole fucking population – slowly, with tits & asses – & in the meantime he's diverted the attention of the people. The problem with Italians, they're all a bunch of sheep. But all countries are pretty much like that. Italians, in particular, are like that – there's a lot of tradition involved, it's hard to come out if you think differently. Avant Garde is not really supported; everybody looks the same. In Rome, or Milan, bologna or Florence, there is still space for art. You will find alternative people – usually all in the same spot."

"It's tough to squat there then?"

"You can't squat anymore in Italy – we used to get 40, 50 people and then barricade ourselves in with food & water. Just stay there for a month then the cops come with their dogs & guns & you just make sure that you fight back for as long as you can until they eventually lose interest. It's hardcore – *nothing* like here. When I came here it was like, '*Oh shit, the law actually sort of protects you.*' If you don't break anything, there's no criminal damage – say that there is a window open & obviously no one lives in the property, if you get into a place & change the lock, it becomes your home. People cannot kick you out – it becomes a civil dispute & they need to take you to court. The police are not allowed to come & kick you out – but now they do it."

"So the anti-squatting ban in the UK is more aggressive?"

"It's harder & harder to squat in London, but we've been doing it for years & years. And obviously a lot of people will say the wrong thing, '*Oh yeah we broke the window.*' BOOM. Done – criminal damage. Well obviously you have to break the window, yeah, because if you find a house with an open window, chances are there's no toilets, no running water. But the law still protects you, in theory. I've seen the attitude of the cops changing a hell of a lot. But you have to know how to play 'no comment.' But if you know they got nothing on you, CCTV didn't see you break in, and you have your story – no comment, no comment – there's nothing they can do. A lot of people don't know that so they start saying 'no, yeah, it was my friend, blah blah blah' – sooner or later you're going to say the wrong thing & that's how they're going to nail you. Truth is there's so much property its disgusting – people've got 5,6,7, houses. Point is the rent in London is ridiculous – it s a joke. Homes should be a right for anybody. Once you're born, you should have the right to a home, to water, & you should have working opportunities, education. It's like £2,000 to uniform a soldier, £95,000 a year to keep someone in prison…"

"Where do stand politically?"

"I consider myself more of an anarchist, but there isn't much difference between communist & anarchist collectivism. The problem with communism is I fear it could lead to some form of totalitarian state. The difference with collectivist anarchism communities is that it can still be organized in communes that not only listen to the people, but are made of the people. It's not like representative democracy that's voted on by a few people that kind of represent us. The problem with communism is that individualism wouldn't be respected enough. I don't really believe in '*majority wins,*' because in the end it isn't fair. In my opinion, majority democracy doesn't really work… I think the problem is how to educate people. Every time you mention anarchism, people are like, '*Oh my god it's gonna be a mess – everybody's gonna shoot each other.*' No – absolutely not. That's not the idea of anarchism – its giving a voice to everybody in the community."

"I've been told that the underground scene in Turin, Italy is drenched in occultism…"

"Turin is the black magic capitol, actually. So its very dark & very weird & the vibe is really, really crazy. I don't particularly like Turin, but its got a very powerful vibe – its not something that I can rationally explain. Milan, there's a couple of really good squats, but the problem is that it's the fashion capitol, so there's a bunch of fucking fake motherfuckers & all this post-yuppie, Berlusconi fuck followers & everything costs 3 times as much & blah blah blah. Florence is beautiful – it's like bologna, a little like Paris."

"Well, I ask everyone this, but do you have a crazy story? Something that happened to you and when you tell people about it they think you're making the whole thing up?"

"Not far from here we found a new squat – broke the window, come down & fucking awesome man – but it was obvious someone was living there, kind of working on the place. It looked abandoned – there were no floorboards, blah blah blah. We left the window open, came back, me & Hannah – we go back and we're like, '*Let's just take that 8x10 amp.*' So I'm pushing it and I hear Hannah go '*AAAAAH!*' There's this dude in the back room with an axe staring through the window. BOOM! Breaks the window with his eyes man looking like fuckin' crazy – boo-wah fuckin' charging and we're like '*AAAAH FUCK,*' you know, and in that moment there was no '*Oh my friend*' – no, fuck you, I'm out that window; fuck off I'm first. So we run & Hannah falls, so I stop & pick her up & were running & I lose my shoes & blah blah blah & the dude is behind me & he grabs me & '*OH SHIT*' and I'm on the ground like BOOM & he's like '*Fuck you fucking burglars what did you take from my house!!*' & I'm like, '*I swear we thought it was squatted were not taking anything.*' He's like '*Yeah, fucking – I fucking swear to god I'll fucking kill you, I swear to god!!*' & he grabs my fucking hoodie and I swear, I fucking saw it in his eyes & I'm looking at him & I'm like… I know this dude. I've sent his dude before man, what the fuck, you know? He starts dragging me & I try to escape but I had a mullet of dreads & he grabs them & starts dragging me back into the house & Hannah, she pisses herself – that's how scared she is. His eyes man, his eyes dude – he was gonna kill me, he didn't care – he break his own window to get into his house faster. So I chicken out completely & I'm like, 'Call the cops man –

call the fucking cops!!' And the cops get there & they're like, '*Oh – hello Mr. Giff.*' And I'm like, '*Mr. Giff? Mr. Giff? OH FUCK – IT'S HIM! Its Roland Gift, the fucking singer of the FINE YOUNG CANNIBALS!!*' He hid the fucking axe when they arrived & they got fucking autographs and sent us home. They didn't do to him anything…"

**(Day III): "a *doom fiend, industrial legend & shabby journalist walk into a bar – somehow they manage to leave the punch-line on the tube…*"

Morning at Keef's – French pressed coffee & an intriguing rant with his Irish roommate whom details the enigma of EasyJet, an airplane company that Europeans have dubbed "*SleazyJet*" because it's uber cheap, drops you a hundred miles from wherever you are actually trying to go & will only let you take carry-on luggage. But the beauty is that when you book months in advance, an airplane flight to Belgium from London is only €15 – most Euro-capitols you can hit for around €30. He also details EuroStar, which is like a bullet train on the Eurail which can get you over the English channel & into France for around €100.

The plan was to get a €1000 month-long pass on the Eurail train system, but that might not even be necessary since I've been given intel on a dozen ride-share sites in multiple languages. The big ones in London, I'm told, are Gumtree.com, BlaBlacar.com & Rideshare.co.uk – as well as Kayak, the "Priceline of Europe."

Craigslist isn't really much of anything across The Atlantic, though you an fairly much live off it in The States. But the German site & its English counterpart – mitfahrgelegenheit.ch & carpooling.co.uk – are far stronger. Further luck is that my high-tech, wifi-laced iPod has free apps for all this as well as language translation software. *Plissken's little wristwatch seems so apropos…*

Keef's Brazilian friend ceases being an unconscious lump beneath blankets on the fold-out mattress, rubs his eyes & slams some black coffee. His name is Wagner Antunes & plays drums in an outfit called LamRatLazIt1st: "Basically I dropped everything in Sao Paulo to come to England to make music; LamRatLazIt1st, its hardcore stuff – melodic. Then I came back to Sao Paulo, we went on tour in Brazil. They came back but I couldn't cause visa problems. I was patiently waiting for this bureaucracy then I just gave up. 4 years later, I'm back…"

"So what's the scene like in Brazil?"

"The scene in Brazil is quite big now – hardcore & punk's the biggest stuff. My first band was a hardcore band called Newspeak. We make two compilations, one EP & a split with Catharsis from Atlanta –

brutal hardcore political stuff... The scene in Sao Paulo is really nice – loads of venues, they really organize... Brazilian culture is completely different then the northeast & the very south. Basically the police are fascist – really, really corrupt. Not as much bad as the beginning of the 80's – we came after the dictatorship, so the police were much more violent. The punk scene suffered so much more then now – you couldn't hang around with a band t-shirt. The skateboarding is something really important to make this scene, because hardcore & punk was associated with skateboarding in Sao Paolo. The first bands, the first vinyl, CD's, t-shirts – the scene is totally based in the American scene. Sao Paulo is an Americanized place...

"What's the deal with Cubatao? Is it like a toxic waste dump city & all the people are mutated & dying of cancer & having flipper babies?"

"Exactly – it's totally fucked. Now they make some companies try & clean it, but no way man. Cubatao man, it's a chemical processing plant – babies born with two heads, two brains... My friend Niño, he's a hardcore drummer. He lost all his teeth because of this company, because he used to work in the chemical stuff. They fucked up the rivers. It's like Mungi – you know what is Mungi? Mungi is a quiet environment, like a swamp. The thing when they built this city – its close to the seaside. They don't realize people would live their after years. It's terrible man, loads of kids dying..."

5pm; back in Camden Town at World's End. Earlier I'd went for a long ride on a public bus getting the lay of the land. Tried to find Big Ben but got fed up with the traffic, hopped off & got caught up in a mob of people waiting to meet Dr. Who [*Tom Baker*] outside a television studio that was cramped in an alleyway...

That soon grew older then Baker himself, so I shot over to the next journalistic target Pantheist. Originating in 2000 by vocalist/songwriter Kostas Panagiotou, Panthiest were one of the first funeral doom bands in Europe & still going steady. They've lived abroad, released a wealth of material and have hit the road touring amongst the likes of doom stalwarts Skepticism, Gallileous, While Heaven Wept & Mourning Beloveth...

Panagiotou returns from the bar clutching some much needed brews, so we kick a few back & hone the verbal chops: "London's a very cosmopolitan town, but the difficult thing, especially when you're in a band, nobody is here to stay – you're here for a few years. You won't find many people who spend their entire lives here. Most people are foreigners. As a band, we don't have a single English person. We have Greek,

Serbian, people from Holland. In the past we've had people from Spain, Australia…"

"Doom is pretty accepted in the USA underground – it's kind of a wedge sound that even the most ardent black or death metaller can agree on, and there is also a huge crust punk following. Even a lot of hipster indie rock types are into sludgy, droning shoegaze stuff… "

"Doom is a very split scene. Everything starts from Black Sabbath – then it became *Winter*, the first album of Cathedral. We kind of fit into that second class – the doom/death side that evolved into funeral doom. More atmospheric, also keyboard – but still very slow, very minimalist. When we get offers for gigs, they are usually very diverse. In a year we played 3 gigs in London, then abroad like Finland, Poland, Latvia, Czech Republic, the Moscow Doom Fest… It's a small scene. Bands like us don't sell very much at all, but they're very enthusiastic people. In the early 90's there wasn't much funeral doom. Very isolated bands – one in northern England, maybe a few in America. So these bands never used to play live, there were no groups, there wasn't much support other then doom-metal.com, which I used to write for. Suddenly all these people were into this music & started talking to each other."

"What was the Moscow Doom Fest like?"

"In Russia, man – these guys are crazy. There was this guy, he was almost like a stalker. He was like, '*Can you sign this, and this*' & he was following me around. And he had a page with him where he'd written some things in Russian & a friend had translated these questions. Like what's your favorite color, what's the meaning of life? I'd come out the toilet & he'd be standing there – '*what's your favorite color?*' Strange, strange people. After the gig he kept sending me emails saying how he wanted to start a family, but he couldn't find a girlfriend, and this made him stop believing in god."

"You originally come from Greece – what is your comment on the current demonstrations? What went wrong?"

"For years they've been living beyond their means – tax evasion, things like that. They call it '*working in black*' when you have a second job that is illegal. The economy was built on a bubble; the country almost went bankrupt. The debt was growing higher & higher & nobody wanted to pay taxes so it started to collapse. It's a sad situation, but if you go to Greece, you will know it when you see anarchists. Groups of anarchists having massive demonstrations, burning cars, smashing things. Otherwise other people are going out – just living, they don't care. That's typical Greek – they live the '*carpe diem*' theory. They have to take austerity measures, which are very harsh. And its not just in Greece – petrol is at its highest, its almost possible to afford a car. The taxes have gone up so much its unbelievable.

"What sort of political environment is at play? Do people take Marxism or even Democratic Socialism serious?"

"In the elections you have like 10% voting for the Communist Party. There was a very strong communist movement in Greece that developed after the Second World War. *[During the reign of General Papadopoulos, then dictator of Greece]* There was a civil war, basically between the government & the communists; there was a strong movement towards the left & a lot of artists that were inspired by Marxism ended up in jail. It's a historical thing, and metalheads sometimes took it over – especially in the beginning. A lot of people in heavy metal, or alternative people in Greece, are often associated with Marxism. Not saying all of them are – there is also far right, in Greece. There's a lot of anarchism, a lot of counter-movement. A lot of people in the extremes, they are joining in on the crisis, not because they believe in it, but because the idea of, *'The government is fucked up.'"*

"Is Italy similar to Greece?"

"The south of Italy is very similar to Greece. Italy is a funny country – you have to be careful when speaking to Italians because there's a massive difference between the north & the south. The north of Italy is like the rest of Europe – high industrial, technologically advanced. The south of Italy's quite poor & similar to attitude in Greece. This traditional, rural structure. Greece – in terms of philosophy & mentality – has always been closer to countries like Russia. There's a strong anti-American feeling. They don't have any problem with individual Americans, they feel America is policing the world…"

Kostas floats out the entrance, leaving me to the rowdy, packed club of drunken Englishmen. Everyone is riled up because a football match is going on that has some sort of deep ramifications for two distinct areas of the country *[but don't they all?]*. No matter – my text message beeper goes haywire because Reza Udhin is now somewhere in the mass of bodies on the upper floor.

Reza is the keyboardist from Killing Joke, one of the most important industrial bands in the genres history. He's also the brainiac of industrial outfit INERTIA & heads up the independent label Cryonica. INERTIA are more of an electro-industrial outfit, as opposed to a nitty-gritty harsh monster. They are somewhere along the likes of Razed In Black or Lords of Acid. Killing Joke, on the other hand, are their own particular colossus & their reputation surely precedes them. The label

Cryonica has been active since 2000, putting out a slab of releases from fellow industrial acts like Octolab, Knifeladder, Void Construct, Swarf & Mono Chrome…

When I spot Reza at the circular tabletop, I'd half-expected a gruffly accented, chain-smoking filthy ol' bastard – instead he's a baby face that could pass for 23. He's got jet-black hair slick from gel; all black clothing, leather pants & boots. And he's totally friendly & smiling in high spirits…

"So How did the Killing Joke thing start?"

"I knew the old keyboard player & he asked if I wanted to join about 12 years ago but I couldn't really do it. I've done 3 albums with them so far. My main band is INERTIA – it'll be 20 years this year. The new album came out 6 months ago & we've been touring for 6 months. We started out in London, did loads of tours – US tours, 9 European tours, 13 albums. Later this year we'll be going to Canada, hopefully the US – Australia, South America."

"How do you feel about the industrial scene in Europe?"

"The scene is good, the festivals are good. A long time ago – particularly Germany & Belgium – used to be amazing. These days I think it's a bit saturated. It's very difficult to get people out to shows in those areas. It's very quiet, I think – too much."

"Are you from the UK?"

"I'm from London, been here all my life. If you want industrial, in the east side is Slimelight – its open until 7 in the morning."

"How does America stack up for you, in terms of touring?"

"Oh I love it – much better then touring the UK & Europe. Doesn't matter if its Killing Joke or INTERTIA. In all fairness The States seem to be more open-minded. Europeans are very dead-set on what they like, or what they're told to like. Whereas The States, they like anything. Europeans, they like all the new stuff & just stick with it. In The States they just go out & find all the old stuff – they're into the history, really into the music."

"Is there a misconception in Europe that everyone in the United States is a hillbilly?"

"Yeah, exactly, but I've never felt that way at all. At one point on tour 10 years ago – we'd tour the USA twice a year – and we'd play in Birmingham Alabama at a really small place. It was great, absolutely amazing – One of the best places we've ever played. Just a small club filled with freaks – goth, metallers, transvestites – anything you want."

"What's the main message you like to propagate?"

The new album is all about people bettering themselves & getting out of negative situations. On the last tour we put a bunch of bands together that would never play on the same bill. The punk scene, the industrial scene – its all quite separated. It's strange, it never used to be like that. Quite a few years ago it was all one without very much effort."

"What changed it?"

"People getting into their own little genres too much. Before it used to be seen as music, not genres. These days people grow up in a particular scene and that's their scene. Its more about the lifestyle & people around them then the actual music, that's the difference."

"Got any nutty stories from the road?"

"On tour once we had a little run-in with the US military around Area 51. We went out there once – followed an old dirt road & drove into he desert. There are signs that say you're near Area 51. We go behind the mountains & just as we got to the edge these helicopters came out of nowhere – just sirens & lights & telling us to get the hell out. Heh heh…

* * *

By 9pm I've fled across town, having been jammed with human cattle in the subway-like Tube. Reza had invited me out to Slimelight – the premier Goth-Industrial club of London for a chat with the owners – but I'd long since promised to make this gig at 12 Bar with Injury Time, Deal With It & Ninebar…

This show is familiar territory; a dirty Irish-style pub linked to a backroom concert area. The show's a monthly put-on by Rucktion Records, who are one of the most well-organized & important hardcore metal labels in the UK. Most the material they put out is Madball/Hatebreed territory – the spin-kickin', knuckle-draggin' beat-down stuff. The chap who roped me into this comes from a band called Kartel. His name is Tom Barry & meets with me briefly before he has to scoot across town to work merch…

"The Rucktion [Records] monthly residency has finally given the London scene a stable hub. Unfortunately tonight has been 'double-booked' & there's another show in Camden so it won't really get going here until that one finishes at 10. Bad communication! It shows that the hardcore scene is still a small underground affair & can be venerable to under capacity crowd issues if people don't stay in contact. The headlining band tonight, Ninebar – they're legends in the London scene…"

"So you wrote a book yourself about the underground?"

"My book centers around the balance people in European hardcore have to strike between work & music. DIY Hardcore is not a music people can live off so they work to fund their tours, print their shirts, pay for rehearsal & at the end of it hopefully break even. I wanted to show that thousands are prepared to do this & essentially work two jobs to keep the scene alive… The book came about when my band played some shows in Portugal & our bassist brought a professional photographer along. Her name's Sophia Schorr-Kon; she hardly focused on the whole '*vocalist-as-god handing out the microphone for the raging throng to grab*' thing. Instead we used photos of guys at their DIY merch stalls, people at the back of mosh pits anticipating somebody crashing into them with worried looks on their faces – the background stuff that people always seem to ignore. We wanted to document subjects at their day jobs & then at rehearsal, creating t-shirt designs, organizing tours, etc. I wanted to document the real hardcore scene in Europe, as there'd been some hyped-up retro hipster crap & felt it was a slap in the face for the people putting in the real work."

"What's the scoop on your band Kartel?"

"We were going for the metal/hardcore crossover but agreed on the need to have our own sound & got a hold of two guys from the scene to do vocals – DBS & Pete. Our stuff has been released through Rucktion records & it's not easy running a band with members all perpetually broke, but I guess it's the standard in UK hardcore… When we started gigging some of these [venues] were legendary, but lots of them have since closed. There was a Jamaican pub in Tottenham, North London, called The Swan that was a real head fuck. You'd be in the back room with all these guys spin kicking to beatdown metalcore, getting yourself all hyped & sweaty & then decide to get some water or beer. You'd then rush through to the main bar & you were hit with a complete opposite vibe – chilled old Jamaicans playing dominos & listening to quiet reggae. It was really funny cause you'd realize how crazy you must've seemed as these guys looked up from their boards with a look on their faces like, '*what's wrong with you?*' Thing was, as the evening wore on & the rum flowed, a few of them would drunkenly wander into the back room & stand there skanking gently as some band were screaming out their bile & people were jumping all over each other. I miss that place…

Tom introduces me to Pierre before heading out the door, the singer from Knuckledust. Coming from Detroit, it's admittedly weird to cross paths with a black guy that has a full-tilt full English accent: "I've been involved in London hardcore since '95; I'm 35 now. Knuckledust started in '96, been playing ever since – no one else was supporting hardcore at the time. We felt we had to. You make friends along the way, family – 15 years later I'm still doing the same thing. We've got two black members in our band, so it's a little unusual playing this music sometimes – people don't expect it. Especially when we starting out man – they heard the name and thought we were a right wing band. And then they hear the shit that we're playing…"

"Rucktion is more of a self-sustaining collective then an outright label, correct?"

"It's non-profit; any money we make form it goes right back into it. Some ignorant people would say all our bands sound the same, but if they actually paid attention, there's a lot more personality in those bands then you could imagine…"

"What are some bands that are exemplary of the London hardcore sound?"

"One of my favorites are Ninebar who're playing tonight – they just capture the London vibe & attitude. Call it beat down, call it whatever. Besides that, Injury Time are doing the typical LBU style –True Valiant from Bristol, Chains of Hate from Wales…"

"What's the bare-bones message?"

"I like to put a positive side, maybe something uplifting to the lyrics that people can relate to, maybe find some sense of hope in it. That's what hardcore was to me as a kid – I was a bit lost & confused & listened to some hardcore bands, those lyrics were the ones that carried me & made me who I am in a way, so I want to give that back."

"There's a massive unemployment rate here in London…"

"At the moment it's very hard for people out here –some of the highest figures that we've ever had. The funniest thing is the serious amount of youth not being able to get employed, coming out of schools, colleges & having no job waiting at the end. The figures there are bigger then anytime in the past. What else are you to do but make money by illegal means? Things are getting crazy out there on the street. But you see the money they put into the policing – if crimes happen the police don't even care no more. It's only if physical harm is being done that they're likely to respond with any urgency, know what I mean? Last month a friend of ours van got ripped off – robbed everything. He had all our backline equipment – broad daylight, High Street – CCTV all long the van. Police said, '*Well we don't have the time or the manpower to respond to this, so if you go and catch them & bring them to us we'll press charges, but we're not gonna sit down & watch the CCTV footage which would have the evidence on it.*' So now they are promoting vigilantes?

And then when that happens, what are they going to do? Throw those people in prison as well? What the fuck?? I can't even remember a time without CCTV, to be honest. It's as bad as it could ever be right now, with cameras everywhere – buses, trains, tunnels, walkways. But the way I see it is they can't have someone watching each & every screen all the fucking time…"

**(Day IV): *"EYE OF THE HURRICANRANA"*

Sunday morning; June 5th, 2011. Today is a day off from the grind, getting contacts in order & continuing to flirt with the gorgeous Latvian girl in the next room that's watching *Fear & Loathing In Las Vegas*. Spent the earlier part of the day acquiring supplies from the 99 Pents store & made it through an open air market that's existed since the early 1800's. There was a bronze bull as a landmark statue & a dinky head-shop that sold over-the-counter Peyote & Hawaiian Woodrose, although I'm unsure if lunging into such a psychological feat is apt for London…

The hardcore show was all it was promised to be, although it was totally strange for me to witness Brits playing up NYC hardcore. Not so much the bands themselves, but the audience. It was sort of this bizarre cargo cult of backwards Dodgers caps & mimicked slam dancing. And all these chicks that were sort of swaying to the left and the right, bopping back and forth, the whole crowd oh so bubbly & English & smiling the whole time with bright white teeth. East Coast hardcore is menacing when participating in the authentic deal on the East Coast, because there are all these tough-guy bulldog's of men, skinheads & such, & so much amped up testosterone. Here it's like you can only conjure images of Simon Pegg, and that's about as threatening as a bowl of wobbling Jello…

Been ditching all possible weight from my travel pack. Such is the golden rule – the lighter the better because even a single ounce depletes the pain of a crooked spine or the possibility of eventually shaping one. If it wasn't for this over the counter codeine, I'd be extremely rough at the moment. This is why Britain would surely kill me – a 30 pack of 1000mg generic Vic's are €2. In the USA, you need a prescription or each pill counts as a felony [**one felony = you can never leave the United States ever again c/o The Patriot Act]. And yes, to any European that will read this one day, even Penicillin is a felony if you don't have a doctor's note. Such is *The Big Shiny Prison*…

Matt is nowhere to be found – he took off with Whitney & Alex to some psytrance rave party on the outskirts of London last night. It's another bizarre coincidence – the only other American staying in this place is from Ann Arbor, Michigan & she knows half my crew from the Theatre Bizarre in Detroit [**the greatest venue in the world & home to the slickest quasi-circus tribe you'll ever meet].

Alex, on the other hand, is a CouchSurfing.com ambassador from Canada; he's built this squat up as under such guidelines & hosts a basement filled with mattresses for any & all whom want to share booze stories. It's a great set-up that, most importantly, has no scabies crawling on the fabric. Alex is literally painted on the wall in homage, with a tag that reads: "In Alex We Trust INC." Other sayings scribbled in sharpie throughout the high-ceiling kitchen include "Life Is Short And Boring," "Fuck Love" & "Death To The Free Wheeling Monkey..."

I lucked out from the cell phone Keef gave me which takes SIM cards. Basically, I get a little chip for every different country at whatever 7/11 equivalent they have. €5 buys you like €10 credit, and since all I shoot over are text messages, this saves me a bundle [**note: to anyone planning to travel here, there is no such thing as a monthly unlimited call plan – every country is divided into their own specific tele-zone region & each country has it's own national version of an "area code"].

Insofar as the UK mission is concerned, it appears that my guy from ANAAL NATHRAKH has dropped off the face of the earth, and both DISCHARGE & AKERCOCKE aren't returning messages. I've got others around the UK, but it's just too pricy – I can't justify $200 USD for a bus up to Ireland/Scotland or an extra $80 to hit Birmingham, Liverpool or Manchester. So long Loch Ness, Black Sun & White House; apologies Arkham Witch, Pagan Altar, Into Sunlight, Esoteric & Bal-Sagoth...

The conception as it stands is to hit Paris next, then Amsterdam, Brussels, Berlin & Prague which will leave me open for any direction by early July. Afterwards it's a loose itinerary that could go any which way, really. But there will definitely be a tour through Scandinavia (Norway, Sweden, Finland) & a roar through Italy, Spain & Portugal. I have a huge turnout of enthusiasm for this project in Greece, but it seems the only way to get there is fly & SleazyJet doesn't go anywhere close, nor are there any direct line for busses of trains. Above all, it's basically WWIII on the streets right now, with anarchists chucking molotov cocktails at riot cops throughout the whole of Athens...

In Berlin I'm set to attend the first BETHLEHEM gig in 17 years at the reputed Under The Black Sun black metal festival. BETHLEHEM is the band that got me into black metal, and this is a once in a lifetime event that people will surely be traveling worldwide to see in person. BETHLEHEM main-man Juergen Bartsch invited me personally & hooked up the guest list, since we've been in contact for many years now.

The post-Berlin target is the Obscene Extreme festival in the Czech Republic – a one-stage, three-day open-air fest of 69 continual grindcore & death metal bands which I've been tipped off as perhaps the greatest metal festival in the world. Where I head afterwards will depend on who I meet at the fest itself, whether it be hopping on tour with a random band or jumping on a road trip caravan to Scandinavia, Italy or Greece...

The trail I blaze will bring me to the one journalistic showdown I've awaited my entire career. No, it's not MANOWAR, it's not even Trent Reznor. The target I admonish above all is **LAIBACH**, for LAIBACH's very existence signals: *"a purifying (EXORCISM) & regenerative (HONEY + GOLD) function. With a mystical, erotic audiovisual constitution of the ambivalence of fear & fascination (which acts on the consciousness in a primeval way); with a ritualized demonstration of political force, and with other manipulative approaches, LAIBACH practices sound/force in the form of a systematic (psychophysical) terror as therapy and principle of social organization."* LAIBACH: *"provokes maximum collective emotions & releases the automatic response of masses; the consequence [of which is] the effective disciplining of the revolted and alienated audience; awakening the feeling of total belonging and commitment to the Higher Order. By obscuring his intellect, the consumer is reduced to a state of humble remorse, which is a state of collective aphasia, which in turn is the principle of social organization..."*

Yes my friends, this has been in the works for a number of years – a legendary showdown between fearless Americano journalist Dr. Ryan Bartek & the pseudo-dictatorial thought engine triad of LAIBACH, IRWIN & NSK. Twice now I've failed in this mission. Once I had an email interview lined up with Ivan Novak for PIT Magazine, which he never got around to returning. Then in Seattle, in 2008 – during the 4-date *Volk* tour – I had a roundtable in-person uber-meeting scheduled through their PR liaison for Hails & Horns Magazine. Yet when it came time for action, they declined at the last minute under the auspice that they didn't speak English well enough & didn't want to come off as foolish.

It will happen this time though, for I am adamant to infect their self-styled NSK territory known to LAIBACHian aficionados as OCCUPIED EUROPE. Because I, like Malevich, like Johnny Appleseed, am now traversing the European continent spreading the seeds of the new art, the new journalism, and they cannot & will not ignore me once again. I will steer a path clear into the heart of Slovenia like a renegade steam engine & they will have no choice but to submit to my demands. For

LAIBACH may be *"the return of action on behalf of the idea,"* but Dr. Bartek is *"the return of the idea on behalf of the action..."*

* *(Day V): *"FENLAND contra NORDLAND contra VINLAND"*

Monday now; back at Worlds End waiting on a guy named Frank from an atmospheric/prog black metal outfit dubbed FEN that's named after a swampy region in England reputed for it's foggy, mysterious landscapes. Currently on the Code 666 roster, the FEN site describes their vibe as: *"An expression of loss and melancholic yearning... to draw the listener into a windswept & desolate landscape, bereft of hope..."*

The day has been raw for Whitney but superb for Matt. When we went on a little grocery store stocking, someone lifted her wallet straight from the purse – thus goes all her money, her passport & any possible access to banking. She's freaked & has to be in Rome within days to continue the freelance photography work that's keeping her afloat...

Matt, on the other hand, who thought his $2000 bicycle to be stolen, had apparently u-locked it in the middle of Camden Town days ago when drunk & simply forgot its whereabouts. So while one hinged on the verge of weeping, the other danced joyously as if a Dragonforce solo exploded in his head...

Frank saunters in & takes a seat – he's a mid-built longhair metal-head with glasses & thick accent, animated & intelligent. He's 31 years old & about to head off to Brussels once we're all wrapped up: "I'm actually going on vacation – a beer tour in Belgium with a couple friends. I'm a bit of a beer snob & enthusiast..."

"Is it true the only thing to do in Belgium is get hammered?"

"Yeah, it's... Not just the beer, but the culture as well. It's got the European café culture so everything is open late & you don't really have to rush to get hammered. It's more a grown up, relaxed approach to drunkenness. Belgium's not a big country, you can drive across it in 2 hours...

"Well tell me all about FEN..."

"We started off in early 2006 – it was myself & my brother, playing bass. We'd been in another band for awhile, built it wasn't properly satisfying us. I think when you're in a band for awhile, it becomes a sort of straitjacket – you feel compelled to play a certain way, there are expectations. I'd sort of moved into a different reality. So let's just sit down, do something more organic. At that point I'd been listening to a lot more ambient stuff, post-rock & shoe-gaze, same with the other guys. Let's just put all this together... We posted demo tracks on Myspace, sent some press releases & generated a little buzz. Got a label offer... After about a year, we realized this whole post-black metal scene was – all these names being thrown out that we're compared to, a lot of people were going down a similar path. A lot of reviews we get, the sort of *'They're just copying Agalloch or Alcest'* – that wasn't the case at all. Yeah, Agalloch, they're an inspiration of similar direction, but they're not looking at whets happening now. Agalloch are looking toward early Ulver, Fields of the Nephilim – same with us. Fields of the Nephilim are a strong influence, they're one of my favorite bands of all time – so we're taking stuff like that but fusing that with the bleaker, more reflective side of black metal. Also adding electronic influences that take it into a different world."

"As you know there's an entire mystique that's important to black metal – have you made it through the Scandinavian territories? How do you feel about those people?"

"I played in a band called Skaldic Curse & we played Bergen. It was cool to meet some of the guys from Enslaved, meet some of the guys from Hellheim & Taake. The guy from Taake, he's an acquaintance – quite a nice guy. It's interesting to meet the Norwegians because you quickly realize why black metal is the way it is & why it went down that certain path. I can't speak for the whole population, but certainly the guys in the black metal scene – they are convinced they're not playing a part. If you're just putting up some veils of mystery, I think fundamentally you're being honest. But what offends me about some black metal bands is that it is an act. You meet some of these guys backstage & they're standing around acting pissed, throwing things around – they wanna be all nihilistic. It's like, *'Look, we're in the middle of sound check – live your misanthropy, pour it out on stage, but this pissing about is just childish nonsense. This isn't contributing to some nihilistic ideology.'"*

"Do you feel the punk scene has that same problem?"

"I think anything where you have a strong aesthetic & overall ideology that has a habit of attracting extremity also has a habit of attracting people who are insecure, people who are just looking for an excuse to behave like an idiot. That's putting it at its most basic level. But the Norwegian guys – there was a lot of sincere intensity there. I don't know if it was a cultural trait or not. They're incredibly articulate, incredibly polite – very, very focused... Black metal means so much to so many different people, but there is a central tenant. You've got the spiked die-hards that look at Alcest like, *'you fags, that's not black metal.'* Well yes it is – its just a different expression. If we're going to say that isn't black metal then you better look at early Burzum."

"So about those French BM terrorist guys – I'm supposed to meet some of them, theoretically. What do you know?"

"Oh, the Les Légions Noires – those guys, I don't know. Belketre, Vlad Tepes, bands like that. Apparently they're supposed to all live in a castle somewhere & they are completely and absolutely dedicated to the black metal lifestyle."

"And they still live in a castle after all this time?"

"I don't know the reality of the situation. They probably all live in a rental somewhere, getting drunk & slicing themselves with knives listening to fucking ANTAEUS or something."

"Where I'm from in the Northwest United States, it's basically a huge rain forest of pine trees. It's called Cascadia. And it has, I reckon, the same bio-regional mystique as Scandinavia. The woods scream black metal, at least visually. But the scene in the Northwest is generally left-wing. Say, for instance, Wolves In The Throne Room – they've kind of gone ahead & started this self-sustaining urban farm commune sort of deal, which isn't that big of a deal considering the population in Portland or Seattle, but in terms of extreme metal – especially black metal – that's quite a departure from the usual attitude of blood & thunder. As far as this self-sustaining anarcho-BM thing, do you think it can be exported to Europe?"

"Let's face facts – in every brutal & blunt way, its just not as cool. You know, the reason the whole right-wing imagery stuff took off was because the whole Nazi imagery stuff just looked – it identified the strength, the self-empowerment. I think that's a more easily accepted message for people who are more socially outcast. Whereas encouraging people to grow their own turnips...

"But this isn't in some lame, hippie-dippie kind of way – this is more a dirty, squatty punk rock approach..."

[Something lights up] Well I respect anyone for gearing to that, the approach is noble, the self-sufficiency stuff I can empathize with. But can it practically be implemented in such an urbanized society? I mean, you try & export that to Mexico City & you'll get nowhere. I don't think that the new wave of extreme black metal ideology is gonna – I can't see it, I can't see it. Look at Drudkh, Nocturnal Mortem, Graveland – despite the fact that they're incredibly right wing, the way it's presented is in such a romanticized, majestical package. You see the imagery; the sort of beautiful sunset, the trees, our *'noble homeland'* – people kind of fall into that. Naïve people can really got drawn into that. Like, '*oh I almost cried* *listening to Drudkh last night – it's so, it's so beautiful.'* And it's like, *'Yeah, well you do know that it's essentially a rallying cry for white supremacists?"* [**see note below*]

"Do you have a question for me about the USA?"

"Is it really full of fat people? Hahaha…"

"Yes. Where I'm from originally – Michigan – it's the fattest population in the United States because it's cold as Norway & there's nothing to fucking eat but fast food because everyone's so poor & no one gets food stamps. And the environment & attitude is that if you receive any kind of help from the government because you are therefore a leech & doing so is a shameful & disrespected act."

"The stereotypes we get over here are of some people who are almost willfully ignorant. Starved of any kind of…"

"They are marching hundreds of thousands strong against any form of single-payer health care or Medicare expansion – like a marginal NHS mirrored system. They're throwing rocks at people, attacking them against some perceived 'communist plot.'"

It reminds me of a working class Tory over here – which is a man who's living in a council house, absolutely broke, absolutely fucked over by successive right wing governments. *'It's all about what you do yourself, you pull your own weight in this world & if you just work hard'* – but that's bullocks. The people telling you that have an invested interest in you staying where you are. They make you feel bad for wanting change. Basically, putting the blame on you for not having achieved that. I've seen a lot of this. Where my parents come from, it's a right wing stronghold. It's just people barking all about, *'we don't want handouts – we make our own fortunes.'* What economical fortune? You're living in a pit. It's this almost medieval peasant mentality."

"Same deal – in Michigan, its almost impossible to even get food stamps unless you are crippled or a single mother with 3 kids, and then you need a stack of identification papers, and they have endless loopholes to deny you. And maybe you'll get $75-$125 bucks. In Portland, you show up homeless & unemployed with no ID and you get $200 a month for six months, that very day."

"So the impression I get, reeling through the stereotypes, is the lack of awareness as to why this situation even is. It seems people would rather sit on a street corner freezing then admit the government should provide them some aid to the situation."

"They have no idea what's going on. The root problem is Cold War propaganda. The entire generation running the show were drilled from childhood onward that Communism was an apocalyptic threat &

any sort of assistance was therefore a symptom of the Red Menace. They actually think that Soviet Communism & Socialism are the exact same thing..."

    **(Day VI): *"ironical haunting from the ghost of a still-breathing baroness."*

Sometime during my walk on Sunday I happened upon a bulldog of a mohawked warrior with a GBH t-shirt. Depressingly, he told me that there is nearly no scene for punk rock in London anymore. But he did recommend one spot – a small indie music store called All Ages Records... The wiry guy at the desk was Nick; at first he thought I was an undercover cop with my reflective aviator glasses, but I explained my deal. Still cautionary, I simply lobbed a rhetorical dung-heap at my country of origin & he lit up like a roman candle...

    "This is All Ages – London's only independent record shop. It's been in existence for nearly 10 years; there was previously no punk specialty shop in London, ever... [*The phone rings, is promptly answered & slammed upon the receiver, sending Nick into a bug-eyed rant*] N' then you got bastards trying to sell you private health care, yeah? We have a fucking national health service in this country & we need to support it or it'll be gone. If we all sign up for private health care like that, we'll end up like America."

    "How much are they charging?"

    "I didn't get that far, because I don't want to speak to these people. How dare they ring All Ages independent record shop?!? Obviously they've got a list of numbers – they don't know who the fuck they're ringing. Fuck off private health care, fucking hell! Terrible. If they all do this we will be America. Terrible..."

    "So about..."

    "Punk rock! Punk rock, yeah..."

    "The CCTV thing..."

    "It's getting claustrophobic in London – they're about to outlaw squatting, completely. Unfortunately we've become very Americanized & that's where it comes from – this apathy, this whole Walmart thing. This whole situation... America's terrible. And unfortunately the people with the buying power are the people. If you don't want Walmart, don't got to a fucking Walmart – it'll close. Like Starbucks. Do you know what happened in Italy?"

    "Nah..."

"Starbucks, you know, McDonalds take over the world. They go to Italy – it's just another country as far as they're concerned. And they open up all these coffee shops in Rome & Milan & all these Italians are amazed by how much it costs, then they buy it and *pffffff* [*pretends to spits it out*]. Starbucks, two months, out of Italy – not a single Starbucks in Italy… Starbucks stopped running a tap in their stores. Did you know about that in America? That was fucking outrageous. Somewhere somebody went to Starbucks & the door was open & they looked through & there was a tap running. The guy said, '*That's right, we were told to run a tap.*' They were told – *worldwide* – run a cold tap all fucking day. *All fucking Starbucks*. I mean, if you didn't have an opinion on them then, surely after you found that one out, you just want to burn them all down. Yeah they paid for the water, but what an awful, awful waste of resources. Fucking hell – this water is so precious & we don't know how precious it is…"

"What's your opinion of Tony Blair?"

"You've go to remember George Bush was a republican bastard, very right wing, and you've got to remember Blair came from a left wing party. He was vilified by our press & the world press. I grew up through Thatcher & Thatcher destroyed the North of England . She closed coal mines that people's dads' dad had worked in – 3 generations, maybe 4 had worked there. These whole towns were built on the pit & she gave them two weeks notice. Barnsley basically closed, Castleford closed, Pontefact destroyed. Take the pit out the equation & all the pubs closed, the shops closed – it was devastation. And then she didn't do anything. And where does she get the coal from? America. Very, very sad… And then she privatized everything – British Rail, British Steel, British Gas, British Telecom, British Water. We had loads of nationalized industries, and that kept us strong. And now the water companies have shareholders & expect to make money. *Out of water?!?* Come on, fuck off, that is wrong isn't it? The whole thing is fucked, it really is. It really is fucked – *big time fucked* – and nobody seems to give a damn. Although I must say there is a horrendous government being voted in… Just the fact that the world is turning into America, that's what I don't like. We're losing our identity. In Europe we had very strong identities, but we don't anymore… There's only punk rock – *that's the last bastion of sanity in all of this…*"

Do I even need to say where I am, once again? I should mention at this point that the entrance sign has but a few key demands – "*No Dogs, No Cycling, No Unusual Pets, No Nuclear Weapons.*" I'm about to cross paths with Mr. Adam Sagir, a PR wiz that runs a company called The Noise Cartel Ltd which is a London based publicity company specializing in the *"louder end of the music spectrum, covering press, online, radio and TV promotion for a variety of different artists, labels, events & brands."*

Sagir has run propaganda ops for a stack of bands including RAMMSTEIN, Children of Bodom & Dragonforce, among others. Like most of these guys I've dealt with over the years, he's just been some vague email address. Thankfully, that little rift gets to change if for one evening only: "Basically we're a PR company – we do pretty much all that fits under the rock umbrella. If it's noisy & good, we'll probably want to work with it. We do a lot of bands that come through label deals. We used to do Nuclear Blast, so bands that came with that – Nightwish, Testament, Meshuggah. We do Spinefarm Records – Children of Bodom, Five Finger Deathpunch, RAMMSTEIN, Killing Joke…

"Well, I'm asking everyone about London, obviously…"

"I've lived in London my entire life & I'll go so far as to say '*here.*' Camden is really for me, as a kid growing up – they used to have Devil's Church every week on Sunday night. It was just a gig – there would always be maybe 3 bands playing – death, doom, black metal, hardcore, maybe a little crust. It didn't have anything to do with Satan really, not a religious cult or something. I'm talking about mid-90's – it wasn't like you went on Myspace to hear a band. I… I'm spoiled really. To be in metal, or any kind of music, growing up in London. I don't think I'd be doing what I'm doing now if I lived anywhere else in England… The more I think about it now, it definitely all started for me at Devil's Church. Maybe I do have Satan to thank…"

"Did you put together the PR gig?"

"Noise Cartel is my company, I started it 4 years ago after I left Century Media. Sort of bumbled around on tour for a bit, tour managing, tech-ing, whatever to make some money before my wife was like '*you're not spending your whole life on the road.*' Fair enough, so I started doing press… The guy that used to run Noise Cartel, he used to share an apartment with a guy named Andy Turner. Basically I just asked if he had any jobs & it took a year of nagging before he's like '*come in tomorrow.*' Eventually it became full time. I was playing in a touring band too – LABRAT."

"That name does ring a bell… [**immediately I have this nu-metal '98 bingo vision]"

"Ironically, Century Media put it out in the USA…"

"Are you still playing music now?"

"I stopped for 6 years – the last show was here at The Underworld. About 3 weeks ago I did my first gig, again, here, with a new band called Dripback as support for Soilent Green. We're playing at Download this weekend, and at Bloodstock Festival in August. I don't have any aspirations of making that my full time job."

"I haven't talked to anyone about Ireland yet…"

"Ireland is a strange place full of strange people. I love it but there's something morbid about it. I was outside this bar & this guy puts his hands up and touches my shoulder – *"Fight?"* I'd done nothing, I was just standing there. *"Why?"* I asked. I guess he just wanted to fight; it was something to do on a Friday night. That happened a couple of times while I was there – it seemed like a sociable thing to do. If you're not interested they don't just beat you up, they're like 'Oh, OK, that's cool.' It was a bit polite, really – a little too polite. Here people'll start a fight with you for absolutely no reason. If you don't want to fight they'll probably be even more brutal…"

"They just want one good one in there to feel accomplished?"

"Like you could just as easily offer someone a pint, that was the impression that I got."

"Is there anywhere in Europe where they aren't totally obsessed with football?"

"I don't think so. I think we're probably worse here then anywhere else – the only time you'll se an Englishmen cry is when it involves football."

"So the RAMMSTEIN connection – I ate lunch with them once. Great guys."

"Of all the bands we work with, they're probably the one I've had the least interaction with. We do the radio & TV promotion for RAMMSTEIN; they have someone else do their press."

"Were you working their album when 'Ich Tu Dir Weh' got banned in Germany?"

"Yes. That really wasn't a concern for us, that song, because – the BBC wouldn't play it here because the lyrics anyway, but most the other people – its in German & they don't really know. We had to work "Pussy" as a single though. You try taking a single called 'Pussy' and play it on TV & the radio – it was over before it begun."

"Were they well aware that it was going to be a failure?"

"Oh yeah – they're not stupid people. I think everything they do is very well thought out, and in hindsight, genius. I was really excited about the prospect of working with RAMMSTEIN – this is great, huge band, we get to work with them, this is really cool – and then the chorus is '*You have a pussy/I have a dick.*' No one in England is going to play that on the radio, its just not gonna happen. That was a bit of a non-starter really. Same with the video – no commercial music channel can play that video.

In fact, the record company didn't want to be associated with this video, so we weren't even officially allowed to work it – not that there was anything we could do with it anyway. But its extreme content probably caused more people to look at it they would've seen it had it been in high rotation… I find them very difficult to work with because I'm so used to bands saying, *'we'll do this, we'll do that'* & being conventional. Something that Rammstein are not is conventional. It can get frustrating at times, but when you see what they've done & look back afterwards – ok, I understand. It's keeping the mystique, the sense of mystery."

"What's up with the Dragonforce live album?"

"We're currently working with them & they'll be supporting Iron Maiden. You know Herman Li? I've know him 16 years – he's one of the guys that used to come to Devil's Church. He was like in every band in the scene – my old band LABRAT, he was in that for a few months. He's such an incredible guitarist that everyone wanted him. But then eventually they'd get sick of the constant soloing. Great, but you can't just do this the whole way through the entire song. So I think he found the perfect vehicle in Dragonforce."

"What's Jaz Coleman like from Killing Joke?"

"The first time I met him they were recording *Absolute Dissent*. He took me downstairs into the basement of the studio & wants to have a talk about press. He's like, *'I'll do anything'* & I'm like, *'Makes my job easier.'* Alright, well there's a lot of silly Q&A's out there that really aren't filled with intelligent questions – like, *'what's the last thing you put in your mouth?'* He's like *'Don't worry – you just set them up & I'll make sure the interviews are about whatever I want them to be about.'* And then he tells me that he'd like to interview people. Ok, that's an interesting spin on it – maybe the future would be you interviewing another band. And he's like *'No – I want that murderer Tony Blair.'* Right, OK. Maybe his idea of what is achievable & my idea is slightly different. ..

"What's your comment on the PR biz & how one becomes a sort of Wizard of Oz figure? A huge chunk of bands that are struggling for recognition are completely aloof to the overall importance of propaganda."

"It's really interesting how it's changed. When I was at Century Media, you didn't email JPEG's to people – you sent a transparent, or photograph, in the post. Cut & paste was literally that – flyer, press pack, whatever. It was a lot more sociable as well; I spent most of my time in pubs or with other people. Now it's just emails. It used to be standard practice that the press person would take the editorial person out to lunch – the sales person would take the marketing person out. A lot of that is kind of gone now. There's people I deal with regularly that I've never met – they're just an email address. I do loads with them & they don't have a face. With email – maybe you feel less obliged to meet people. I'm not on Facebook, but I could see one becoming obliged to add them – you know what their family looks like, last Sundays BBQ – its weird… The internet has really changed the way that PR press works. I didn't know many independent press people because most worked for a label. The labels & magazines, between them they dictated what the kids would listen to, because that's how they found out about stuff. The kids – their favorite label or magazine would tell them what to check out. As a kid, maybe I'd see Phil Anselmo wearing an EYEHATEGOD t-shirt & I'd get into them, or the thanks list on an album. Now you don't even have to work to find new music – people are constantly pushing it in front of your face. You can hear anything you want within seconds without paying for it. So now I think the media is playing catch up with the fans. I don't even need to play a note of music to know someone will write about them – all I say is they have 500,000 Facebook likes, or 500,000 YouTube views. I think the power is with the people now. It's a lot harder to do those cynical PR campaigns without talking about this Wizard of Oz shit. You can do it, if you have a genuinely good product that people are going to get excited about. Now, if you try to do that with a crap band – I don't think a Coal Chamber would stand a chance in this day & age – it would be over before it'd begun…"

**(Day VII): *"MEDICALture Shock"*

I've got this problem with my teeth. It started before I'd left America, this whole business of spitting blood. It was really bad once I got here, sitting on a ledge with Matt, sucking on my molar & spitting crimson. Gruesome as it gets.

Basically the last push of my wisdom teeth had come roaring through, shoved all my teeth to the front & relined my jaw in one week. Got too drunk & flossed with wax apparently sitting on the shelf for 5 years. Cut the shit out my gums & thought using tons of mouthwash would fix the problem, but all alcohol does is repeatedly clean a wound & kill all the bacteria which accumulates to heal it.

As a slave of capitalist health care, I'd a hard time believing that a hospital would actually exist anywhere to help you. Gums on fire, I approached a sight that was not a mirage to my eyes, but rather a jackboot-to-the-throat insult lingering from my homeland. Here was a public hospital 5 times the size of any I'd seen in the USA, with gigantic plastic letters spelling out its name like a used car lot: "**ROYAL FREE HOSPITAL**."

It was more surreal then a rotting Detroit drug house advertising "FREE COCAINE" in glowing neon letters. There was also a 5 level parking garage which read "FREE PARKING," unlike America where you pay $10 for 3 hours? They were legitimately there to... *help me?* This thought, this abstract reasoning...

Ok, there GinGrinches – _you win_. I did have to pay a small bill (*in the mail*) because I wasn't a UK citizen – something like a staggering £30 (*snicker, chortle*). But the truth is that they didn't even ask for proof of identification; they weren't remotely concerned with sending me a bill. The doctor, he was like: "*We'll fix you right up, no problem.*" I was so shocked by his kindness I wanted to buy him a lavish steak dinner. And diagnosis of a nasty case of gingivitis, he handed me a prescription of the strongest meds on the market...

At the medicine window, the sign read "*all prescription £7.*" $14 USD?? No matter the sickness, it was the same nationally guarded price. I neatly wept... When I turned to one of the Brit's standing in line & remarked on the price in awe, she misunderstood my temperament & actually replied: "*Yeah – outrageous charging people this, isn't it? Bloody wankers*"

Well, if I drank any alcohol whatsoever with this stuff I would pass out, possibly die. So sadly my life's dream of chugging wine non-stop in Paris & wearing a red beret amongst a bunch of Frenchie's chortling: "*Honh-Honh-Honh – Fuck Amer-eee-kah – Honh-Honh-Honh-Wee-Wee*" was firmly out the window…

* * *

My last action before shuffling off to Paris tomorrow is a punk gig in the south end; the last of the dingy punk bars in London. It's a place called The Grosvener [***pronounced grove-ven-ner*]. I'm about to have a long ramble with a cat name Max Ferrin from a sXe anarcho-punk band HELLO BASTARDS, whom recently did a tour in Palestine working with Anarchists Against The Wall – a protest group in opposition to Israeli brutality…

HELLO BASTARDS' site describe their mission statement as a band created to: "*give voice to our views and beliefs, and to encourage punk music to become a political threat again. Punk nowadays means nothing – it has been dilapidated & absorbed by the system. Most bands do not have a message & most bands have forgotten that punk music is political. Hello Bastards are a vegan band & strongly support the animal liberation movement. We believe in the liberation of all species, whether that means humans or animals. To us there is no difference & we do not place emphasis on one struggle over that of another, to us all liberation struggles are equal and feel that a holistic approach means a thorough and consistent standard of ethics…"*

"Every member of the band has retained sXe ethics. We feel that straight-edge is an important part of liberating yourself from the addictions of society. We understand the history & the importance of the straight-edge movement, which is why we sometimes feel so disillusioned with the current state of the scene. To us being sXe is not about drinking Coca Cola, wearing Nike's or eating meat – it seems to have morphed into some Capitalist consumerist subculture. HELLO BASTARDS exists for the sole purpose of spreading a political message. If it were not for this, we would not be a band. We do not like to label ourselves after any political movement. However, we feel that anarchism is the most natural & innate movement which exists. Music is the vehicle that we use to express our ideas and emotions; music without a message means nothing to us…"

Max Ferrin shakes my hand & we munch on venue donated pizza before his side project STAB takes the stage: "I have an Italian father, a French mother, but I was born in Argentina. I've been living in London for the last 6 years; I'm the singer in HELLO BASTARDS & also a band called STAB. BASTARDS' started around 2005 with a bunch of guys from South America living in London. From the old lineup it's just two of us – myself & Jefferson from Brazil. New people – Santiago, our bassist from Israel, Amy from Germany & Herman who's from Poland. So it's a little like The United Nations, here in London…

"So this intense Palestinian tour that you guys did…"

"The thing with Palestine & Israel – it started with us being politically conscious & trying to approach the situation from a different point of view then the anarcho-punk scene. Even though we are against flags – even though we are against nations – what's actually happening in Palestine and the oppression of the Israeli government is completely unacceptable. So we decided to take a position to support the Palestinian struggle. We had the luck to have Santiago. Our bass player, he's from Israel & part of the Anarchists Against The Wall organization. It's based in Tel Aviv – they support the Palestinian uprisings in the West Bank. They go in as human shields during demonstrations or just help by any other means. We decided to go to Israel, and then Palestine, because it was the right time to do it. It's easy to be in the position to talk about things in a book or watching a movie – but its completely different when you're on the front lines. So we decided to go to Israel to play some gigs & also the Palestinian territories…"

"How difficult is it to get through the border? I'd assume cavity searches are quite popular with those people…"

"Before you get to Israel, you have to be prepared not to have any equipment & not to have anything related to political parties. You cannot be wearing an anarchist t-shirt – it cannot be in your luggage. You have to try to not look alternative. As soon as you reach Israel, the international airport, as soon as you get off the plane – even before immigration – the IDF, the Israeli Defense Force, are checking your passports. *'What are you doing in Israel, where are you staying, do you have any political affiliations?'* You pass through that, and then you have local police asking the same things. 15 meters ahead they check your actual passports. Immigration – of course they're gonna ask you the same things. At that point they put two stickers on your passport – one green & one red. If you pull a green you are free to pick up your luggage. If you pulled a red someone from immigration is going to escort you to your luggage, they're going to check your luggage, and ask you more questions. And only then can you actually get into Israel, which is how the country sort of feels as a whole. Being in Israel, you can feel that it is very repressive in a way. We stayed in an Arabic neighborhood in Tel Aviv and it feels… I would say oppressive, because there is a constant harassment by the government to the people who live there. They were actually bulldozing some of the houses. Not even specific properties – sometimes just to make the street bigger or to make a park, but of course this happens all the time. Very specifically its illegally forced on the Arabic people in that area…"

"What about Palestine itself?"

"We started to go to the occupied territories. At the time there were local elections in Israel and this village – half of it was in Israel & half in Palestine. The village was 100% Arabic. It turns out the far right party in Israel decided they were going to monitor the elections of this village. The elders and the people of course didn't want this person monitoring the elections, so the goal was to block all the entrances to the village at 4 in the morning. It was very interesting to be participating in the blockade, especially when there's 40 or 50 IDF with machine guns pointed at you. It wasn't violent, but it was direct action. We successfully prevented this guy from getting into the village – the police said the conditions were not actually met for him to be in the village because they could not ensure the security. After that we went to the house of one of the organizers. We were able to socialize with the Palestinians in a different environment, in a different way – a more human way. And while we were there, there was the news that some other people from this right wing party actually made it to the main school of the village. So we're rushing to this school to try and kick out this person, and at that point things started to get more violent. The IDF, even the local police, they started to fire tear gas, rubber bullets – I'm talking about kids, 10, 12, 16, 20 to 40, 50, 60 years old who were defending… If you think about politics in Israel, they are on the right end of the spectrum. And to say these guys are far right, that says a lot about what kind of people they are. The situation deteriorated and we needed to leave the area. It was our first taste of how things actually run in Palestine…

"What about the protest at The Wall?"

"After that we decided to go to the Anarchists Against The Wall demonstration. There are weekly demonstrations against the partition of this village in two – they've lost 70% of their land due to the wall that Israel is erecting in the occupied territories; it's actually all Palestinian land… The demonstration itself, they meet on a Friday afternoon, gather all the people from the village & just walk to the land where they are constructing The Wall. That's it – there is no violence. As soon as you leave the boundaries of the village there are IDF units all over the place & they start to shoot with rubber bullets, sound grenades, tear gas. Also they use live 9mm ammunition… One of the rules of the human shields is to remain in the front to prevent the IDF from shooting the Palestinians. As soon as we started we were actually bombarded with tear gas, rubber bullets, sound grenades, whatever you can imagine. It was very unprovoked – situations where they use extreme violence in situations where there is no need. When they started to throw sound grenades we needed to retreat inside the village and the IDF came looking to arrest people."

"That's extremely surreal."

"It was surreal because you're in a city where people are just wandering around buying groceries, having their kids with them, and the military is entering into their village. It is very sick – these people live with this every day. Then you see 5 your old kids throwing rocks at their cars, and its not like it's going to do anything, and then you have guys from the IDF shooting them with live ammunition. To be living this every day? This is very tough."

"In the United States people are very apathetic & without a clue as to what's actually happening in the Middle East. What we are repeatedly told by the media is this impression that the Israelis are the 'good guys,' and that Palestinians are the 'bad guys.' Especially Arafat

– he was viewed as a monster, and by default, the Palestinian struggle garnered an implied aura of terrorism…"

"I need to say that, luckily for us – even though the media is useless because it's not meant to inform but to misinform people – I believe that in the UK at least, in general in Europe, there are a lot of people actually supporting the Palestinian struggle. At its most basic it's a humanitarian struggle. We've had maybe 40,000 people demonstrating in London; there are a lot of organizations abroad. There a lot of actions being taken against Israel so I need to say the context in Europe, in the UK it is a little bit differently then the way you're painting it in America. There is much more awareness."

"The Arab Spring, which is just really gaining momentum now – this past week the Israeli's mowed down a bunch of protestors staging a demonstration outside The Wall but on the Syrian end. But they were working under that Cairo-styled banner… Also, we don't have Al Jazeera in The States – it's implied through the corporate media that you are a bad person if you watch it, that they only show videos of American soldiers being decapitated, that they are in cahoots with al Qaeda, et cetera."

"You have to take it into context – every country is different, and there are different reasons why every population is uprising against their particular tyrannies. If you're talking especially about the incident that happened – the Palestinians entering the borders from the Syrian border, the Israeli reaction is interesting because it's the first time the Palestinians actually entered the border in a long time. If you look at what they're were doing, it is completely innocent. They just want to show that it is still their land. And, of course, the end result from that side is just bullets, bullets, bullets & bullets & bullets & bullets – just killing people. It shows this criminal use of violence & how the government solves its situations. Fatah and Hamas, they are trying to create a united front between the two of them to get recognition of the Palestinian State from the United Nations. The vote is going to be happening really soon. Even though I want to remain positive, I don't think it's going to happen. There are too many things at play & Israel is going to be doing a lot of lobbying to prevent the UN from recognizing the Palestinians. Even if it happens, it will not bring the borders back to 1967 like America, other nations are proposing."

*[**Note: At the time of writing, the Palestinians have no choice but to request a UN vote in September 2011. This vote is to ratify a unilateral declaration of Palestinian statehood. If approved, Palestine would then be a fellow member of the United Nation whose territory would include all of the West Bank, Gaza & East Jerusalem. Therefore making the Israeli*

occupation a 'legitimately' criminal occupation. However, Barack Obama has already signaled that he will veto any such resolution on behalf of the power invested unto him by the people of The United States of America. At partition in 1947, Israel was allotted 55% of Palestine. The Jewish state now controls 78%...]

"Do you have a question for me about America, something you don't understand..."

"Sometimes I don't understand American culture in general. I find it so focused on Christianity – and you all fall on Democrats & Republicans, like there is no alternative. I'm not even talking about an alternative to the whole system, I'm just talking about an alternative to the Republicans & Democrats. It's amazing how America is a country with so many people, so many bands saying all things, so many people are aware & know what's going on, but they still cannot form a unified front to tackle the system..."

**(Day VIII): "*Vive Gay PARIS!!!*"

Thursday morning & I wake up in the sort of place that 15 year old punk rock kids have wet dreams about. It's called "The Deathdrop" – a squat that was formerly a tavern but could never muster much business, being hidden from public view in an area coagulated with small industrial factories. About 20 crusties live here now & throw gigs out the basement – most recently a secret gig with DOOM...

The mid-level floor is caked in posters & silkscreen flags, windowless & illuminated by strings of Christmas lights. The top floor is the living area with a huge industrial sized kitchen where we all ate a vegan feast late at night. This is another hookup, thanks to Keef, basically. He'd recommended I talk to an Italian guy named Enzo from a band called GRIND THE ENEMY, but when I called earlier in the week he was unavailable. Just so happens he lives here & I'll interview him shortly, but right now he's appearing in court after being subpoenaed over an associates' legal transgression...

I'm alone here, hammering away on a community laptop. When I look deeper into it, all of my contacts for France are scattered throughout the country. In Paris I have a few black metal guys, a more "Ozzfest Territory" metal band called ASHKA, a prog-death act dubbed Underflesh & an NSK operative I'm thrilled about meeting, for LAIBACH's only responsibility as the engineers of human souls is to: *"remain irresponsible,"* for LAIBACH *"cannot concern [itself] with the fulfillment of other people's expectations. We believe that in art [all] morality is nonsense, in practice it is immoral, [and] in people it is a sickness…"*

Enzo shows back up, this tall & muscular Italian guy with long black dreadlocks & a penchant for broken English. He feels kind of silly in the shirt & tie he had to slap on for court, so he switches to more comfortable crust gear, makes us some vegan lunch & we head into it…

"You just came back from the court…"

"It's kind of like a Big Brother thing here 'cause there are a lot of cameras everywhere & they really control you. In fact at court this morning they were taking out all the Facebook mails & phone calls that they recorded – like hours of stuff. Fuck that…"

"The police actually used Facebook as legal evidence?"

"Yeah, the detective downloaded all the Facebook stuff – like messages, anything – the files were really big. So yeah, it's the new way to fuck people up. I was shocked when the guy said, '*Alright, this is the Facebook file.*'"

"Do you think Mark Zuckerberg is directly working with Interpol & the CIA?"

"Yeah. Also, if you want to close your account, they keep everything – all your private stuff for years & years. Anytime the cops ask for stuff, they have to give it."

"Tell me about your band…"

"We started about 3 years ago. We play stenchcore influence – the band is called GRIND THE ENEMY. The lyrics are pretty simple – to give a message that is complete hate against society. Its like nothing original – just pure hate. It's not intellectual stuff – just pure, simple, hate & anger."

"Where did you grow up in Italy?"

"Southern Italy – Napoli. I've been in London 5 years now. I used to squat in Italy, since I was 16. The people in the area, they're not like mafia, but they're not really nice with punks. They see diversity as a danger – they want to take the shit out of the punks. It's not easy life, and squatting every night we'd be like fighting with them – petrol bombs & fighting, fighting & fighting. And we moved from there cause it was taking our energy, our time; we couldn't produce anything. Even to have a gig was a big risk. So we moved to North Italy, to an old squat. We took over the place, start to do gigs, anarchist stuff, meetings. We had a few bands playing there – sort of a punk picnic every year."

"Does everyone hate Berlusconi?"

"Ooooh yeah. He's a fucking twat man."

"I have this idea for this book to go to Preddipio, which is the birthplace of Mussolini, because that's where his crypt is. I've heard it's like this Old World Fascist town where people still salute you with 'A'Noi!' There's supposedly a volunteer guard forever on duty protecting Benito's crypt 24-7, 365 days a year. I just kind of want to go up to him and ask why."

"There's still places in Italy where old people say, '*Oh when Mussolini was in power, it was the best time.*' It's like, when do you die? Old creep."

"Tell me more about the difficulties in squatting Italy…"

"To squat in Italy is pretty hard. You always have to have a barricade because anytime the police can come crush the place & arrest you. There was a nice squat in Naples but its not there anymore because the communists & the mafia took control of the place. The mafia people, they came in & kicked us out with guns…"

"What does anarchism mean to you?"

"I don't consider myself anarchist, to be honest. Less or more, I don't try to be a part of this society. Anarchism is a big thing – when I was young I used to tend to be more '*perfect anarchist*' but this is wrong too. When you say, '*I cannot do this, this is not right, this is not what an anarchist would do*' – I found that to put stuff in front of you, in front of other people. I don't think that is right. I like to feel free to drink a Coca-Cola if I just want to. For me anarchism is just respect people, try to live together – simple. If you come in my house & smash my house & say, '*this is freedom, this is anarchy.*' I say, '*NO – you are a fucking idiot.*'"

"Do you have a question for me about America?"

"When people come back from America, they're always complaining about how they've been treated. Like punks – not complaining – but saying, '*We had an amazing show but in the end we've been left out the venue.*' And they gave us maybe good money, but they were left by themselves. They didn't know where to go, where to eat, where to fucking sleep, you know. And I just ask myself why? What's wrong with these people? They invited the bands to play. For me, when we organize a tour or anything, we make sure – I make sure – that the band feels welcome. You have to guarantee at least a place to sleep & food. I don't know why Americans cannot do that…"

* * *

As I make my way to the end of The Tube, I cannot help but notice in the most hyper-exaggerated sense the omnipresence of CCTV. When you decide to compartmentalize such awareness in the back of your head, it's easy to dismiss Echelon peering through every crack of cement about you; everywhere the ominous black lens, recording your every move...

A manic rush now for Pacal, my rideshare to Paris. Tube after Tube, hitting a bad switchover, having to turn around on another train – crazed text messages from him to be at the prescribed airplane terminal or he'll leave me behind. But the phone dies beneath these tunnels disconnected from the reach of satellite's...

Closer, closer to the deadline – inching towards the abandonment my hard-won £30 ride into France...... *Up the elevators, down through escalators... Darting past sluggish tourists bumbling in my path... Sweating, sweating, panting & beading...* !!BAM!! – made it. Two minutes to the chagrin of time...

As I stand atop the parking garage, green army coat shielding me from the light summer breeze, I can view all of London in the distance like a concrete abstraction. Shining sun, rolling lakes & fields of the countryside... The future never so bountiful...

Goodbye sweet London, one day I shall return into your crescent arms... Onward comes Pascal & his little Toyota, his backseat packed of fellow travelers... Just one man vs. FORTRESS EUROPE & 1600+ hours to go...

"...*dans l'étreinte amoureuse de la France, je voyage désormais...*"

PARIS

6.9.11PARIS 6.14.11

II. *"l'humiliation de l'illusion piétiné par le fantasme d'évasion"*

The *Cimetière du Père Lachaise* stretches for kilometers, tombs sprouting as bountiful foliage. One of the eldest cemeteries in Paris, 'tis the domain of Chopin, Abelard & countless innovators of progress. Unlike so many visitors my interest was not the inauguration of the dead, but something crudely juvenile – the age-old quest to smoke a joint on the grave of Jim Morrison...

For every teen of my homeland influenced by *Cheech & Chong* ritualism, this action is sacred. As Adam of Eternia would lift his mighty sword in reverence to Greyskull, us stoners flash glass pipes conjuring the fuzziness of The Lizard King...

Although there is a lack of green on this occasion & the clouds mesh the sky to an ever-gray, equilibrium is found. Droplets of H2O begin to plummet from the sky, causing my British companion to remark ever so snidely: *"Well 'ere's one for your book Bartek – you can say that once we got 'ere, the heaven's literally started to rain..."*

Back in London, atop that epic parking garage, Pascal & his little Toyota zoomed up. It's interior carried two Brits – both of whom immediately knew who I was, having read the forum posts on Gumtree. Pascal's silent annoyance was an ominous indicator of the character of the French; his reserved aura was politely knee-jerk to my American loudness...

Crossing into French territory the only resistance encountered were two UK border guards. As they bobbed around the vehicle verbally bouncing *"Cheers, cheers, CHEERS, cheers cheery-ho CHEERS"* they both dusted the wheel with UV-specific brushes like mad painters seeking chemical traces of explosives. Once clear, we drove right in – not a single passport glance. As Kunal explained [**my fellow passenger & guitarist of the band Youth In Colour]: *"No one cares because there is no issue of immigration – no one wants to live in France..."*

For a man who once nearly took a one-way flight to Paris in desperation of escape, this seemed an implausibility. A fellow Detroiter had also warned me of this deep winter suicide mission I was contemplating: *"Ummm, Bartek... You are aware that Paris is a modern metropolis these days, right? That whole world of absinthe poets – it doesn't exist anymore. Just another bloody, awful thing you can blame on the Nazi's..."*

As if the extinction of Henry Miller negates *l'aventure de Paris...* It's all Miller's fault, anyway. Just blame him for everything, because if it wasn't for *Tropic of Cancer*, I wouldn't be living this terrible way. I look back at Seattle and my long stretch of homelessness in the Northwest. Everything in Miller's world mirrored my own; I could only view parallels at every turn. Ever lost in the process of random materialization whilst swallowed by the blacktop abyss...

Forever haunted by an outstretched heart fruitlessly yearning for the embrace of a Euro princess while ironically surrounded by flake Americans & reading volume by volume the diaries of Anais Nin while planted firmly on the curb. It is the Romantic Paris I seek – the pulse of Cendrars, the madness of Lautreamont, *je vais avoir des relations sexuelles avec Mona Lisa…*

** *"singes capitulards mangeurs de fromage"* **

"...they full on believe it the Chicanees. They're like these little children with big old man's heads. And they just fucking steal you, or steal the children, which is what faeries used to do in Britain. This friend of mine, he's gathering as many Chicanee stories as he can from the local area. And he's beginning to believe it, because it's just something that everybody…"

Jason Michel is fired up on mythology, munching on oriental delicacies: *"In Thailand, for example, my Thai boxing teacher – they all believe in ghosts. So the all have the little spirit house, land spirits or whatever – it comes from the animus traditions. There's a story I heard – they have this equivalent of a vampire. The top half is a woman, beautiful woman, and the bottom half is just entrails. I cant remember the handle of this creature. My friend, she was in a hotel 4 floors up one day & was looking out the window & out the window there was this girl sort of looking at her, and there's no balcony. And she kept going, not thinking she was on the 4th floor. And then she said 'Oh, its someone looking at me' & her friend came in from the other room and they both freaked out. Apparently they both saw it…"*

Jason & I are in Versailles, not far from the Royal Palace with gold plated gutters. It feels good to share company with someone from the same world. Not just the language, or the metal/punk gibberish, but because we both know what the world actually is. Not the phony foundations of power they sell us on the newscasts, but the Bilderberg/Bohemian Grove cabal that really run the show...

We both know the ship is sinking; we both know to what extent the power-hungry toads amass their war criminality. Agenda 21 sparkles in Jason's eyes & Moloch twinkles in mine. The world teeters at the precipice; Europe hangs by a thread, dangling over the venomous snake-pit of unsalvageable bankruptcy...

With the lust of death the globalist power-wielders initiate their maniac plan of elitist eugenics, infectious vaccinations, microchip mandates, drone strikes & murderous designs of population control. 6 billion heads on the chopping block & no guide but the Georgia Stones...

Vacation means you don't have to scream anything at the person you're trying to converse with or be looked at like a lunatic for reciting any of the awful wisdom you've accumulated like a cat mangled by curiosity. Vacation means they already know that the leaders of your country are a bizarre pagan cult hell bent on world domination & armed with HAARP, their veritable *Deathstar*. Vacation means you don't get funny looks for explaining that every year since 1888 the majority of United States Presidents, Congressmen, business leaders, media moguls & military brass have had their own secret, evil Burning Man festival at a Black Magic campground called Bohemian Grove in Northern California...

That they all wear hooded red druid outfits & have a mock child sacrifice beneath a 40 foot stone owl which many claim is Moloch, the ancient Babylonian god of war & human sacrifice. That contrary to everything you've been taught, the world is apparently caught in the crossfire of a clandestine pagan war. That the Illuminati is not a figment, that Trilaterals actually are over Washington, and that the Bilderberg Group is actively plotting the death of 6 billion people, yourself & all those you love included... Vacation means you are in France...

Jason & I are eating at a Chinese place with the buffet-style stainless steel trays where you just point at slop & they scoop it on your plate. He refuses to eat French cuisine because he thinks it is as identically rancid as the indoctrination of their culture. He prefers the cooking of his Italian girlfriend, whom also despises Berlusconi. While she was lovely, her kids were a little disappointed in me – they expected a grizzled crust punk with a 6 inch mohawk glued up like a fin...

We spent the night having dinner with two Southern Italians in proper *moda Italia*. The suppers are prolonged affairs ever ripe with appetizers & *"plenty-of-a-red-a-wine-a"* – plates of pretzel-encrusted hot dog wieners, deep fried tofu poppers & a hearty collage of chips. I was so stuffed with *hors d'œuvre* I could barely attack the main course…

In terms of Paris, Jason is my Bob Hawk. He's a Welsh guy with a proper, Bond-ian UK accent & an impressive repertoire of martial arts maneuvers. Jason's been ensnared in Paris for far too many years, stuck in his own bubble of solitude; an old-school metalhead that teaches English to French businessmen as a living. Last year he'd snagged a copy of *The Big Shiny Prison* & interviewed me for his zine *Pulp Metal*, leading us to this confrontation here...

After devouring an Egg Roll, I proceed with the usual questionnaire: ***"What're the best ghost stories of England?"***

"You got things like the Headless Horseman, all that stuff. The one that I actually based my book *Confessions of a Black Dog* on – I actually had this dream about the thing and it really affected me. I had this book when I was a kid called *Monsters, Ghosts & UFO's*. The Creature had a single, Cyclopean fire eye. When I was a kid that scared the shit out of me, like Hell Hounds; there's a ton of black dog stories up in Northern England. I've been fascinated trying to connect this dream to that creature, and its supposed to be some portent of death..."

"Ever go to Edinborough & Loch Ness?"

"My father took me up there. Can't remember if I saw Crowley's old place – I was too young. Apparently Crowley did the Ritual of Adrenalin which is based on this very intense magickal ritual where you're summoning up demons & all that. And he stopped doing it halfway through, so the story goes. The legend goes that something came through & a lot of locals, to this day, say the place is haunted..."

"What do you think of David Icke?"

"The Lizard People, heh... If you look at Prince Philip you can kind of see it, haha. When Icke went to Canada or the US, the Jewish anti-defamation league accused him of saying Lizard People was a synonym for Jews. That says to me, '*Who's the paranoid one?*' David Icke talking about 6 foot Lizard People – he's accusing the Queen of England. I guess that means Kate Pendleton is getting penetrated by some sort of balding, tentacle cock, hahaha."

"Is David Icke a national joke in England?"

"He is, but a lot of people go to his lectures man..."

"When he's not talking about The Lizard People but about the New World Order he's pretty spot-on..."

"Yeah, he's talking about the banksters, the Bilderbergers, but then he goes into Lizards – its hard to convince people when your speaking about something rationally & then bringing in a bad sci-fi plot. It's like a bad episode of *Dr. Who*."

"So about the French..."

"I'm probably not the best person to give you an objective point of view…"

"Ok, give me an unbalanced view – I mean, its your perspective…"

"I do find them to be pretentious; I find them to be very close-minded. The younger people are more – and maybe this is the world over, because of globalization – culturally it's given people more of a sense of an open worldview… I'll give you an example – there was a French guy in town & he's in a Thai restaurant & everyone's eating banana pancakes and fruit & he shouted at the waiter for not bringing a pan o' chocolat. '*I want a pan o' chocolat!! I want a pan o'!!!*' & smacking his fist into the table."

"What's that?"

"Chocolate bread – he wants his chocolate bread. Well they don't have anything like that in their culture, and why should they? But that's the sort of French thing – I find it very statist. It seems to me there are two kinds of French people – those who've actually left the country & gone abroad. When you meet them, they're quite lovely. They've seen the world. And then you have the ones who've actually never fucking left their sofa in their hometown & their still fucking their high school girlfriend & this sort of thing. But as French culture goes, to be honest I'm not that interested. Paris is very conservative, more then London, for example. You can tell by their fashion. Here it's a lot more sheik…"

"Are the French disliked abroad in Europe?"

"Nobody likes France – everyone thinks they are a bunch of arrogant bastards. And their reputation is justified to a certain degree. I'm generalizing of course, but one thing I do know is that in Paris everyone is shit-scared of everyone else. If you smile at somebody they almost cower. I think theirs is not a culture of chances. I think they have everything on the plate – they're protected, completely, and they're closeted by the government system. That's why you don't have as many private business here because the taxes are incredible. You hear a lot of the protests recently over things like the retirement & it's the people who are privileged enough to retire at the early age. Its not the private sector. The private sector, it's like everywhere – they have to make do. But the protected workers, they shut the place down to a standstill. The French have an adolescent attitude towards the state – it's a thing that supports them like a father or a mother, yet it's the thing they rebel against. This completely teenage way of looking at the state… But hey, you might have a different perspective – I'm just a grumpy old English teacher."

"Henry Miller – no one really knows about him in the USA because our public schools don't touch him with a 20,000 foot poll. You

have to get deep in literature to discover him, because with Americans, if there isn't a big movie fictionalizing his biography in a smash-hit way, there is little to no attention. The only reason I found out about Miller is because Henry Rollins talked about 'Black Spring' during the Black Flag days."

"Even though Henry Miller was better then most French writers, he was still an American. But he came to France, along with the rest of The Lost Generation. Hemingway, Ezra Pound... I've never heard a French person talk about Henry Miller. But in England, we talk about him. People recognize who Miller was & you have that sort of, "*Was he a dirty old man?*" We all had *Under The Rooftops of Paris*, and that first chapter where he has the naked 13 year old girl on his knee, heh, heh."

"Does everyone hate Celine?"

"They don't hate him – he's more of an embarrassment. He's sort of a taboo, which is a shame. French people are very politicized in this left-right dichotomy. They young people, yeah – they say the UNP & the Socialist Party are a bunch of cunts & we want our country back. But here, most people are either right or left. You don't get too many pragmatists like you would in England. Here they would see Celine as someone that was a Jew hating Nazi. So its very political in France – you couldn't have a lot of English TV comedy shows that make fun of everything. They are obsessed with their own French-ness. On TV they are always told France is the best, France, France... so yeah its very weird. But then you tell them, '*Yeah, the French couldn't cook until the Italians came over & told them how to do it...*' Allesandra was saying that she heard a teacher telling a school group that Machiavelli was French. Know what I mean? *French bah-stards...*"

** "nous ne faisons pas qu'en France" **

8pm; waiting for the show to begin at Star Café. It's one of the only possible places here a metal band can actually play live. It's the upstairs hall to a small bar, one that generally holds karaoke, pop music & traditional French gigs...

It's a sleepy time drag, twiddling my fingers & waiting. The headliner, Underflesh, whom I interviewed earlier & invited me to this gig don't speak much English. It was a pretty down-the-middle dialogue that reinforced the absolute lack of metal radio or TV programming in this country – *there is nothing, at all*....

Metal is spit upon as low-brow, same with punk & industrial. The most popular stuff is dance club techno, French-language hip hop – the art scene is so stuffed-shirt that the Underflesh guys have no knowledge of it. Paris is all fashion & Styrofoam cuisine…

As Jason described, the Parisians are an isolated bunch. Everything about them is a concealed, impenetrable womb of Frenchness. However, I'm convinced that if I play the "famous metal journalist guy" card, or the *"Obama is a monster of equal or greater stature to Bush"* thing, I might just find myself doing well…

Maybe my own personal writing will have that *party favor effect*, since my pimping of French literature might prove catastrophic. *"Oui, mon petit bout de femme magnifique! Comment pensez-vous de Monsieur de Sade?"* **5 finger slap-splash. *"Excusez-moi monsieur, que pensez-vous de Louis-Ferdinand Céline?"* **Handcuffs clank on the National Socialist provocateur. *"Superbe femme qui vole mon coeur au premier regard, que pensez-vous du Anaïs Nin?"* **"Que faites-vous, un homosexuel ou autre chose?!?"**

Jason had scribed me some French phrases in case the cops were to harass me for sleeping in the park, or if I'd needed to find an embassy. One of these was basically a *"can I crash on your couch tonight"* that went something like: *"I'm traveling with very little money & hoping not to have to buy a hotel room – I was wondering if there might be an after-party once the concert is over, etc..."*

Trying not to be *"hint/hint, nudge/nudge, wink/wink,"* I handed this phrase to the Underflesh guys & said *"hey, is this correct?"* And they all kind of read it, and when they reflect upon the concept *"after-party"* they all kind of looked at each other befuddled, like they didn't know how to respond, or they'd never heard of it. One of them kind of stared off into space for a second, comes back & says: *"We don't really do that in FAH-RAHNCE – I think that's more of an Irish or German thing…"*

Jason was correct-a-mundo – the French have things perfectly organized. They have their social time, return home. It's not like this sporadic, open mess of existence you'll find in America where you'll wake up to dogs barking in the streets & people just showing up to your house without calling & you got a buddy kicking you in the back saying, *"Get up asshole, drink this fuckin' scotch…"*

Well, the Underflesh guys did get the hint & arranged for me a spot to crash. Upstanding Parisians, might I add. But if I had it my way, I'd be back with Jason griping about Francophobia. I miss the rotten bastard, already nostalgic to restart the day when earlier we took a stroll beneath the *Tour Eiffel* [*which when spoken in it's native French tongue sounds like "Tour Awful"*] & underneath this Awful Tower no sign of romance was to be discovered – only twenty French Legionaries with AK-47's & flak-vests protecting the landmark from *la menace du terrorisme...*

This was a clear departure from my first hint of Paris with Kunal & his buddy. We'd arrived in Paris suddenly, dumped out at *The Arc de Triomphe.* We quickly made our way to the apartment of a girl Kunal hadn met through Couchsurfing.org. She let us in, kissed everyone on the cheek & soon vanished, leaving us three strange men to celebrate with fresh-cut hoagie sandwiches...

In the morning we made it three blocks before somehow walking into a zoo [*Ménagerie*]. Apparently you only had to pay admission when exiting, so we simply hopped the fence after digging on the tarantulas & were soon strolling amongst the bank of the Seine... We made it into a business district cramped as Manhattan. Prices were sky-high on everything from chocolate-coated wafers to mayo & cheese sandwiches. Before our pilgrimage to Jim Morrison, we hit the gallery of guerrilla street artist Space Invader, who's traveled the world anonymously plastering tiles onto the buildings of every capitol...

Ok, the Underflesh gig... Jason dumped me at the Star Café after we'd made a pact jokingly dubbed *"The Versailles Treaty."* If things go horribly wrong, I simply make the call & hop a train to his apartment. I can only do this once though, because I don't want to overstay my welcome. The reality (*hard-fought, no less*) is that it's me vs. the street for 6 more days, 6 more minutes, 6 more seconds. *Regardez ce que vous avez commencé Mr. Miller...*

A procession line of metal dudes & their ladyfriends enter the concert hall & begin kissing everyone's cheeks from left to right in traditional greeting. Then they came at me, these 10 girls going ****mwoa-mwoa**** & laughing as ridiculously hard as I was. Thankfully the metal dudes [*after kissing all the other metal dudes*] decided to switch over to the American male handshake...

Underflesh took the stage, belting out a slick, machine-like death-metal decimation. Their vibe was somewhere between Gojra, Scarve & Mithras (*if you carve out the industrialized parts & add in a ton of groove instead*). Plenty of finger-tap quasi-solo's – black metal nods & atmospheric interludes stringing sections together...

The Belgian band was supposed to play next, but they are still stuck in traffic, leaving Normandy's NOEIN to fill the gap. The crowd is starting to pack the hall, and it's growing sweatier by the minute. The singer from NOEIN is a polite French girl with skeleton finger gloves in her early 20's that instantly turns into a monster the second the drums start blasting & grinding. The further the set progresses, the more her eyes go to that other place. Furious! NOEIN pummel onward with an expert blend reminiscent of Gojira, All Shall Perish, Chimaira & even Strapping Young Lad at times…

A break between loudness as the Belgians set up their equipment. NOEIN guitarist Adrien Leboulanger & I sit at a booth downstairs rapping about the uphill battle of a metal band in France: "We are from Normandy, like 100km from here. The name NOEIN comes from Japanese anime – it's basically the story, you know, metaphysical space & time, kind of a weird universe. We created a whole story about a corporation that controls everything from economics, education, government. They get the technology to create clones so there are factories of human beings you can sell. The song 'Crystallis,' we have a music video – it's the awakening of one of the models. It's an adult body with no mind – nothing, you know – she just wakes up and discovers sense, sights…"

"Metal here is obviously a minority, and it seems that no one really speaks good English."

[Chuckles]. "That's typical French. There's kind of a phenomenon – in France, metal is not well known. You cannot find metal radio & there is no metal channel on TV. You don't hear about metal in newspapers or anything – its underground & always been like that. The French bands have difficulty getting out of France & most French bands play in France only. You cannot expect to live on your music."

"Do you know about the Peste Legions?"

"I've heard of it – they were burning churches & stuff, some racial crimes. I don't really know about this – its part of metal but it's a part I really don't like. I don't like the black metal voice; the philosophy is kind of weird, right ring – kind of Nazi… Sometimes you can have the signs, the symbolism, it doesn't mean that they are really racist but its not always easy to know the limit. That's why many people who don't know the limits believe that every metal band is satanic and that's why we have some politicians in France who wanted to forbid the Hellfest last year based on the argument that it leads people to kill each other, to kill themselves, to hate people – just based on some lyrics that are like '*burn the priests, and famine, and bury them in camels shit*' or stuff like that. '*Yes, yes – we have to ban this event, even though it has worked well for the population. It is not possible in a catholic country…*' But this was all just advertising for the festival."

"Are there WWII monuments in Normandy?"

"There's not a lot left over – some cities were completely erased 90% because of World War II. There are some old monuments, churches, but the culture – the Viking culture – is still alive. There is a big boat like Vikings & people all dress up, so its kind of the Normandy culture. There are new bands now – like black metal but Normandy black metal – but its kind of weird for me because its like nationalism."

"Everyone in London hated Paris but said the rest of France was OK…"

"Paris can be a great place when you live there & know it. When you come from the countryside like us you come once or twice a year and its, *'My god its too big, I'm completely lost.'* The Belgian band tonight, they got stuck in traffic & completely lost for 3 hours. Paris is kind of a nightmare for that. People in Paris suck, really, they are not friendly at all. So even if Paris for the world is a classy, elegance, fashion kind of thing… I wouldn't live in Paris, but its great to come here sometimes to play & confront another audience."

"Do you have a good story? It can be about anything…"

"I went to Portland, Oregon last summer for two months…"

"I live there right now, actually."

"Really? I love Portland – it was really, really great. One side is more posh, the other side is grunge, tattoo shops. I went their because I was a French student with two American kids that spoke French. On the plane there, going through Montreal, I recognized Devin Townsend. I kind of hung outside the airplane bathroom with a paper and a pen, waiting for an autograph… Of course, no one else knew who he was on the plane."

"You can live anywhere as an EU citizen, right? If you could live anywhere, where would it be? Many people back in The States would kill for your position."

"I always wanted to move & I've been in lots of countries in Europe because I'm in theatre – that is my other passion. But I'd have to say Portland, really."

"Really??"

"I've always said to myself, yeah, the USA, you hear lots of things & I don't really want to go there – you know about George Bush & we really hate him – I guess you do to, or…"

"Yeah, <u>A LOT</u>"

"And people are like, *'Americans are silly – why would they vote for such a loser?'*"

"Because Die-Bold rigged the elections."

"Yeah I know, I know – they cheated, so… I didn't really want to go to the US but I had the opportunity to work there. I was really, really surprised in a very good way – how kind people are, how open-minded. Something that struck me the first time – I went to buy food & the guy at the counter was tattooed on the arms, had piercings everywhere. You will never see that in France – it is not possible."

"The rest of the United States, you won't see that as much. Rarely, in fact."

"I met a girl that told me she was from Texas & about how Portland was into ecology, green stuff & told me about the law that forbids buildings higher then 30 floors. I went to the beach & someone told me that's where they shot *The Goonies*."

"Yeah, Astoria…"

"There were so many shows for so cheap – I saw Divine Heresy, Fear Factory & After The Burial for $12 bucks. In France that would be like 30 euros… Portland – I think it's the greatest city I've ever visited outside of France."

"Let me get this straight – of all the cities you've been to in Europe, you would take Portland over any of them?"

"I think so, yes. Really, really – I love Portland…"

** *"avalé par la grande prostituée"* **

"Paris is like a whore. From a distance she seems ravishing – you can't wait until you have her in your arms. And five minutes later you feel empty, disgusted with yourself. You feel tricked…" Beneath the city I coddle my wounds as a gypsy wails the accordion. The Frenchie's stare blankly at the floor as subway tiles whiz by; unable to follow the maps I let the subterranean train take me wherever it feels right, like Parisian roulette...

Watching the gypsy hammer away on his instrument & the denizens of Paris not give the slightest *baiser*. I see quite plainly the frank equation – 1 million gypsies in Europe & nowhere for them to go. It is a real problem with no real solution & it is no stereotype that they live in packs like a pyrate tribe. How I burn to infiltrate, their secrets. Everyone I speak to of Romania, they say: *"don't even bother."* Gypsies are impossible to break the yolk of, for they are like wild men, mountain men whom live deep in the woods. They'll rob you, assuredly, and every inch of their natural Romanian/Ukrainian habitat – the crops, the animals, their communities – are coated in radiation from Chernobyl & will be for the next 6 billion years…

Last night I let something essential leave my spirit. Each city in Europe represents, at least symbolically, a plague of the soul which I must kill off level by level. In London, for example, the morning I went to NHS I'd awoke from a powerful dream. I was in the company of a lost love of my youth – we were both adults though, in our early 40's...

We were outdoors in a meadow of vivid, brightly coloured fauna. There were children everywhere as if this were a colossal picnic gathering. A tree sprouted in the midst of the meadow, fruit spawning from its branches. Dandelion seeds floated through the air mimicking light snow...

Generic as this vision might sound, 'twas ripe to the bone. The woman & I, we'd beaten the grimness of our collective past. The war was over; we were free & first time I'd felt it. She squeezed my hand as concretely real as anything could ever possibly be. And then I woke up...

Opening my eyelids & detecting Brit accents on talk radio, I realized that I could at any point hitch a ride to a mega-hospital & they'd do anything they could to help me, for free, because that is why they went to college – that is why they scrapped so hard to retain such knowledge & skill. Even the lowest man, the one's fishing through trash cans seeking minuscule scraps – these people were exempt from the terrorism of absolutist greed...

Last night was one of those breakthroughs. Yes, I could've gone with the Underflesh caravan, but I wasn't interested in sitting around struggling to make basic sentences – I came to see Paris. So after my chat with Adrien, I left blaring LAIBACH's *Francia* on my iPod...

I began to wander the shore of The Seine, the major thoroughfares of tourist flurry. I charted architecture, as always – a Metropolis ripe with history you feel like a ghost world beneath the foundations, yet those a pretending to admonish it are just as removed from the spirit of this past as the North Koreans are the current events of world history...

I was in search of some elusive enclave of shops & bars; some miniature Camden Town, even if for two blocks. Such a thing exists in every major city of the world, even the most hick – *but not Paris*. You have to dress like a Metrosexual Gucci & fight your way to the tip of the echelon to even be noticed. Just laser-lit clubs with dress codes, bad techno & shitty hip-hop. All I wanted was a bag of Cool Ranch Doritos & to roll out the sleeping bag ...

After 6 kilometers I found what appeared to be a massive park where some hobo's had popped tents while others drank wine beneath the gazebo. The gnawing hunger in my guts kept me moving, so I went in search of a 24 hour market – any little shop with a sandwich or candy bar... 5 kilometers on foot & every shop closed. The 24 hour lotto-liquor party store phenomena was apparently an American notion. Another 5 km

& a failed attempt at consuming a half-rotted orange until I discovered a McDonalds where even the $1 burger clocked in at $12...

The only other restaurant open, apart from a handful of high-class steakhouses, was dubbed "Classic American Hamburgers." From the outside it looked like a Coney Island with neon lettering, but its interior was a destitute farce. Just another Americanized cargo cult with Frenchie's playing make believe at an elaborate wine-sipping joint where a basic entrée of burger & fries hit $30 USD...

Here I was on a Saturday night in Paris during peak tourist season, having fantasized about escape here over a decade & this is what I find myself doing – picking through a trash can only to score a handful of caramel corn & a half-eaten Chicken McNugget...

It hit me like derailed locomotive – Miller was dead & my Paris [*aka Seattle, 2009*] was infinitely cooler by every possible means. I recognized, rather painfully, that I'd already done this before & with so much more elegance. I'd already lived the vagabond dream to the hilt, ironically obsessing over this legendary city of romance the entire time. My faux-Paris had unbelievably trumped the authentic by unfathomable kilometers of glory...

And it was in that trash can, on that fateful Saturday night, that I exchanged the last shred of any fictional longing in return for a half-devoured Chicken Nugget...

It took another 10 km & a detour around the Louvre before I discovered another park, absolutely exhausted. Some scattered homeless were already passed out on the lawn, so I wrapped myself up & went out beneath a tree. I awoke to someone lightly nudging my back the next morning, & turned over to view a black police woman blathering something politely in French. I nodded, pretending I understood. She wandered off & stood at the edge of the park supervising the exodus of the bums. Soon as I stood up & stretched I realized where I'd actually camped out – *smack dab in the middle of City Hall's lawn...*

** "*l'art à l'image de l'état*" **

Sunday, June 12th – apparently a national holiday on par with Memorial Day. The crowds are thin & the only English speaking person I've met was a girl from Florida, whose body language departed so heavily from the robotic, cold French. She was wincing her eyes at bus schedules & when I asked her Paris opinion thus far she near exploded: "*It's horrible, it's so fucking horrible...*"

I'm sitting outside the Black Dog Pub – *the only metal tavern in the entire city* – waiting on an NSK Operative, who like all NSK Operatives are thus charged with the task of further rendering the NSK State is a global one which in turn incorporates all other countries & systems of the world as its sub-directors, thus defeating the possibility of epigonism...

The LAIBACH people pushed him through to me, I think. All this was hatched in such a flurry I didn't have much time to keep tabs; I just kept sending out emails & jotting down names/numbers/cities. Paris has been an extraordinary bitch because all my French contacts are spread throughout the country & nobody knows anyone in "*Ugly Paris,*" because as a rule of thumb they won't even come near this bastard colossus...

In terms of journalism, it's slim pickins'. There is a totally bizarre "*even I don't know what it is*" electro-pop-quasi-industrial project called Dragonfly Lingo that makes videos with image stills of a woman in a white nylon body suit & Bowie-like *Aladdin Sane* makeup & the videography is heavy on the insect symbolism...

There's a straight-forward indie rock band called The Saint Cyr & a sort of "Ozzfest mash-up" metal band called ASHKA with a mohawked female singer. There's a worthy black metal band called OTARGOS & a fairly mediocre thrash band I won't mention by name. And, as per usual, there's a trying-way-too-hard industrial metal/rock guy whose videos are some of the laughably bad of the entire post-Spooky Kids imitation lot...

My main target is Black Metal Band X, probably the best French BM band I know of outside Blut Aus Nord & Merrimack. I could never get a hold of any of the Les Légions Noires people though – you know, those black metal terrorist guys who reputedly live in a castle wearing corpse-paint & leather 24-7 & are constantly doing black mass rituals with severed goat heads...

I was looking forward to meeting Merrimack, but the guy dropped off the earth. He promised conversation last month after he emailed me back with: "*sure thing, as long as you quit spamming me with all this fucking political bullshit.*" Some people, they just don't want to know about Bohemian Grove & The Owl people. Anywho, I've always felt that SPAM in the name of revolution isn't really SPAM at all. If anything, it's a process of, *dare I say,* Spamvolution?

So the NSK guy I'm about to meet – he goes by the codename Valnoir and runs Metastazis, his own graphic art company that's done work for Morbid Angel, NSK & others. It's imperative we start with the disclaimer listed on his site which floats next to a severed, talking hand: "*!!ACHTUNG!! to all our clients to be or not – **METASTAZIS DOES***

NOT OBEY IT'S CLIENTS. Metastazis does not carry out its clients' every whim. And Metastazis does not add more Blue just because the client doesn't like red. Metastazis is always RIGHT, because the world of our process is logical, because all of our decisions are justifiable in accordance with our own criteria, and because we observe a coherence within our work. You come to us for interpretation, to speak in your place, to decide and to act there where you have no words to do so. We abhor criticism coming from those who are not within measure to criticize…"

And there he is, *the* Valnoir, turning the corner & stomping up to me exactly as I'd pictured someone of his ilk. He's got a tight grey suit & black tie, pant legs tucked into knee-high Jackboots – one of which has a clicker on the heel ala *Jean-Baptiste Emanuel Zorg*. Valnoir's got his hair pulled back into a pony tail & is wearing black leather gloves with a skull ring pulled over his left ring-finger, combo complete wtih a shiny black cane. The only thing missing from his ensemble is a monocle …

    "Ello Ryan I am Valnoir. You must excuse me, I was at a party last night. I don't normally dress like this." He immediately lightens up – an animated metal guy for sure. He takes me to a Subway Sandwich Shop first before eventually reaching a fancier restaurant with typical French waiters buzzing around like the bees of a hive. One of them presents to me a small glass bottle of Coca-Cola, pops it & fills my glass...

    "I was born & raised in Paris; I wanted to become a graphic designer since maybe 7 years old. So I studied graphic design for 5 years in Paris... I've been pretty obsessed with black metal since I was 15 years old; the first album I bought was *Ceremony of Opposites* from Samael – second was *Battles In The North* from Immortal & *Suomi Finland Perkele* by Impaled Nazarene. It was kind of the Golden Age in this period. The fact that we didn't have internet gave it this magic aura. It was extremely difficult to get any information – no gigs, just a few gossips about killings & church burnings. The only way to contact these guys were to write mail.

    "What was your first real BM gig?"

    "I was 16 years old & it was Dissection, Gorgoroth & Satyricon – all these mythic guys. So I always felt very close to this radicalism inside black metal – it was dangerous – should remain dangerous, which it is not anymore. This radicalism, it's not only music – it can be terrorism. It's militant, you know. It's what makes a a difference between black metal & any other kind of music…"

    "Well, I'm curious your progression from nothingness into this higher echelon of graphic designers you've found yourself in. You have quite a repertoire."

"So graphic design, anytime we had a subject to work on at a school – even when you're trying to work on a publishing campaign for, like, fishing trout – I would try to put some black metal & gothic elements in my work. It was of course extremely stupid and immature, but I couldn't help it. All my teachers kept telling me *'don't keep doing that, otherwise you will never find a job if you keep doing this crappy metal stuff.'* And I wanted to prove that I was right. When I got my degree, I wanted to be freelance which is a pretty bad idea when you are just out of school & don't have any contacts. You struggle to find clients & I still wanted to work with this black metal design. I wanted to work for the bands that were mythic to me. After 7 years of struggle, I made it. Last week, I just found out the guys from Samael were interested to work with me – that is a pretty fucking big vindication. Samael were the ones that got me into black metal, and now I cannot ask for money – it's free, you know... I worked for LAIBACH recently; I worked for Morbid Angel, for Black Dahlia Murder and, you know, huge American bands. I can make some good money sometimes, but it's not the goal & I think that's why my work finds some success, because its honest from the beginning to the end."

"You play music too, correct?"

"I play bass in CNK – it used to be black metal, but now its more like a metal version of LAIBACH with industrial, militaristic kitsch. CNK stands for Cosa Nostra Kollective."

"Tell me about French black metal scene..."

"I think I probably met all the guys involved in serious black metal bands & I've worked with a lot of them. I respect some of them. sometimes I hate the guys, but I make a difference between the work & the person. I think we have some very good bands – Deathspell Omega, Alcest. Peste Noire, ANTAEUS – those are the bands that I respect the music & the guys."

"NSK – what are your experiences with the collective?"

"The story with NSK is very interesting regarding graphic design. One day I open an issue of French design and the entire issue was devoted to New Collectivism, the graphic design department of NSK. 'WOW,' I thought at this moment – graphic design can be that. So those guys gave me the will to become not just a worker, but to become an artist in graphic design with my own personality, motivation & politics. I already heard about LAIBACH but I was not much interested. With NSK I was really obsessed – I was looking for books, but at this point it was difficult to have any information on the internet. I was so pissed off not to find anything that one year I went to Ljubljana just to meet these guys from

Irwin & NSK. I love propaganda design, totalitarian design and NSK is the best studio worldwide to use totalitarian art & political art & to mix it with contemporary art. They do it perfectly. Plus the fact that they are extremely skilled designers – typography, drawing, everything. NSK is timeless.

"I'm just as obsessed, but people in The States, people in general have no idea what NSK is…"

To sum it up, I could say that NSK is an art collective – it tries to draw bridges between art & ideology in the 20th Century, especially totalitarianism, and to find relationships between both. It's not that simple, but that's the most simple way I can describe it."

"So about the blood-drenched WATAIN poster you did…"

"I was talking with my guy who has a silkscreen workshop & I asked him, *'Could we maybe we could print in blood?'* We almost did it too – he bought a bucket of pigs' blood but he forgot it in his workshop for one month. WATAIN were the perfect band – they told me *'maybe you can mix this pigs blood with a little bit of human blood – forget the pigs blood, lets do it only with human blood.'* So he wanted to do it with the blood from the members of WATAIN, and this would've been the best solution, but the problem is sending human blood in the post office – it's something pretty complicated, pretty risky, & the blood would coagulate before it arrived. So instead we extracted my blood and a friends – about half a pint."

"Do you know of any other occurrences where this was used in graphic design?"

"As far as I know we are the first ones to silkscreen a poster with human blood. It brought me a lot of attention – people in the design world came to me with this story."

"The punks have anarchism, black metal has Satanism which is basically the extreme metal version of spiritual anarchism… What does Satanism mean to you, if anything?"

"There is no global definition of Satanism in my eyes. I am not a Satanist but am Satanist friendly, because I share a lot of things. Satan is a metaphor who stands for a lot of values – rejection of Judeo-Christian moral values. or any kind of submission, in fact. I'm a total atheist so anything related to supernatural – this is the only thing I do not like. I don't think you can claim to be a Satanist without a little supernatural spirituality, and I don't have that."

"Do you feel alienated by French culture?"

"No, no, no, not at all. I hate French people, but I love French culture. I'd be stupid to reject that. France has been the lighthouse of the world for centuries. I feel bonded, definitely. I like when people see my work and tell me it looks French – '*It's good & it looks French.*' I'm pretty happy. When you go to graphic design shops in Tokyo, Bergen or New York, you see exactly the same books, the same works on the walls – the globalization of graphic design, I fucking hate that, you know? I like to find Japanese books in Japan, I like to find American books that way. I want it to look French – it is my personality & my culture."

"I went to that Space Invader exhibit the other day, which you might've heard of. Have NSK done anything similar in terms of guerrilla art?"

"The only time that NSK made street art was during the war in Yugoslavia. And Slovenia, for 5 days it was war. During these 5 days, people from NSK were printing posters & putting them everywhere. It was like bloody soil/fertile earth – some very provocative, violent images. It was a very intense moment... I like the concept of street art – its different then showing your work in some shitty bar or gallery...

"WATAIN, it seems more then ever, is a band who means what they mean & takes no prisoners. Of the black metal bands you've met, who are the ones really serious about extremism?"

"You should go to Trondheim [Norway]. I don't have direct contact with those guys, but there is a radical black metal scene who considers the rest of Norway nothing and they try to keep it alive. Every winter there is a festival & there is no light – everything inside is darkness. Dead animals everywhere, some of those guys exhibit severed heads on stage, human heads they stole in like cemeteries – they have dried skin on it. So there you can find some very intense guys. I've heard the music is not that good though. Not shit, but generic. You cannot expect those guys to have a modern sound."

"When is going too far going too far?"

"As soon as it's justified, there is no limit. They should act as violent as it is, as long as it's justified. I don't like free violence. The assholes, I hate that. It's like in art – everything has to be justified. If you use discolor it has to be justified, if you use this form. If you kill this guy it has to be justified. If you burn this church it has to be justified. I don't have a big problem about that – and I think radicalism is the past now. Of course it's sad that they burned all those wooden churches – they were stunning, but if you are radically against Christianity..."

"What of this legendary French black circle?"

"Mutilation, Valcutrary, Artopus, those bands. You should talk with one of the guys from Alcest & the singer of Soro Dolorosa. They used to be friends with that circle in the 90's. I don't know that much because I was in Paris & this was happening in the south. As I told you – no internet, no information, no nothing. We heard some guys were living in a castle and were doing nothing but black metal & were real fucked up."

"The CNK cover with the guys kissing – is that a shock attack to freak out the black metal guys?"

"The singer is kissing the guitar player but the reason is a pretty famous picture. During the Soviet Union there was a tradition that when the leaders of the countries met – like Yugoslavia, USSR – they were kissing each other on the mouth."

"TITO & Stalin made out?"

"Yes. There is a very famous picture of Leonid Brezhnev & the leader of Communist Germany [**Erich Honecker] – they are like kissing each other on the mouth. We made exactly the same picture – the same glasses, same haircuts, the hand on the shoulder. Of course our fan-base don't know shit about that because they're too young. If you ask their parents, they know that. Of course it was about the politicians. Come on, who's shocked now by two guys kissing? Who gives a fuck about that? Do we live in North Korea or Iran? It shows the attitude though, of course, because metal guys are the most conservative ever & we've been called even a homophobic band because of that. Some guys thought we were making fun of homosexuals – this kind of nonsense, you know. We wanted a cover pointing at totalitarianism that does something sexy, you know? And something very French, because we are supposed to be gay in France. So look, we are gay, look. And we thought it was very funny because the album was called Ultraviolence Uber Alles & the photo session was good fun as well, because they had to kiss like 50 times. Kiss once again, kiss all day – kissing, kissing, kissing, kissing…"

"In The States we have the expression – at least the handful in that know – that RAMMSTEIN are a 'Poor Man's LAIBACH.'"

"We have exactly the same expression… Of course RAMMSTEIN's main influence – at least visually – is LAIBACH."

"And they also use the black cross…"

"On the last tour, the keyboard player of RAMMSTEIN was dressed exactly like the singer of LAIBACH, with the hat, the beard, the chest – everything, you know. LAIBACH is RAMMSTEIN for the adults, and RAMMSTEIN is LAIBACH for the kids. They do not have any adversity against each other – they appreciate the fact that they work together in a way."

"You do know that the NSK Black Cross is also used for the Anarchist Black Cross, which is a prison abolitionist movement?"

"I didn't know about that... The origin of the cross is the black cross of Malevich. Malevich was a Russian suprematist painter – the most famous painter of the Russian Revolution avant garde & one of his most famous painting is the black cross. LAIBACH uses that because it was the Avant Garde of painting but also related to the Soviet Revolution. So its art & politics gathered together."

"Well, I ask everyone this. Do you have a crazy story for me – it can be about anything..."

"10 days ago I was in Belgrade, in Serbia, to give lectures about my work & Ratko Mladic was arrested. His nickname is 'The Butcher of Bosnia' – he's the last mass murderer of Milošević on the loose. He killed like 6000 people in two days, he was the worst guy ever. There was a huge demonstration with 10,000 ultra-nationalistic, Nazi guys in the street. Of course I had an appointment with a girl down the street, right there, at 9 o'clock. And we saw this manifestation occur. You know, a Serbian Nazi – 1 Serbian Nazi = 5 French Neo-Nazis – huge fucking men. & the fact that they were all involved in the war. And you have 10,000 guys gathered like that, and you are right in the middle with all the streets are blocked, swarmed by 10,000 Neo-Nazis. And it turned into a riot – the army was there, it was really scary as fuck. It was a civil war atmosphere.

"As dicey a situation as they come..."

"For another story – last summer I went to a republic called Abkhazia. It's an unofficial settlement still at war & this country is only recognized by Nicaragua and Russia. For the rest of the world its only part of Georgia. When you want to go to this country you have to go to Russia and then into Abkhazia. But we knew this guy working politics in Georgia so we had a special pass to cross the border. We spent time in bum fuck Egypt trying to explain to these Eastern officers that we are French & American tourists and that we were on holidays. 'Holiday?!? It's a fucking war here!!!' So we saw the trucks from the United Nations going there, covered in missiles. We were there with a Russian friend, and they really hate Russian guys. So you have to cross the border, then the river, to end up in this town. There were customs officers waiting for us in the middle of nowhere, smoking: 'Velkome to Abkhazia.' Everything in this town was destroyed – war, just war, you know? So we drive two hours to the hotel, and the second day we are death threatened 3 times. We wanted to see the woods, so we are walking through the woods & a drunk guy just stopped us & told us in Russian: 'If you go to the ruins I'll cut you.' Alright, let's just turn back. 10 minutes afterward & we've been followed by 15 guys – drunk, champagne bottles in hand. So they are following us, gathering, gathering, gathering & they stop us, back all 3 of us against the wall. And the boss of the gang came to us, 20 years old, tough guy like that — the whole arm was fucking burned. My friend from New York, he's got a lot of piercings around his mouth – *"We don't like that at all. The old guy from the village, he don't want to see you with that. So I shoot all of you in the head, like that – we don't do that here. So now, you take that off."* 15 guys like that, civil war, anarchy, no cops, all that. The only cop cars we seen just drove by – 20 year old kids in white shirts in a police car. So he takes off his piercings, and the guys, they just vanish…"

** *"mémoires en ce qui concerne les salles de la justice"* **

Monday, not far from Black Dog. Soon I'm to meet ASHKA, and later Black Metal Band X. I hung with Valnoir last night; his apartment was decked out in NSK paraphernalia the way a Los Angeles gang-banger would pimp out his low-rider with fuzzy dice & chopper rims. The Black Cross of Malevich was everywhere, glued to the walls & made of shiny black tiling. Even the bathroom was an NSK exhibit., shower, toilet & all – ferret taxidermy with Santa hats & mannequin halves with gas masks...

The apartment building itself had us cracking up – the entrance way's tiling had little black swastikas. This was none of Valnoir's doing, of course – this apartment was made in the 1800's, so this was most likely a hangover from Vichy France. You know the stereotype about Germans being meticulous – you could almost see the blitzkrieg shift from lightning war to intense home decoration overnight. First they occupy the city, then they occupy the tiling. It's like you could almost envision SS Troopers on their knees, hacking away at the floor: *"Jah, vee must make zis look guut for ze Fuerher, jah... Klaus, vere ist zee epoxy? Vere ist mein chisel?!?"*

Soon I am with ASHKA drinking beers at a restaurant outdoors. The main speakers are Laurent, the bass player *[a tall black guy in a Slipknot shirt]* & the mohawked hellion Syhem Angel, whose hair is bright pink today. She became their vocalist in 2008, at 15...

"Are the prices here 3 times that of, say, Toulouse?"

"Maybe not 3 times, but two times. Paris is expensive…"

"What of the French metal scene?"

"It's hard to survive & to exist. In France, people are not much fond of this heavy metal music. The culture entertains more traditional French music."

*"**mainly R&B & hip hop…"*

"When you are looking for some money to get your finance your rehearsals & recordings, it's difficult. Say, Universal Records – they don't want to invest in a French band. Plus everybody that is 15-25 years old is just downloading music for free."

"**& all the bands working in France are signed to labels in Germany, England or Spain – but never, never in France."*

"There are some people listening to this music & coming to the gigs, but for some reason it is very difficult to bring this music to the people in the media."

"Tell me about the lyrics…"

"**This is the story of a girl who's completely schizophrenic – it's a concept; the difference between the little girl & the monster. It's two persons on stage singing the same lyrics, but when you look at it you can see two different people at any moment in the song."*

"The music of ASHKA emulates violent moments with some cool moments, we wanted to have these two sensibilities collapsing & colliding with each other. It's the basic concept of duality – duality of music, duality of the soul… The idea of ASHKA is to have this contrast. The songs are not too technical, mainly because on stage we want to be free to do whatever we want – jump in the crowd, stuff like this. For us the gig is very important – you're in this with your body & your soul – you give everything,. You must be there, so there was this idea of instinctive music – like Nirvana, for example. It's easy to play & you can do whatever onstage."

"What do you have to say about the Punk scene here, or squat culture in general. Does that exist in Paris?"

"**Yeah, but its really underground, the squats & stuff. But its not huge."

"Well talking about globalization, Facebook culture erasing traditional culture through unified mentality…"

"**The French people are so conservative its unbelievable. They see somebody like me with tattoos & stuff – 'My god what is that – it's a monster, it's a freak.' I have pink hair, so… In the tube, in the streets, anywhere."

"We were talking about Amsterdam earlier & I swear I just smelled some weed drift over to this table – what are the marijuana laws here?"

"I am a lawyer appearing before the courts in criminal law so I will say that yes, in Paris there is criminality like every big town. I think that Paris is not a very violent city compared to other American towns. All in all, Paris is quite secure."

"So you are her lawyer if anything bad happens?"

"Ha! It's pretty funny, and its something no one understands. At work, I cannot speak about metal, because it's a very conservative working environment. They have bad ideas about this music, so I just don't talk about it. And with metal people I don't talk much about my job. All I know is that I love both – I've been listening to metal long before I became a lawyer."

"What's the weirdest case you've ever had to handle?"

"The thing is in dealing with criminal law, people's lives are in your hands. And sometimes you know the client is guilty. So first you've got to make a strategy & to decide whether or not you will plead guilty or not guilty. If you plead not guilty, you have to be very good & you have to be sure that there will be no information of proof against you during the trial. You can also plead guilty, but you have to invest in the client – then the aim of the strategy is to reduce the sentence. So it depends.

"Ever have some really guilty, evil bastards you refused?"

"I remember a guy that came into my office and he told me a story about a girl that was working with him – the girl said he tried to address her sexually. The first time I meet people, I'm just asking them questions. Everything is confidential; I keep the truth for me. Well, he was lying to me – I knew he was cause the statements didn't add up. But I had to do my job. If I don't do my job then I should not have accepted the case. So I said I cannot defend you properly – I must refer you to someone else. Sometimes I've to refused to defend certain people. Say you have a man, 30 years old, coming to me saying, '*Some people think I have raped a child.*' I look at that & realize I will be judging my client, because I have moral ethics. Each time I have this moral problem, I recommend them to another lawyer."

"You got a crazy story for me – it can be about anything…"

"***When I was like 11 I was a huge fan of Green Day & two years ago I went to see them at the biggest venue in Paris in front of 16,000 people. Billy asked me to come on stage & sing with him… Well, there's a video on YouTube..*"

"No, no – hahaha…"

"***No, it was me, it was me – my singing was OK, but I felt sick and… I vomited onstage in front of 16,000 people.*"

"Did people clap?"

"It was a mix between horrified people & ones that were really insane, screaming '*Yah, you rock!!*' Never again. Never, never, never again…"

** *"tout est permis et rien n'est sacré"* **

I am crouched outside the deli market, attempting to fleece the Frenchies. My baseball cap is laid on the cement & tilted upside down, attempting to catch a few ¢ as I wait ever so humbly for Black Metal Band X...

I've been careful to only speak French to the panhandling victims, giving a polite *"merci, merci,"* to every €.10 dime drop. Probably made €2 thus far, enough for bus fare but not food. I was going to spange *The Awful Tower*, but I've been told you can get deported if you *déféquer* on their bread & butter. Here though, on this deeper Parisian stretch, people could give a flying fuck-all...

I've never been so bored of a people or of a city – millions of inhabitants & I feel locked in solitary. Thousands rush by like disconnected automatons; you cannot pick up an auric trail from any of them, these repugnant, vulgar bullfrogs. I don't wish to be another stereotypical American Francophobe, but I cannot shake the feeling that the naysayers were right all along – Paris is the world's biggest museum & filled with complete assholes...

I see him; he sees me – black metal guy from Black Metal Band X. I sneakily remain in background as passes me in leather pants & biker jacket, stomping towards the Black Dog Pub where we're theoretically to meet in 10 minutes...

But he sees my hat filled with hustled change & *I know* that *he knows* it's really me & gets tight in his steps. He wants to ditch out & turns the corner hare-quick with a no-neck-motion back glance of the eyes I easily spot. He's just going to run off through the alleyways as to avoid whatever journalistic trap he thinks he's walking into; when push comes to shove, run from the lefty.

I try to talk to the bartender, but he only speaks French. When I pull out my little notepad of French sayings – the one with *"I'm a metal journalist from The States writing a book – you have any friends in bands that speak decent English I can interview?"* he shakes his head 'cause he doesn't know anyone. So I wait, just to be sure, for 4 hours. I flash my little notepad sayings to everyone that comes inside, but it's useless. *BM guy won't even return a text...*

So let me get this straight – it's OK to burn churches, sacrifice goats, slice yourself into oblivion, play shows with decapitated human heads on stakes, snort cremated ashes, promote the gospel of Satan & the destruction of all morality/religious faiths... *but to hustle a couple Francs out the Frenchies is sacrilege??* Bullocks... *"Même si vous étiez sur le feu, je ne ménagera aucun de mes urines pour éteindre la flamme..."*

AMSTERDAM

III. *"vaarwel rode lichten van Amsterdam,*   *je*
          begravenis komt in september"

She glides from backstage with the grace of a track-marked heroin stripper, the sort of breed you'd expect to headline the sleaziest trucker dive in all of Missouri.

This angelic Eastern European immigrant; this time capsule of global economic desperation where even the most sparkling of cherubim will initiate unspeakably barbaric *modus operandi* for cold, hard cash...

The audience chuckles in dimly lit atmosphere; her silhouette flanked by crimson curtains of the vaudevillian stage. The crowd, most of whom are tourists, sit uncomfortably next to their girlfriends. The nude dancer glides as ballerina; nervous laughter rings in hushed giggles. The shame in her eyes flashes with nocturnal feline shine as the 19 year old pops an abrupt squat & swings her legs wide open, exposing us all to her *picka*...

She unveils a mighty Cuban cigar & stabs it in her mouth, strikes a match, takes a puff, then swiftly rolls back in a yoga-like stretch. She then sticks the burning tobacco cannon into the lips of her *pošva* & puff puff puff go the smoke rings in perfect circular dimensions, her *sticchiu* an industrialized smoke stack. The crowd explodes in unrelenting laughter, unable to compute the sight which is awful beyond mere mortal description...

Welcome to Casa Rosa, the seediest, most disturbing sex club in all of the Red Light District. It's even a little much for me, the impervious beacon of filth that I am. The very lengths this poor girl will go through to buy baby formula, or more likely, an 8-ball of gutter glitter. I simply can't help but to wonder what the actual job interview was like...

Pussy tumor leaves the stage. The crimson curtains swing shut & soon reopen to a black couple fucking on a rotating platform. Their pelvic thrusts are a highly choreographed, professional dance – ballerinas of coitus & screwjuice. The man smacks her lightly on the face, representing the merry lunch limbo of S&M. Nervous laughter continues to erupt as the fuck ballerinas hammer away in perplexing cheap thrill sideshow. *Wat was het sollicitatiegesprek uit*...

** *"het echte centrum van europa"* **

London was not my first choice as an introductory capitol. They spoke my language & my contacts were bountiful – I couldn't go wrong & didn't go wrong. With Paris, it was a romantic head-trip assuming the planets would correctly align...

Amsterdam though, this was the #1 target all along – the main "vacation portion" of my trip. As a teen of the 90's, Amdam was the most hallowed of destination spots to the American outcast. The stories one would hear of the sundry sex & drug freak-outs – the tribes of crust punks littering the streets like an autonomous bastion, the squat complexes & hash bars with pounds of psychedelic mushrooms laid out like lunch meat at a delicatessen...

That even while openly tripping the cops would do you no harm; that when reading the very decals on their squad cards it'd basically spell out the word "POLITE" in the English language...

I was expecting a far more dastardly enterprise, because the reputation that precedes Amsterdam makes it sound lawless as the El Ray of Tarantino folklore. Instead, the Red Light District is considerably tame, and this sex theater Casa Rosso I got suckered into... Well, I'd assumed it was to be humans morphing into wild beasts behind mirror-glass windows for shameless horn-balls sticking quarters into random slots...

Not that I've been disappointed with Amsterdam – in fact I've been so ridiculously stoned on White Widow I'm having trouble calculating how long I've actually been here. That's the trickiness of Amsterdam – it's like one big mall created for slam-banged stoners where sugar-coated Belgian Waffles & dark chocolate Devil cakes are pushed in the front-line of your vision at every turn. The core of the Red Light District is an expertly crafted tourist trap built upon the exploitation of famished blood-shots...

This ancient town spins itself like a web; one of the only major Euro capitols untouched by WWII. When the Nazi's came roaring through, Holland remained a weak collaborationist state [aka "let's just do whatever the crazy people say & this will all be over soon enough"]. Therefore nothing was actually burned to the ground upon Gotterdammerung & the architecture reaches back to the major 16th century expansions. Canals lodge between the major thoroughfares in a fashion comparable to Venice; the Royal Palace rests at the end of the strip, gutters coated in gold lining...

At any turn you're likely to find yourself in some vampirism head-trip; cobblestone alleyways of Gothic architecture pointed eerily like medieval steeples.

Indeed, once one passes the old Church in the dead of night you head down claustrophobic alleyways where glass windows pop out from every nook. Behind them prostitutes in skimpy lingerie smile at you with the ever-beckoning curled finger, like harpies drawing you into their cauldron of HIV doom – a vampire coven out to suck your blood, not a flesh appendage like a milkshake through a straw too tiny for accurate traction...

I'd pulled in from Paris around 5am, soon alone on chilly, vacant streets. Garbage drifted aimlessly through Downtown streets – titanic piles of cigarette butts, ganja roaches, empty pot baggies & McChicken wrappers. Twas the aftermath of the ever-raging bestial party, the crisp morning air tinged by the stench of spilled beer & stomach juice soon washed away by the Soon Dutch Street Cleaners in bright orange get-ups...

Corporate Franchise XYZ opened it's doors, allowing me free access to WiFi. I looked deeper into the squatter scene & found a YouTube video explaining its ease. With the laxest squatting laws in the Western World, in Nederland all you had to do was break into a building, set down two items, call the police & simply explain how you now live there, utilizing these two items as articles of evidence.

You are then the rightful owner of the building until the landlord files a complaint against you, which then takes months in court to resolve. That's it. No riot cops, no hired goons or mafia guys sent by a corrupt landlord. Amsterdam was The Vatican of squats...

I encircled the first portion of the Red Light District near Dam Palace, since these seedy areas are contagion across Amsterdam. The Red Lights signify the sex & drug industry, as not to confuse any conservative tourist from wandering into the sort of place that would make Pinocchio turn into a donkey...

Of all the ganja dens I'd encountered, one stuck out like a mutilated thumb – CAFÉ 420, dedicated to the unrelenting awesomeness of Frank Zappa. It was like diving into the glossy pages of *High Times* magazine. It was the most cozy of them, reminding me greatly of some dive bar in Southeast Michigan. It had polished hard wood tabletops & a two-century-old bar top of identical construction. Dimly lit, smoky & forever playing classic rock, I'd found my HQ for the week...

I observed the menu with the gigantic bud leaf silhouette. Some of the grandest strands produced by mankind were available. A dime bag of White Rhino was €12; high-grade space cakes were €10. At all of these hash bars, they sold cannon spliffs of hash & tobacco as single purchase blunts in little plastic tubes ranging anywhere from €3-€6…

Not that such smoking was my style – the Europeans all puff on mixed half-tobacco spliffs & think you're mad to smoke straight buds. I bought myself one of these cannons, took a timeout & wandered up to the barkeep – a friendly, tall Norwegian lady named Jane in her late 20's: "I've been working at 420 over 4 years – it's a coffee shop in the middle of Amsterdam with long traditions. This building is over 400 years old. It's been a bar tradition the last 100 years. 4 years ago, the laws in Amsterdam changed – you can only carry one license, it's a choice –you want alcohol or illegal drugs?"

"The law… did a new party bring that in?"

"It's a complicated thing because when you discuss it – first of all, cannabis is illegal in Holland as well as every other country. So when you have a law like that you can't really make other laws to regulate the use of this drug because it is illegal. When Holland introduced the smoking ban, they went with the lightest version of the law saying you cannot smoke tobacco in a café but they couldn't really pass a law saying you can't smoke cannabis, because it is already an illegal drug. So in Holland the law is one thing & the practice of the law is a completely different issue. We have controls any time from 1-4 times a year where the officials come over. It is a beautiful collaboration, but it is also strange to see the uniformed official people come in with their own scales, ask you permission to search the premises & weigh how much you have. You're not allowed to have more then 500 grams in your shop at any time. You have that, and no minors – they're really strict about that. They come over, they say, '*thank you very much*,' and that's it…"

"Well, I might as well give you the floor to say whatever you want on this situation, because to be honest, I haven't smoked in weeks & I'm fried out my gourd…"

"Whenever you debate drugs, you have to take into account the consequence of the drug & the consequence of the drug prohibition. The law is that the drug is illegal, and the rest is regulated. Now we're allowed to sell an illegal drug, and in the last 3 or 4 decades its been a beautiful system. It's completely divided the hard drug & soft drug community. In Holland, over the past 20 years you've had 0% increase in heroin addiction – there is very little recruitment when you compare it to England, which has had a 1000% increase. Holland has nothing to prove – the numbers are all there. Still there is pressure from the conservative government, conservative countries where Holland is not seen as '*everything is alright*' from outside. All the rules make sense & if everybody followed them, that's what you get out of it – the numbers. The use of cannabis among Dutch people is lower then any country surrounding it. So if you think about the theory of prohibition, there is something that's not right."

"Well, is there general political pressure to cool it down?"

"The thing that happens – funny enough, around election time – you have some kind of big case that not only reaches national attention, but it goes worldwide. This latest one was the 'Weed Pass.' A couple years ago we had the famous school rule which said your coffee shop cannot be located within 250 meters of a school, which is another debate in itself. Extremely funny, but a complete waste of time. There is a front that says *'we're cracking down on the coffee shops,'* because Holland is the sore thumb of Europe."

"Is the conservative mindset the same as the United States, where they are being propagandized to fear for their children?"

"Yeah – their whole campaign a couple years ago, people's general opinion on cannabis was: *'It's pot, it's weed, it's ok.'* They launched this thing where *'It's not weed anymore – it's 3 times as strong then what you smoked in college, these kids are getting fucked up, they're getting psychotic.'* That was the word – skunk & psychosis. So this is also putting pressure on the Dutch government to keep it down but I think also this is a way for politicians to flirt with their core electorate in the media.

[**Guy looks like he has a seizure, falls off chair & she gives him a Coca-Cola]…

"Do you play psychedelic referee here often?"

"Kind of."

"What's the worst bad trip you've ever had to deal with?"

"There was this guy, maybe eastern European, came in with his bag – typically straight into town, took a little bit too much. He had a pain in his back & asked for something. So I said we have, you know, Dr. Ganja, and if you need something stronger you gotta find a pharmacy. So he had this bong, and then he knocked the bong over, and had this *'What the fuck'* look & I'm like, *'duuuuude.'* So I went down & talked to him. I asked him *'I see your smoking & I bet you didn't have breakfast – did you do anything else?'* Took some mushrooms – classic, you know? No, no, no – they are afraid to admit it. And I'm like *'It's OK, maybe you need to find your hotel.'* So he stands up & he's like *'Am I moving, am I moving?!? Am I bleeding? Oh god, now you're tripping me out…'* It's a longer story, but that guy – I'm just trying to figure out where he's at. He looks pretty deep in. That's actually a beautiful thing – sometimes when you have a special connection, if they experience some fear & you have to calm them down, you know? That's the worst – when you have a group of them & '*oh my god, call an ambulance…*'"

"I knew these people – they locked themselves in a closet and were back to back crouched in darkness with their fists held up crying for hours awaiting demon hordes. Like really? Are you serious? I've seen soo much of this crazy shit. There was this one guy, a dishwasher at this restaurant I worked at, and he ate a ton of really powerful acid & got lost in the redwoods of California. He was completely lost for days, flipping out like a changeling of the night amongst these massive redwood trees, you know?"

"If you want to keep your coffee shop license you're not allowed to advertise. So you cannot put any merchandise on your menu. Websites cannot say 'cannabis.' It cannot have a cannabis leaf on it – it cannot say get your joints here, 2 for 1. You're supposed to be able walk on by & worst case scenario you pick up a little whiff of Christmas. That's it. I wish I could say the same for the sex industry – passing through you're subjected to a little bit too much."

"When did they outlaw mushrooms?"

"It was about 2 years ago."

"In the interest of a truly democratic nation a lot of people are conservative by nature – do you think that saying there should be a legal age to do this is fair & legitimate to pacify the whole?"

"I think 18, because at a younger age your brain is not physiologically there yet. I give you my blessing to try it at age 18, but I think people should wait as long as possible…"

"What do you think of Paris?"

"You know Amsterdam is a buffer for many people – people will start or round off their Europe trip here. And if you have a middle age American couple, married with children, they say in Amsterdam they had a great time. People speak the language – maybe the Dutch service is more direct & harsh, but still you can deal with it. They have a weekend in Paris & then they come to Amsterdam– they're always '*thank god we're back.*'"

"Amsterdam is renowned for its squatting culture…"

"The most famous squatted street is the Spuistraat – there's a great bar there called The Minds. It's like punk, skater, kind of trashy but really cheap. You can't miss it – the squatted buildings are completely graffiti'd up."

"How about art communes? Are they creative squatters as opposed to junkie squatters?"

"I'm not sure, because I am an artist. But, you know, a lot of people I've met have made their way through all of Europe with

CouchSurfing.com – but when hey come to Amsterdam, they hit a brick wall. Amsterdam is too small with too many people wanting to live here, so the renting conditions are crazy."

"Is this the last gasp of Amsterdam? I know they are about to make all drugs illegal unless you have proof of legal residency here in The Netherlands."

"Look around now – how many Dutch citizens do you have inside? Zero. I would have to turn down 99.5% of all my customers because they are not Dutch residents. And these people are gonna go wherever they can get it & their gonna have to patrol up & down the streets looking for anybody that looks half Dutch. And then you know what? At some point I'm just gonna get a jacket with big pockets. And then boom, you're on the street selling with the crack dealers. *It is a solution to a problem that does not exist*. This system is really tight & so regulated – you do not see any minors in here."

"Well, I'm sure you've met all sorts of random people coming through this place. Who was the most interesting?

"One of my favorite stories – the first time I came to Amsterdam it was the first time I really experienced what it was like to smoke & not have to hide it. One evening I was walking along the sunset – *a beautiful evening* – and there was an outside seating coffee shop. And I thought I'll sit down & have a joint, and there was only one gentlemen sitting there. I had a feeling that I knew this guy but I never met him before. I found out later that night that it was John Sinclair. Writer, poet, musician, political activist – one of your fellow countrymen…"

** *"het kameraadschap van detroit is oneindig"* **

Amsterdam, Day II; early morning @ Corporate Franchise XYZ soaked from rain. By 7pm yesterday I was so horrendously baked that it was useless to hold a conversation with anyone or try to go anywhere else except hash bars. I kept packing on levels of fuzziness which eventually led to that bizarre scene at Casa Rosso...

I veered away from the main stretch & headed down the quiet back roads of those Venice-like canals trying to find somewhere to sleep. The streets were like a ghost town, window lights reflected off the rippling water like phantasmal bonfires…

The city was bum proof – no awnings just compacted, flat-interfaced buildings. I walked 10 kilometers to find the dumpster of a construction crew. It was chilly & I'd wrapped myself in my camouflage tarp like a burrito. Hidden from view I slept well until it started pouring rain, sending me moving about 40 minutes ago…

As I'd learned yesterday, everything once heralded about Amdam was on its way out. The squat culture was being snuffed; Couchsurfing.com was spammed to oblivion over the past 2 years. The squats no longer took unsolicited strangers & you'd be arrested for sleeping on the street. *Vondelpark* was illuminated & cop infested with nightly sprinklers…

My interviewee situation was grim – Marcos from Deinoychus was in Germany; Severe Torture couldn't meet until Tuesday & the only way to them was a 2 hour train ride south. Sylvester from Fondlecorpse was in Rotterdam an hour away, Jorn from Soulseller Records was busy all week. There were a number of others as well who, like clockwork, weren't responding to my text messages or emails…

I made the decision to skip Brussels & head right for Berlin. I still had a few more days to kill before I headed off to Ruigoord – this legendary autonomous squat community on the outskirts of Amdam that has been in existence since 1973. At some point the Dutch government evacuated a town which then sat abandoned for two years before the freaks declared it their own territory…

They've been living there ever since as a generally Dutch secret. For an idiot tourist Americano, the locals would do anything to put you on the wrong bus, the wrong train just to prevent you from ruining it. They didn't want every rube fresh off the plane showing up, let alone clubber jocks from across Europe…

Well I am me, of course, and I know the secret route – I have my pyrate map. And this weekend there is an open-air, three-day quasi-rave. So long as I volunteer to work it, I get in for free…

The tip? Well, that came from a random Detroit refugee at Café 420. This older guy named John, he'd been living in Amsterdam for years. Just kind of hanging out, perpetually stoned & working on poetry…

I caught his Midwest accent & we struck up a conversation about nightmare Detroit. I brought up Abbie Hoffman's *Woodstock Nation* that I'd been reading shortly before taking off for Europe, about how this Hoffman vision I still retained in terms of counterculture, which Mr. John surely agreed on in principle…

We got on well, ranting about Henry Miller as the king of American literature. Said he wrote a blog for Metro Times, the big local weekly free newspaper in Detroit that was the main competitor of Real Detroit Weekly I worked at nearly 5 years…

"een uitbarsting van chaos, haat en angst dat eindigt met de totale vernietiging van de mensheid"

Hiëronymus emerges from the alleyway smiling wide. We shake hands & head towards the nearest hash bar for a meeting that's been a long time coming. Hiëronymus is a famed painter of extreme metal album covers & easel masterworks. He is also known to the world as a propaganda front man for record label New Era Productions & audio terrorists STALAGGH.

If the reader is ignorant of STALAGGH's existence, then might I cliché say you should fasten your seat-belts, for nothing I can say will do possible justice to their purist malevolence: "I never thought I'd ever live to be an artist. I started by studying archaeology – Viking age from 1992-1998. I got my masters degree in '98, but all the time I kept painting. I started working as an archaeologist and it was very boring work, very laborious work, being in the full sun…"

"Like Indiana Jones?"

"Yeah, but a lot more boring, finding nothing and shoveling in the dirt all day. This was not what I wanted to do with the rest of my life. So a friend of mine, he was a radio presenter, and I did some radio work as well. He financed my gallery in 2001. A huge surprise for me – people wanted to buy my painting for 3,000 dollars! Wow. So I said '*fuck archaeology, I'm going to be a painter.*' So I did that for the next 3 years & the gallery became so successful that it took away all my time to paint. So I quit the gallery, became a full time professional artist & I've been doing that ever since. I also did a lot of album covers. I did a painting listening to *Battles In The North* by Immortal & I sent out a photo to Osmose Productions and said '*maybe its something for you.*' Three days later they phoned me and said '*we want to re-release 'Battles In The North' because the cover with the guys in the snow is kind of lame, is it ok if we use your painting?*' So I did it for free. You know Marduk, the artwork for 'Fuck Me Jesus?' The nun with the crucifix? Osmose Productions had so much trouble getting that cover printed. No one would do it – not United States, not Holland, not Germany. The only country in the world that had no problem with it was Israel.' Haha! Jews couldn't care a fuck about a nun with a crucifix…

"Where'd you go from there?"

"I got more offers from more bands & started writing some articles and making drawings for *Slayer* Magazine, the zine from Norway. Those were the heydays of The Black Circle – Euronymous, Dead, all the crazy stuff. A friend of mine had a label called New Era Productions also in

Holland, so I started making covers for them. Our theme was music, art, ideology & no politics, because some pagan bands are right wing & we didn't want to be associated with anything political... one of the releases of New Era Productions was Domini Inferi (a Funeral Winds project – these are real Satanists). They had on the cover this big statue of Christ in the neighborhood where they lived & smeared feces on it & its called *Excrement Terrorism On The Holy Trinity* or some thing like that. No one would print that of course – they had to send it to the Czech Republic & printing factory called & said, "*We're gonna call the police on you*', because the cover of your release,. So they had, like, do-it-yourself artwork, and on the back he's peeing on a statue of the Holy Virgin Maria..."

"I'm quite aware that you know all sorts of these ghoulish black metal guys here in Holland..."

"In 2005 there was a concert & the headliner was [**name *withheld to protect the guilty parties*]. They're very secretive, they wear masks, I don't even know who they are et cetera – as they play they start throwing something on people, something everyone thinks is dust. People were getting chunks of it, getting it in their beer, drinking it. It's like ashes or something. And I look closer at this beer & it's a piece of bone in there. And then they were throwing dead mice & blood & everyone was covered in that. And then I went backstage and asked the organizer – '*What was that stuff?*' He's like, '*human ashes.*' '*Human ashes? How the hell do you know that?*' And on the table are three urns. They just stole them at a cemetery the night before! And they were throwing the ashes into the public. The owner of the hall also noticed the urns & got really pissed off & then the police got involved. There were reports on the news, the government, the house of parliament – they were asking questions. '*This is too much, this shouldn't be happening in Holland – why is this happening in Holland?*' I mean, people were drinking it, drinking human ashes. That was really fucked up!"

"Yeah, that is pretty ghoulish..."

"Another crazy Dutch act is LUSTMOORD – they never record, they only perform live & always perform completely naked. One song, its called 'Rape Me.' And they're all guys, smeared in animal blood – it's a completely insane stage show."

"So they're so kvlt they refuse to record an album?"

"Yes – its all about the live experience."

"What does that name translate to?"

"Lust of murder, or murder out of lust. The reaction of the audience is always very interesting. One time they opened a right wing skinhead show & didn't tell people what they were exactly. So yeah, they're playing this Rock Against Communism gig but it was a full of skinheads, hahaha, and suddenly 5 naked guys come out & they're like '*FAGGOTS, FAGGOTS!!!*' & they were really trying to attack the band. The skinheads had to be held back by security – '*fucking faggots, fuck you!!*' heh, heh, hahaha. LUSTMOORD couldn't even complete their set. Then they also did a normal black metal concert recently, but most metal heads are very hetero. They're like, '*I can't watch it,*' heh ha, '*I see a penis,*' haha, & then they start masturbating on stage, hahaha…"

"Keep 'em coming – this is gold…"

"In Holland you've got a very Christian black metal band called Slechtvalk. They are really into Christian lyrics & have a plan to try and convert people who are almost impossible to convert. They want to reach out, haha, to the people who are into Satan. So they said '*we're gonna start a black metal band.*' And the music is really fast, almost like Immortal. But we also got a thing in Holland called the Black Metal Mafia, like the inner circle of Norway. They're not nice guys – they're gonna fight and use drugs. They're really dedicated Satanists… You know, I'm an atheist, I'm against all forms of religion. I don't believe in anything So there's this concert with Slechtvalk & guys from the Black Metal Mafia. What they did, they shit in a bowl, like a big bowl full of human shit, and saved it for 3 days. They went to the show & the guy who was singing – he had a long beard – they smashed the bowl into his face. It as all poop – he was covered in shit. All on his beard, in his teeth. So when that attack happened, with the shit, they had to evade because there was a mob of Christians trying to beat them up…

"Is there such a thing as going too far?"

"You know, grave desecration – I would be very angry if someone did that to my family or friends. For me, that's too far. Also burning churches – that's too far. Those churches were built a thousand years ago. I'm against all forms of religion – but it's a monument, its a piece of art. It happened to me the same. I had an exhibition at a university – the studies of art history, they asked me to exhibit there & was opened by the professor of modern art. The gallery owner called & said there have been threats – there are Christians that are upset because your work is satanic & you must remove it. Satanic? Are you kidding? Hahaha. My work is not satanic – I make dreamy, strange paintings. There was one of the god Cernunnos which was a Celtic god & he has antlers on his head & a big erect penis & he's ejaculating into his own mouth – but its very subtle. I said '*fuck them, it will stay there.*' And a few days later I got the call & they said they did damage to my work. They wrote on the wall in chalk "*dirty satanic work.*' And took a knife & slashed a few of my paintings. And those are people who study art. They got expelled, of course, and I had insurance for the paintings. Luckily I could restore them. The good thing was I got a lot of press because I made a press statement: "*My work has been attacked by Christians.*' It was in all the newspapers…"

"What are the critical reactions to your work?"

"Mixed. Art people – I actually hate modern art. You know the story about the emperors clothes? Most modern art is that – you go to the museum and '*oh, it's a nail with a piece of wood.*' It's nothing interesting, aesthetically. I really don't like minimalist concept art. Its made for a society of elite that think they know… Art is for the people – they've been enjoying it for centuries. But now its like children's drawings are suddenly art. So I try to bring back the old values of art, from the 17th century. I use old techniques & try to create something beautiful. And those academies & museums hate my work. They say its old fashioned and not new. Why does it have to be new? When people see my work, I want them to feel something – if it's a dark emotion or fear, something they can relate to – it's most important for me. So I don't get recognized by the mainstream art, but people that are into underground art or outside that scene, they really like my work & that's more important to me."

"You mentioned some 'toilet paper technique'…"

"Like this painting here [*shows me one of his STALAGGH prints*], what you see is the white of the canvas. I just take a piece of toilet paper & I start rubbing so the canvas comes back again. The harder you press with the toilet paper the whiter it gets. This painting I made in less then one hour. Normally it could take you a month to paint something like that, but with the technique I invented with toilet paper – one day it just clicked…"

"How'd you get involved with STALAGGH?"

"When I worked for New Era Productions I got sent the demo CD & said, '*whoa, this is some crazy stuff.*' The story behind it, with the mental patients, its some really interesting stuff. There are two main members, and one of the guys works in a mental institution. And he said, '*it was quite easy to get the mental patients because I work there.*' Scream therapy, he asked his boss – '*Can we try scream therapy?*' So the boss said, '*If the patients want this, they can scream as long & as loud as they want.*' So we did 300 copies on 7" vinyl & it went over really, really well. The famous cover painting, it's my own face – but I made it more dog-like, like an animal. It became a best selling album, to my surprise."

"A lot of people reading have no idea about STALAGGH."

"Yes – some people think its fake, or whatever, but they are really serious about what they're doing. If you listen to GULAGGH, its very well made *[**GULAGGH is the second entity in a proposed trinity of work, following STALAGGH]*. They used a classical music producer – if you look at the back it's not his real name, but it's actually a very famous composer. They started in 2000 as STALAGGH. They said, '*We're going to do 'Projekt Nihil,' 'Projekt Terrror' & 'Projekt Misanthropia' – and then they're going to change the name to GULAGGH.*' I've met them a few times, as well as one of the vocalists, the guy who murdered his mother. He was a very strange person; he was abused when he was 7 by his uncle. And his mother knew this & she just let it happen. I think he was 16 or something when he grabbed a knife from the kitchen & stabbed his mother like 30 times. He had so much hate – because of the abuse he became a psychopath, cold, no emotions. When I first met him, his eyes were, like, dead. You have a sparkling in your eye, but he was like a shark. Dead eyes, just staring at you with no emotion. He was a very intelligent guy – studied Japanese. When he killed his mother he got youth detention & was held in a place for people with mental problems who commit crime. You know, when you hear 'mental patient' you think, like, retards. He was much more intelligent then normal people... He had such a background that he couldn't get a normal job. He was working for a funeral home, had a nice girlfriend, but he got into an accident on the way home – he smashed into an electric box & was electrocuted in his own car. So his life story is very sad. Had a terrible youth; had lots of detention & prison time & finally, when he gets a job, a kid on the way, a nice girlfriend – he gets killed at 32."

"Was he a fan of the STALAGGH recordings?"

"He was really proud of the record. I talked to the guy for 3 hours– he really liked me & my artwork. I met some of the other guys too. The guy who does the screaming faces artwork [**points to Pure Misanthropia CD he handed me – limited edition, 13/300*], he's 44, a lot older. He's an artist who is schizophrenic – he has been in an institution for 20 years. He's a very nice guy, originally from Germany, very intelligent, but he believes in aliens. He has an arm tattoo he calls the '*alien mothership*' symbol. It almost looks like a rune... He said when the mothership comes around the rune starts glowing. And the mothership calls him & he goes with the mothership & he actually believes that he's gone a few days but is in a psychosis. It's really, really fascinating. His apartment is filled with all kinds of strange drawings, things he found on the street, and he always sits in a chair smoking & the walls are completely brown from all the smoke. Sometimes I shave his hair as I want – he has really crazy hair & he gives me an electrical razor & I make patterns for him. He doesn't mind – just strange drawings on his head. I visit him once a month, and I just take anything he says seriously. '*Did the mothership take you?*' He also collects pictures of Hitler. He's not a Nazi, he just keeps pictures of dictators. People are shocked when they see it. He makes a 100 drawings a day sometimes…"

"How do I find this guy?"

"I asked him about you, but he's scared of people. It takes a lot of time – he gets panic attacks outside. So bad I saw him sleep for a week afterwards. He doesn't come out sometimes for weeks…"

"Holland has a reputation for weirdos. What are some Class A examples?

"The first person ever to be sentenced for stalking in Holland – he just goes to someone's front door, rings the door, they let him & he doesn't leave anymore. He just starts living in their house. And he's such a big, threatening guy – people, yeah, they can't kick him out. And when they call the police, the police take him away. He gets out & comes back and starts sleeping in their bed, starts eating out of the fridge. And at 50, he was convicted of stalking. He lives in his car & just drives around & starts living at people's houses."

"Ok, back to the whole STALAGGH/GULAGGH thing…"

"How GULAGGH was recorded – it was improvised. All the instruments – the violin he saxophone & the trumpet – were done by professionals but you cannot hear that they are professionals. GULAGGH had the idea to have them play as if it were their first time & just forget everything they've learned. Just play violin & let go of your emotions. Portray yourself being in a GULAG camp – the terror and the horrors & just close your eyes & play what you feel. But don't play riffs, don't play music. And some of them just could not do it – it was impossible. No notes, just do what you feel, portray the horrors of life. Only a few could do it."

"Some people would see the name of the – well, group, I guess, even thought they refuse to be classified as such – and think there is some right-wing political message. A lot of people may not know that a GULAG was a Soviet prison camp, and that a STALAG was a Nazi concentration camp [**note: the GH at the end of both stands for GLOBAL HOLOCAUST]."

"People say its' an attack against communism or fascism but its not – they wanted to portray human suffering. That's why they use mental patients because they didn't want some black metal vocalist to act like he's suffering, they want people who really suffer. That's why they took me as an artist because I'm also not 100% mentally stable, hahaha…"

*"What are the major differences in sound between the projekts? [**Note: STALAGGH refer to their works as 'Projekts,' not 'Projects.']"*

"GULAGGH is completely different – these are screams from children. It's like classical music, speeches from Stalin, mixed with the sounds of people condemned to the work camp & they used damaged women & children from the youth mental institution. It took them 6 months to get permission to record there – the children were all under 12 & suffer from all kinds of mental disorders. But the composer was quite famous, so he wrote a letter saying that he wanted to make an opera, a classical piece based on the screams of children. *'Ah its very interesting, the children will love it.'* But they had no idea – still have no idea – that it was for GULAGGH. So they went there & used about 30 children, like in a group, and they recorded... Really, it's fucked up – mental patient children screaming their lungs out. It hurts you, listening to them. And one girl, the composer said, *'It's really sick, this girl was like 8. She was screaming while lying on the floor, clawing on the floor – bleeding – as she was pulling out her own hair.'* Around 24 minutes in you hear her screaming – it hurts you, the sounds coming from this little girl. She was sexually abused or something... And they also used prostitutes & women who were raped. So you hear lots of women & children, because the Vorkuta camp [**in the Arctic Circle] had lots of women & children..."

"Is there any way to possibly top this?"

"For the next album – this has never been done before – they're gonna use the born deaf. So people who've never heard sound – they're gonna put them together in a group & let them scream. So they can't hear themselves & I've heard a sample – *far out!* Like animals. It's so weird – and no one has ever done it before. They cannot hear themselves or the others. It's really, really fascinating, and with a full orchestra. You've got a little but of a scoop there, because almost no one knows this..."

"So maybe like a whale underwater?"

"Yeah, that's almost what it sounds like. The composer, he phoned a deaf institute & said *'I want to make an opera with deaf people.'* HAHAHA!! And the children who worked on the GULAGGH Vorkuta album, still they have no idea – hahaha... You know, the staff kept calling – the children are really excited, they want to hear what you did. Finally he made a composition in one day, just playing piano with some of it mixed in. Of course it was OK, and the children didn't know that they are really on that CD..."

"What do you have to say about mid-90's Amsterdam – you know, the city in its prime, during The Golden Era..."

"In 1990 you'd see a naked guy cycling his bicycle & instead of a bike seat he had a dildo up his ass. He was just like cycling through the street like it was no problem. And no one cared."

"Usually I bring up GG Allin in interviews just to get people going, but, you know, STALAGGH really 'take the cake,' as we in the United States say, so..."

"Years ago there was a GG Allin memorial concert with several bands performing in this squatter building. They were all extreme left, anti-fascist guys. So when they stamped you to get in, they stamped you with a huge swastika on your hand. Ok? For extreme left? We go in & they are playing videos by GG Allin – all left wing punk guys with mohawks & anti-fascist symbols and the band that came and played were called Johnny Cohen & The New Age Nazis. The vocalist, he had a mirror & made this swastika out of cocaine and he sniffed it in one go – it was a really big swastika too. And he went completely berserk, wild as GG Allin. And then the strange thing happened – the vocalist starting calling out *'Sieg Heil, Sieg Heil'* & doing the Hitler salute. And all the extreme left wing guys, they were also doing the salute. You know, what the fuck is this? And I ask my friend & he says – *'because we can finally do it ourselves without being arrested.'*"

"So it was a protest against fascism using fascism?"

"Yeah. It would've been a great picture – a hundred anti-fascist punk guys with Mohawks all giving the Hitler salute... So the stamp was real thick & black – it almost looked like a tattoo, and I forgot I had it on my hand. We went into a bar and there was this black guy & this black girl sitting at the table and, eh heheheh, and I grab a chair from their table & he says *'go on, go on, leave me alone,'* and I'm thinking, *'what a strange reaction'* and then later I realize, ah fuck, he thought I was gonna try to beat him up or something, hahaha... I mean, how are you going to explain what just happened in order to apologize? He doesn't know who GG Allin is or this extreme left wing, hahaha..."

** *"het kenteken zei fris en had dobbelstenen op de spiegel"* **

Back at Café 420; Jane works the hash bar & John types poetry. I'm with Roogier Droog, mastermind of industrial black metal titans Weltbrand & former guitarist of Funeral Winds, the longest running black metal band in Holland. He's also a member of the notorious Dutch Black Metal Mafia & knows pretty much every guy in the extreme metal underground of Western Europe...

I pack the pipe of a 3 foot water bong & fill the chamber with white smoke. Roogier watches the vapor rise to the top with a grin. "Ok, so I've never smoked a bong before..."

"When I pull the pipe out, just suck back everything in there." Roogier wails it back, coughs his lungs out, & snaps back to our mutual dialogue. *"That'll probably be good for now..."*

"I haven't smoked for years, so I'm probably gonna get hit by a hammer..."

"We'll start easy – just tell me about the band..."

"These days my band is Weltbrand – its kind of like industrial black metal with a really sarcastic undertone. We fuck around with politics, but we're not right or left, like LAIBACH or CARNIVORE. We are evolving, rethinking things, because once you make a few black metal albums, you've basically done it & it's not so much a challenge anymore. The booklet itself – for some reason people thought we were on the right wing, racist, whatever. I mean we are politically incorrect, that's for sure, because we're just assholes with a bad sense of humor. But with this album, to be fucking around with communism, haha. From a black metal point of view we take all these clichés about how these guys are supposed to think & were really wondering why communism was such a taboo because what Stalin did made Hitler & The Third Reich look like a kindergarten. That taboo needs to be broken, in my opinion."

"No one in the United States know who LAIBACH are, or what NSK is. I'm going to try my best to meet with members from IRWIN in Ljubljana, since LAIBACH is, you know, near impossible to interview in person..."

"Yeah, I love them – I have most their albums. Especially the image – it's such a mystery... The first band I did was Ordo Draconis, it was more of a melodic black metal thing, even though that didn't work out in the long run. I left that band in 2001, and that's when I joined Funeral Winds, which is one of the longest running black metal bands here. I did that until 2007 & did some session work in the meantime. For the last years I've been working on Weltbrand; it's like the 3rd album right now..."

"I come to Amsterdam finally, expecting something much different from what I've walked into. Mainly, the rabid commercialization. Is the old Europe disappearing?"

"Nah. When you come here it is very extreme. And where I live, yeah, it's a media town. You have a few streets in the center like that but the rest is OK. But this is also Holland & very modern. So you see a lot of American stuff here. When you go to the eastern countries, that's way more laid back – it's not as flashy."

"Do you have super underground black metal castle shows here as well?"

"Well you don't have castles here, but in other countries I'm sure they do. Cause even here they rented old spaces out in the middle of nowhere for private gigs. It's actually quite fashionable in the music scene. Like anytime we play Germany, it's usually those kinds of things. You walk into clubs that have crappy systems, sound guys that don't understand metal & don't speak English at all. Over here it's very professional. I have to also say that I kind of isolated myself a little. I'm not in touch with many Dutch bands anymore. Most of our friends are from Germany, especially in the East. It's the best scene for us – it's more like home then we have here."

"Got any crazy tour stories for me?"

"There's always a few insane stories when you get on the road & get into messed up situations. Or like people protesting you – they are very left wing over here – which is a pain in the ass with black metal because, you know, you are automatically Nazi in their eyes. And I really don't know what to do with it…"

"How do you feel about Brussels?"

"It's nice – it's a little like Amsterdam, although not as flashy. I don't go to Brussels much because I don't have any friends there, I'll play Antwerp or Gent. Belgium, its got its old villages and cities, and when you drive on the highway its very desolate. Abandoned factories, old buildings & lights, you know?"

"The 2012 stuff – you think the world is gonna explode?"

"Something is gonna explode for sure, but I'm not really a 2012 type. I read the stories & I'm amused, but you know, we had this guy always in the street waiting for the world to end waiting for the ascension & on that day he felt like a total dick. That's basically what these same guys will be doing next year. So I watch it from the side with a smile. All this tension & they have enough weapons to blow this whole world up. I think that's a far more realistic thing to expect then some 2012 death cult."

"What do you think of Napoleon?"

"Actually I haven't got into that topic yet. Of course he's interesting – like an earlier version of Hitler. But, you know, we still see Hitler as a war criminal and Napoleon as a great conqueror. So in that way it's even interesting as a reflection of how the European military has changed over the centuries. I read a lot of WWI topics."

"What's the most blasphemous thing you've ever seen?"

"There are some extreme things that I've seen but I cannot really talk about it, it's a… let's just keep it as that."

[**It is then that I realize we both unspeakably baked] "In terms of interesting, intelligent people in underground metal, who do you think I should talk to during this trip?"

"I would go to Juergen Barstch from Bethlehem. He is great, a very realistic character, cause he's old & bitter like me. Definitely talk to Secrets of The Moon – they have this avant garde slow type of black metal sound, like an early Samael vibe…"

"Are Bethlehem well known in Germany? Because no one knows them in the USA…"

"Yeah, in Germany they are quite popular – there are quite a few fanatics. They've really sold a good amount of CD's & have been around for 20 years."

"Is Sweden over?"

"I would say Norway is – the only thing I know of are the Trondheim guys, like Celestial Bloodshed. There's a lot of bands that are fresh & extreme. Apart from that the Norwegian guys – they are walking around like they invented it all & feel like they are the most important thing in the world & every time you support a Norwegian band, like 1349 or whatever, you get treated like shit. A lot of these guys act like rock stars & there's nothing extreme about them anymore. That's why I like the Swedes better – they have something. We're quite the same as Germans and Dutch, but the Scandinavians are a bit more reserved. You really have to get the conversation going & pull the answers out of them. You know, say whatever you want about WATAIN, but they still have the fire. The bigger the get the more fucked up they get & that's what I really like about them. They are always getting more fucked up & crazy. They always say *'we're gonna do it until it explodes in our faces.'*"

"So what else would you like to talk about?"

"I don't know man, you just get me so fucking stoned. I can answer a few questions but apart from that, it's a bit game over now. It lasts for about a half an hour & then you can speak again…"

"Tell me about the Lustmord thing"

"Weird bunch, haha. I don't know if I can take the shit 100% seriously but I like the invention of it."

"What do you think of GG Allin?"

"He brought danger back into rock n' roll & took it with him to his grave – what the fuck's not to like?"

"What is your comment towards the occult in general?"

[Pauses for a second, with an ultra-stoned moment of revelation in his eyes] "I used to be really into it… But the older I get, the more nihilistic I become… I'm not like a hard-line guy with a hard-line attitude.

Still got the attitude, but I don't use the theory much anymore. You slowly get this '*me against the world stage*,' this thing that's growing & really eats you inside. Most people really mellowed. You lose a bit of the fire of the youth & get more bitter."

"You got a crazy story for me? It can be about anything..."

"Well, you know, I'm the kind of guy that when I die you put a stand up comedian at my funeral like a roast... Back in the early Funeral Winds days there were quite a few ghoulish times. These guys were like having this shit-fetish, like smearing shit all over this Virgin Mary statue, you know, in front of churches... And there's almost being run over by a car by Will Smith, you know, in Amsterdam – hahaha. Of all the fucking black people that can run you over, it's got to be the fucking French Prince, haha. Come on man – it's like insult to injury, hahaha..."

** "terug te keren naar de aarde" **

I awake surrounded by the tricycles of children inside a circus tent covered in mud & grass, stinking like bonfire... Ruigoord, the pinnacle thus far. Had I not volunteered for kitchen duties, admission would've been €60 Euros. Had I not volunteered, I would've never discovered the pleasures of Hagelslag...

These Dutch cats, they turn everything into a donut. They layer every piece of bread, every slice of fruit with globs of butter & dump on chocolate sprinkles. I must've ate like 6 boxes of this delicacy which Americans only regard as a topping to frosted cake. It never occurred to me you can just avalanche them on meat loaf...

I could only envision being chased by Nederland mobsters through the cobbled alleys of Amsterdam & ditching the armed thugs by chucking said sprinkles all over the stone walkway. The gangsters instantly drop their guns, bumbling in that specific Dutch way towards the dark chocolate mess of tasty flakes: "*Jah, vie must eet de Hog-gull-slaag – Jah, Hog-gull-slaag...*"

Ruigoord, this counterculture apex of Western Europe... Goon Americans would label it a hippie commune, and certainly there is a staggering amount of purple clothing & dangling bells. But the vibe, the reality is something in itself. It's less a hippie-dippy pipedream & more an artist's compound flowing with psychedelics.

It's the closest thing I've found to mirroring the Theatre Bizarre territory in Detroit. At Ruigoord you find an entire civilization of bizarro tribalism segregated from Europe, encapsulated by a community of a few dozen. There are about 10 scattered houses, acres of open land & sacred relics of legendary acid freak-outs...

To reach it one must take a local train to the outskirts, hop a bus through 15 minutes of factories & windmills, and then spot a pointy steeple of a medieval-looking church emerging over trees – the world's _only_ squatted bar church, used as a concert hall & community center...

Summer 2011 is their final run, for they know the end is ominously approaching. The threat of looming expulsion from government authorities has breathed an explosive life into their aching providence.

What was once a tiny hidden village surrounded by glorious acres of meadow has now been completely surrounded by industrial factories. Every year a new refinery pops up, a fresh steel mill or textile plant. Like strokes of chess the corporate forces move their pawns, biding their time. Many feel this is the final thrill before the bulldozer greed-kill...

It was 3 days of this madness, whilst camping in a tent & freezing the entire mud-caked time. Hundreds of tents, gigantic bonfires, DJ stages, art areas; throbbing masses of dancing Latvians, Poles & leathery Dutch...

The volunteer coordinator pulled a tarot card, describing my spiritual mission of the weekend. The cosmos had recommended my elemental "*return to the earth*." He told me of the quiet spot far from the masses – a plot of land deep in their wooded area along the trail of lethal & poisonous *berenklauw* plants specific to Holland...

On the final night, I decided for one final go-round of ye olde rave glory. I popped something designer & with Dutch cohorts followed the trail towards the sacred spot, past the deadly vegetation. My body began reacting badly & I soon had waves of "*The Fear*." The sod of solitude presented no recourse...

We just kept walking, walking until I settled & we'd returned to the encampment. I spotted the raging bonfire as gray day turned blackest night. I rested close to it's embrace, staring into the flames. I let the bonfire abduct me, it's primordial vacuum fusing the embryo of chaos. My vision became tunnels of star-like shapes... *Damn, it probably was laced...* Freedom at the cost of nothing more then the suture of the past... *I needed not a return to the earth, for I had eclipsed it's orbit. I was no longer part of it but rather something separate & viscous in energy. My elemental totem reigned vibrant in the vortex of kindling, raw in the searing blue of 1000+ Fahrenheit... Want ik was de feniks, geheel herrezen...*

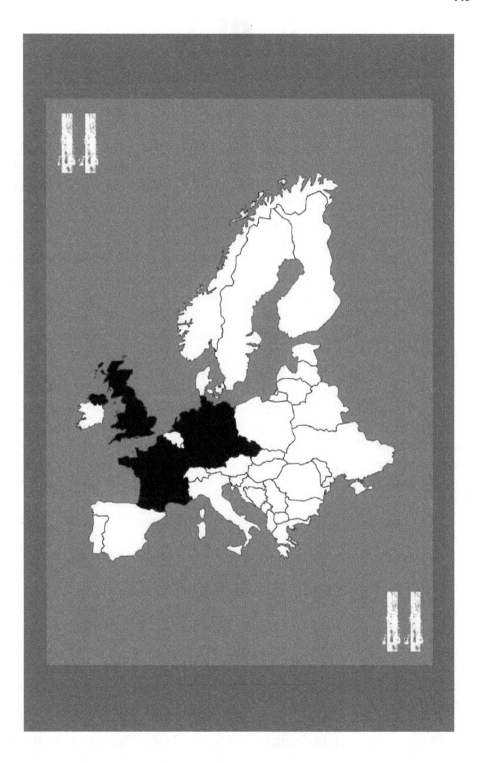

BERLIN

IV. *"solidarisch beschmutzen wir das grab des faschismus"*

Will Carruthers is the closest vocal mimic to Keith Richards I've ever encountered. Not that he's an intentional doppleganger, per se, because there's nothing in him that wants such a thing. I'm sure plenty of dumb Americanos have said something to this effect, which has surely drove the man up the wall over the years – the same way people meet me & banter nonsense about EMINEM in some hair-trigger response of pop culture.

It's just that gruff, chain-smoking/slang-heavy tone of Northern England: *"I think it was professor down at Berkeley, or a journalist, n' he was trying to pitch this Fukushima story to his paper, n' they're like, we're not interested in this – nobodies interested in this. Don't even fuckin' bother pitchin' it. It used to be consensus – but no, that's not news anymore. But who wants to know about it? I don't fuckin' want to. I still feel compelled to look at it, but I don't wanna know. Who would want to know that shit?"*

I, for one, have kept it bottled throughout this journey – but if there ever was a man to illuminate unfurling Armageddon to, Will Carruthers' is as pitifully blatant a target as a glowing, neon moose: ***"Yeah, that might be true, but it's still looming heavy. Once the meltdowns happened it took 3 days for all that shit in the atmosphere to hit us in Oregon. And immediately everyone Portland had flu-like symptoms, but no one was actually sick. It just kept lingering; we started calling it 'The Portland Flu.'"***

"Yeah, the radiation. It fucks with your immune system. It does, I'm tellin' you."

You are fucked from every angle by an invisible enemy..."

What we're talking about should be no surprise to anyone who is actually paying attention. See, when that 9.2 earthquake rocked Japan on March 11th, it crippled three nuclear power plants in one blow [*the Fukushima Diachi complex*]. All three plants experienced total nuclear meltdown & have since released staggering amounts of radiation that are so unfathomably high the highest-tech equipment mankind possesses cannot gauge it...

These aren't nuclear meltdowns – *they are nuclear <u>melt-throughs</u>*. Something, you must understand, has never before happened in all of human history. The radioactive ooze inside the broken reactors is so uncontrollably hot that it's burned through the containment units as to steadily melt a hole through the crust of the Earth. Just Imagine the blood splatter from James Cameron's *Aliens* & insert Mother Earth into the equation. If these volatile streams of toxic ooze burn their way to underlying volcanic activity, then the chain reaction could make the entire complex explode, thus sending a portion of the world into a sort of nuclear winter & making parts of Indo-China uninhabitable …

As the guts of Fukushima hollow their path through Terra Firma, all groundwater & soil it connects with will be coated with lethal, mutating radiation that will last for billions of years. In response to this problem, Tepco – the Corporation which owns these reactors – has admitted that they cannot in anyway coat these plants with concrete & forge a makeshift band-aid of lead & cement like the Russians did at Chernobyl.

You may have heard the plant workers were dumping seawater inside the reactors with fire hoses to keep them from exploding, and this part is true. What they haven't explained is that every time they stop, 50 years of spent uranium catches on fire & releases 1000 times the radiation of the Hiroshima bomb.

At this point, in June, Japan has been coated by an estimated fallout that is equivalent to 20,000 atomic bombs & that the rain coming down on the Japanese people clocks in the same as a highly targeted dose of aggressive chemotherapy. The sewers of Japan are now clogged with raw sewage on par with near-identical levels, but you must ask: "*Where does radioactive sewage come from?*" Well, from people shitting pure radiation…

What you also don't know is that the Japanese government – at the behest of the Obama administration – has dumped this radioactive seawater [*which registers at 7.5 million times the legal limit*] directly into the ocean. This factoid comes from the Chinese government's official website, who recently posted this as a warning to their citizens. Their discovery is that a 250,000 kilometer slick of radiation is now floating in The Pacific [*aka 100,000 square miles*]. And this lethal, eternal sludge is on a time frame to coat the beaches of Hawaii & the entire West Coast of The United States by 2013…

One speck of these radioactive properties [*like plutonium or cesium*] will absolutely kill you & could easily be ingested in a piece of fish, seaweed or rainwater. Once you have one of these particles in your system, this mutates you a cancer-radiating death totem for all those surrounding you. When you die the particle lives on, buried with you forever; eventually flushed out through decomposition into the soil/water that in turn finds its way back into the population…

Researchers are pulling car filters out of vehicles in Seattle & said filters are setting off Geiger Counters – the data shows everyone in the Northwest has been inhaling 5 hot particles of radiation a day; the Japanese 30. The data also indicates that the evacuation levels of Chernobyl are now permanent life in the soil & water supply of Tokyo – in some cases registering 30 times higher then the Russian calculations…

The US government's answer has been to stop testing the rain & raise the "safe levels" of radiation intake by 300% [*the Japanese raised it 2000%*]. In reality, the rain in San Francisco recently tested at 18,000 times the normal level, and particles of Plutonium have been discovered in milk as far East as Vermont. It's being found in the tap water of virtually every major USA city & where it's been strongest the death rate of newborns & infants [*including miscarriages*] has shot through the roof…

If you want to know why Obama's hair is now gray, why he looks haunted as Mussolini in 1945 & goes golfing every weekend rather then stand up against the GOP, there's your answer. He knows it's game over, is gliding through the motions & ignoring the inevitable explosion… I'm sorry, but enough radiation has been set loose as impact every living being on Earth. Again, I humbly apologize to inform you of this, but when reading the books of Dr. Ryan P. Bartek, you submit to The Red Pill upon entrance. *And don't even get me started on Bohemian Grove…*

Carruthers was a mystery figure; an anonymous email from a UK filmmaker I'd met during *The Big Shiny Prison*. I was told to hunt him down at once, yet I'd erroneously waited for two days of rugged uncertainty here in Berlin…

Will is something of a legend among "indie rock" circles – as in The Golden Age, before the Nuthugger Mafia. Most might know him from Brian Jonestown Massacre where he's played bass a number of years, or the far crazier *(& way cooler)* Spacemen 3. Carruthers joined that noise rock bastion as bassist in 88; one of his first gigs was the *Dreamweapon* live album. He performed on the discs *Playing With Fire* and *Recurring* & toured extensively…

Afterwards he hooked up with other Spacemen 3 guys in the space rock outfit Spiritualized before taking a long hiatus. He drifted the UK working odd jobs for 4 years, spending his free time "*hunting down go go dancers – preferably one's holding large bottles of vodka.*" By the late 90's he'd joined The Guaranteed Ugly, toured the USA with Spectrum [*opening for The Flaming Lips*], then recorded an EP with The Silver

Apples. Freelovebabies is the name Carruthers is now releasing his solo work under, coming off The Brian Jonestown Massacre stint of 2008-2010...

Back to your regularly scheduled broadcast of radioactive doom: "When I was a kid, me & mah family are from Southfield – it's near a nuclear reprocessing facility up on the top west coast of England. N' it's like fuckin' Springfield around there. It's a nuclear industry stronghold. I used to work up there for a bit, but I got away with it, you know, unlike my family in the area. It's the only place where I've ever been accused of being an undercover Greenpeace. Well if I was undercover Greenpeace I'd look like you."

"Were there 3 eyed fish?"

"There's a lot of fuckin' cancer, a high rate of childhood cancer, a leukemia cluster. And they try to prove that the cluster is in no way related to the huge releases of radiation in the Irish sea which have been detected far away as Norway. I used to work there at a bar n' serve all the nuclear industry people their dinner. Used to put a fuckin' suit & tie on. Be like *'what would you like for dinner tonight?' 'Mussels.'* I'm like, *'what a good choice.' 'Enjoy, I got 'em off the beach mah self this morning'* n' his face would go [**bugs his eyes out*] hahaha. You know that I know that you know. Fuckers man, & they don't afford to give a fuck... They had a visitor center for re-branding & advertising the industry & this guys all proud faced & ask what do you think of all this? *'Well if it was so fuckin' safe you wouldn't need to spend all that money to convince people that it fuckin' was.'* N' he reacts bad like I just jabbed 'em I the fuckin' chest & says *'you think I would put peoples lives at risk?'* N' I'm like *'listen mate – you're not in a position where you can't think any different then you already do because you built your whole life believing this.'* If you start thinking,' *'yeah, I did kill some kids,'* how the fuck are you gonna live with yourself? They 'ave a built in mental defense & they can't afford to believe anything else otherwise their whole life will be seen for the shit it is... You see the W.H.O. figures about it they attribute deaths to be very few. But the W.H.O. were in league with the International Atomic Commission n' they were not allowed to pull out anything without first consulting the Commission. Alright, so they've come to this conclusion tat there wee like 30 deaths. Prove it then. Cancer doesn't ha pop-up with a lil' sign that says 'Made At Chernobyl' – you just get cancer. & nobody knows why –could be smoking, could be this, could be that. But, you know – I mean there were big clusters around here. A lot of that shit fell just north of Berlin & it's still radioactive. That shit – Cesium 131 – the half life on that is some'n' like 35 years. You know, your looking at 150 years for that shit to go away, and then the Strontium – the reason they stopped all the atmospheric testing was because they were finding fuckin' Strontium in it. You know, Strontium 90's a mutagen. You know one lil' particle can sit in you forever. Might not do anything... But it might. And nobody can prove one way or the other conclusively the health risk of fuckin' radiation. They'll tell you that radiation safe and – Ann Coulter, she's fucking classic. Shit's safe, its good for you. If it's safe & you got a kid, what do you want to feed that kid – a spoonful of wood or a spoonful of depleted uranium..."

Did I mention that we're in Berlin? It's Friday now, June 24th, having arrived a week early. After the travesty of Paris & the blown out, sluggish dead-end of Amsterdam, I simply skipped Brussels & went right for the kill...

Germany is special to me for a variety of reasons – chiefly, the symbolic defeat of Fascism. Second, I was partially indoctrinated by German industrial. Third, Berlin is widely considered to be the counterculture apex of Europe, breeding some of the most gorgeous women on Earth...

That much said, it should've began beautifully & effortlessly, as indeed the dawning hours were. I'd hopped off the Eurolines coach near a park with a glistening lake where Germans were walking dogs & doing yoga. I snagged cheap brews from the petrol station, since it was now legal to wander around public openly intoxicated & wanted to follow the letter of the law to a tee. Imagine the brilliance of staggering around a mall in pajama pants, scratching your ass & staring at mannequins sippin' whiskey. This totally insignificant action held so much gravity & balloons in maniac scope when you realize the bus & subway are automatically factored in...

The notion from the go was to march right up to The KØPI like a punk rock soldier & present my case to whomever looked semi-official. I was intent to volunteer all my energy & live some dramatically crust existence of haggard bliss, because as everyone explained, it was the squat to end all squats...

The KØPI is the surrealistic wet dream of every 14 year old punk kid worldwide. It'd been around since 1990 – an ex-Soviet Armory the punks took over shortly after The Wall fell. They stormed in & declared it liberated, quickly rendering it the Anarcho-Hive of the continent. 21 years later, KØPI 137 is the crust paradise of Earth – the grindcore equivalent of the Egyptian Pyramids…

The anarcho-complex has 5 stories, hundreds of rooms, every syndicalist trade comprehensible incorporated into it's vast autonomous web. Perimeter fenced in by a hybrid of barbed wire & concrete, the guts of the yard wrap around an overgrown Urban Forest that shields a labyrinthine maze of tents & trailers…

I approached the gates of this beast in the pouring rain, soaked from head to toe. One lone figure on the steps was there to greet me; a hard-edged, 19 year old Eastern European crustie stinking like armpits & missing teeth. He's flanked by street dogs that playfully wrestle each other in the mud: *"Look man, I'm a journalist from The States writing a book on punk rock – I'd like to volunteer, maybe interview some people if that's cool. Who should I talk to?"*

The crust gives me a misanthropic, powerhouse death-stare: *"I doun geev a fukk,"* snarling his jaw like a Texan Grandpa spotting two homo's french kissing. *"Look man, I'm on the level – I'm not some cop or anything. I left the USA cause it's a nightmare & I fuckin' detest most those people & I never wanna go back…"*

Misanthrope snarls again, with a vertical eye-scan: '*I doun geev a fukk – you kum in heer drest like dat? I doun geev a fukk.*" Ok, now it is true that I might've not appeared so much with the in-crowd, per se. I hate feeling obligated to wear an Exploited shirt just to fit in cause my attitude is very "*nothing to prove*" – but yeah, sure, OK, I could've flanked myself with bare-minimum punk-o-flage like a Choking Victim hoodie. Stupidly, I approached the haggard one wearing a hodge-podge of leftovers cause everything else had cat-piss sweat-stench from 3 solid weeks of armpit ragging…

I had on soaked green khakis, a short-sleeve black dress shirt & was wearing tennis shoes. Not goony bright ones mind you, but mud-caked sneakers (*I mean, you can't backpack Europe in army boots – it's just too damn painful*). The janky, see-through raincoat I ground-scored at Ruigoord didn't help much either, or the sleazy bright-red beard that'd grown in. I must've looked like some misplaced pro journalist wearing a garbage bag for protection…

"Look man, these aren't my normal clothes – my shits dirty as fuck. I traveled all the way from London just to volunteer. You seriously going to tell me to fuck off?" Shit-head gazes down at his own stereotypical scum-wear to prove a point of grime & continues shaking his head: *"I doun geev a fukk, I doun geev a fukk…"*

So this leaves two options – either I strip naked right now, diarrhea shit all over the yard & roll around in my own feces spray screaming *"fuck Jesus Christ, FUCK JESUS CHRIST!!!"* or just come back tomorrow when shit-head will probably have overdosed in a corner & starving dogs'll be eating his flesh piece by piece…

I abandon The KØPI & it starts raining hard, flooding the streets. It's cold & miserable; no one speaks English. I'm in something of a warehouse district with graffiti & barbed wire everywhere. Am I to seriously sleep beneath an awning on Köpenicker Strasse & not Crust Eden? Some possible death hood in East Berlin awakening to the ghosts of the Stazis?

I burned so fanatically to inaugurate Berlin with anarcho utopia; some expertly choreographed Red & Black colossus within the tomb of historical Fascism. But instead I got a 19 year old kid too punk rock for his own good. *Bloody hell – if that isn't the bottom line of punk rock anyway*. You search for Freak Zion & the bottom line is always that same angry kid telling you that everything you represent sucks because you're old…

So I made the call – Mr. Florian Engelke (*of Ingurgitating Oblivion*). He directed me through the complex of subways. London was simple, Paris got strained, Amsterdam was raw but Berlin is annoying as a Rubik's Cube where every single color is isolated from it's kin. Every street in Berlin has a different name per block, and all are indecipherable run-on sentences. In the USA, we just pick one street name & it's a straight line that'll run until it hits a body of water of a dead end 700 km away. Here every block changes it's name half way through…

The next day, before Florian headed off to work, he'd hashed me a map of various stretches to investigate with alternative culture, bars, record shops, etc & left me in Kreuzberg. The first place I entered was a record store who's owner didn't have much to say but recommended I converse with a Polish girl named Ajka who worked down the street at a silkscreen print shop. Once there, I was again sent after her by a coworker. I chased her lead through streets of a Metropolis too dynamic to describe by mere American estimates. Berlin was something between Chicago, Paris & Manhattan, fused with a distinct Portland vibe…

I'd arrived at a KØPI-like artists complex called RAW [*phonetically spoken "ARV"*]. It was a sight to behold – hundreds of artsy freaks toiled on collectivist projects, but not one lick of English was spoken. It took an hour to find Ajka & by the time I actually did she looked totally confused why I would go through these insane lengths to track her down on foot all day. I really didn't have an answer, except that I was going with the flow. Random chance & I heeded the call – but I didn't realize how much effort it'd entail…

Well, Ajka played in a punk band called Insuiciety, but she wasn't in the head-space to give a spontaneous, powerhouse interview. She did, however, invite me to a doom gig on Saturday & offered a place to crash if desperately needed…

I got some grub, took a nap; gray skies cleared & I headed to a coin laundry with full bar. Just breathe, relax, smell nice; find the nearest metal/punk bar & just be social. Buy people drinks & make them like you, offer them cigarettes. Something'll give…

Normally I'd be interviewing some band, but the bitch with Berlin was the same as Paris – I had next to no contacts & no one spoke my language. All the major enthusiasts were spread throughout the country & none of those people seemed to know anyone in Berlin…

Seeking the easiest possible "*in*" to my tribe here, I go for "The BIG Metal Bar" – Paul's Metal Eck [*German for tavern*]. Blasting Motorhead on the outdoor speaker, the bartender spoke no English & the cheapest beer was €6. The guy at the next stool was from The Hague on his first vacation in ages, having just kind of showed up to Berlin spontaneously. He'd been having a rotten day because no one spoke English & kept buying round after round…

We met an Italian couple who unanimously railed against Berlusconi & soon wandered off into the night singing Ramones songs. Holland took a cab & the Italians let me crash for 3 hours before they had to work. I stumbled from their apartment seeking a public park which was quickly located but it was too chilly.

I slipped into one of the Internet cafés that flood the Berlin streets – high-speed PC's & only €.50 an hour. The anonymous email guy gives his street address, never explaining who he was. I soon get lost on loop trains & buses & have to turn around twice & take another train one way & then hustle down the street still showing up an hour late. I quack the buzzer & Keith Richards emanates from the intercom, wondering what took me so long.

That's how I met Will, with his Northern accent & Sherlock hat & the 20 year old girls chasing him around like a fan club: "First time I came to Berlin was in 1989 when I was touring with Spacemen 3 – we did a big European tour as far north as Sweden. We played in East Germany so we had to go through the border. That was weird – I ended up with a lot of American soldiers who were all smoking this hash. He's like '*you wanna come to the base after this gig?*' Fuck it, why not? We just sat there drinking with all these American soldiers until 6 in the fuckin' morning.

But Berlin was just a free-for-all then. Germans used to have to do conscription for a year, or public service for a couple years, but if you moved to Berlin you didn't have to. So all the fuckin' refuse-niks & the weirdos & the fuckin' punks suddenly come to Berlin to get out of the national service. So you ended up with real awkward squatting in Berlin & to a certain extent it's still here…. The first time we went into The East [**Iron Curtain era] we 'eard how fuckin' dodgy it was. Our driver was being all militant like *'we're 20 clicks to the border, get your passports out.'* & we're taking the piss outta this guy mercilessly. Eee's all paranoid like ee's gonna get hit in the head with a pistol. So we get to the border & we're about to enter the deadly & evil east right? We steal 'is fuckin' passport & drew like dog ears on 'em & a little dog nose & put it back into the pile of passports. So he hands the passports to the communist border guard – the guys looking through the passports all serious faced & gets to this guys passport & he starts laughin'. And the guy, our tour manager is like [**gives the 'shitting his pants' expression]. Hahaha. So that took the edge off. And then we went down to Hungary in Budapest & it was still communist at the time. We were like, *'ah shit, the communist east, we 'eard all these fuckin' stories growing up with all our propaganda'* and you get there & imagine people in gray cities walking around broken. The guy fuckin' waltzes out the venue, right – dressed in a nun's habit with fuckin' swastikas tattooed all over his face & a fuckin' psychedelic helmet. Eee's like *''Ello, welcome to Budapest!'* & we're like, *'What the flyin' fuck is goin' on 'ere?'* It's like the weirdest dude I've met the entire tour – & he was alright, you know? It was like at the time the first McDonald's ever opened in the Eastern Block in Budapest & there was a cube going around the block – and it was the same price for a Big Mac & fries as it was to go to a really nice restaurant with linen & tablecloths & a three course meal. Just fuckin' unreal…"

"Ever done salvia?"

"I've smoked salvia & I like salvia a lot."

"Most people just have horror stories about it."

"I guess it portends upon your idea of *'fun,'* right? I'm more interested in Ibogaine – I've been reading about people quitting methadone habits, long term abuse problems – 'sposed to give you a long high look into the more uncomfortable areas of your past."

"Do you enjoy bad acid trips?"

"I don't believe in bad acid trips. They're like nightmares –they're just trying to show you what you're scared of. If you make friends with your nightmares, they're not so scary. Ask every lil' monster what it wants… I've got some interesting information to pass on to people regarding doing shows while under the influence of LSD. I didn't experience any of this, but for the sake of the law & for the future, this is all a fictional account of what might happen if you were to dare to attempt to playa show under the influence of psychedelic drugs. Basically I was told of this show in Glasgow & he was playing, & there was a lot of strobes, & so this band he was playing in spiritualized, he said that there were like fireballs coming out of the strobe lights n' he was dodging 'em. First rule of playing in an acid state is always dodge the fireballs. & also when you look down to see where you're playing & you have three fuckin hands. It can be quite confusing but I've been told that it's nearly always the hand in the middle. & the roadie, 'e was fuckin' flipped out – doing this weird tribal war dance around these two terrified indie kids in the middle of this Leeds nightclub. There was like nothing in his eyes. So I might've been under the influence of LSD myself so this might've been a little disturbing – I went up to the stage guys that are normally very attentive & polish your guitars & – this particular time he's taped weird hieroglyphs everywhere on the stage, like weird magical symbols in gaffer tape – some sort of arcane roadie magick he was involved in. I went up to him, wears my bass? And he looked me straight in the eye and with a kind of fucking deranged look he beckoned me with a weird roadie finger into his domain and my bass, with all the little fuckin' weirdoes hangin' out – he'd completely dismantled it. Now I might've been trippin' at this point or not, depending on the legality of the situation..."

"As far as music stuff goes, what's your main project?"

"My main project at the moment is renovating a farmhouse just north of Berlin. Which isn't very musical, except when I see what I'm doing... I'm in a band with these two Germans – it's a punky, trashy kind of band & it's good fun. I'm doing a lil' solo thing with my loop pedal. I do a little bit of spoken word things sometimes – I'm fucking determined never to do the same thing twice in my life. It seems at times that when every moment is captured – you go out & someone's always taking your picture or recording everything I'm like – I'm really interested in the unrecorded moment – it seems like the rarest thing. It drives me fuckin' crazy, sometimes you go out & it's snap snap fuckin' snap, you know? It reduces the world sometimes."

"Have you been to Iceland?"

"No, I never have – I got a lot of friends there though n'd' love to go. They're very odd people & they're great to get drunk with – they're one of the few people I can drink with & don't get terrified around me."

"Do you freak out The Germans?"

"I freak out most people. N' if there's a bad phase of the moon, I get difficult."

"People get goofy with me too – 'you have no volume control, you just keep going n' going.' Well I have vocal chords & I wanna use 'em."

"Yeah, you gotta keep that shit in shape, right?"

"What's your spoken word stuff about?"

"Well, especially when you're dealing with a non-English speaking crowd, then the spoken word's really hilarious. Just anything is difficult, and when everything is difficult, I feel all is well with the world. N' it's kind of nice to trail off into some stream of consciousness thing. It's pretty fuckin' boring when you see some dude on stage & he's thinking *'oh how is this gonna work for my career.'* Career? What's the fuckin' point in a career? N' that's what he's vying for. The most you can hope for is some, like, dreadful advertisement. So, you know, if that's the fuckin' peak achievement I'd rather be on the building side slinging fuckin' bricks. I do what I like, you know? That's why I did it in the first place is cause I liked the freedom for me-self & no one tellin' me what to do. So if you're prepared to sacrifice that – selling your ass to some fuckin' advertising agency – but what's the fuckin' point? I can't understand it… I'm less interested in speaking about touring – I'm interested in speaking about shitty jobs 'ave had to do in order to support myself as a musician. I've got a feeling those stories don't really get told these days. You just don't 'ere 'em – stories of people working in factories, all that lower class art has just dropped off the fucking radar. You got rich people tellin' all the stories now, I think."

"What's the shittiest job you've ever had?"

"Oooooh… I've had some shitty ones. The sheet metal factory was pretty bad – that was a fuckin' horrible – I did that one for a year & a half in Berlin… Cleanin' toilets, that was pretty fuckin' bad – it was at a folk festival & it was 36 hours in 3 days…"

"Where's the weirdest place you ever woke up on tour?"

"It wasn't on tour – I was coming back from a party & I woke up in a tree once. A tree yeah, over a river. I vaguely remember walkin' home & thinking *'ah that tree looks really comfortable. I'd got my legs wrapped around it – do not fall off the branch.'* You know that thing where you can give yourself commands just before you fall asleep & your subconscious mind follows itself. Like do not fall off the fuckin' tree. And in the morning I hear the traffic, like demons in mah dream."

"What do you have to say about the indie rock scene?"

"Back in '89, the independent scene in the UK was really fucking healthy. Indie now, what does that mean? And it's like a brand of music? Shitty music…"

"The new brand of 'alternative,' just like in the 90's."

"Yeah. Back then, you'd look at the independent charts and there's be punk bands & pop bands, all sorts of different fuckin' bands. Because they were independent record labels. But now it's like indie fuckin' schmindy – what does that mean? It just gets so dull – it's damaged… Now the independent record label is as fucked as the independent record shops. They've been pushed out because nobody buys anything. It's not like your wanting to ride around in some helicopter but it is hard when you've been on tour for 6 weeks & you come back to no job & no flat…."

** *"der hass auf das ungeliebte und unnatürlich"* **

Within 20 minutes it'd morphed from sublime vacation to a 1970's disaster movie. Will & I were now at a cinema-themed rock bar, having spent the day acquainting me to the peacefulness of Berlin.

Earlier, we strolled calm streets where soldiers once goose-stepped; phantom visages were replaced by baby carriages. We continued through lush gardens as he explained the attributes of the fauna: *"Chew this you'll fall asleep, feed this to a lil' lady & she'll miscarriage, smoke that root & you'll see lil' pink men…"*

We passed the hill where The Wall once stood – not a scrap was left, nor did anyone seem to know what it's former dimensions were. We strolled by the secret prison of The Stazis, the Communist Guantanamo Bay; nothing remained but an abandoned brick building spray-painted with anarchy symbols & dried urine…

But it's night now & many American women are at this movie bar. Will has an autographed bass hanging on the wall, and he's definitely attempting to get me laid – introducing me as the famous Detroit writer guy to these attractive young ladies. They're certainly excited to talk to a friendly American that has something to say, unlike the cold, chauvinist Germans they complain about…

This one girl, we hit it off brilliantly. She was from Chicago & I once lived there too; She went to Columbia College, I went there briefly too – upstanding taste in music, literature, vice versa. She'd run away & was living 3 years illegal, nervous about visiting her family in Illinois & midway through arrangements with lawyers who claim they can't really help her…

But then I fucked it all up. After all the NWO, Bohemian Grove & FUKUSHIMA talk with Will today my inner Alex Jones dropped out in a rustle, like a rattlesnake springing it's venom not to kill in prejudice, but because it's the creature's very nature...

I mentioned something about "*the Japan situation*" & tried to back off but she really wanted to know, like they all really "*want to know*," being all "*oooh your hiding something from me*," flirty tickly-pokey "*tee-hee-hee*." And then she gets pissy cause I won't tell her, like they all do, so, well...

Without much of a response, her eyes water up & she hurries into the bathroom, leaving me alone again & watching the "*Look Up, Hannah*" speech emanating on the projector. It was a moment of panoramic déjà vu, thinking about all my folks around the globe & how they will react once everyone starts looking like lepers...

My impromptu date comes out the bathroom, having just wept in a stall: "*I'm a real person, you know? I'm not some dumb bimbo. I know exactly what you are telling me... I had no idea, no idea. I can't look the other way. I'm accepting this – this is horrible, this is horrible, if what you say is true, everyone, everyone, my family – this is horrible...*" And in a flash, she bolted away to drink with her friends & ignore me & the monstrosity I unveiled on her fragile psyche. *And things were going so well...*

Will & I ended up at an apartment of another highly attractive female that'd run away to Berlin [*this time from Portland via the Midwest!*] but luck did not aid my lonesome soul. Instead, I ended up taking a taxi back to Will's apartment with an exceedingly intoxicated Carruthers. Early blue-hued morning, pigeon flocks coasting the skyline, both of us reeking like cheap booze. Will hit some eternal spike and in certitude, in reserved acceptance, he muttered: "*This town'll kill you Ryan. This town'll kill you...*"

** "*tickende zeitbombe der menschlichen einsamkeit*" **

Saturday night at the big doom show. It's a coffee shop with a cramped concert space. The bands are sludgy & loud, reaching from Iommi's subconscious crypt. The headliner, PYRAMIDO, are a bunch of Swedes & have been in existence since 2006. Don, the bass player, is a former member of Deranged during the *High On Blood* era [*easily one of the best death metal records of the 00's decade*]. Tonight is PYRAMIDO's last show of a 15 date run...

"Tell me about Sweden – in The States we have a tendency to think every single person is in a metal band."

[They laugh at me, the Don begins]: "Sweden has a pretty weird scene because people are quite good at playing, I suppose, and it has a lot of context. And without playing live, you can record an album easily & release it, especially these days. But the live scene is really bad in Sweden for metal bands; as a metal band you have no chance to play anywhere"

*"**Outside of the hardcore scene, there's no metal scene to talk about…"*

"No, not at all. There are many bands but no bands playing live – the only chance as a small metal band to play in a venue is an opening slot for someone bigger on tour."

"Not even like sports bars?"

*"**No, not at all. It's very rare."*

"We've all played in hardcore bands before, so its natural"

"What's been the weirdest moment on this town?"

"In a little village in France there was a little bar in a village and we couldn't play louder then 100 decibels. And we were without a PA system…"

*"**So you can't play that quite, you can't hear anything. The drummer have to, like, tap his sticks & his snare."*

"You could basically only hear the drums & the owner of the bar actually came down and told us to stop…"

*"**I think it was like 10 or 15 people, like drunks without fingertips"*

"This one guy there was like the typical Russian grind guy from a mine or something – he lost his fingertips & one eye & he was old & like yelling at everybody in French & trying to do things with the drums while we were playing. So our singer had to, like, get him away. It was pretty fucked up…

*"**When we got there, this was this cat lying in the street dying. It set the tone for the whole tour…"*

"Is France the shittiest place in Europe for a metal band?"

"Yeah, as far as we know…"

"The reputation that Sweden has is that everyone thinks melodic death metal or black metal – is that played out or…"

"Actually I think there are so many bands because its been so hyped, which means that everybody between 15 & 18 has a death or black metal band & they are so good at playing because they practice so much – they are technical to the point where its what older players dream of, and they have really expensive equipment. But they are sort of fucked up that within a few years they will not be playing their instruments anymore."

"**Like the whole melodic death metal thing – that's played out for sure, so there's no discussion there. Hardcore is the big thing right now, especially in Malmo, where we live."

"It's a really strong scene with bands that tour Japan, United States & Europe all the time. I mean, regular people in our city haven't even heard of the bands but nonetheless they've sold so many albums & toured everywhere."

"Is Stockholm as lively as its made out to be?"
"**No."

"It's hard to get a regular punk show because everybody wants to be a little hip and in the scene. Like its cool to play a rock club but nobody bothers to put up a small show."

"What's the next step?"
"We're playing a benefit show in your hometown for homeless cats, haha…"

"**We didn't think it would happen, but its kind of nice."
"Like old ladies selling homemade toys that look like cats…"

Ajka's phone is off & chances are she went bar-hopping but is still close by. These German bars never relent though – last call is 6am, if you're lucky. I'm too tired to fight my body anymore; I discover a scaffold covered in plastic sheeting, giving all the camouflage I need to roll out my sleeping bag & avoid street view…

I awake to a 6 foot 3 Romanian trans standing close to me, staring at me, having been lurching there who knows how long. With blurry vision, I can make out dreads colored purple & green, smudged lipstick, black fishnets & a tiny pleather skirt that's as rigid as a plastic dandelion. He/she has got these converse sneakers but the front halves are cut off exposing gangly, dirty toes that are nail-clipper mangled & painted all colors of the rainbow. They apparently have crystal meth in Berlin to…

I give he/she a Camel snipe [*USA slang for a half-smoked ground-score*]. Methy eyes continue to survey me as I roll up my sleeping bag. I offer the t-girl crackers, and "they" shove a way-too-huge stack in the mouth & tries to chew them rather comically, crumbs raining from the lips like moist hailstones. The trans tells me about his/her love of Romania but how he/she can never go back because of family abandonment, soccer hooligans, the police…

** *"darlegung der wiedergeburt einer stadtn"* **

Florian Engelke speaks some of the most grammatically correct English I've heard anyone roll off their tongue, all in that prosaic Brit tone. Fluent in German, he exudes a sharp attention to detail in all matters of his business work & artistic merit. He is the humble example of finely-tuned German discipline – that sense of efficiency most stereotyped. His approach to music is the same way.

Florian is guitarist of Ingurgitaing Oblivion, the super-tech/genre-blurring beast whose *Voyage To Abhorrence* ranks among my top 100 death metal releases of the Zero's Decade. They massacre with a central weight as heavy as Stephen Hawking's antimatter theorems...

"We founded the band in 1996 & started off being open-minded kids listening to My Dying Bride, Anathema, that sort of stuff. The first record we did in '98 & that sounded – we had kind of romantic lyrics about nature & all that. It was definitely more influenced by the black metal scene. I think 3 years later – I mean I was totally into the 90's death metal but there were tons of sludge & doom bands around as well. We took on that sort of style as well, but then we incorporated more tech metal, death metal [*which evolved*] into gloomy, complex, evil death metal. We wrote lots about Hindu thought, religious topics – definitely not glorifying but rather the opposite – nothingness, nothing as all – loads of Nietzsche & Schopenhauer. That's what the bands all about. The next albums going to be released by Diabolical Conquest best in Mumbai, India... We're not really into this front-noise, high-speed sort of stuff. I appreciate it, but after awhile it's repetitive. As a structural element its interesting if you repeat riffs – say that you have some meditative atmosphere going on – but I think generally... I like bands like Gorguts, for instance. I think that's a good approach, or Ulcerate from New Zealand. They definitely took a Neurosis element into their sound which is really interesting. It's got blast-beats, gravity blasts, but twisted elements. And not twisted in the '*you're so brutal, you play at 300 BPM*' & that sort of business.' But it's really intelligent, deep, interesting, progressive music. Otherwise, I think the scene grows old & there is a need for innovation because it can be tedious. And that's what certain bands should bear in mind more. Repeating the same thing over & over again is just not interesting."

"You grew up in Germany & Northern England..."

"Berlin is a really interesting place I think – just so many things going on. Loads & loads of punk, grindcore & death metal, classical music. Culturally it's a just a really vibrant place. What I like about Berlin in particular is that loads of people try out things – they have an idea, develop it & try to make a living with it. So they are a very idealistic people. It's a very easy going, inspiring atmosphere it's not grounded – people are not stuck. They don't get stuck they just are curious, almost childlike in this."

"This is the 'it' city in Europe, but I hear there are no jobs. Do you think it's easy to crack into Berlin if you're just showing up, or is it a hard city to ground yourself into? Are people scraping by or is there a good quality of life?"

"It really depends on what you want & where you come from & whether you're diligent, consistent & qualified. There are loads of courageous people opening up cafés, galleries, restaurants, so forth. And they go out of business & they try something else. Berlin certainly does not have a reputation for a thriving, prosperous job market. The unemployment rate is dreadfully high in Berlin but then inspiration & courage is high as well if you compare it to Munich or Stuttgart =, for instance. People in Munich or Stuttgart earn much more and that's why people go there. But its not inspiring or interesting – it's OK-ish."

"Do you think Berlin as the artistic capitol of Europe is the ultimate symbolic defeat of fascism?"

"Yeah, I think it's a very symbolic place. Different people have different perceptions of what it stands for, but it definitely stands for the defeat of fascism. It's quite a basic, essential idea. It leaves behind the oppression by change. Most of the people that come here are aware of the historical significance. I think any people are just enchanted by this atmosphere of change. But of course, historically, and you want to find out more about the history of democracy, the abominations which took place under Nazi Germany, architectural ideals, and state related ideals & the way they changed in the past 70 or 80 years – this is the place to be."

"About the fall of The Wall – I have the impression that some of older people may sympathize with the communist ways…"

"It really depends on which generation you belong to. The end of 30's people, early 40's – they still have vivid memories of the communist/socialist past in astern Berlin. You meet loads of them & they're normally nice people with characteristic traits of sticking together, being very open. Kind of verging on the point of being a bit naive with their openness & directness. They miss certain things having to do with the GDR – mainly comradeship, supporting one another. Those are very basic emotions which were quite present in the GDR. I think the younger generation, people born 1988 or '89, they did not experience it consciously. Certain discrepancies & prejudices still being present. You know, more jokes about Western German people, capitalist ideas, then being different. But basically they blend in perfectly – there is no big discrepancy any more, especially with the younger generations."

"When I was growing up & would think Germany, I'd always think Kraftwerk – this post-industrial, streamlined militant look. You know, RAMMSTEIN, the nihilists in 'The Big Lebowski.' And I get here & its not the case at all. Is any of that sort going on? Being puzzled about this as an American, do you think people here have a tight grip on what America is really about, or are they just scratching their heads as well?"

"Yeah, there are pre-conceived ideas. You have to come to the place to actually experience this. That's the best thing you can actually do, and as you'll find there are certain stereotypes & and find out that clichés are usually pretty condensed & it's an extreme trait they made look extreme."

"What of stereotypes in Europe itself for Germans?"

"I've never really had issues having to do with prejudice. I was raised in a family with very open minded parents – they belong to this renowned '68 generation. They grew up begin hippies & they traveled to America a lot, they went to Woodstock. They are actually quite fond of The States, absolutely anti-fascist, very liberal left wing people. So I never really had these sort of ideas. Ok – when I went to France, this & that got shattered, but I never really gave it that much thought. I mean, I think about mentality the way cultures have been differentiated but I never went to a place and thought it was '*supposed to be like this.*' It's not an issue for me really."

"Ok, the last of the 60's sort of commune holdovers – Ruigoord, The Tachales, The KØPI even. It seems like I'm showing up at the last gasp for a lot of these things & what I would consider the idealism of the counterculture. All this cracking down on squats, the art movement –maybe not in a violent manner, but they are definitely clamping down. It seems Europe is moving more & more to the right. Of course in America that would still be the moderate center, but it's right wing compared to Europe..."

"I don't know whether there is a general tendency. If you look at, for instance, the Netherlands. That's a nation that formally used to be rigorously involved in colonialism. That's whey there is a high level of foreigners living there – that's why they have to deal with integration issues. There is a large community coming from Muslim nations & they have to deal with loads of situations there which is quite different then in Germany. Germany is quite inexperienced when it comes to foreigners. So people are less experienced, the political system is less experienced, but if you look at Scandinavia – still relatively left wing & relatively liberal. There is loads of Neo-Paganism bullshit going on – that's extreme of course but politically its still relatively liberal. I think due to the sub-prime crisis people rely a bit more on conservatism because they think that could be part of the solution – sticking to old prudence, values, that sort of thing. That's where there is a short term tendency. But as a whole, I'm not too certain if there is a general right wing movement in Europe now. Definitely not in Germany. People who are dealing with such topics, they might oppose & say that's not true, but then they deal with underground movements like the NPD, a very right wing party in Germany. But they are nearly bankrupt & there is quite a significant awareness to such movements. Politicians react straightaway & boycott & ridicule that. So I think it sounds like a good story, you know, '*oh yeah, there's a right wing tendency*' but I wouldn't really confirm that."

"But in some countries?"

"Absolutely – there are issues, and I'm not saying you should ignore them, but I think a tendency would be an exaggeration…"

"In the USA extreme metal is a little more right wing 'shoot first & ask questions later' politically, more working class – if not redneck – kind of mentality. Do you think the European scene by nature is far more open-minded or left wing?"

"Yeah, I agree. I mean, there are definitely bands who are naïve, who are just assholes really and they think… A certain time a go, there was *rotten.com* – they loved all these gory pictures & put them as their album covers. And that was kind of a vehicle to shock people. So basically a marketing move, right? Definitely the case in Germany as well. After a decade people wouldn't complain about the band hailing Satan – it didn't work anymore. And sometimes Nazi imagery does the job as well, and I think that's just plain stupidity. Also claiming that the swastika was used in France & other parts of India as well, different cultures. Well, of course it was, but we're in Europe & it's got a different significance & there are thousands of symbols you could use. I think the difference is in Europe people are still very aware of Nazi Germany & the significance of such symbols & that it just absolutely distasteful to try and glorify this. You know, this romanticized idea of Nazi Germany – the esoteric, the mysticism, the quasi-realistic approaches of the regime. People that identify themselves with Hitler's vegetarianism & believing in the feudal society, Atlantis, you know. And Himmler, who was very esoteric, very spiritual. But I think that's not a particularly serious approach. Yeah, it's interesting, but just watch a *Hellboy* movie and it'll serve you right. I think it's not responsible, it's just stupid. What I don't really get is those black metal bands, the Neo-Pagan bands that make use of such symbols. But if they are to make use then they must take the responsibility & give it proper explanation & to have the balls to justify certain things. I think it's cowardice when people say: '*Oh, we're not political.*' Well the symbols are, and the responsibility you must take on is. They are political symbols which symbolize absolutely abominable atrocities..."

"How do you feel about Napoleon? Is he seen more as a historical figure, as opposed to a maniac like Hitler or Stalin?"

"Napoleon is associated with France and... Once you get into history, and profoundly you'll find he terrorized people in different countries & there were millions of causalities related as well but mostly territorial & political reasons. He's still associated with France & there's still a romantic idea of Napoleon. France is associated with illumination, democracy, so it's not the same level. And I think it is not the same level politically, because Stalin & Hitler – they are just another level of efficiency & brutality when it comes to the organized slaughter of people..."

** *"der hohe preis der alchemie"* **

I'm back on the strip of bars & shops not far from Carruther's apartment, eating swarma-like sandwiches with members from El SSchlong. Turkish Pizza – the el cheapo delicacy available at food carts throughout every inch of this megalopolis. If it is true that you are what you eat, I will soon become a product of Istanbul...

Another one of Keef's people [*did I mention that FLOWERS OF FLESH & BLOOD are killer?*], Leah Hinton formed El Schlong in a New Zealand suburb in 2003 before moving to that country's capital in 2005. Quickly absorbing drummer Jordan Tredray into the lineup [*who now sits before me with Turkish Pizza sauce dribbling down his chin*], El Schlong relocated to London embarking on what they describe as "*the slowest world tour in history*," as in moving the group from capitol to capitol for months, or years, at a time.

El Schlong's brilliantly quirky *The Baddies Are Coming* was recorded April 2008 & sprawls across the musical spectrum, moving from the metal to the bizarre. It is like "Satan in the bath puzzled by the ginger pube on the soap," or so they describe it. The animated video for the title track won second place in the "Handle The Jandle" video awards in 2010.

In August 2010 they set off for the Southern Hemisphere. "Time/Place" was recorded while in New Zealand & released in May 2011. A snapshot of their two years in London, the album "*expels a darker and slightly foreboding mood and further explores the band's fascination with dynamic movement.*" A few months ago they returned to their sluggish world tour, relocating again to Berlin & have thus toured extensively playing 31 cities around Europe & UK, bringing their tour count up to 47 cities worldwide…

The drummer Jordan has this crazed bi-hawk thing going on & spends his nights giving "alt culture" bar tours to vacationers. Leah is a mess of blonde dreadlocks – a public school music teacher in Germany that takes great pride forcing her students to listen to Mr. Bungle's *Disco Volante*: "As soon as we say we're from New Zealand, people love us. Everyone wants to be your friend. I don't know why."

Jordan Treday: "**It's our countries reputation, as a tourist destination…*"

"And maybe just cause we're so far away. Maybe we're exotic, I don't know…"

*"**And erotic…"*

"This tendency of European politics more xenophobic…"

"I don't have much knowledge about that, but the UK is fucked…"

*"**Certainly the general Englishmen is very cynic…"*

"But, I mean, look at 'em. They've been colonizing the whole world & now because of it they get overrun with an influx of people coming & the system can't cope with it."

"Is there a general anti-UK sentiment in Europe?"

*"**No – a lot of people want to go to London."*

"But it's not the most popular country, that's for sure. You know, it was the top dog for so many years. Same as why a lot of people dislike the states because it was the top dog for so long,."

"What was the London experience like for you?

"When we first got to London we'd just go up & talk to anyone because New Zealanders generally do that & when I'd start talking to random people they'd look at me like I was mental, like I was going to stab them. This girl must be scamming me, she's going to rob me.

*"**You will at some point, in a London lifetime, assume the fetal position and cry for mum."*

"Was playing in a band difficult, in terms of logistics?"

"We had no van, so every gig we played we had to bring the whole junk pit – everything on The Tube. So you got hundreds of people trying to squash in…"

"Haha. Have you had better luck in Berlin?"

*"**So we get this gig right – we don't know any of the bars' reputations. And we get this gig and I'm putting up flyers at other bars,*

and this guy comes up n' says 'no you can't put this up here.' why the hell not? N' he brings out this whole folder – cause a lot of metal bars around here are specifically anti-Nazi. They have this 'no Nazi's allowed sort of thing' – ad it turned out this gig was like a biker gang head-club funhouse.

"So basically our first gig here was at a Nazi bar, haha, and we have no knowledge of this. We walk up to do sound check and there's just like 4 or 5 tattooed tough fuckers just running around. N' we're like *'oh god, whets this?'* And this one guys comes through n' says *'listen – meat... potatoes.'* So they cooked us like prison dinner haha, like steak n' potatoes."

*"**This woman comes downstairs, like this mangled looking drug addict, she's got a gang patch on as well. They ate like burger patties – no bread or anything – just burger patties, slush n' potatoes., And then there were two other bands, like Russian bands, because Russia is known for sort of..."*

"And the Russian bands were sort of weirdo Russian folk with some crazy flukes & they put on these dresses & jumped around – it was just the weirdest most awkward, awkward moment. N' of course they got all of their mates to come. And they had this room full of motorcycles. N' so you had one particular Asian, he was quite effeminate. I think he was, you know, got a man call n' stuff. But yeah, it was weird..."

*"**We got out alive... And they had these round tables where they obviously had conferences & meetings. And, you know, the seats were all kind of stuck to the ground at the bar & they had plastic cups & no glass anywhere. So, fuck it, we played anyway, and this guy comes up n' says "that was the greatest gig we had in 5 years."'*

"So we put that one behind us, n' ever since then everything has been fine. It's just interesting that these kind of half-hippies from New Zealand ended up at a fuckin' Nazi biker bar."

"Is Berlin the ultimate symbolic defeat of fascism?"

*"**Yeah, its kind of imploded on itself."*

"All the Nazi stuff is pushed out east to the suburbs & whenever any of that tries to come to the city the shit really flies. They really can't play any places."

*"**They got like festivals for anti-Nazi awareness. Because you got kind of these Hitler fans that shave their heads & wear suspenders n' have that image sort of thing n' then you got this underground black metal scene who aren't so much racist but just more... It was [Anonymous BM Band] really – they did an interview & at one point the guy started ranting about niggers & stuff like that and then in the punk community –*

anyone wearing a [Anonymous BM Band] t-shirt couldn't go into the KØPI or these bars."

"Back to the scene…"

"We came to Berlin because we thought there was a huge metal scene here, but actually upon getting here – compared to punk – the metal scene is not so much, we're from a small city in new Zealand, and the punk & metal scene was all the same thing. When we came to Europe it was quite different because they are so separate – punk & metal are quite separate. I mean there are the borderline crusties but in Berlin they really are two separate entities. We've had more fun playing in the squatty scene, but that's more affiliated with punk & hardcore. Hardcore is huge in Berlin, they love it… The problem with us is that we don't fit into anything – we're more weirdo so people who don't like metal, '*Oh you got screaming & stuff.*' And people who like metal, '*Oh you got weird bits. You know, you're not tough all the time – what's this soft shit?*' Despite the fact that Berlin is touted as such an alternative city, I think its only alternative to the point where people choose a genre and they stick to it. All the punk I've seen here is absolutely standard punk & all the metal is standard metal."

"I've used that term a lot too – weirdo. Is that what they say in new Zealand as well?

"No, it's just what we're called – '*wow you guys are weird*' – you can't find a subgenre name for us. Someone the other day asked my friend what we sounded like and he said '*psychedelic weirdo metal.*' Our old stuff was more Opeth meets Mr. Bungle. But the new record is completely different as well."

"***After listening to a lot of Gojira, Obscura, and you know, Devin Townsend & all that shit – it progresses even more, but we influence ourselves. You know you're gonna do another album and you have to make it different. This new album has the same amount of interlude-y sort of weird things going on, but it's also a lot darker, and is actually heavier. And I also think we got influenced by living in the UK. It was a hard time – not like 'oooh, cold, tired hungry.' This new album – it has a lot to do with the human mind & the idea of time & place, the evolving of the person. Also, the three of us are quite different people – you know, I'm quite into the occult…*"

"And I'm like all about science & fact."

"***There was once a time when I was quite younger, and I had to defend what I'd say – you know, 'aliens are real, alien are real & preach, preach, preach…'*

"N' I'd say 'shut up Jordan'"

"**But the point I'm making is that the album is quite meaningful for my point of views & Leah for her point of views, because she wrote the lyrics & they're really relevant to what I'm into. Like Alchemy, sort of time/place progression & evolution – all he crazy, weird shit going on."

"Back to the message – I'd like to think we've got a similar message to Jesus, which is just being a cunt, basically…"

"**Being a good cunt…"

"About the occult & whatnot – people hearken back to Crowley often. Is there anybody that is relevant today that I should seek out in Europe?"

"**I kind of delve into that world – I like Crowley, I believe magick's real, I like 'The Satanic Bible,' but UI don't read it because X amount of people follow it I'm curious why people are into these little pins. Anyone that's traveled the world & has all these little adventures & stories to tell I like. That's why they always come off as crazy because nobody wants to know if magick is true & is it was true they wouldn't want it to be proven because it would ruin the stock market."

"What's your definition of magick?"

"**Intention based on positive thought, or sometimes sacrificing a goat or a virgin… But I have figured that it is quite possible to manipulate the ether and get what you want through the power of positive thought & intention. I have to say that The Satanic Bible was a huge influence for me because it made me feel less guilty about feeling animalistic sometimes. You know, when all this magickal shit was invented they didn't really have science and now we're figuring out how through vibration you an manipulate water molecules & shit like that."

"Even old whats-a-mick-call-it that came out with the theory of a lot of modern physics he was also a firm believer in alchemy & he firmly believed he could make his urine into gold. In fact Isaac Newton, he spent more of his time on alchemy then he did with science and he came up with the modern thought of physics…

"**He used to rub mercury into his hair, because in astrology, the planet Mercury control your thoughts. So he thought it was a logical thing to think…"

"He was a fuckin' nutbar, if I might say so…"

"**He used to be paralyzed by thought & he'd wake up in the morning & sit there for hours…"

** "gegensätze ziehen sich an" **

If you're keyed into the right vibe, Berlin moves faster then the rapid weight loss of *Jimmy Tango's Fatbusters*...

Leah Hinton took me back to The KØPI last night & while I never made it into the squat complex, we did see a hardcore punk show in the murky basement venue with the moldy, sweating walls. I was given free beer, free smokes & made buddy buddy with the bartender before meeting a few crusties that'd run away from Detroit [*Trumbullplex cronies*] & were also backpacking Europe. We drank & smoked merrily, watching a Deutsch version of Cronenberg's *Naked Lunch* on the projector screen outside...

The KØPI lives up to it's reputation – it is for punk rockers what the Lost Boy fortress is for Peter Pan's tribe. Except Captain Hook, in their case, would be a riot cop sergeant covered in storm-trooper gear & his pyrate league the Nazi douche-bags the KØPI-based Antifa scuffles with in street battles...

It is now Tuesday, June 28th; hot & humid as Germany gets. I'm at a Tiki Lounge waiting on Texas Terri (aka Terri Bomb), an old-school punk vocalist of Texan lore. Also a cat that goes by the pseudonym A.L.X. from a New York based band called Love Crushed Velvet. Later tonight I'm going to be interviewed live on Berlin Metal TV, which I've been told is a sort of Germanic *Wayne's World*...

I have come to the opinion that Berlin is the greatest city in the world. How efficient; how educated & respectful. Never once have I felt threatened, though rather haunted. I do not mean this in a dark, internal way – I mean quite literally. So much history exudes a curious energy & if you are a person in tune to such theoretical subjects, you will understand the magnitude once you encounter it...

I've had a number of strange things happen so far in terms of poltergeist activity. One moment came at Florian's in the dead of night. I'd fallen asleep listening to the *Tron Legacy* soundtrack & began dreaming of a haunted house, searching through dusty, dilapidated rooms with broken floorboards & smashed windows...

I woke with the strong impulse of someone inside Engelke's apartment, and when I slid my eyelids open there were flies on the windowsill. I got a magnet-sharp impulse from the hallway & swung my head to view the door handle turn itself & push wide open...

Texas Terri strides up; a skinny, cartoony, chain-smokin' old school rocker that has that LA vibe ever-flowing. She's in her 50's, a punk singer originally from the territories of Fort Worth & Austin [Texas] who's forever compared to icons like Iggy Pop, Lux Interior & Wendy O. Terri Bomb has developed a reputation for wild, scantily clad stage antics including regular performances where she would rip off her shirt to only be censored by electrical tape reading 'TXT.'

Back in Hollywood she formed trash rock band The Killer Crows in 1984 & then later Texas Terri & The Stiff Ones. With an eventual new line-up Terri released the grimy *Your Lips...My Ass!* album which was produced by Jack Douglas & featured MC5's Wayne Kramer. Terri has been in Berlin now for 4 years...

"Why'd you come to Berlin?"

"Because I couldn't afford to go to Stockholm at the time. Berlin's a cool city, but not for me to live. I think it depends on what you're looking for. I'd like to move to London because I need to live in a city that's big, full of opportunity & stuff to fill my head This place is too far gone for me, creatively, and I need to go back to a country with my mother tongue. I've been very frustrated with my musical endeavors over here. This is just my opinion & my reality, but musicians on the mainland of Europe – they're not that good, at least for what I need. The people I work with, because I'm very serious about what I do & I want people to play killer – they don't understand the higher standards because the thermometer of their standards is stuck at this standard, when in the US – I don't know why, we just breed higher standards. Same with people in the UK & Sweden. It's been frustrating – I haven't put out a record in7 years. Last year I got invited to play 10 shows with the damned so I started flying over to the UK more. I knew I was dying inside here, but then I finally realized I'm in fuckin' handcuffs creatively. You know, the American in me – we're brought up to be go-getters, knock everyone out of the way & do our fucking best & excel. At least that's what I got out of growing up in America. I pretty much shut down here..."

"What are some cities in Europe that have impressed you?"

"Stockholm, especially in the summertime. The color of the sky is the most beautiful cobalt blue. My heart just fills up with excitement just looking at the fuckin' sky. Also the water in Stockholm – the regular drinking water – is the best I've ever tasted in the world. I love the people there... Here, you try and smile and The Germans do not smile back. And France, *cha cha cha*. I was at dinner with some Americans & one of the girls had a German boyfriend & we were talking about when they went to America. He was saying how annoying it was when they went out to eat & the waitress kept coming up & asking if everything was alright. He was so sick of smiling – it was just making him sick, how friendly everyone was, and that he never smiled so much in his life. But you know, it's just different cultures; I just can't relate to this culture… In Stockholm, you think that maybe people are cold at first, snobby, but they're not – they're just a quieter group. But they are all so creative its unbelievable. It's really a joy to be around them. There my soul gets fed; here my soul is starving. Berlin's a great place to visit & tour through, but not a great place to live – at least for me…"

Alex (aka A.L.X.) is in his early 30's with short black hair & a *die Scheide* tickler goatee. Alex is on an acoustic tour of sorts, hoping to gain some exposure Europe so that his full band may travel in due: "I've been doing this since a teenager, did a slew of other projects in the past. The last solo record that I did I had Cindy Lauper's drummer as a producer, and when I put together a touring band for that I ended up hooking up with Tommy Price, who was a drummer from Joan Jett & used to play with Billy Idol before that. So Tommy & I got a band together with Jimmy Bones, who was the old Black Hearts guitar player. For some reason I just fell in with Joan Jett's musical footsteps, but we're making a different sound. One of the things I've noticed with those guys, when we were playing that last A.L.X. solo record – the live act had such a different feel then what we made in the studio. The studio record consisted of songs I wrote on the acoustic; live it was much more muscular sounding, it just had more balls to it & a different texture. So we formed a band around it called Love Crushed Velvet. Spent a year writing, another year recording. We got a great guy to mix it out of the UK that'd done a bunch of Depeche Mode records, some Verve & Placebo… [*starts going back & forth with the waitress in German*] You know, unlike The States you have to make your own iced tea everywhere…"

"How do you feel about Berlin? And you're obviously speaking German…"

"My mother's German – I was born here, in East Germany."

"Did you get duel citizenship?"

"No, because back then I could've come back & they'd say '*you have to go in the military*.' It's what I've been meaning to do for years, but I'm like you – I'm on the road all the time & live back in New York. But I've spent a bit of time here in the past few years; I have family nearby. For logistical reasons it makes sense… For me, the scene here – Berlin is one of the best cities in the world right now. The vibe is fantastic, it's not expensive. The summer here is just amazing. I love New York though, because once you live in New York, the problem you have is you can't figure out where you want to live after that – except maybe here. The hard thing about New York is it's a difficult place to be an artist & even more difficult to be a musician. It's a great place to make music, but it's a really hard place to pick up a following because there's so much competition for peoples attention. First of all you have a zillion bands – like anything in numbers, the majority aren't that great. But the hardest thing is everybody's got so many options – there's just selection overdose. Some good friends of mine, they're huge in Asia – they'll play to 10 or 15,000 but in New York they're lucky if they can get 40 people to show up. That's what the scene is like there, and that coupled with the cost of living…"

"What is the overall message of your music"

"Every album that you make has a different impetus behind it & it's all about where you are at the moment. Love Crushed Velvet – we try to capture New York through our own particular prism but in a real rock n' roll kind of way. The real modern day craziness of New York. So we poke fun at reality TV, the attitude – poke fun at flashy, pandering culture.

"Have you traveled abroad in Europe?"

"Yeah, through my family background. My father is also Polish so I've lived here for awhile, lived in Vienna back in the early 90's. So I've always had musical roots in Europe. If you're looking for a scene in Croatia, it's Zagreb. Croatia has – it's a funny place because they're really not into western music the way they are in Western Europe. But they are very into local Croatian bands & cultural music. So you go to a show & 70% of the time you recognize nothing,. The Croatians are very insular in that sense."

"What's the oddest experience you've had traveling?"

"This is 20 years ago traveling as a kid. This was right before Yugoslavia broke up, I was hopping around transit buses, hitchhiking everywhere just trying to get a gig. And I'm at a bus stop & I got my guitar strapped on my shoulder & I find myself surrounded by 10 Yugoslav army soldiers – by myself, punky haircut, ripped up clothes. I don't know a soul, I don't speak their language; I'm gonna get thrown in jail, 10 guys are just gonna beat the living shit out of me. So one of them says to me in broken English: 'You play the guitar? Play something.' And I didn't know what, so I'm really thinking how to come out of this without a broken nose & a broken jaw & having my shit confiscated. Well, I can't remember what it was I played, but they ended up liking it – 'play some more, play some more.' 5 songs later we're like best friends – these guys escort me around the entire town with a private guard of sorts. For me it was a cool thing – like 120 soldiers taking around. I guess they thought they were with some western rock star or something. I'll never forget that…"

** *"es ist party-time ist es hervorragend"* **

Somewhere in former West Berlin, I think, and Jens from Sinner's Bleed is making us pizza. It's now Wednesday, the 29th of June, & I have only a few more days to go before Under The Black Sun. It'll be an epic metal campground with 2 full days of unrelenting black metal – BETHLEHEM, Fides Inversa, Atras Cineris, Setherial, Baptism, Bloodline, Kratein, Shores of Ladon, Thorybos, Lugubre, Massemord, Monarque, Winterblut & IMPALED NAZARENE...

While I'm geeked to see IMPALED NAZARENE [*the kings of blackened deathpunk aka "Nuclear Metal"*], the real prize is BETHLEHEM, who are my favorite black metal band of all time. Some would scoff at that, but let it be known that I got into black metal not from Dimmu, Cradle, Mayhem or any of such ilk – it was the *Gummo* soundtrack that got me hooked & BETHLEHEM are headlining Friday night with their first live gig in 17 years...

Last night's show on Berlin Metal TV was quite the *abenteuer*. The ringleader Hansmeister Krause invited me to the Orwo Haus on Frank Zappa Straße, a sort of heavy metal version of The KØPI, though nowhere near as epic. It was a giant complex of band rehearsal rooms in a warehouse section filled with metal/rock bands – many are of the "Berlin Metal Legions" association...

The show was a live-stream 2 hour broadcast hosted by 6 metalheads ranting in German as we sat on a big couch ala *Wayne's World*. We drank free beers provided by Berliner Pilsner & barreled through nearly 150. At some point they made me sing my acoustic cover of RAMMSTEIN's "Ich Tu Dir Weh," which is banned here for it's S&M filth. The German girls in the audience giggled at my choppy translation...

One of the hosts was Jens Staschel – vocalist of Sinner's Bleed (*& ex-Defeated Sanity*), both of which are top-tier death metal bands from Berlin. He'd dragged me back to his pad last night & following an afternoon of Supermarket pizza, we rolled across town to visit his co-conspirator Lille Gruber, the mastermind of Defeated Sanity...

Lille's the sort of long-hair that's perpetually in a guttural death metal t-shirt, spending an average of 10 hours a day playing guitar & creating these maniacally technical arrangements like a mad scientist in his laboratory. Defeated Sanity was formed in 1994, inspired like so many of their ilk 1990's USA death bands. They eventually teamed up with

Grindethic Records for the albums *Prelude To The Tragedy* & *Psalms Of The Moribund*. The latest disc *Chapters Of Repugnance* – a concept album dealing with "*some of the most cruel deeds in the history of mankind,*" has just been released through Willowtip Records & features AJ Magana [*of Disgorge fame*] on vocals…

Says Mr. Gruber: "I was in Bavaria, in the south of Germany – I grew up there – and we started the band there. I was in more of a provincial do-it-yourself world – a small village & didn't know any people who were doing metal. I went to study here in Berlin & kind of changed the band around, found Jens, Jacob & Christian… When we write a song it takes about 2 years for it to be finished. We're moving stuff around all the time – its not like rock song or something that you do in two hours. Its like a little masterpiece – everything has to be perfect…"

"The USA tours you did – how'd they go?"

"Crazy stories are always happening. Last time what was really weird was when we played in Baltimore, our guitar player & driver were standing outside in a really bad district. There are always crack people running around. There was this guy & he talked to them about some other guy that betrayed him with drug stuff & they saw how he was digging in the trash and he hid a hammer there – I think so, because he was searching. He apparently found a hammer & then he killed another guy with it"

"On the street?"

"Yeah, and the other guy had a knife."

"And they were fighting to the death on the street?"

"Yeah, and I didn't think of it as – I thought it was harmless, like a little thing – yeah, I saw the police line, a little bit of blood. Christian saw it & they all had to go to the police station, then it came out that the guy died. That's was pretty much the craziest thing we ever witnessed on the road."

"As far as music in Berlin, metal in Germany – what impresses you these days?"

"For me it's very hard, you know, because I'm into the brutal death stuff & there are only a handful of bands. You know, the gore brutal stuff, like what we do – just a handful of bands. The rest is more in the old school way. For Berlin I still have to say Sinner's Bleed – it's pure death metal. I really can't find too many bands that are really sure of what they want to do. But Sinners Bleed – they're coherent.

"Have you played Russia?

"Yeah, 4 shows. It's crazy – people are very receptive of foreign bands, but also when the locals play they go crazy. It has the most beautiful women in the world, but the most ugly landscape."

"What is the message of the band?"

"I treated this subject a little bit differently before my dad died. I found it really funny, and I still find it sometimes funny, goregrind bands making fun of this disease or that disease or anal sex with a hook through the mouth or I don't know. But we never wrote about this – we actually started out always with a message, not just dumb making fun of misfortunes or whatever. We're more like, '*What is the reason why we do this stuff?*' First, it's a fascination of death & morbid stuff. And it's a little philosophical. I think the best things to give you an example – on the last CD there's a song called 'Calculated Barbarity. It's about the development of high tech weapons & the paradox of a really smart person writing blueprints of crazy technical stuff & using his intellect for something barbaric – like a fragmentation bomb. Little pieces that go through every part of your body. It's just for killing people. So it's a pretty big contrast in my opinion. You have to be really smart to make that kind of stuff, when in the Stone Age you could just take a rock and *poufff*."

"Have you ever been to Austria?"

"Yeah, when I did session drums for Belphegor. The streets are extremely clean – everything is very square. But I guess the underground people are a contrast to that – they are really extreme. That was actually the first time I came to the US, was as a drummer for Belphegor's US & Canada tour."

"What are those guys like?"

"Heh – extreme. They're not lying about their lyrics – they live it, you know? The rehearsal room smells like goat."

"Haha..."

"The rehearsal room was a goat place before & there's goat heads all over the walls & black metal posters & everything."

"Do they do weird black mass rituals?"

"No, no no no. I mean, who does that shit? I think short haired people that listen to Wagner – they do that. I recently posted that on Facebook that Satanism is of the insane. They impregnate their women just to have a baby to **squish-squish** and to fuck the holes & stuff. Satanism, if you take it seriously, and being an asshole, being evil – then you are evil. Crowley said the best thing for sacrifice is the male baby, so innocent human baby."

"How was the tour with Belphgeor?"

"We played with Krisiun & Unleashed. We stayed with Kirisun in one RV – 9 people. That was pretty intense. And the toilet – you couldn't use it. Or just to pee & then it was so cold the pee froze & stuff. But I would say it was my only rock star tour. I saw the whole groupie stuff, because in brutal death metal it is a myth – no one ever gets laid, haha…"

** "vielleicht ist es die tennis-schuhe" **

Friday, July 1st, 2011; 1,121 hours to go – one of those infrequent moments where being "*entrapped by the dimensions of time… where every millisecond is spontaneous origami & menacing as the ominous, black obelisk*" really wears thin…

I'm at the Under The Black Sun fest stretched out on a patch of grass, staring at a grey sky moments from drizzling. I am incurring what some might describe as nervous collapse. Not that I'm a *schwächling*; I'm simply drained. A lesser man would bow out & hop a plane for The States in a desperate attempt of refugium…

I'm caught again without a tent in a steeply priced camp staffed by non-English speaking workers. I'm also surrounded by 500 black metal guys evenly split between classic long-hair, biker-leather types or skinheads with white laces & Burzum t-shirts...

So it is what it is. I like individuals, I like music, but I'm not going to pretend to be a BM scenester. This is why (*despite being a guy who at one glance is obviously into metal*) I'm being scanned at with xenophobic gazes. Yeah, even me – the blonde-haired, blue-eyed, shaved head Americano with the green army jacket... Well, if anyone wants to play the Satanist card, I'll gladly embarrass them with my track record of fiendish diabolism...

The whole thing set me off into a dark trance, brooding over the past few days. After hanging with Lille from Defeated Sanity, I attended a local show with the Berlin Metal TV guys . I recorded a useless mess of choppy English interviews & saw a headliner named Placenta that were way too screamo for my tastes…

The gig cleared out & became a techno dance party for teenage kids. I slept a few blocks away in a woodland patch that smelled like urine, as if all the drunks would habitually use that soil as a wobbly toilet. It was the best I could do in terms of avoiding police; I awoke sucked dry by mosquitoes & bumpy with spider kisses, then spent hours unsuccessfully trying to find the Immigration Office...

I made my way to the Deutsch Historical Museum. It was monumental in scope – every period of Germanic history sliced in expert levels. True creepiness is not the shit production of an early Darkthrone release but the Black Plague exhibit itself...

One turns a corner & finds themselves in the Nazi period – NS propaganda posters & NDSAP handbooks, personally signed proclamations by Hitler & SS uniforms displayed on mannequins. Dramatic models illustrating gas chambers & mug shots of petrified, crying Jews staring at you from the criminal abyss of history...

After a somber walk of terror, I ran into a mob of juveniles weeping. Must've been a student field trip, the very moment they confront the reality of their monstrous past with the same parent-approved delicacy we Americans approach sexual education. The true horror of it consumed me, surveying the bawls of a 16 year old sweetheart... *In der Hölle brennen Adolf...*

I left the museum feeling empty, shaking in the climate. What I wouldn't give to be beside a warm, English-speaking body on this gray day suffocated by Fascist Imperium. After yet another fruitless assault of emails – including overtures to folks in Prague, Warsaw & Krakow – I had nothing to show for it. No ride-share to Czech, no more interviewees in Berlin & no solid plan what to do afterwards...

Since the month-pass Eurail train plan was out the window, I hedged my bet on hitching a ride after Obscene Extreme with whatever random band might be on tour.

If that didn't work, I could bum around Poland/Czech for a week, maybe hit Slovenia/Austria before heading up to Scandinavia – or simply attempt "The Southern Campaign" through Italy, Spain & Portugal. I wanted Athens but the only way in was a ridiculously expensive flight – there were no buses or trains, since all of Greece was cut off from Europe by the former Yugoslavian countries. Greece were also in the middle of a half-repressed civil war, with mad sporadic riots...

Obsessing over the next *wendung des schicksals* I gobbled Turkish Pizza, drank cheap booze & attempted to find a cinema with English sub-titles. There was a bad German dub of *Transformers III* but was it really worth €15? Tried to nap under a bridge but the construction crew nearby busted out jackhammers; tried to call in a squat favor but Ajka, Florian & Leah were all unavailable...

My brilliant plan? Head into the outskirts of Berlin into suburban territory, find a hole-in-the-wall bar & mingle with the common man. I'd been informed of such coordinates earlier this week, but I had to catch the last train West. As I raced through the terminal, ducking tourists & Berliners, I ran into the loopy Romanian Trans! *Duck, swish, zoom...* Off to the edge of Berlin – emerging from the train station was like coming out a bunker. I was surrounded by kilometers of woodland...

I walked & walked & walked through the night, finally discovering a normal looking street where everything was closed. I was starving; the only respite was a Burger King10 minutes before closing. For kilometers the road was black & lights were out. I gave up & posted a one-man encampment beneath a train-track bridge, sleeping soundly to the occasional rush of exiting semi-trucks...

Ok, now – Under The Black Sun. To reach it I had to take a shuttle through cattle farmland & the ticket booth people could find no mention on guest-list. I tried to phone Bartsch, but he wasn't answering. A security guard in army fatigues took me to the stage for clarification, but none of the BETHLEHEM guys were around...

If I wanted in I'd need to shell out €60 Euro's [*$75 USD, my budget for an entire week*]. Who should appear to my rescue in this remote German field? None other then Roogier Droog, of the Dutch BM Mafia, who was randomly working as a stagehand...

I headed off to investigate the encampment. No matter where I went, I stuck out like a ripe case of sausage toe. I tried to chat with a cute Polish girl at a picnic table, but her boyfriend soon came up with a territorial air. He was wearing a Confederate Flag belt buckle & a t-shirt that read: "*Hatecore – It's More Then Music*" with the "o" in "*Hatecore*" a sniper bullseye. He made me hit his vodka that was gooey from spittle backwash. When I said I was from Detroit, he remarked: "*Good to get away from all those niggers, huh?*"

Day II & sitting in the cafeteria. The guys from IMPALED NAZARENE eat lunch by themselves looking as out of place as I do with some of them wearing Soccer Jerseys & baseball caps. I've tried to find an opening to talk to Mika Luttinen, the vocalist, but none of them have stepped out to smoke...

Almost everyone is sick or hung-over, since it's rained nonstop following BETHLEHEM. All the bands were pretty much straight-forward blasting with cascading textures. The standouts were Fides Inversa from Italy & Monarque from Quebec – and the Canucks were more of a blackened thrash band.

BETHLEHEM was interesting – great projected video feed of morgue footage in played reverse with coroners actually putting the guts back into people. BETHLEHEM had a good run but you could tell they were still rusty. The vocalist did his best to mimic the pained howls of

Landfermann while the group wore the white uniforms of mental patients. They played plenty of classic material from S.U.I.Z.I.D. & Dark Metal, the guitars still wailing that specific no-mid Marshall stack echo/reverb psychedelic tone...

I waited backstage for mystery man Juergen, awaiting the answers to so many odd rumors. In the end though he was all tied up backstage, so I didn't get to ask him much of anything. When I finally cornered him, he remarked in a very spaced-out tone: *"Oh Ryan – you're Mike's friend, yeah?"* referring to one of my buddies who does vocals for his industrial side-project Stahlmantel.

Bartsch seemed lost on what I was doing: *"Sorry I wasn't here earlier, we've been sitting in the hotel room all day drinking water & eating apples."* And then he kind of trailed off into head-trip oblivion, gazing to the upper right corner of his vision. He snapped out of it, squirted mint droplets on his tongue & blew sine minty breeze in my face with the smiling, innocence of a child. *"We can do the interview tomorrow, yeah?"* **"Sure Juergen, no problem."** And Bartsch wandered back into the band cabin, ever-remaining the great scatter-brained mystery…

The tap water is brown with rust – a bottle of water is €3, but black coffee is €1. I tried to start a conversation with a fairly normal looking guy with short hair, but he soon started talking about secret white power festivals they have to hold clandestinely because of *"the thought police"* & that I should talk to all these bands that seem to include the word *"honor"* or *"pride"* in their names. He wants to know what it feels like to have *"a nigger for a president…"*

Nazi creep drags me outside to interview some black metal band guy who gives the typical black metal guy interview where he name-drops some Nietzsche books he probably half-read & didn't quite understand & then tacks on the standard: *"devil worship as a symbol = personal growth = mysticism this & that = private rituals I cannot tell you about because whatever bullshit reason."* This dunghill of gibberish is topped off by describing the liberties of his homeland: *"We still have freedom of speech – the leftists can say 'fuck off Nazi' & the Nazi's can say 'Sieg Heil,' like in the open. That is what I like about Country X…"*

Hours later, still raining, still no sign of Bartsch. As much as I want to see IMPALED NAZARENE, I've no tent & the rain will continue indefinitely. I've been holed up in the carpeted lobby of the cafeteria, sleeping on the floor with French Canadians…

Two of the girls are backpacking Europe & staying in Berlin – they want out as desperately as I. I'm pretty sure they're a lesbian couple but aren't saying so, since we're not in a realm so friendly to queerdom. This doesn't help when a thrash metal hermaphrodite (or mid-way trans conversion) comes in the door sopping wet, denim vest covered in patches. Black metal guys give mean looks, laughing to themselves; angry homophobe rednecky vibes are on the rise. The psychic energy of the room feels totally uncomfortable for everyone, and it amplifies both myself and the gals making a run for it to head out. *Die Blicke auf diesen Menschen ins Gesicht...*

We split up the cab fare back to the train; they're avoiding taking me anywhere in Berlin, 'cause wherever they're staying is selective. I haggle them & they spill their guts: they're staying with a famous death metal musician guy named: <u>*Lille Gruber*</u>. So I call Mr. Defeated Sanity & ask if I can crash, then hand the phone to the girls – grinnin' like Wise Ass Champ of The Century.

As we clank away on that train towards Berlin, I gaze out foggy windows at canopies of Pines. Those needled steeples whizzing by – these trees were no longer black metal trees. For the first time since I'd devoured *Lord of Chaos,* they were not troll-infested forests adorning so many a record cover in stark gray-scale. These pines were now happy trees, like the paintings of Bob Ross...

PRAHA

PRAHA

V. *"Obscene Extreme & the Legend of Battlefield Trutnov"*

Blessed be The KØPI & their armada of vigorous, high-strung Antifa. I am back in CrustLand, whose inhabitants are filthy & gloriously scented because the purchase of deodorant would in turn do harm to chemically tested monkeys & elevate the   margins of yet another soulless corporation…

Sometimes reversals of fortune relay themselves effortlessly. I should've put more trust in following the signs… When I met Enzo [*from Grind The Enemy*] in London, he'd jotted down some Italian contacts I didn't bother to investigate until the proper moment.

Things had come to a severe low after the pizza party at Lille Gruber's. Having burned out my leads in Berlin & a ride-share to Prague pushed to Wednesday, I was once again stuck in a European capitol with the thrill of it long having dissipated. I'd two more days to kill if I were to save €60 & be given a free place to stay in Czech by the college vacationing drivers…

Think, think as it pours rain once again, as you walk empty streets on a chilly Sunday evening… Best I could come up with was head to KØPI. It was a dead scene, most hiding in the 150 room squat fortress I'd no contacts to enter. The bar was thin with hung-over crusties speaking every language but Anglo-Saxon. I ate some of the Food Not Bombs vegan buffet, volunteered for dishes, then sifted through the mess of handbills on the table. *Antifa this, anarcho that, Marxism here, IWW there, yadda, yadda, Red/Black everywhere, etc, etc & then **BLAMMO**…*

On Tuesday night, REPULSIONE would be playing – yes, **REPULSIONE** – *the only powerviolence band in Italy* & the highest recommendation Enzo had bestowed. He'd fingered Lorenzo as the #1 guy to talk to in Italy, their ringleader/drummer and also a concert organizer from Bologna…

I sent a text & sought shelter, since I didn't know: *"Darf ich bitte schlafen auf dem Boden?"* I went to the Hostel five blocks away & booked my first room of the trip. €20 for shared quarters, but I lucked out & had the entire thing to myself. It was incredible to sleep in a bed once again, to let my aching back unhinge itself & sit in the shower for an hour. I slept 13 hours; I'd assuredly survived the most grueling of the trip. The rest was all catharsis & motion…

Monday afternoon en route to El Schlong's flat, I get the reply from Lorenzo: *"Hi Ryan very nice to find your message. Enzo told me about you, your trip and your project. It will be very nice to meet you tomorrow at KØPI and if you want to <u>come with us on tour</u> you will welcome. We will play also at <u>Obscene Extreme Festival</u> in Czech. Keep in touch – we will arrive in Berlin this evening..."*

So here I am @ The KØPI, having teamed up with the Italians – and my oh my are they ever Italian, beginning half their conversations with: *"Please-a-excuse-a-my-shit-a-English."* Matteo is a pro wrestling fanatic, Andreas a stoner/rapper. Lorenzo's speaks with his hands & builds every sentence to monumental proportions the way a Milanese businessman would try to sell you a life insurance policy. And Gulio... Well Gulio barely speaks English & mostly nods & smiles & chain-smokes rollies & is always sporting that a sleaze-rocker bandanna & buckled pyrate boots without socks & cut-off black denim shorts & a leather vest with Misfits skull...

Tonight is a grind spectacular in the moldy basement venue with the dripping walls. Two other touring bands have converged for performance – FEASTEM [*of Finland*] and CHIENS [*of France*]. The show is much welcomed, but the real pleasure is being treated as one of the musicians. This equals endless free beer & complimentary sleeping quarters in the secret band room. You slip through the back corridors plastered with bumper stickers & graffiti, head up a retractable flight of stairs that leads into a hidden attic without windows. Pitch black, it's filled with a dozen stinking mattresses – and plenty of snoring, intoxicated crusties...

** *"vita tra i dinosauri"* **

Prague now, en route to Obscene Extreme. After leaving the KØPI we drove straight to the gig in Czech; it was a tiny venue with €1 beers & a gaggle of grinders speaking whatever language they do in these parts. The promoter (*who also puts together the Fekal Party fest*) led us to his apartment after, dragging Matteo, Andreas & I downstairs under the auspice of a quick beer but instead held us hostage with tall brews until 6am...

Watching the sunrise from his 10th floor high-rise, one could view all of Prague laid out in 9 segments. That's how they divvy up the postal service – nine clustered neighborhoods. This is how we got lost searching for the venue last night – never thought to add a Prague 3, Prague 8 or

Prague 9 to our GPS search. The view from above seems a forest with 9 random spots of civilization...

Lorenzo begins our exchange as we rattle around the tour van on this perfectly sunny day: *"As a band we was born in 2003 & started playing some style of Italian hardcore. Hardcore born in the middle of the 90's – it was a typical Italian sound. Maybe '94, '95, there was some good bands. In USA no one knows them. Powerviolence, in our opinion, is a blend of different styles. Maybe grindcore, fastcore, some crust, maybe mid-tempo songs. We is mixing these different influences, maybe like some American influence like Man Is The Bastard or Iron Lung. This is our 5th tour – the 4th in Europe & we also made a tour in Greece."*

"Do people use the term mincecore or stenchcore much?"

"I think here in Europe the mincecore masters are Agathocles. We also do a split with them, but in my opinion is much closer to crust. I think its not so fast. Stenchcore..."

Matteo: "**Is an attitude – a type of slower crust."

"What are some standout moments of this tour so far?"

"The places I remember for very great moments, maybe the gig in Greece because I seen that those guys have absolutely no money, ok? Those guys are very poor because they have very hard economic crisis but you can find everywhere good equipment, ok? I've seen very young people at the concerts. I remember that in the North of Greece, a bunch of little guys maybe 13 or 14 years old – we cannot play because we have to go home because our parents are waiting for us. This was strange... Maybe our worst moment ever was in Germany 3 years ago in a squat managed by anarchist students, ok. I don't know why during the pogo dancing when a Swedish band was playing some guys from the squat thought we was too much violent dancing. And they start to say that we was like macho, ok? And we have to sleep in the van because they don't want us. But you know how we are, I think we are not so macho. Haha..."

"Tell me all about the Italian scene..."

"Ok this is a good question, but I think in Italy we have had a lot of good places, a lot of good bands. You can find anarchist. You can find left-oriented places that are in contact with the hardcore punk scene. I think now there is a crisis past 6 or 7 years because maybe people have lost interest in this kind of music. Maybe we have had electronic music wave at the beginning of the century. And then the trend is some kind of dub reggae & you can see that there's no new people, young people at the gigs. I feel sad about this. For us, its our life – everyone of us has grown in this scene & we feel a strong affection. I have seen a lot of interest & motivation, but I think we have to wait a little bit of time & things change because the situation is very hard. The economic & political situation is worse then the 80's, so we have a lot of causes for being angry. I think we have the motivation to protest. It could be a good moment for hardcore music."

"**Maybe problems are strictly to places that are few. We lost some very important places in the scene in Italy. I seen in the young generation less interest. People go to the concert to pass the night & not with the sense to put in work. Also maybe a problem is the growth of social network. People stay at home & listen to music on computers & stay in touch by chat & don't know."

"I'm just curious what the ararcho scene means to you..."

"Everyone of us has his personal opinion about this, but I think that I start to listen to this music because discovering punk & hardcore, it was like a light in my brain. Ok, this is what I am. I remember when I was child, I feel a little bit solitude in my life. For me, DIY, punk, hardcore means we meet up a big family of people. I understand this scene – I have met a lot of people like me. This was for me the motivation. I don't want to use excessive words, but I think it's something that saved my life & I think it is positively creating an alternative society where you can trust everyone.

"How do the different subcultures relate in Italy – is there a stronger unity between the punk & metal people?"

"In Italy no one is interested to promote music, ok. There's no place for play and this situation is the same for the bands who play every kind of metal. Death metal, black metal – no one is interested to invest money in music. So this is kind of music that is not strictly connected with the DIY scene, they are maybe forced to embrace the DIY mentality. Often in these years many underground thrash metal bands play with us & they have not our mentality because they have in their life the metal dinosaurs, ok? They are forced to play in the squats or the places of the anarchist. So maybe this is good for people to understand what we mean by DIY. In Italy, you see a lot of these guys embracing the DIY mentality...

"Are there physical confrontations with fascists in Italy?"

"**Last year, they grow up – 10 years ago they were few, in their own bars & zones of the cities. Italian society is easy that this idea can grow in young people. They hate toward immigrants. They have a sort of squat they use & have used towards Italians. They give people homes, they give people food, to Italian poor people & this is a way they grow. It is a sort of provocation, but this is the same technique they use with the

Nazis in the 30's. When the nationalism grows, the hate towards immigrants – they use it to push fascism in the minds of people..."

** *"drak přichází"* **

The phrase "Obscene Extreme" is a hallowed one, echoed intercontinentally. You catch fragments of it on message boards, claims of it's standing as the ultimate metal fest. But when you live in America, the chance you'll actually meet someone that's lived through it's madness is slim. When you do, they are almost always in a band that actually graced it's stage & when asked their eyes spark up with the potency of a towering lighthouse...

Communication is immediately lost; everything spills out in awe-struck babble rendered incoherent by fantastic recollection: *"Well what was it like?"* you ask plainly, and the response is always a mess of: *"dude, you don't even fuckin' know bro, it's like fuckin' – dude, fuckin – just holy fuckin' shit bro, really bro, holy fukkin..."*

All I knew was that some bad ass metal fest materialized once a year in Central Europe. It was vague to me, since I'd no means to attend it. Why put yourself in a sulking situation? That's like a 5 year old getting hyped on Santa's North Pole workshop, having a seizure over the possibility of all those imaginary toy stockades It's like just stick with your own fucking Christmas Tree, alright kiddo? Don't get too spazzed up about sugary providence...

When I elaborated to interviewees during this trip that not only was I going to Obscene Extreme but that I had guest-list & a backstage media pass for all three days + plenty of drink tickets – people acted as if I'd won the lottery...

Wanting to keep the lineup a secret until I arrived, I didn't even bother to look at the flyer. I really didn't want to know – just let it happen. Moments before we pulled into the band parking lot, I finally let the REPULSIONE guys fill me in. And, well...

First thing's first, because it really is true – *<u>Obscene Extreme is the greatest extreme metal festival in the world</u>*. Nothing touches it. Sure, I've never made it to Maryland Deathfest [USA], Wacken [GER] or Tuska [FIN], so my response may be slightly skewed – *but I doubt it*. Prior to OE attendance, I'd pegged the L.A. Murderfest 2007 or Milwaukee Metalfest 2004 as my top tier metal fest experiences ever. But Obscene Extreme, it just dismembers them all. It's like comparing the Adam West *Batman* to Christopher Nolan's immaculate conception...

There can be no explanation of Obscene Extreme in conventional terms. What I think of, when examining these past three days, is an epic cartoon of everyone in attendance stage-diving, moshing, freaking out with a mushroom cloud exploding from the stage itself as if the painting were a mix between *Where's Waldo* & the album art of Terrorizer's *World Downfall*, ANB's *Agorapocyalpse Now* or Napalm Death's *Scum*...

The festival takes place in Trutnov, a rural suburb of Prague at the "Festung Battlefield." It is not the site of some legendary WWII skirmish as I'd assumed, but fairgrounds dubbed *"Battlefield"* because to survive Obscene Extreme is to survive a ridiculous war composed of thousands cannonball stage-diving relentlessly – all in ridiculous costumes, or plainly naked. How many in banana costumes & crash helmets? How many bloodied & torn, smiling with missing teeth? They just keep going. Even the kid I helped up that landed on his head, who actually tore his ear half off in the process – jumped right back in with it half-dangling from his skull...

OE begins on Wednesday – *"Freak Day"* – when the weirdos of European punk & metal begin to pop up the tents for this Ruigoord of grindcore. To establish encampment & share some drinks, get bizarre, freak out on mushrooms, run around naked & get redonculous. This sets the tone for a celebratory, life-filled journey in opposition to all the shitty downers in metal culture. You will not find tough-guy *"you looking at my girl?!?"* gibberish – no pretentious spandex, no unfriendly Johnny Evil bullshit, no metallic hardcore mobs of jocks with crew-cuts seeking fisticuffs...

Thursday it officially begins & does not stop until 3 am Sunday morning. Day after day – from 10am until 3am the following morning – you are assailed by non-stop grindcore, death metal & the occasional noise band or freak-show act. All bands play on the same stage for 20 to 45 minutes & everyone uses the exact same back-line & just plug their instruments right in. Only 10 minutes separates the band performances – one after another in rapid fire procession. In between, the loudspeakers jam polka or *Pulp Fiction* soundtrack...

Since the fest is open-air, you will find people passed out on the lawn at any given hour. Drink, mosh, stage-dive, pass out, return to action – thousands doing this circular pattern, like insane lemmings begging for blast-beats... The campground is fairly massive, flanked at every edge by merch booths, campers tents, bonfire pow wow's & vegan food carts. It's crusty as Tijuana dumpster, as if the most illuminated of Planet KØPI were gathered & shit out in a random Czech field...

But down to business – the real meat & potatoes... I'd be sitting through BRUTAL TRUTH, Entombed, Impaled, Squash Bowels, Magrudergrind, The Varukers, BRUJERIA, Putrid Pile, Benediction, Fleshrot, Lock Up, The Rotted, DROPDEAD, Mincing Fury, Rotten Sound, Entrails & SKITSYSTEM + dozens of other bands I'd never even heard of & will never, ever get a chance to see live in the USA. My eardrums got an erection just pondering it...

** *"žádný odpočinek pro zlý"* **

To try & write a show review in conventional terms is useless – you can only pull from your experience the peak flashes. I had attempted to interview a ton of bands, but all you can really drag out of such an event are tiny, pre-conjured snippets, like a press junket on a massive scale. 10 minutes to talk to a band before the next one starts, and both the interviewee & reporter have their attention immediately flagged to the stage. I must've recorded 15 useless interviews lasting 6 minutes a piece...

Like CHIENS, for instance. I can't even make out what they said. But what I can say about them, however, is that not only are they probably the greatest grindcore band ever to come out of France, but they are easily one of the most savage grind bands I've ever seen perform live...

What I wish to offer is a succinct description of the peaks flying through my recollections like stealth bombers. The Obscene Extreme rains upon the psyche like anvils – one after another the peaks come, raging like PCP-laden wolverines. Of the 69 bands that played, all were stellar in their own unique fashion...

The fest began for me on Thursday, around 5pm. Once REPULSIONE & I were situated, I parted ways & marched straight through the crowd to backstage, just to make sure I wasn't tripping. One second you're helplessly homeless in Berlin; the next you are loaded with beer tickets & surrounded by Danny Lilker, Shane Embury, Cristo de Pisto & LG Petrov. All of them are electric, because Obscene Extreme is for the Grindcore Mafia what Bohemian Grove is to the Illuminati...

The first band I saw was FEASTEM, who played with us in Prague last night. They were just as killer in arena sound as they were the primitive bar PA. Next was NAPALMED – a screeching noise performance of home-made synthesizers & amplified devices while the members wore lab coats. Pandemia followed, harvesting the pit with death metal fury. SQUASH BOWELS stomped out to the ever-enlarging crowd, slaying with a pulverization historically reserved for a 1920's Texan slaughterhouse...

GRIDE, who I'd never even heard of before, destroyed the crowd with in an all-out grindpunk assault. The mighty ENTOMBED played next, who in a strange way felt like hard rock due to the hours-long barrage of grind I'd just endured. That mirage slowly dissipated, and here I was again with the nastily tuned machine that was chiefly responsible for the sound which is described worldwide as Swedish Death Metal...

MAGRUDERGRIND followed, upping the ante after midnight when night had coated the sweating mess of half naked, beer-soaked bodies of crust-affiliated warriors. The drunks continued to stagger about, slamming into each other, stage-diving nonstop in a huge cauldron of dirt that was the front row...

Everyone filthy & bloody, joyous & free, Benediction thundered on. The old school tore it up & then came the HELL SHOW – an S&M/circus freak spectacle of women hanging on hooks through their back flesh & fire breathers galore. I soon made my way to the hill & passed out with all the other victims of Battlefield Trutnov who surrounded me like corpses of Gettysburg...

Day two; wake up on the hill, say hello to the REPULSIONE crowd & all the folks I've graciously met. Make it to the stage around 11:30 for three grind culprits in a row – Dislike, Nominal Abuse & Porno Infantil – all followed by the death metal juggernaut Razor Rape. Enthrallment, this slicer of a death metal beast from Bulgaria, had that Brazilian death influence screaming between the lines. LAUTSTRUMER, a sort of rocking hodge-podge of darkness came next, which showed us some of the old DRILLER KILLER guys in new action. UK death metallers FLESHROT disappointed no one & were soon followed by the thrashy b-deat grindpunk hybrid D.I.S. of Southern Cali...

It began growing dark again. The encampment's numbers were about several thousand by now making it a veritable Disneyland of the grindcore elite. For the first time I had found others that actually danced like me – gyrating around frantically like they were being electrocuted by the blasts wailing like Morse Code. We were lost protons that had discovered our nucleus; we regenerated from the grind-pocalypse the way fauna grows to the light of the sun...

Rectal Smegma made a bold attack & ENTRAILS zoomed past like an L.A. Drive-by; Extreme Smoke 57 pulled the noise-core card, Last Days Of Humanity lived up to their name & Putrid Pile lopped an avalanche of just that upon us... Everything changed dynamics once The Varukers took over – it was Punk Supremacy hour and angry, animalistic

& anarcho as ever. SKITSYSTEM appropriately followed & Rotten Sound brought us back to the grind barrage...

The big assault that everyone was waiting for now loomed on the horizon – BRUJERIA. Word don't really do justice to how fantastic these guys were. Shame on any who consider them a joke band... At the end of their set they covered "The Macarena" by Los del Rio. This was classic in itself, but what shoots it to the moon is the fact that half the pit – like literally 70 people – actually climbed on stage, slam danced or otherwise pogo'd to this notoriously catchy 90's dance anthem. BRUJERIA were laughing so hard they could barely play their instruments...

Following an almost impossible-to-top performance was IMPALED, the finest Carcass clone in the biz, who firmly held their own despite so many still massively dazed from the tribute to Los del Rio. GRONIBARD came next, who I'd never heard of until this very moment & soon found to be the French answer to Norway's Turbonegro. Not by musical standards, of course, but from their unrelenting homo-eroticism. Radical Queer Grindcore from a French band whose name translates to GROINBARD – you know, minstrels of the cock. 20 people in the band, running around the stage in a freakish display of Gender Pyrate bravery. The singer came out with a devils mask & pink fairy wings, declaring: *"Fuck you – wee are vrum Fah-rance!"*

No nonsense early 90's pioneers of Swedish Death Metal INTERMENT followed, clearing the slate. Moments before 2am, the crowd began thinning out from most people assuming that we were heading into the *"all the big bands shot their wad early, now we have to sit through the misfits lingering in the shit time-slots because all the other bands bigger or more important want to drink."*

That's when CHIENS came on, immediately freezing the lessening crowd in their tracks. The people boomeranged & with huge applause witnessed one of the best performances of the entire day. The carry over worked perfect for REPULSIONE, who quickly blasted into their two-bass powerviolence attack. The crowd roared, giving their full approval...

GORE AND CARNAGE followed. Halfway through their opening number, I was grabbed by lone hands from the crowd. It's dark, it's vague, but I know that insane grin... Ah, good old Matt Rozyci! The Chicago escapee had left London some time ago & was freshly primed from a grueling bike-ride across the width of France. *Je to o čase...*

Day 3 & 30 minutes before the opening band. Obscene Extreme promoter Curby & I relax under an empty field tent, drinking coffee & anticipating the day: *"I work on the fest all year long & it's really difficult before it starts because I want everything perfect. I'm not nervous about the money or the budget. Doing a really good festival is not as easy as everyone thinks because its like this year we have 69 bands, a lot of logistics, all this shit. But when that first band starts, its really great. I hate these blockades at the big festivals because it makes no sense. That's why we do it totally different, a unique festival – it's still a very punk way we do it. Bands this year – I was happy to see Entombed & Benediction – I couldn't believe my eyes. I like them, right, but they are so good live. And last night, Brujeria – have you seen this happening at the end with the 'Macarena' & like 60 people? Dancing on the stage & Shane Embury dancing & Jeff walker? So funny man. Then Impaled – there are so many good bands; even the bands playing 10am are great. The fans here are real fans, not people that just what to drink for a weekend. They care about bands, they care about music. And the bands, they don't just take the money, play, drink & leave – they stay here the whole weekend backstage hanging out. I got a really great feeling – it's Saturday morning & we don't have any big problems. We have great weather this year. Have you seen any aggressiveness here this year? No. The punks, the hardcore, the metal – they grind all together. No one gives a fuck if you are different..."*

The day flies blissfully – The Afternoon Gentlemen, Brutally Deceased, Komatoz, Powercup, Haemophagus, Unkind, Death Toll 80k, Collision, Assessor, Wrathcobra, Onanizer, Mesrine, Visions of War, Zubrowska, Instinct Of Survival, Psycho, Inhumate...

It's so peacefully turbulent; this hybrid collection of the alienated. Everything materialized perfectly once ISACAARUM hit the stage, with the blood & leather & spastic facial features of the vocalist. This is a surprising example of a band being Ok on record, but being an unstoppable tank live. The Rotted oozed their Brit gore-grind next, followed by a super-obscure gore-grind act dubbed DEBUSTROL which deliver a volatile knock-out...

Things hit a high note once Lock Up hits the stage. Let's face it – you can only have heard so many bands. This was my first encounter with them & they sledgehammered my face to a pulp of nothingness. BRUTAL TRUTH finished the job, playing a darker, sludgier, more experimental set...

When DROPDEAD begins I am backstage. DROPDEAD, the sXe fastcore legends from Boston, are "The Big One" which people have waited for all night. This was their first time ever at OE & as the vocalist looked into the crowd, his expression reflected that he's never quite seen anything like this. The vocalist ranted some Animal Liberation/Vegan stuff & then they tore right into it. I was standing next to the guys from Brutal Truth, next to lock Up, next to BRUJERIA and all of us were like little kids in total awe of this band. DROPDEAD flawlessly delivered one of the most solid punk performances I'd ever seen. The aftermath of every song was like a *Wrestlemania* coliseum chanting *"holy shit, holy shit"* in response to some acrobatic devastation...

LE SCRAWL perform this avant-saxophone-noise-grind set before I come back to reality in one final push of *"go crazy in the dirt cauldron & slam into people like a 16 year old asshole since we're all gonna die anyway so let's have some fun & bleed..."* On comes Melancholy Pessimism with their goofy *"we mainly speak Czech this is why our band name sounds totally awkward"* stigma. Well, this band I expected nothing of rocked my world, earning them a place in my top 20 personally witnessed death metal performances ever. The vibe was indescribable – everyone was to the primitive & nothing existed but our mad cauldron of lunatic slam-dancing...

As GRUNT took the stage, with their S&M grind aesthetic & rubber suits & whatever bizarre sex rituals they were intent on performing, I could no longer regain the balance of gravity, for alcohol had taken it's toll. The bodies were laid out like the dead of a war, the camp bonfires were smoking craters of spent ammunition. The rain began to pour heavily; crust punks everywhere with arms outstretched like the sewer escape of *The Shawshank Redemption*. I crept into the empty kinder-grinder child tee-pee & hijacked it, laying my bruised & mosh mangled carcass atop a wood palette, magically drifting off to last nights *Reservoir Dogs*-like glimpse of 4 crust buddies wandering off with arms around each others shoulders in eternal friendship, the one in the middle cloaked in a full-body cow-suit, grimy utter dangling from below...

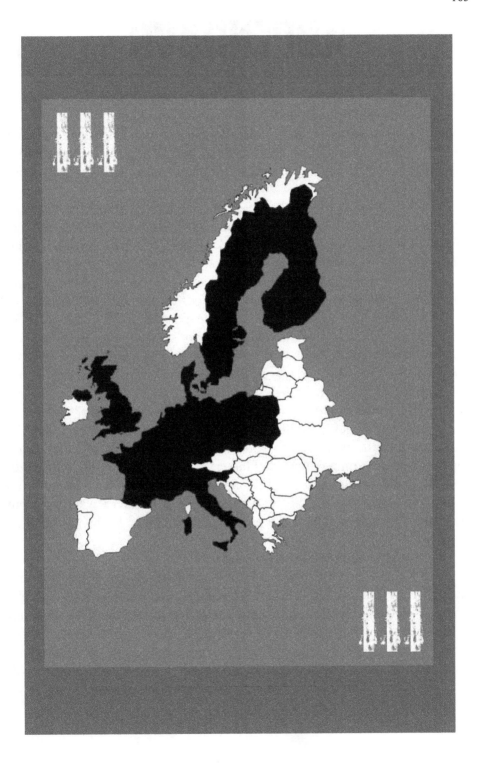

KØPENHAVN

VI. *"ungdomshusets skygge tager fremtiden som gidsel"*

Charlie is an eruption of *smavý* hurling towards Planet Vulcan. We've already crossed through bullet riddled Poland, through Germany with their €6 Petrol Station beers, over the ferry boat into Denmark. We are t-minus 30 minutes from Copenhagen, cruising along a dark highway past lochs shining in moonlight...

Charlie, who gladly abducted me in the aftermath of Obscene Extreme, is the dread-locked leader of long-standing grind act ABORTION. Laughing, laughing, he clamors in his thick Slovak accent: *"Slovakia, the underground scene, it's really good. A lot of people have no money to buy the gear, and they are burning for this they want it – the rest of the world they got everything, they got money, but no interest... In Copenhagen, mainly you can hear the crusty bands... With ABORTION, the lyrics are political & about the stupidity of people – how we hate each other, how we want to fight all the time. You have-a white skin, you have-a brown skin, you have a bigger nose then me. Mostly stupidity – the government, desecration all over the world..."*

"What was it like growing up in a communist country?"

"That's difficult, so difficult. For example, if you are under 18 years old, and the police catch you somewhere on the street, they bring you home & say to the mother and father: '*Do you care about your child? Because if not we will take him.*' You cannot have long hair, because it's against the idea – the socialistic, communist idea. When I went out from the country I was just looking around and saying, '*hmmm... that's-a-freedom.*'

"So what of this Christiania place?"

"When I go to Denmark, I don't know anything about Christiania – my girlfriend told me, '*It's a kind of freedom.*' She was really saying this. '*Ok, ok, I go try.*' The first time there it was like Christmas. They help out the homeless, you know? Soup & everything for free... Christiania, for me – really, really good & relaxed. You can get good hashes & good ganja, haha. And the people – talking with the people – it's so nice. No one will try to fight you, even if you're shitting into the coffee or something...

** *"heldigvis fanget i grebet af historien"* **

I walk into the autonomous region of Christiania with the air of a stranger pulled from fiction. Perhaps these streets make everyone feel legendary – as if here comes the destined rabble-rouser with that lone wolf Leone swagger...

Perhaps it's just København, a city which breeds the truly Nordic. The capitol of Denmark since the 15th century, it is a Medieval fortress town built upon islands dubbed Zealand & Amager. You feel in a kingdom for you are in a kingdom, literally...

Christiania, on the other hand, is the kingdom of the freaks. The Danes call it *Fristaden Christiania* [*translation "Freetown"*], a communal, anarchist civilization smack-dab in the middle of København that stretches 85 acres. It even has it's own flag – a red banner continually waving on the horizon with three yellow discs representing the "i" dots in Christiania...

There is a feeling of immediate peace once you cross it's perimeters, this magical mutation of counterculture ambiance. It's like a miniature castle world containing the spirit of 1969 San Fran, a psychedelic aura hovering within the territory like the mist of fog...

Christiania is is utterly segregated from the EU; the Danish government legally regards it a commune, but the area is regulated by a special law which transfers its legal supervision to the state who pretty much does nothing. Any legalities are mainly a formality of chaperonage existing purely on paper...

Originally a naval wharf that squatters occupied in 1971, Christiania is comprised from former military barracks [*Bådsmandsstræde*] & ancient city ramparts. The ramparts were established in 1617 & reinforced during 1682-92 to form a perfect defense ring. While the western ramparts were demolished, the remaining half not only protect the anarchists from aggression but are considered among the finest surviving 17th century defense works on the planet...

The barracks of Bådsmandsstræde housed the Royal Artillery Regiment, the Army Materiel Command & ammunition depots. Infrequently used after World War II, the barracks were abandoned during 1967-71. The outermost defense line [*Enveloppen*] is connected to central Christiania by a bridge across the main moat. Four gunpowder storehouses have been revamped & renamed "*Aircondition*," "*Autogena*," "*Fakirskolen*" & "*Kosmiske Blomst*" [*Cosmic Flower*]. The Danish post-WWII execution site can still be seen where 29 war criminals were gunned down; while the execution shed is gone, a drain for the blood remains...

After the military evacuated, the area was only guarded by a handful of watchmen. On September 4th 1971, anarchist squatters broke down the fence; by September 26th, Christiania was declared open. Over these past 40 years, a new civilization has been built from scratch. Christiania now has its own electricity plant, theater halls, athletics buildings, yoga center, crust centrifuges...

The mission statement offers the following: *"The objective of Christiania is to create a self-governing society whereby each and every individual holds themselves responsible over the well being of the entire community. Our society is to be economically self-sustaining and, as such, our aspiration is to be steadfast in our conviction that psychological and physical destitution can be averted."* The only law is non-violence; the only bans forbid stealing, guns, knives, bulletproof vests, hard drugs, biker/gang colors & private vehicles...

The big gripe of government & social culture clash comes from the drug trade, which is purely Cannibas. White drugs were never part of the manifest & are not allowed in Christiania. Ganja on the other hand, this has been central to it's core. Pusher Street, while no longer a brazenly open entity, still has guys with huge black bricks of hash. If you want it you can get it, so long as it isn't being snorted, injected or smoked out of tin foil...

It seems that only a few spots in Christiania have been corroded by the normalcy of the EU; years of worldwide reputation have bred a few tiny shops which confine the inevitable tourists to a specific bottle-neck, leaving the compound a vast mystery...

As for this early morning, the streets were empty but for the traces of jazz emanating from a concert building. Which one I cannot answer, since they all have functionary status. Again, that lone wolf Leone swagger – wandering into this place felt like a Wild West town, as if I should've had a cigar in my mouth & a multi-colored poncho...

But instead of stagecoach stops, you have murals painted on everything, steel sculptures, oddly shaped houses, cobblestone streets. You have coffee shops & barter town markets & marijuana bushes just growing like wild rag-weeds out of cement cracks because people discard so many seeds they just flourish haphazardly.

It's by the jazz building where I find an old man with a white Santa beard & a blue suit coat with no tie smoking a tobacco pipe. Avoiding the initial mistake of The KØPI, I don't bother approaching him in any semi-official way. I just characteristically start rambling on about Frank Zappa, which the man offers plenty. We smoke some brick hash, then one by another random occupant of the jazz building come outside & mingle...

Within 20 minutes, I'm plenty stoned & it's just myself & one authentic resident of *Fristaden*. He's a German guy that methodically smokes a monster of a hash spliff with me, making his points by striking the lit ashes in the air like a teacher poking at a school-board. The German tells me the way to get rich in Europe is by finding people with automobile troubles online, then call the junk yards & act as the middle man shipping necessary parts because it's always about €100 cheaper then they'd expect to pay. Says he makes €10,000 in one go & hasn't worked in a decade. Tells me it's not so hard to get married for a green card, because most European women want American citizenship & will gladly trade national frontiers...

When I explain I'll be going to Stockholm next, he does everything he can to persuade me otherwise. Tells me it's a nightmare of persons disappearing, cops beating people, white slavery. About how it's completely illegal to sleep on the street & if the cops see I have red eyes, and assume I've smoked pot, they have the legal right to cotton swab my mouth on the spot...

Since all drugs are considered identical felonies without distinction in Sweden, having a gram of grass is the same as a kilo of heroin by rule of law. So they will just put you in prison for 2 years over a little ganja. You don't even need to possess it, you just need it in your system. Sweden, he says, is a nightmare world – but nowhere even close as shitty as Norway...

** *"denn er hatte schöne schuhe"* **

Hours later; denizens flood the market place but are soon repelled by harsh thunderstorms. As it pours from the sky, I accept morning coffee & newspaper time, ironically trying to read Danish. Many locals do the same, all of us sectioned off in a glass encasement that works as a sealed smoking section that you cannot smoke tobacco in. It's like a mass morning clam-bake session...

The older gentlemen reading a paper next to me, he's been scribbling tings down in a notepad for the past 20 minutes. Somehow I bumble into his bubble & ask about ear & consumption in the media which is enough to kick-start a diatribe. His name is Kai & has a strong & proper Brit-like accent, though I do believe that is common with the Danes...

"I just had an American visiting for a fortnight – an old scientist of 78 from Pennsylvania, and it was kind of scary what he said. He was very black in his vision. He really sees no future for the US & I think that we have to do what we have done so far – invented things. But the Chinese are able to produce those things for a lower price then we are. Well it's logical – a developing country seeing the light. We [Denmark] are a broken welfare state with great costs on everything. You know, panic always breaks loose – and behind panic there is only fear…"

"Tell me about your writing…"

"I'm a journalist; I'm 60. I turned 18 in '68 – grew my hair long, wearing sort of Indian clothes. Since then I've been writing about subcultures through the 60's, 70's, 80's, 90's up until now. I was a music editor, photo editor – I met all the pop stars, rock stars, directors, actors, writers, painters, philosophers. In '98 I quit my steady job but kept working with subcultures & also unions, politics – especially Social Democrats, which are closely connected to the unions. I've been a ghost writer & also a spin doctor; I've produced magazines, done radio – I've worked for the state, the government, advertising – even football magazines because I wanted to change the typical sort of sports journalism. The newspaper tells about the game but I tell about the fan culture because it's so similar to what's been built around music. On the way I found I had this way of telling about right now & the future that wasn't political, that wasn't intellectual or religious, but just building on the last 60 years."

"Do you think through pop culture terminology you can reach the masses greater then through any other academic fashion?"

"It's an entire unit – you can explain anything. Especially talking to people who are fans – we are not citizens anymore, we are users whose way of liking things are idolizing. And this pop culture, it's absorbed everything. I think the old establishment is in the midst of finding out what happened. We are talking about '*paradigm shift*' all the time, but nobody explains what it is – they make it so complicated that its unbearable. Really it's a very simple thing. I mean, what did I find out in those 40 years that I'd been writing about society? Well, the old world is driven by necessity. You were born & you have to do the same ting as your father. But in my life necessity has never meant anything. You can't look at society being driven by necessity, but instead being driven by possibilities. The paradigm shift is so simple – instead of asking all the time '*what's the problem?*' we have to ask '*what is the solution?*' When you ask, '*what's the problem?*' you drown yourself in problem. If we did the same thing with solutions, that would be constructive. Problems paralyze us – then fear comes in…"

"Let's talk about the spherical nature of pop culture as a sort of matrix. Do you see propaganda the same, as maybe an even larger sphere since propaganda can be taken into any context be it the

advertising of ideas, of religion, or lyrics of music, or even communication between individuals?"

"Well pop culture was kind of invented that way. Propaganda, the first time you saw that as mass pop culture was Adolf Hitler. He staged reality as a Wagnerian show."

"Do you think, in this sense, Hitler was the first rock star?"

"I think Hitler invented 'stadium rock,' yes, I do. He created those big rallies with this Wagnerian staging. And we always get a hint of a feeling like that in those environments. The feeling is always stimulating & if we have to talk about Adolf Hitler, I think he said something that a lot of people agreed with & I don't think we have done anything good it he last 60 or so years without talking about it. We're not allowed to say anything sympathetic – I agree there isn't much to say – but he said something a lot of people agreed with about the Jews. I talked to a lot of Germans about why they voted for Hitler & one of the best reasons I got was an old man who said, '*They had nice shoes.*' Nobody had nice shoes at the time. When these people were sort of role models, the people – they saw nice shoes, nice clothes – this must be good. They didn't like what they were saying, but they liked the shoes… The main part of propaganda, telling people something they need to hear – it can be in a good sense & a bad sense. Propaganda is always bad, it rocks half the picture away & makes the other half rosy and fantastic. I think we have to stop thinking this way."

"Aliester Crowley said that magick is only the process of using the power of will through all means to manipulate reality. Looking at propaganda in that context, do you think that propaganda could be considered a highly stylized black magic? Like black propaganda, false flag operations, the spread of misinformation wielded almost like sorcery?"

"Magic in our times is computer technology. Maybe its related to propaganda… The good thing about propaganda in our time is we are able to look through things. In the 30's they weren't able to do that. If people had actually seen Hitler they would never have vote for him, because he looked stupid. In the stadium Hitler was a tiny speck on a massive stage – they could only hear him & the sound was manipulated. A guy like Mussolini, the Italian parallel, he was a totally stupid dumb-bell but nobody could see him. Pop culture, you can use it for all the bad things you have in mind, but you can also use it for all the good. Pop culture is neutral – it's like time. And time is just a thing that goes on – you can't blame it on anything. It has never been so obvious then today, that in pop culture we go really close to people – tabloids, gossip press. We are now acknowledging that we are people – not ideologies & more fluffy rhetorical stuff. People that create everything."

"So tell me about Christiania..."

"They're having a 40 year anniversary here in September. The story goes that they kicked down the fence. The reason why they kicked it down was because they couldn't move their arms because they'd been beaten by police sticks. They squatted a place two blocks away, but the police came in & cleared them out, beat them on their shoulders. It was a military area, as you can see. There's approximately 900 people living in here – sometimes 750, sometimes 800... The most important thing that Christiania has given is a meeting place for people who think in different ways. Of course they come here because Pusher Street, because you can buy hash. Christiania has always been linked to that. It's kind of changed now, because for the first time Christiania is actually buying this place.... You know, this place has been a training ground of police for 40 years. The hashish – it's a good thing, in a sense, and a bad thing, in a sense. The fact that it's here has made the youth attracted all these years & kept this place alive... This place is run by consensus, almost like the UN. If you are violent here, you end up at a meeting with the community & they talk about what you've done. And they fine you in the way the find suitable – you could be thrown out for 3 years, for instance. But you can come back. They try to rule in a another way then democracy does, in a talkative way. The golden rule is no violence, no guns & no hard drugs..."

** *"her kommer ballade"* **

Somehow she appears moments after the thunderstorms – Miss Korana Jaleca, cruising up on her bike, the vocalist for Slovak Charlie's other grind gig Solid Noise. I am soon to find out that Korana knows everything about everything. At this point though, this particular moment of time, I don't know much except that she's well connected in Copenhagen & has reflective aviator glasses & thick blonde dreads. You have her pegged for an anarchist Queen Bee at first glance...

"I mainly do projects for fun. If it gets about 'the scene' it leaves this very stale taste in my mouth. Solid Noise is one of those bands where everybody gets to contribute. We haven't even played live yet, and we've been together a year & a half..."

"Is there an industrial scene here? It really seems to be lacking in Europe, to my surprise."

"POSH goth club that used to have industrial nights, but in the manner where people dress up and... nobody who actually likes industrial wants to go there. They play crappy industrial. I went once and regretted it, really badly… I think there are quite a lot of good bands in Copenhagen but it goes up & down – periods where not a lot going on & fractured, but I think right now – for the past few years, it's been…"

"More punk oriented?"

"Yeah, kind of – but it's a lot of the same people changing genres. At the same time it's fractured because people who are really into one thing tend to cluster together."

"You came from Yugoslavia & actually experienced it before the break-up of the state. What was it like growing up in a communist country?"

"Well, that's kind of a common misconception because it wasn't really a communist country."

"Well, TITO had a third way which was more a true socialist path…"

"It had a mixture of economies – it was never closed, as was the case in others. You didn't need special permits to get in our out, it had a thriving tourist industry. It also had poverty, but in a different scale. It had a rather good health system & good infrastructure. I think its weird in that sense – if you look at the Western countries or the Communist countries, its like a blend of those two. So it had its own weird development with history that you can't find anywhere else when it comes to the economical system – almost like what the EU has now. It's also a country that has a lot of different cultures. I think its quite hard to compare to something."

"TITO is villainized in Europe to a certain extent, but I know a big portion of the ex-Yugoslavian population is generally sympathetic."

"He was definitely not villainized as I remember it, but I was a kid. I do remember when it started falling apart – there were a lot of people older then my parents who survived the Second World War – he had this kind of semi-idol…"

"Like a war hero?"

"Yeah, exactly. And if you ask them everything bad started happening after he died. I think if you look beyond the fact that at several times he had prosecuted dissidents – I think the main population felt they benefited. But still, I'm not going to idolize him. It took forever to actually be one republic, the whole territory. One part belonged to the Austria-Hungarian Empire, this part to that – the whole time it's more or less been this war zone because it has this central placing & everybody wants it. I think for a lot of people it became one nation & that had great significance. I think that when it started breaking up, that was a huge shock to a lot of people.

"What do you know of the gypsy culture?"

"There are about one million of them in Europe, and it is an ongoing problem. Its not one that most Europeans recognize or confront. They really do have shitty living conditions. For instance, in Hungary, there has recently been this revival of this fascist party, can't remember the name right now, but last year they had these death squads – like real death squads – who would drive into these areas with gypsies & burns houses & shoot people, stuff like that. It actually is a very huge problem."

"I hear there is a rise of extreme nationalism in Hungary, specifically…"

"Absolutely, but also in Western Europe. In the Balkans right now – especially after the war – they were extremely nationalist. It's something I actually experience when I go to visit family."

"Are you big into 80's thrash?"

"Oh yeah. Denmark didn't have a music station, but Yugoslavia did. So I grew up with 80's thrash. I don't know if you know the original '*Headbanger's Ball'*…"

"Of course – and 'Beavis & Butthead,' when they actually showed the videos. That's how I found most my stuff as a kid. If it wasn't for both those shows, who knows what the 90's might've been like?"

"Exactly! And I think this maybe why I like so much industrial because…"

"Yes, yes – people that should get industrial or see it the way we see it, thyey never had these shows as a psychological backdrop. Like now – you have all these young kids but they are like fashion goths with cheesy zipper pants & clubber girls with fake hair extensions made of yarn. You know, 'Beavis & Butthead' is where I found Ministry & most people found KMFDM… But, ok, back on topic. What is a stereotype about Copenhagen? To be honest I had no conception or stereotype, because this is one of those vague countries, especially to citizens in The States."

"I'm not sure. My experience has been when it comes to people coming from the US, they have a more idolized view of Europe – especially when they are aware of their own government's mischief. I'm perfectly aware it is worse in that sense, but I think just because something is worse doesn't make the other thing good enough. I think there's this problem where you view something as the worst case scenario & then everything else not as bad becomes permitted. I still think Europe is in really shitty shape & its just getting worst – the growing nationalism for one… When I came to Denmark as a kid, as a refugee, it was really shitty then. The hidden story about how badly you get treated in Europe as a refugee or immigrant – it doesn't matter if you are from Europe, you come in that sort of role. I was in a lot of these really shitty refugee camps where they pack two families together in these 16 meter rooms."

"Where were these places located?"

"All over Denmark; now there's only a few. It's still a system where you were treated as if you were a complete moron. In order to get mail – which I thought was dehumanizing – was that you had to give your number & not your name. I think Europe has always sold itself on its civilization & humanity, but when it comes down to it, we're just much better at hiding it & having structural things that seem a bit different. Denmark – we have this social system where we don't have any poverty line. And one of the reasons we don't have an official poverty line is because the number of the people below it would be huge. So basically, it would mean students would have to – we have these grants we get, students get money – but we get half the number you would get to be above the poverty line. *'Students are temporarily poor.'* What the hell does that even mean? I'm not sure that you can divide poor into, *'Well, its only for a few years.'* So I think that it looks better on paper then it is, and in a way that makes it more extreme. Its difficult to resist something which is hidden then something obvious. The Danish system right now – the politics resemble one of those populist movements like The Tea Party in the US. You have politics based on fear. So when you constantly have to demonize & create your own political identity as a contrast…"

"Are Europeans watching The Tea Party like a horrific sideshow?"

"Yes – but I think it's the same with all those extreme Christian radical movements. That one church that loves to go out picketing funerals…"

"Yeah, the Westboro Baptist Church. We protested them in Seattle & the drag queens were in full force, all glittered out, just blowing bubbles at them & dancing around in speedos making out with guys to freak 'em out."

"I think we have a few of those in Denmark but the number tends to be less then some well built organization. The born again Christians, they tore down the old Youthouse because they were convinced everybody was possessed by demons [**The Youthhouse was Copenhagen's equivalent to KØPI]. There is this whole revival of the Christian Danish culture in the past few years, which is just horrific – everybody has to have Christianity in their schools. You can decline & remove your children from that course, but it is a subject in primary schools up until 9th grade. It actually has the largest number of hours in terms of classes that are given, besides Danish & math, when you measure it over a 9 year period. But that is part of this whole nationalist, '*we mustn't succumb to the Muslims*' thing that's going on. I wish I could say something that was less depressing..."

"What do you think of the black metal scene?"

"I had this friend when I was 18 & and we used to drink a lot of Icelandic booze & listen to black metal. He has a lot of goods stories 'cause he's from Norway. The scene in the 90's was completely fucked up – he said they actually had territories in cities where if you went to this or that bar & they knew you were affiliated with this or that band, then you would just get your ass kicked. They actually had these violent gang-like tendencies. So it's not only the few knife stabbings we've heard of. They actually had these in-fights that were massive & people would get badly hurt... It's a personal issue because I really do like metal but I have a problem with a lot of the scenes because I do think it becomes this chauvinist crap & I'm not there to get my ass grabbed, I'm there to listen to music..."

And Korana, who understands perfectly that all art is subject to political manipulation _except for that which speaks the language of this same manipulation_, takes me to the crust barracks of Christiania. It's another lengthy building – most likely a former soldier's quarters – and in order to enter the top floor, we had to climb an unfinished steel fire escape that ends just a few meters before a docking bay-like hole in the concrete...

The interior is an obvious factory of anarcho-syndicalism; the top floor akin to an editorial office. The main room has about 10 computers, xerox machines, printers, etc – it's something of a zine command post. In a magical spurt I become a megalomaniac newspaper baron & have all these crusties running around hustling machines to make a stack of *Big Shiny Prison* flyers. I'm tossed an avalanche & am deflated back to proportion...

While Korana hammers away on the cell phone setting up interviews for the coming days, I meet her personal comrade Mr. Marcus Rock, who is a younger guy in his early 20's. Marcus has that notorious cut-though-the-bullshit analytical Nordic mind & says he's been in, "*about 15 bands, none of which have ever recorded anything. Now I play in Scavenger Brats, which is a speed metal band – also Shit Comet. There hasn't really been a scene here for speed metal, ever, I think since Artillery... Maybe 6 years ago, there was a lot of punk a lot of fast hardcore, like 80's American hardcore bands. Then there was the eviction of the old Youth House...*

The Youth House, which Marcus just name dropped, was the Copenhagen equivalent to The KØPI – it ended a few years ago with the biggest riots this town had ever seen, at least in modern history. Marcus & Korana were neck deep in the saga; they promise to introduce me to key figures... For now, Korana takes me on a tour through the woodland trails of Christiania – past the Nazi execution shed, past the *Fakirskolen* & *Kosmiske Blomst,* down rows of houses built expressedly against stringent Danish code & their Frankenstein Monster lop-sidedness...

*** landskabet er drømme, og vi er dens hjernespind ***

I recall something Kafka once scribed about the writer as a sort of living dead thing, an unnatural element whose greatest responsibility is in servitude towards his greater function. This epoch was, of course, mixed in with the terrorism of family tradition, thus producing feelings of beetle-like metamorphosis...

In terms of this greater function, the main question is critical in nature – is it's *modus operandi* directed towards a malleable crucible of enlightenment? If not for God, is it for history? History by which it's very definition offers no reward except the theoretical praise of distant men who, in turn, will be perpetuating their own morose sham of critical academia?

Art is not a means in itself; it is simply a vehicle to explore life more abundant. Sade's legacy was not the Ark-like flood of filth but the sweat-soaked madness in the catacombs of *Charenton.* Miller's triumph was not the banning of his life's work in 80 countries, but his diminished salvation in the streets of Paris. Van Gogh's greatest accomplishment was not the *Starry Night* but the passion of the ear...

I ask myself what might be posthumously said of me? How many centuries before resurrection from the annals of quote/unquote *"music writing?"* Such is the problem of academic ingestion, never the discrepancy of art in itself. The great work remains the rock; the academics as barnacles desperately clinging through parasitic dependency on a landmass incapable of offering the sustenance of the flesh...

Art is of the vacuum; it is a symptom of life which effortlessly materializes the absurdity of the great nihil. Only the catharsis of art has any intrinsic value, properties which by their very nature are frozen foreign to the spectator. Completeness cannot be measured by any individual other then it's creator; vast halls can fill paintings that stretch from Genesis, but their physical existence is meaningless – only the gears employed of are importance...

...and Korana, who speaks 5 languages, who has read all of *Being & Nothingness* & processed it with ease, who is learning Russian so she can read Dostoevsky in his natural tongue, is now showing me Copenhagen under the starry night. Somewhere along the canal, moat, whatever you call these remnants of castle city, the moon shines on rippling water & she is terrified of the loud, territorial geese which now encircle us menacingly from the concrete embankment...

** *"trolde er også mennesker"* **

Of all the bands that could have swept through Copenhagen & slept on Marcus' floor, my sleeping bag spot is the same as REPULSIONE's, who came roaring through here just days before I met them in Berlin...

Somewhere in the groggy realm of half-sleep I contemplate these rabid layers of karma as Marcus & Korana peddle me towards the first interview of the morning. Like *E.T.*, I'm situated in a wagon basket on front of Korana's bike with a bullseye-ringside towards oncoming traffic, being splattered by the early morning hard-rain...

Yesterday had been a golden sun; we three had gone cycling through Copenhagen, met integral players of the Red Tape record label, casually drank with drum-synth prog-noise duo Chainsaw Eaters & received reports of a DIY crust venue in Prague that was an abandoned nuclear bunker 50 meters below the surface of the Earth.

Ok, *aaaaaaaaand* ACTION – Emil Munk of Melting Walkmen, when asked to explain what he dreamed last night: *"Well I have this constantly returning dream – its kind of a classic. The main part is me just going to the top of a mountain but when I get to the top there's a field. No one is there & I just walk around. It's like a valley, and I'm just trapped in this grey field. I walk around all alone & get to the edge of the mountain. For some reason I get a push from someone & I start falling towards the earth. 10 meters before I hit the ground – the picture, my vision scatters & moves to the side & there's this red handle, like an emergency break – and I can pull it & I wake up. I've had this dream like 150 times in the past couple years."*

"What do you think is the significance?"

"I don't know – its kind of control of my unconsciousness? I'm not really sure. It's interesting that I wake up when I want to, and that it keeps coming again & again."

Well – tell me about the band..."

"The band's called Melting Walkmen, formed in 2008. We're 3 guys who all had a background in hardcore punk &wanted to do something different – try to take out the upbeat thing, take it down a notch & more gloomy, more atmospheric. In the beginning it was inspired by Joy Division – classically structured songs with an internal, dark exploration of the human mind. We met Chainsaw Eaters & found out our music was collaborating well so we started playing a lot of concerts together, and The City Kill as well. Red Tape [Records] was formed – we did a split 12" with Chainsaw Eaters. It's nice but it sounds a lot like Warsaw. So we took more atmospheric expression, the noisier parts of Sonic Youth…"

"Do you think the more out there, bizarre stuff is more prevalent in Copenhagen then traditional punk?"

"Yeah, I think that's the tendency. 10 years ago, hardcore punk was dominating everything. I'm not sure what the reason was, but the last 4 years, there's been more room for experimenting."

"Is ICE AGE the big export?"

"Yeah. They're a really young band but have been able to penetrate the underground & mainstream media playing huge festivals, great reviews in the biggest newspaper in Denmark. At the same time it's 18 year olds who don't give a fuck about anything & don't do interviews. They're kind of the big name right now."

"What's the lyrical message of Melting Walkmen?"

"We all come from hardcore punk, where our messages were more political. That's not the case with Melting Walkmen – its more introvert. We're dealing with mental states, disillusion of existence. We want to put frustration in music… In hardcore punk, I think Jello Biafra did it very well because he had this satirical, ironic approach. But I don't think the music, the lyrics of something like The Exploited is interesting because there's not much to look for – its pure energy & that's it."

"You think Dead Kennedys are the ultimate punk band?"

"Yeah, definitely – and the lyrics, that'd be the number one."

** *"ekkoer af det endelige opgør"* **

Across town, we properly dissect *"a five megaton comet of pure shit crushing into the earth, obliterating every living being on it."* Marco Malcorps, whom is Marcus Rock's brother in arms, is now telling his tale. Marco was grafted into the life or death struggle of the old Youth House, known better to the free world as *Ungdomshuset,* located *Jagtvej 69* in *Nørrebro…*

"Basically we started out wanting to try the whole powerviolence thing. Hooked up with Marcus & the other guys playing fast crappy songs

*and... At the time I worked at a café [**in Christiania] & Marcus & I started talking about music. One thing let to another and lo & behold, SHITCOMET was formed."*

"How would you say SHITCOMET in Danish?

"The Danish version would be '*YOUTACOMEET.*'"

"***Marcus: We talked about doing a tour with a new name for every country – in Germany it would be 'SCHIESSEKOMETE.' In Sweden it would be SKITCOMET...".*

"Tell me about Copenhagen..."

"I think if you talk about brand in terms of DIY, the 'Copenhagen brand' is really strong [***Copenhagen's "brand" is often cited as "K-Town," the nickname referring to its proper spelling Køpenhavn*]. Which is why it annoys me when a band like ICE AGE – the mainstream music critics [*Marco huffs a huge breath of faux-enthusiasm*] '<u>*Punk rock is reborn in Denmark!*</u>' What?? Since 2000 we've had one of the strongest brands of international punk rock in the world & now you're trying to tell me punk rock is reborn? This band of all bands that suck Jesus' ass?!? I really don't like it. I think its bullshit beyond belief."

"Same problem with Detroit – 'ooooh White Stripes, ooooh-woo-hoo-haa-hoo.' I mean, they're OK, but, fucking, come on man. The end-all-be-all?"

"But you have to give ICE AGE kudos for the fact that they always try to mention some of the other pretty good bands from Copenhagen. But I generally think that the bands getting the most hype are not worth the hype they're getting."

"Were you a part of the Youthhouse?"

"Yeah – regularly since 2000."

"So you saw the big fall..."

"Totally. The short version is in '81 – after a long shortage of housing for young people & a shitload of squattings in Copenhagen – the city decided to give the squatters movement this house to appease them & have them not do anymore squatting actions. They didn't give them the actual deed of the house, they gave them the right to use the house. And there was peace for a time... Around 2003 – out of the blue – the city decides to put the house up for sale without informing us; nobody knows until we read it in the paper. Obviously, as this case unfolds, one of the things that comes to light is they asked the guy who was in charge of the deeds for the city, he told them not to do it. '*I never have trouble with these kids, they pay their bills on time, there's no troubles, so I think you shouldn't do it.*' As we would find out during the next 7 years, everytime the city heard something they didn't want to hear, they just put their fingers in their ears and went '*la-la-la-la-la.*'

"So what sparked the final descent into chaos?"

"Eventually it was sold to a woman who owned this company & when journalists started digging into it they found out there was no board, only her, thus making the company illegal & making it needing to be disbanded & the assets foregone to Faderhuset. And Faderhuset – here we are – turns out to be a Christian sect. Crazy ass born again Christian – they're insanely right wing; kind of like the American Christian right but in a Danish context. They've been characterized as a cult by a Danish institute that does research into religious nutjobs. Basically, what sets them apart is that Jesus bestowed upon them his powers so if they want a new job, they will have it, because the powers of Jesus will give them a new job. And its run by this crazy, crazy woman called Ruth Evensen, a spawn of Satan if I've ever seen one… She had the house evicted on the 1st of March 2007. Those days are kind of hazy to me… 2 or 3 days later & Marcus was in jail, I was spending all my time on Anarchist Black Cross stuff not sleeping, not leaving the office… It should be said that the reason it was evicted was because this woman – she had an epiphany that this house was filled with demons & all of us were possessed by demons. So Jesus was telling her… She changed her story a couple times. When this whole thing started, we put a huge banner out front that said: '*FOR SALE – including 500 psychotic rock throwing autonomous punks from hell.*' And the first story she told the press was that she drove by, saw this sign, and god told her to buy the house & save us. But at some point I guess somebody told her, '*Hey, you're on TV – you come off as kind of a nut*' so then she changed her story to, '*We've always had our headquarters in that part of town & thought it was a really interesting building.*'

"Did people handle the threat of the raid fairly well?"

"The strange thing is that it was in times of adversity that the house functioned best. When we had an external force pressing down on us – even though it was stressful, I can honestly say that those last 6 months – I've never seen that place so active, people coming from all over the world. But the general feel wasn't everyday '*we're so depressed*' – it was very organized. Watchers on the roof, people cooking, huge demonstrations – people preparing in every conceivable way for the inevitable. The house was fucking vibrant, it was alive. And that might be my fondest memory of the place…"

"So how did the raid go down, exactly?"

"The house was evicted by a fucking anti-terrorist squad really early in the morning, rather brutally I heard from the people in there. A couple days later a big crane tore the thing down. The eviction led to the hugest riots Copenhagen has seen in over 100 years, lasting around a week... The last 6 months, up until the eviction, I spent a shit-load of time there – every day we had shifts, cameras around the building, so we had 8 hours monitoring. It was really stressful because you knew it was coming & you knew it was gonna be crazy as fuck. So when it finally happened it was surreal... Those days were strange; it's like something I experienced in another lifetime..."

** *"aldrig glemme at spørge en viking, hvad hans holdning er"* **

The last of rapid fire interviews brings us back into the realm of black metal with an unrepentant Viking kick. The guy's codename is Ynleborgaz; he heads up the respected ANGANTYR, known for their work on uber-kvlt label Northern Silence Productions...

Ynleborgaz, at least in his press photo's, is suited head to toe in spiked leather & corpse-paint; in person he's got a goatee & long brown hair pulled back in a tail: *"It started as a young teenager listening to heavy metal, thrash & punk. When my friends & I found out about the first wave of Norwegian black metal, we got really into that. That was in '96 & nobody wanted to play this style of music. So I decided to do a one man band. First of all, there was no one to play with, haha. Secondly, I wanted to be in control & not compromise. So this started in '97 & the first album came out in 2000. In 2006 I got a lot of requests for festivals so I hired some friends to play live. We played Rock For Roots, a couple 100km from Berlin, Played Under The Black Sun last year... I also have another project: Make a change... Kill Yourself. It's a melodic, depressive... I create all the music, do the singing, but the lyrics are from a friend of mine..."*

"So I take it the bands message is pretty blatant..."
"Heh..."
"Is there any BM scene in Copenhagen?"
"In the 90's, and after the turn of the millennium, there was actually quite a big scene. I think its declined – there used to be head-bangers, drinking beer. Now all you see is glam & sleaze, people having rockabilly tattoos & stuff. It's not like underground black metal here anymore; the death metal scene in Copenhagen is much bigger. There is one metal club called The Rock. All the bands that come through here not

big enough to play the 1500 people venues play there – like 800 maximum..."

"What's the message & overall theme of Angantyr?"

"The Lyrics reference certain points in Scandinavian history – fictional events based on actual happenings in the Viking age, or maybe some events in the UK, because the Danish people had a lot of land there. Norse mythology is really interesting, I've read about it all my life. So I created some characters that could have been there, that period, and tell stories about them. And about their rebellion against Christianity that's trying to take over everything."

"A lot of black metal bands play up the Satan thing, but you have more of a pagan, folky edge..."

"For me, black metal is rebellion against religion, against Christianity. One way is the Satanist way. I'm not into it myself, I never was, but its still a rebellion against Christianity. So from my point of view its OK – I just don't..."

"Who are the real deal in BM that are super fucking serious into the occult?"

"Last year we were on tour with HORNA – they were serious about their music & all the things surrounding their music as well."

"Ever been to Trondheim?"

"Yeah, once."

"I hear that the ultra-serious bastion of BM comes from them today. This guy in France told me about gigs with severed heads dug from graves. Heard any stories like that?"

"I've never actually heard of anything like that. When I visited it seemed like a small community; it seemed like there was no underground scene at all. The closest thing to 'not normal' was the university which had a backpacker's hostel – that's as diverse as it got. But that was 15 years ago..."

"I hear Oslo is extremely boring..."

"Its pretty natural that black metal is born from there."

"Ever hang out at the Youthhouse?"

"In the mid 90's I was there for some concerts because there was some death metal shows, a lot of punk shows, but I was never part of that culture. They also frowned upon the likes of me. They can have their culture, and I'll have mine."

"Did you do a tour with Taake?"

"Yeah, same tour with HORNA."

"What were the Taake guys like?"

"They were musicians, above all. The main man – he's doing everything in the studio himself, so its only live members. They didn't seem like tight friends, but they were a tight outfit. And very good at partying too…"

"We've been talking about dreams today – what's the last bizarre one you remember?"

"Usually I dream of people turning into animals & trees & stuff. I don't really think about it that much – I don't think it symbolizes anything in particular."

"Are you a total atheist?"

"Yeah, I would say so. I really have not experienced anything that has convinced me of the opposite. What you see is what you get – and that's what I see."

"What do you think are some stereotypes about Denmark?"

"I heard Oprah Winfrey did a show about Denmark, and she called us the '*happiest people in the world.*' And, well, I'm not gonna disagree with that one. Denmark is a very safe country to grow up in – there's always an economic net somewhere; the welfare system is really, really good. If you don't have a job, you can easily get enough money to live, and also a lot of help to find work. And education as well – most of it is free. In Denmark, the possibilities are open to anyone. I think it's a really good country to grow up in. I never thought about living anywhere else. I just moved to Sweden 3 months ago [from Malmo]. Another thing – the health care system, also a safety net…"

"The Swedes can only have like 3.5% beer right?"

"Yeah, in the shops. You have to go to a special, monopolized store to get your alcohol & its super expensive."

"As far as the Norway thing – do you have a cut-off point where extremism goes too far?"

"I don't have a cut-off point – there's nothing that I think is too much. Black metal is about extreme. Back in the days it was everything you could do to be so much more different then everyone else. And the more 'normal society' loathed you, the better. So in extreme black metal, no cut-off point."

"So tell me about this record you handed me earlier."

"All the titles & lyrics are in Danish – Martin Hannford did the artwork & the albums on Northern Silence records. The title means 'betrayal' in translation. The intro, you hear some church organ with lots of reverb, the door is kicked open, you hear some footsteps, axes being drawn, the organ player is beheaded & falls on the organ. Some of the people of the cloth are getting killed by Viking warriors, but at the same time the citizens of the city that the church controls have found out about the Viking rebels' hiding place so they send an army there & kill everyone & burn everything, blah blah. Because, of course, there was a guy within the Viking camp who betrayed them & their position. So yeah – when the main character returns he comes back to a burning village, corpses & everything, and then he decided to do the same thing to the enemy. Infiltrated their city under false pretenses. And that's what this album is about. His woman, who had a baby many years earlier on my other album, she's sent into the enemy city to work undercover. They have this leverage point on her – they know where her baby is, because it was taken years ago..."

"Ok, the Taake thing. I saw this post he sent out about the Antifa guys, that they were going to start a war at one of your gigs. Now, I've had this problem too – I was in this borderline black metal band for a little bit that had no racist content whatsoever – not even any 'burn churches, kill Christians stuff' – and the Antifa people in Portland actually targeted us. Like they were gonna come fight us or picket our debut show. They were just seeking an excuse to start some shit because they had nothing better to do – it was totally ludicrous. Was it the same deal on your end?"

"Yes, that is right. There is very much focus on the right wing black metal, or just black metal in general. To the Antifa all black metal is National Socialist. Now, I'm talking about the German Antifa – they are really destroying many live shows for many bands that have nothing to do with Nazism. And they've also been hunting Taake for example, HORNA – the show we were on with that problem on the tour was canceled. It's always the same stupid thoughts, you know?"

"You know, a lot of people have this opinion when they're younger where it's like 'yeah, burn churches, cool, fuck everything.' But those same people grow up and now are like, 'but you know, that was some great architecture,' haha..."

"It is something that made a message, you know? I don't see it much different then the Christians burning down the heathen monuments. Of course, we're living many years later, but... When I was a teenager, I was the same. You know, burn the churches – all the Christians have to be killed, cause that's exactly what they did to our ancestors. But what good will it do? Nothing really..."

STOCKHOLM

VII. *"land of giants // ashes of ásgarðr"*

The Øresund bridge is a mythological *Conan* sight, especially in the pouring rain. It appears the handiwork of giants, this beast of concrete & steel... It is the first identifier marking your entrance through the Gates of Scandinavia – the longest road & rail bridge in Europe, connecting Copenhagen to Malmo. The water base is foggy & exotic; you half expect the Kracken to twist it's tentacles from the depths & mangle this colossus to uncharitable fathoms below...

Riding through Sweden on a Eurolines bus, this somber 6 hour trek – the entire country resembles Novi, Michigan. Same pine trees, same gray feel – same drudging landscape & construction yards housing tractor equipment & caterpillar hi-lo's...

The scenery changes to modern metropolis as I'm dumped off in the heart of Stockholm. Despite the futuristic architecture, what remains is the grating & depressive psychological aura of Michigan... Pushed through to another random capitol with nowhere to go & in no mood to play *"metal journalist guy."* The Swedes are going to be *"properly scheduling"* bastards, I know it – and timid in the face of my American loudness...

I begin with a string of bars & convenience stores that looks lively enough. The street resembles the northern part of Downtown Seattle, like Queen Anne or Virginia & 2nd. There is one rock bar with beefy biker bouncer, but entrance is in Kroner & equals like 6 euros; the cheapest beer is the same. The 7-11 equivalent only sells alcohol until 6pm & it cannot exceed more then 3% alcohol due to Nazi booze laws. Furthermore, drinking on the street is a crime the same as sleeping on the street, and if the bit about the cotton-swabbing cop is right I'll be quickly imprisoned from lingering K-Town THC. *Cheers to Nordic, Oklahoma...*

There's a cute black metal 20-something running the checkout at the Hema equivalent. I ask her where the freak bars are, and she's confused. I say, you know, *"like punk rock,"* and she says I'm in horrible luck, because punk rock is not popular in Sweden & I won't find much any of it. These people don't recognize metal or punk as the same planet whatsoever; it's all melodic death or hyper-blasting corpse-paint here, as is expected of their heritage...

Hoping to avoid cops I try a hostel but it's like €50; no one has responded to my emails or texts. The big dogs of Swedish extreme whom I assumed would come out in droves are static as a piece of lumber. All these years worshiping a black hole... Korana & Marcus no longer exist; Lorenzo & REPULSIONE are figments. The Obscene Extreme has fallen into a history distant as Gettysburg, but a war victorious without the firing of a single shot. *Exhaustion*...

Stockholm seems cobbled by giants. Buildings look the shape of massive thrones in *vampyr megalopolis*... Twisted lampposts & endless cement steps; the sky a strange velvet, purple hues jutting through the air... Tonight I slumber in this land of giants cold & alone, hidden from lawmen more ominous then those of Tijuana. Hidden behind this steel bread cart in an alley doorway, it will soon be raining... *Utmattning*...

** *"bara in och ut"* **

Day II & Failure I – *Café 44*. An ironic failure at that, because previous truncated attempts have led me to curb any remaining fluffiness to my approach – *just go exactly where you know they will be*. Without any hesitation, I woke up & hauled ass to Café 44, Stockholm's reputed anarchist café/infoshop. It was closed for months & not to reopen until September. Disgruntled, I called the most enthusiastic of possible interviews...

Representatives of Invidia Veins soon came by, which were a few younger guys from this melodic death metal act. They generally reinforced everything that's been said in terms of Swedish tepidness: *"Swedish people like rock, but metal is more like extreme rock, so there a lot of people dropping off there. People like Bon Jovi, but when it comes to heavier stuff – they drop off, the heavier it gets... You have The Anchor, the Harry b James, maybe Café 44, but those are the only three I can come up with. You send the record and maybe you get an 'ok, you can play in half a year.'"*

Before taking me site-seeing through the castle complex & old town tourist spots with plush Viking beanies, the singer added a nice bit on Chernobyl: *"When I was young my grandfather, he lived like 250 km from Stockholm. Chernobyl blew up, because the nuclear reactor was pushed too hard. Parts came up, some landed in Sweden, where my grandfather lived. 10, 15 years of my life we couldn't eat blueberries or mushrooms in the forest cause there was a risk of radioactivity. My mother had a teacher in biology, and he was out with a class, measuring the ground, teaching the kids and found something weird. So he tried to call someone at some government something and tell them – he didn't get an answer but after awhile he noticed he was right because they actually came out with it to he television, not to eat something from the forest..."*

If Paris taught me anything, it's *"just in & out"* – if things are grating, then split. So without any further rumination, Gothenburg is out & so is Norway [Bergen/Oslo]. Norway, admittedly, has been on the skids since London...

Handful of reasons, but mainly that everyone has deflated Norway in their descriptions of it & I want to let it remain this mythological heavy metal land in my head where Slayer is playing on shopping mall speakers & people dress as viking in their every day street clothes & trolls still live in magickal forest canopies & all mountaintops resemble that *Blashkyrth Mighty Ravendark* video with evil looking dudes in leather thrashin' axe 24 hours a day...

I don't even want to see it. I don't want to know what's it's like to pay €10 for a bottle of water, or €20 for a one way bus ride across town – even when meetings with Gorgoroth, Motiis, Pantheon I & Shining are thrown into the deal...

Gothenburg, on the other hand, is manageable; widely considered the freak city of Sweden [**Stockholm is more like the Munich to it's Berlin, or the Reno to it's Vegas*]. Gothenburg is the gritty, working class industrial city that breeds hardness, although I cannot imagine it being some destitute Cubatao. For now I have a few major targets in Stockholm – Jonas from LIFELOVER, Erik from General Surgery & Dadde from Wolfbrigade...

Helsinki though, this is a major coming stronghold – FINNTROLL, Beherit, Enochian Crescent, Dodskvlt, Moonsorrow, Battlelore & Korpikilaani. I'll be ditching for Finnish shores soon after this weekend, as I already have a rideshare with a random backpacking Australian. Said I only had to throw €30 on the Ferry...

** *"precis där vi bör vara"* **

Wolfbrigade are one of the most important punk bands in Swedish history. I know they will never be judged as so by any establishment ruling, but everyone that knows what's up knows very well that Wolfbridgade have made some of the nastiest, crustiest, down-n-dirty metallic d-beat Sweden's ever produced...

The drummer Dadde & I have made our way to a bar/restaurant off the beaten path, having met at the subway train. The day has grown brighter of weather & the realization that all the women here are exotically

European – they all have the facial curvature of porcelain dolls: "*I grew up 4 hours away – that town, so many good punk bands... Are you familiar with Anti Cimex? Their old singer was the first singer of Wolfbrigade, or Wolfpack, as it used to be called. What Discharge was for the UK, Anti Cimex was that for Swedish hardcore... I've been in Wolfbrigade about 10 years; the band was formed in '95. The only two members still from the original lineup, they'd a death metal band called Obscure Infinity. The singer killed himself, so they went on. They were death metal kids but grew up listening to punk. So they started crust bands with death metal – one of the first to mix melodic death metal with hardcore. Like Tragedy, they're huge now, but they were influenced by Wolfpack. So it's a circle... Officially we're on hiatus, but we've been working really hard writing music for a new album. We know it ourselves so well that if we say yes to gigs our writing process stops. It's frustrating because we've had so many great gig offers. Next year will be a new tour.*"

"What's the new material like?"

"It's back to the Wolfpack sound, but improved. We're gonna record in Gothenburg where the first two Wolfpack albums were recorded. I think the new material is more death metal then crust, but there's still plenty of d-beat. Our lyrics have a semi-political approach even thought they can be a bit vague and dark. It's Personal but it's always about some sort of struggle. The new records is more metal, better production – it's coming out in The States on Southern Lord. I don't think we're gonna do a full 3 month USA tour, but we've been offered to open for Municipal Waste. That would be fun, but we – I've reached a point I guess comes with getting older. I have a job I'm pretty satisfied with. I don't want to tour that much either. Our guitar player just had a kid, we all have jobs. Since we're kind of trapped in the DIY/hardcore/crust scene, we're not getting rich from playing live. I've had crusties coming up to us and saying like "*you guys are nice, you guys have clean clothes.*" Not being disappointed, but expecting something else – like long dreadlocks, something like that…"

"Do you wish your music was more accepted by metal audiences abroad. It seems you're relegated to the punk scene…"

"We played a few metal festivals & so on, so I think our name is – there's people familiar with us. Being on Southern Lord is only good for us. We'll probably get a bunch of shit from hard-line DIY crusties but I don't care. It's our band, we do what we want."

"I don't see Southern Lord as a major label."

"I don't either. We've jumped label to label for so long, I just want to stay. That's always been a problem – distribution. The feeling is that we have good communication, they respect us, we respect them. We've worked with good labels, but its never been 100%."

"Were you surprised by anything in the USA?"

"I was surprised by how well organized everything was, even though it was DIY. But still, there are things that you never question at all here in Europe – you get food, beer, places to stay. That wasn't included in the deal over there. Even though there were people who took care of us, shows were good, but there was other people coming who made food instead of the actual promoters. I try not to be superficial, so I didn't have a stereotype about how the Americans were supposed to be. Its such a big country.

"Did the largeness of America unsettle you? As in the WalMarts, the SUV's..."

"No – it's just kind of fascinating. Just bigger, better – the slogan of The States. I don't get offended by it in any way. I could get offended if there's Americans who think they are better then me because they are Americans, but I haven't met anyone like that."

"We have house venues all over the USA, but it seems quite apparent that Europeans can't really get away with that here, mainly because the houses are so compacted due to thousands of years of mass population?"

"No, the cops – the neighbors will complain. You'll get thrown out of your house or squat. There's one place that's shown up here in Stockholm that's like the punk venue, which is more of a European style squat. They have to be out in the suburbs pretty much, more of a warehouse where there's no neighbors. Their second closest neighbors are like the Hells Angels, so no cops show up there. I'm not sure if they appreciate anarchist crusties..."

"Are you tattoo artist?"

"I work at a shop and I might become an apprentice. I've been working at different tattoo shops the past 2 years. I've always had an interest in body art."

"Is Sweden a place where they won't hire if tattoos show?"

"I read that Stockholm is the #1 city in the world for people who are tattooed. It's getting more accepted, but I still get looks from people in the subway. I think its more curious instead of offended. Of course I can get a bad conscience if I'm standing on a street & there's a really old lady walking by looking really scared. I don't want that, but I can't blame her. This wasn't normal when she was young. There's more jobs where you can actually have tattoos.

"What's your favorite tattoo?"

I really like this Illuminati thing on my hand [*Points to a sort of "Novus Ordo Seclorum" Freemasonry thing*]." Stockholm has become – it feels like our audience & gigs have moved to more commercial bars. For two reasons – one is that there's no one that has enough energy to run these punk places that are going to be shut down all the time. Two is we're getting older & don't want to stand in dirty toilets."

"Do you think if any of us are standing in 20 years, our kids could never live up to how hardcore our generation is?"

"I don't know – I've seen '*Crabcore*' on Youtube. Are you familiar? Just look it up. I felt very old seeing that."

"As in slam dancing meets the crab walk?"

"Yeah, and the music is horrible. It, like, offended me. I felt kind of like how my parents reacted when I played punk & metal. You can't even hear what they're saying…"

"Scandinavia is the undisputed home of satanic black metal. Did the punk scene look at this like a big joke in the 90's when all of uit broke out? And is Burzum identified as a white power band up here?"

"If you go back when Swedish death metal was created – the early 90's with Nihilist, Entombed, all those bands – they were punk rock kids listening to heavy metal. And there was fights between death metal & the Norwegian black metal – the more satanic… I think the Swedish death metal scene were considered wimps, or gays or faggots or whatever they used to call them. I might be wrong, but this is the impression I have… There's been a few fights over the years over & the shit talk. I think in the early 80's you were supposed to sing about anarchism, anti-war if you were in a punk band – the same way you were supposed to sing about Satan if you were in a black metal band. Over the years it progressed… At least for a while the crust scene was super pc – '*metal bad/punk good,*' you know? And there was no crossover whatsoever. Our band, Wolfpack – there was shit talk that we were Nazis 'cause we had wolves & iron crosses. Bands like ours, we were on metal labels. Then something happened, mid-2000 I think more punks started appreciating metal again & the other way around. All of a sudden they seemed to see past the politics of satanism, anarchism… I would say our band is socialist & very to the left. But we're not the pc kind of band in that sense. We have different opinions, we're individuals. We don't want to sign under an anarchist paper…"

"What do you have to say about Helsinki?"

"There's a lot of similarities with Swedish people – they're more outgoing, but that might be because they're more drunk then we are. The

Swedes are kind of shy, not very outgoing in general. If you're too outgoing you're pretty much considered a freak."

"What do you have to say about Café 44?"

"Here in Sweden, a lot of the bigger bands – this is one of the places they started. Even big pop groups do secret gigs there. Metal gigs, sometimes, like Napalm Death played there & it's not even 200 capacity. Hellacopters played there, Entombed played there. Café 44 is significant for Stockholm's scene in general, even though its considered more of a leftist, anarchist café. The venue part is talked about with a lot of respect..."

** *"hur kan du säga MILF på svenska?"* **

The Swedish, they actually listen to you. They do. It's a little freakish, admittedly, when in the United States you are so accustomed to people talking to hear themselves talk. You begin a sentence & they hang on – *they follow you & speak better English then you do.* I'm sorry if this sounds generic, as it will to any European, but it's important to note...

We're all at Garlic & Shots Bar – Dadde & half the Wolfbrigade guys & one of the big dogs from grindcore act Splitter & a bunch of other perfectly fluent underground folks. The Australian shows up baked from Hash & looking to party, your typical surf-loving party down slightly jock but still goofy enough to be likable Aussie...

I try to keep him at bay from Dadde, who is a little reserved & possibly neurotic with strangers, but the Australian barges right in talking about this glorious intercontinental *"Fuck Mission"* he's on & doing his damnedest to hunt down as many wild packs of MILF Cougars as possible. He's out for *slidan* trophies, cruising around Europe without a license in a Dutch van he bought for €300 that was probably stolen in the first place. All hail the Schengen Agreement...

I step out with the guy from Splitter, a crusher of a grind act that's been around since 2003. They've toured Europe several times & also east coast of USA: *"We here in Stockholm have a lot of good bands, famous bands, but the scene is really bad. Its hard to put up shows, no one shows up, no one cares in Sweden. This is why we go abroad to play. Most of the shows with splitter have been outside of Europe and in the old Eastern Block – they're more die-hard but at the same time its mainstream, more accepted, not as underground as here in Scandinavia. In Czech republic, people come from the office wearing suits. It's like grindcore is a passion of their life... Prague will never be the same as Berlin. Berlin is so multi-cultural, multi-subcultural, and its so easy to find a place to live. In*

Sweden it's really restricted. People in Stockholm are mostly lazy. In Stockholm if there's a show people hardly ever turn... One of the best times I had touring with Splitter was touring with Napalm Death. They're like the most down o earth guys I've ever met. I was not that big of a fan, yeah I know they started the whole thing, but when I met them and saw them live everything changed. So amazing live, really into it. Probably the best time I had on tour ever. It was supposed to be 10 dates in Czech/Slovakia/Ukraine, but our vocalist broke this thumb in the middle of the tour. Just some hardcore Splitter fans, wanted to pull down our vocalist. They expected to catch him, but they just moved. That really sucked..."

** *"en dag aporna kommer allenarådand"* **

"Get up!! Get up!!" The old lady is tugging at my shoes, trying to get me to drink more vodka. *"Get up!! You are only in Svee-den once in a lifetime, get up & drink!!"* I vaguely snap out of it, wrestle with what little room I have on the bed only to get blocked by The Australian who's face down & hogging the entire mattress... I torpedo into slumber, only to be awakened sucked back to reality – this time by The Old Man: *"Get up American!! Get up!!"* The Old Man is tugging at my shoes, trying to get me further wasted. *"You are in Svee-den – in Svee-den you drink more, you drink more & more!! Get up!! drink!!!"*

Hours later I groggily awake, leaving the Australian face down & drooling on the bed. I tip-toe down the stairs & the old folks are passed out on the couch – but the famous Swedish rapper Mächy is wide awake with the air of a hammered Russian demanding you drink with him to oblivion. This block of a man with a whiskey jug in his hand, he's the sort of guy you just don't say *"no"* to. So I ask Mächy for coffee & he fills it with half vodka...

After a rugged sip I gaze down at the coffee table & remember the paranormal episode a few hours ago. Aussie & I, we'd ended up at this party after hopping in a random taxi at the bar. All these nicely dressed women, they led us to a designer flat where we all discussed movies & travels, continuing the alcoholic torpedo...

We all kind of looked down at the same time – the beanie-baby Shark, which moments ago was resting atop the plastic tree in the corner, was now firmly in the middle of the coffee table. There was no explanation – it must have floated through the air & dropped itself there of its own accord. The girl quickly apologized, saying this sort of nonsense happens all the time...

But Mächy, this concrete slab of a fellow – he struggles with English in a belligerent stupor. He flashes tats with the Mächy logo & a Swedish saying that translates to *"Don't Be Like Us."* He asks to see a flyer for *The Big Shiny Prison* & when he views the Statue of Liberty with the skull for a face, he asks if I'm *"a communist."* Reassuring him I believe in democracy, he then plays me his form of Swedish rap. I didn't even know there was an underground for this, this expert flowing in *urgey-burgey* language...

** *"du kan inte leva så för evigt"* **

Across town now, a gray day harbor-view & somber moment of pure journalism with the main contact point of the day. Mr. Erik Sahlström of General Surgery [*and ex-vocalist of totally rad thrash band Serpent Obscene*]. We meet at Corporate Franchise XYX not far from the Old Town strip...

Sahlström is a classic long-hair/death metal t-shirt guy, very polite & humble. While General Surgery started as a Carcass cover band in '88, they soon evolved into... well... being the ultimate Carcass clone. Not that there is any shame in replication – Carcass laid the foundations for such a plethora of styles it's like pointing the finger at a rock band for sounding like Zepplin or Sabbath. One might say General Surgery pushed the Carcass aesthetic further then ever previously attempted...

"We did the Maryland death fest a few times, we've done a West Coast USA tour. We played LA Murderfest in 2009... At the moment we are writing our third album. Kind of laying low I guess. We've been touring the last 4 years quite a lot. Since 2007 we've done 60 shows. We don't do any long tours – the longest was 10 dates. Just a few of those, usually weekends & one-off festivals. We all agree that this is at the level we want, just keep it like this. We have our lives here & don't want to be on the road all the time."

"Did you grow up here? Are you happy here?"

"Yeah & yeah, I would say so. I really like Sweden. Not too many people, so for me – I'm not a big fan of big cities. I think Sweden is a really good country to live in every way I can imagine"

"What do you think of the stereotype that Sweden is this heavy metal land?"

"It's a strange thing. With the metal scene, considering there are so many bands & that most are pretty good. I think its easy to get into playing music. When you go to school you get free rehearsal place, music lessons from your community school. It's really cheap & easy to get into music if you want. When you're a kid, you're always encouraged to play at school. When you're a teenager its so easy & that's the big reason there are so many bands. I don't know how that works in other countries."

"Did the largeness of the USA unsettle you?"

"It's another thing that struck me about America – the East, West & middle, it's all so different. It's like being in Europe – very different from Stockholm to Spain. When I first went to the US I thought it's the same all over. I never understood that until I got there. I got to Florida, to Miami, and you can't walk in the streets; only criminals are walking the streets. You have to take a bus or a car, and everyone has a car. I thought that was very strange."

"You never see people riding bicycles in the USA really, unless it's like Portland, which is more like Amsterdam."

"Up there in the Northwest, that was the part where I felt most comfortable. One of the weirdest places we played was in Arizona, in the Mojave Desert. It was like a youth center where the kids hung out. There was like 3 or 4 older guys that came to see us. The kids didn't really understand what we were doing & we didn't really understand what we were doing there. It was strange."

"Were they metalcore kids with the quaffed emo hair?"

"Yeah, more like that. That felt awkward – we always have the blood, stuff like that, but that was I think the only one where we went up & played in our t-shirts. There was no point getting drenched in blood when nobody understood what we were doing."

"Is there a deeper message hidden inside the gore?"

"No, not really."

"What're your favorite lyrical lines in gore-death?"

"I think all the Repulsion lyrics are really awesome, and of course Carcass. It's a pretty boring answer with this one. Gore lyrics though, it's the best entertainment. There's no personal meaning in General Surgery, just a little story about death & just blood & guts. It's pretty silly, really. How you say, tongue in cheek?"

"What are the kids into in Stockholm these days?"

"Here in Stockholm, the metal fashion is the glam, sleaze thing – its been that way for a few years now; the sleaze kids are all over. But when you go to Gothenburg its more the 70's rock, that kind of hairdo & denim vests."

"Do they call them 'Denim Demons up here?"

"No, I haven't heard that – its more of a led Zepplin thing."

"Is Stockholm a better all-around city then Helsinki?"

"No, the other way around. Actually Finland – metal & rock music is very popular in Sweden right now. The Sweden rock festival is like 20,000 people. And there are like 4 other festivals that play metal music that are 5 to 10,000 people. The Big 4 was like 60,000 people. Iron Maiden played to 60,,000 people. The summer last year they sold over 200,000 tickets to hard rock or metal events in Sweden. That's a lot of rock & metal – but in Finland its even more so. Finland is a rock country for sure. But the problem is even less people live there then in Sweden. Helsinki is smaller then Stockholm. There's so much forest and wilderness in Finland, but the people are more melancholy; that's kind o the personality. They're very quiet & mellow until they drink, and they drink a lot. I would guess on the whole, Norway, Finland & Swedish people are very quite & down tuned, but in Finland more so – they are the epitome of that. Swedish people are probably the most open socially within Scandinavian countries. Norway, Sweden & Denmark are almost the same people, the same language. But the people in Finland are more Russian, Slavic. They have a totally different language; the environment has had its psychological mark. There's studies showing that the further north you go the less people are talking, and I would say that's absolutely true, in Northern Sweden – very few words in a sentence."

"When the Norway thing happened, you were here at the time. What was the Swedish metal scene's reaction…"

"I was in my early 20's. The metal scene took two directions – a lot of bands followed Entombed & played sort of death-n-roll stuff, mainly the older guys. They really had no connection to this black metal scene. Maybe they thought it was a bit over the top, a bit stupid. But at least the teenagers, it had a really big impact. Everyone was playing black metal at that time, from 93-96. At the concerts people were trying to be as evil as they can. And people are standing in the corner looking at each other, nobody was actually having fun. Actually there was a few of the bands that trying to be the coolest guys, beating people up,. Compared to now, there was a lot of violence at the shows. I saw quite a few people get beat up, hit in the face with a bullet belt for wearing the wrong shirt. Pretty strange scene; people were not working together. I was talking to the guys from Merciless. They were saying the metal scene was growing into something that people didn't understand – so different compared to the late 80's, early 90's. It was about going to shows, drinking beer, having fun & then it was no fun at all. At that age I was probably the most into metal in my early 20's. I'm 35 now, so if that would've happened now I would have more perspective on things. I think for a lot of people in Stockholm there was Gahenna. They changed a lot of things cause they were playing black metal in the vein of Venom & were old school – also Nifelheim. People were into Darkthrone, the forest romance thing, and Nifelheim said, *"Nifelheim is a chainsaw through the forest."* Gahenna was like *'we drink beer & play black metal, & we have fun.'* The bubble burst in '97. People realized we cant do this anymore – it's impossible to go on hating each other…

** *"kokain i ansiktet av Mona Lisa"* **

Following my collision with General Surgery, I made my way to *Grundbulten* – the DIY anarcho-punk venue in a warehouse district at the edge of Stockholm. DOOM were playing [*as in the hallowed UK crust band*]; a few of the Wolfbrigade guys were hanging out. It was cheap & real as this country gets. It was like a basement tavern; dark & dingy, walls painted black with pentagrams spray-painted everywhere...

I cannot evade the seemingly forced etiquette of the younger kids, as in 30 Swedes looking at each other for what to do next, and everyone kind of throwing their fists in the air & mimicking in unison. *Or maybe I'm just old.* Maybe this is the way you probably looked at 16 to some jaded 30 year old bastard...

Moments before DOOM finished, I snuck out the front & built my little campsite in the patch of trees. Slept well in fact, waking to the clearest of cobalt skies. Made my way across town & here I now am, with Carl Mydia of thrash band Exekutor sitting before me. I was hoping to meet with Jonas of LIFELOVER before slipping off to Helsinki, but as Mydia explained, Jonas is *"special"* & you must take him as he comes...

Says Carl Mydia, guitarist of Exekutor: *"We didn't decide to play thrash metal, it just kind of happened. Of course I didn't speak to the other guitarists sober for months & in that drunk period the band was being created. So it was lots of drugs & stuff, but it gave a lot of inspiration. Right now were gonna do a full length and play in Germany, Finland... In Stockholm there are many bands but not much clubs. There is kind of a... 'conquering style' among the bands, and that's not very good. So we focus on being friends with all the bands to create contacts & such. We are a network playing together now, maybe 10-15 bands, so we can create whole evenings. Soon we are doing a festival called Mosh Mofo Meet."*

"What's that translate to?"

"Idiot Meeting – haha…"

"What do you think created the competition in Sweden?"

"It's a cold country. In Germany, everybody likes everything – really good country for music. In Sweden they are not social – they have their own place, their own band, and trying to be very true to the music, so they release only 100 copies on their record."

"Cause they want to be a kvlt as possible?"

"Yeah. Some people just dig themselves down being 'true' & not releasing pictures, not playing gigs, only releasing 100 demos. That's it – they don't get anywhere."

"On a day to day basis, are people cold or is it only the metal scene?"

"No, only the metal scene. The punk scene is very left, and the metal scene doesn't care; people are kind of different. The metal scene is very progressive, because it eats all types of music. There is no 'pure metal' – people have the will to evolve."

"Is there a rivalry between Sweden, Norway & Finland?"

"Swedish black metal people don't like the Norwegians and such – but in death metal & thrash, it's a much happier music style. It's a lot of *'honor'* in black metal. That's why I couldn't play it – it became too much. We're just focusing on playing thrash, partying, having fun, you know? And it works."

"[He laughs as I say every word]: Living in The States you hear about Sweden as this metal capitol of the world, people are telling me when you're in a mall, the elevator music is Slayer."

"No, is not true... But everybody knows Black Sabbath, Alice Cooper, Slayer. Those guys, those old people out there, they know. The black metal scene is – a lot of people listen to black metal. But the bands that are playing, the old bands like Bathory, Gorgoroth, Darkthrone – they are kind of nice guys, but the people that are listening to black metal make it called as such. It's the audience, you know? If you talk to Fenriz, he is a nice guy. He doesn't cut his arms."

"What other countries in Europe are really into metal?"

"I hear in Italy, and in Spain as such. As soon as you have this Thor's Hammer tattoos, leather & studs, distortion on your guitar – they love you... I think the Swedish thrash scene will be a new wave of music in Europe & the world. I think we have a high potential – Executor, Conflagrated, Divider, Nuclear Torment."

"Is Madrid more of the metal city?"

"They have some extreme death metal bands there. I think they are consuming more music then they are producing. In Sweden we create, we don't listen to much. That's Swedish stupidity..."

"There's a real paranoia here that if normal people on the street smell pot on you they'll call the cops. Even if the cop suspects you are high, he can cotton swab your mouth."

"Yeah, everything that is illegal is the same. Cannabis & heroin is the same in Sweden. Some groups of headbangers just drink. Some smoke, some take cocaine, but there's not much cocaine in Sweden. Almost no heroin. When your out playing, people want to sell all the time."

"I was really into Berlin – what do you think"

"In Germany they like ideas – in Sweden we only like our ideas. Heh, heh…"

"How old are you"

"19"

"Can you start drinking at 18?"

"People drink here when they are 12."

"Is it like France, with wine at the dinner table?"

"No – we drink vodka & beer. People don't drink wine very much, only girls, sometime. Me & my friends, if we say were '*Doing French*' this evening, we mean we're not going to get very, very drunk – we're just going to be a little drunk all the time. That's '*Doing French*' in Sweden."

"Is there a movement to try & end the alcohol ban?"

"That happened at the beginning of the 21st century. The Swedish people were about to die, because they were drinking so much – like a half liter of alcohol per day."

"I hear the Finnish are extremely drunk."

"Yeah, that's why we like Finland. You can buy everywhere in Finland, and is way cheaper,. And Estonia is as such. We understood that drinking in Estonia is not good. It was like Auschwitz – everything was grey, there was no people. The food was tasting like shit. The toilets weren't clean, you know."

"Did the people…"

"They looked like they were living in prison. People was not out on the streets, they were in their houses. We went to a market that only was selling alcohol – a whole market. It was called 'SUPER-ALCO.' And you could buy six pack of vodka. And when you opened them, they were not these kind of things like a screw on Coca-Cola. So when you opened it, you couldn't end it. You have to drink it, the whole liter of vodka. That's how they drink… I have some relatives in old Russia, and that's like the 15th century over there. There's no electricity, nothing. Some houses they don't know who lived in that house, they just took it when they got there."

"What's the weirdest show you ever played?"

"We were playing in my hometown, 40km south of Stockholm, and we did not get any money but we got free beer for the whole night & it ended in the hospital. The whole band... My liver was damaged, totally, it didn't work. Because of an overdose, it was like 20 beers straight into the blood & through the liver. The heart was about to collapse – totally near coma & death. I woke up in my home next morning, still drunk as fuck & thought I was the best person in the world. Smelled whiskey in the whole room. The whole evening is black. And I know it will happen again.

"You have compulsory military service but it's easy to get out of, right?"

"You say '*I miss my mom*' & they're like '*OK, go home.*' They asked me questions, to see if I would go in the military. The last question was '*can you take orders?*' So I didn't get in."

"You should throw a fest called 'The Acoholocaust" with free beer."

Ha! Soon we'll be releasing a one track album called *Hellbitch Highlights* about the nice metal girls out there. And we'll do Mona Lisa on the front, take up her lips like that, & paint some cocaine under her nose..."

HELLSINKI

VII. *"suomi fennoscandia perkele"*

You know you are in Finland when the moment you step off the plane you are flanked by smoking sections *inside* the terminal... I thought I was doomed in Stockholm, Aussie having never booked us a ferry in advance. Everything was sold out for 4 days & if I were to make that Helsinki-to-Milan plane then we'd have had to scramble-drive through the icy reaches of Siberian Scandinavia – through the Northern tip of Sweden & over the Finnish border – in a 36 hour non-stop jolt of driving.

     Was I really about to take the Aussie's cougar *"fuck mission"* into the secretive, severed headed shows of Tampere? That would've been some real Ivan Reitman shit... I left him there – the Australian & his Dutch deathtrap of a van. What was the use anyway? The women he's gunning for all spit Black Eyed Peas rhymes & worship Ke$ha. I came to Finland for corpse-paint, not Avon blush...

     Helsinki does kind of look like Amsterdam, vaguely. It's got this Prague vibe, but supplanted on an exotic harbor with streets in a language that seems a blur of English & Russian. They lump all the words that comprise a sentence into one big word; every sign is a Porthaninkatu or a Karhupuisto or a Djurgardsvagen which changes every half block making Helsinki even more difficult then Berlin...

     Metal City HELLsinki... The street clothes are very Eastern European – a little on the neon side & plenty of those silk shirts with designs of komodo dragons or *Dragonball Z* characters. The shops are like blocky, black glass skyscrapers built for midgets & glued together with the lopsidedness of a Las Vegas casino. Or the perfectly sealed, plastic shopping centers of urban Tokyo... It is in the bear park, flanked by street names like Agricolagatan, Viides Linjen & Flemingsgatan when proves it's worth.

** *"vaaroissa psykoosi ja meditaatio"* **

You brace for another Stockholm, expecting ragged defeat. Send a dozen texts & go right to sleep, curled up in the public park & surrounded by street names like Agricolagatan, Viides Linjen & Flemingsgatan. One hour later you wake, rub your eyes – but this time nearly everyone has replied & brought that much more traffic along with them...

Enochian Crescent was formed in Finland in 1995 by guitarist Victor Floghdraki [*aka Karri Viktor Suoraniemi*], the man now driving me to their rehearsal space in his pimp ass convertible with the top rolled down...

I've heard them all, met many & interviewed many, many more – and Enochian Crescent are one of the only black metal bands that I actually *listen* to. When you weave together the tapestry of their whole, Enochian Crescent do not sound like any other BM band. That distinct Finnish vibe is raging; plenty of traditional instruments & native tongue, but they still permeate a blackened death juggernaut that is structured differently in terms of tone & atmosphere. The sound remains exotic but never in a corny, forced sense. It is a pure, natural strength through & through...

"I haven't done a live show with a full unit in nearly 5 years, and it drains man, it fucking drains. People don't understand – when you play live & you hit that spike & the whole world goes away, it's like a drug."

"It is. I totally agree – that's why I still love doing this shit. Sometimes, in the wee hours, when you haul heavy shit back to some van & think '*why the fuck.*' Then you think of the hour before when you were on stage & on fire & everyone else was on fire, you can't describe it… Its funny how its turned. Before you got something from the record sales & something from the gigs, and now its basically what you get from the gigs, it covers the costs. If you want to walk away with a little something you have to sell shirts. That's a double edged sword, in that you have to invest in the merchandise in the first place."

"A lot of people in the USA just live in their practice spaces & lie to the management that upkeeps the building – is that standard practice in Finland too?"

"Yeah."

"Ha! Good. Ok, well, tell me about Enochian Crescent…"

"We started out in 1995. My band Wings was playing at a festival, met the singer & had good ideas about what black metal should be; that it should have a deeper meaning then superficial theatrics. But still it should be somehow visually shocking even & cause some reaction in the crowd, but also the music should be varied, not the ongoing noisecore trend with bad production & every riff sounding almost the same."

"What were the ways, in particular, which you wanted to define yourself from the rest of the black metal pack?"

"I think if you asked me that question 10 years ago I would be much more verbose. Nowadays I think we've been around for awhile, so our back catalog defines us – no other band sounds like us, no other band does what we do. It's not arrogant to say this, but we are in our own bubble. Before it was hard for other bands, even the Finnish scene, to swallow us because we were so different. Nowadays things have grown…"

"Being a black metal band in Finland, I know there were rivalries between the Scandinavian countries in the heyday…"

"I think the old rivalry, when there was a sort of a war – it was basically teenage kids calling each other & saying empty threats. Impaled Nazarene were part of that, in that sense. The vocalist said he jokingly exaggerated stuff. I don't know how serious the Swedish & Norwegians were, but he admitted he was just stirring up shit. And I think in the old underground zines, things tend to get exaggerated easily. I must admit that many of our old interviews – especially if the questions weren't very interesting – we started to fabricate stuff just to, you know, make it more interesting for everybody. It's a kind of – if you have an extreme scene, its so easy to cause reactions. If the chances are there, some people will always grab it. So I think most of the war thing, it's a lot of noise out of nothing. And the stuff that was happening in the Norwegian scene, that makes it all sound so much more serious. People were getting killed & churches were actually being burned. I think that's something that lends more credibility to everyone else everywhere then should've been given."

"As far as direct anti-religious action, what happened ?"

"There were grave desecrations, stuff like that, but not as much as in Norway."

"When all that first happened, what was the perception in Finland? Was it in the newspapers?"

"No, it wasn't; the media was surprisingly quiet about it. But there were some fringe happenings in Finland – some drunk killed another drunk while listening to Norwegian black metal. Like '*ritualistic murder, blah blah blah*' headline. Every time a grave was knocked over, they got big headlines. But nothing from Norway except maybe a small insert. I think in Norway it was much bigger, of course. What I've seen from the tabloids, there was lots – even national television. But for us, in the underground, we knew the people. We were writing letters back then. I remember Bard Faust, I was pen pals with him. So it was kind of interesting – the guy you kind of know is all of a sudden in jail. But then again, when you know someone only through paper, you basically don't feel… He went and killed somebody. Ok. You don't really think about it.

"Tell me about the scene in Helsinki…"

"What is special about Finland, these past 10 years, is that metal music has been breaking into the mainstream. It also brings in people who are not so much into the metal itself, just hanging along to get a piece of the imagined success, the perceived success. The album I just gave you was #1 in the Medplast Charts last summer with 1000 sold. So the record sales are so down, the money we got out of it was nothing. I guess someone would see that as, '*They're number one*' haha, they're driving convertibles, haha... The Finnish scene, most take their shit very seriously; they're almost spiritual about black metal. If you think about Beherit, they had this mystic approach. Now Baptism, Behexen, even us – we have this spiritual level also. You have dedication among the bands, a non-compromising attitude..."

"Tell me about the spiritual side of the band..."

"'Religious Black Metal' – I think this is a good term to describe Finnish black metal all the time. In that sense, the prime movers in the bands, the lynchpins – they've been reading all the time, studying old mythologies. Basically not a formal spiritual practice – they have some sort of belief system or agenda they want to push through. Somebody can be a hardcore Satanist & say '*I just want to be with The Devil*.' And that's superficial. I think the most lasting & prominent bands have really studied something and you can read it in the texts and feel it in the music."

"The keys of Enoch – how does your band mythology tie into it?"

"It was & still is a thematic that has been intriguing for us. Basically, in the *Old Testament* there was a prophet called Enoch. But there are only a few chapters there & lots of stuff was left out. Everybody talks about *Revelations* & the end of the world prophecies, but in the *Old Testament* – the *Book of Enoch* – there's actually a lot more about that stuff. And the Nephilim, how they inter-bred with humans – ivery impressive texts because its thought provoking, its evoking, and I don't wonder for one second why they were left out. It doesn't really fit in with their other teachings. Also if I jump a little forward in the 15th century, the British guys – John Dee, he got the Enoch language deciphered through crystal gazing. Dee was actually an occult scientist. He met up with Edward Kelley who was good at getting messages from the other sphere. So they had a dynamic duo in that time & deciphered this mystic language, from some beings that claimed to be angels. With the internet, you get information from occult practitioners all around the world. Lots of old texts have been transcribed & can be downloaded in PDF form. It's all readily available if someone wants to look into that..."

"A lot of this goes back to Sumeria, Nibiru, 2012..."

"I think geometry, the numerical things – nature is nature, and humans invented the numbers. Whatever meaning we put in the numbers reflects the human existence. I don't think we will see the end of the world in December – at least not a concrete apocalypse..."

"Do you thick someone crazy will do something crazy just because they've been programmed with this number for so long?"

"Most definitely. There are doomsday cults all over the world. I just read about one in Russia where they moved to Siberia & built whole villages there. They live secluded from the world on a strict vegetarian diet. Nothing harmful – no TV, no smokes, no alcohol. They worship their living god, who was a taxi driver in Moscow. And then he moved there & founded a new religion. And thousands followed. *[**Sergey Anatolyevitch Torop a.k.a. Vissarion (Виссарион) heads the 'Church of the Last Testament' in the Siberian Taiga. He has around 4,000 followers (called 'Vissarionites') in 30+ villages & about 10,000 followers worldwide. Vissarion claims to be a reincarnation of Jesus Christ & teaches financial abolishment, veganism & the impending apocalypse]*."

"Do you have any good stories about touring Russia?"

"I haven't been there – I value my life that much. I've heard stories – bands whose drivers just disappeared with all the money & they had to go through Moscow's underground with all their gear in the middle of the night. It's Wild West, but the sheriffs are bad also."

"Will Russia join the EU?"

"I think the EU is really falling apart at the moment – I don't see Russia wanting to join. I think the monetary unit is about to implode – Greece, Ireland, Italy & Spain are really deep in their own shit. Belgium is following & Great Britain has all this debt they can never repay. What's left its France, Germany, Finland – they are the payers at the moment."

"What are the stereotypes of Finland?"

"Well we are silent, we don't have facial expressions – some of these things were true but the world has opened up, so maybe we should update our national stereotypes. We like alcohol, that is true, and we like out metal music, that is true. And long winters tend to create a brooding sort of people..."

"Is metal culture bigger here then in Norway or Sweden?"

"Well, at least locally it's going through the whole of society. Even in elementary schools it's OK to play metal. So I think its pretty much throughout every layer. Even in the deepest hick zones in the country you will find a radio station that plays metal. When I was a kid, what was called heavy metal back then now sounds like pop. So I think the general perception of 'what's extreme' has changed. If nowadays you turn on the radio & hear Morbid Angel you wouldn't be surprised, because it's accessible."

"About living through The Cold War, with the fear of Russia invading…"

"Mmm-hmm. In the 80's I was about 10 years old, and nuclear war was one thing all over the place. Veterans from the Second World War were still telling their stories about how big & bad Russia was. So of course you grew up in fear of Russia. Just look at the map – we are one tiny speck against one huge country, and the first the Red Army would march to. At least I lived on the west coast & we had a 3 hour ferry ride to Sweden, so it was interesting to get a glimpse of the more liberal culture. In Finland everything the political leaders were doing was in fear of Russia. Sweden was much more open then & under Western influence. It was difficult time, and I was very, very happy when the Soviet Union collapsed."

"Were there huge parades?"

"No – we just opened a bottle of vodka & put the knife on the table, heh heh…"

"Was there a Finnish equivalent to Joseph McCarthy?"

"No, it's kind of funny – the communists were never in power. It was always the Social Democrats & the Center Party – but they were treading on thin ice considering Russian politics. The communists tried at coup in 1918 – it was Finnish Whites against Reds. The Whites won & the communists were never in power after that. The Red Fear nowadays is racist fear, or the dominant liberal feminist green thinking & everything else is basically – even though it would have nothing to do with race – you are stamped a racist so easily if you're thinking anything else that isn't fitting into the modern values. And it's kind of funny that they promote they are liberals but nothing else is accepted. They are everywhere promoting supposedly free values, but if you think otherwise you are a racist or a Nazi, or a conservative, which is just as bad as Nazi these days."

"Even if you're moderately right wing?"

"Yeah, and what's even more shocking is that even if you are progressive & oppose their views, then you are conservative as well. So that's unfortunately where I see Europe heading. But that's politics & I've been trying to avoid politics – but now I've been rudely awakened. That's shocking for me…"

"Do you have good paranormal story?"

"Do you know the band Death SS? I heard that during one invocation ritual, a dagger poked out an eye from one of the guys. But I don't know if that's true… Other stories of ghosts, visual manifestations, moving objects – they're around. Other stuff about demonic invocations gone wrong & people's lives going to hell after that… I think there are forces beyond our normal scope of vision & understanding & different religions have different names for those forces. We don't normally see them or feel them, but when you subject yourself to something you can get incensed. Modern psychiatry calls it psychosis & I've seen that – when people become entirely different persons. It's kind of unsettling. You see people who are very sound in mind just collapse totally without any drugs or alcohol, but from going too deep into some spiritual practice. I'm not even talking the occult."

"Is yoga practiced by people here in the occult circles?"

"I used to do yoga intensely for a few years, even went to India for a month to check out what it was like there. I witnessed some pretty intense happenings, but even in Finland people that went too far with meditation went into complete psychosis or became other people when they met some 'enlightened ones.' And then you see people after this 'enlightenment' & they are wrecks. And that's something I wanted to avoid – putting my personal well being into the hands of someone else or some kind of presence. I don't trust any guru or occultist or anyone to fuck with my mind, spiritual or physical. I myself have luckily been avoiding this shit. I've had some interesting experiences with, what's it called… I had this one experience in my mid-20's. I was with this man & woman who were into the occult, and we had this group meditation experience and you put as little of this ointment on your wrist – I don't know what's in it, but most likely psychotropic. It was pretty intense. There was this guy, we were having the same vision. After we started talking – I saw him & he saw me out there on a spiritual plane. Basically, it was a tombstone planet, and we saw one another there. That was, I don't know – mind boggling. I can't say eye-opening, but to connect on that spiritual level… I know people who've seen ghosts. I know people who claimed to have been possessed. There is definitely shit happening… I'm getting Goosebumps thinking about the subject…"

** *"koskaan sanoa ei humalaisen venäläisen"* **

Day II: @ The PRKL Club, which is the first place you want to go in this town. It's essentially the big metal bar, open all day, all night – everyone hangs out here. The owner of the club was one of my main contacts here, but as my luck characteristically has it he's out of town until TUSKA [*the big metal fest*] starts this weekend which I again, characteristically, was unaware of & thus booked my flight to leave the day before it begins. *Huom Itselleni...*

Last night I hung out with Sami from Bestial Burst Records & noise band Will Over Matter, who was as soft spoken as he was a literal giant. He must've been 6 foot 8 & his girlfriend 6 foot 4. They took me on a tour through Vaasankatu Street, which is the major hang out spot of the city. We drank at the local bar, bumped into one of the guys from Deathtoll 80k still nursing his hangover from Obscene Extreme, and ended up meeting a Norwegian girl named Betsey from Boobie Sue & the Skavaböle Bastards that graciously let me crash on the couch...

Today is all *milk from da mudda's teet* – effortlessly, might I add. I have an interview scheduled every coming hour. I had a quick chat with Ceaseless Torment [*brutal oldschool thrash ala Kreator/Destruction*] & met with Matias of black metal slicers Dodskvlt, who all reaffirmed the need of Satan in ones music & fairly much every major topic so far in this book. Matias & I set up an extra interview with his side project Anguished, which he claims features one of the craziest female vocalists in metal that no one's heard of anywhere but Helsinki...

Mitja Harvilahti from Moonsorrow – the genre-bending, super-epic, melodic-death-doom-pagan-folk amalgam – wheels up on his bicycle. The Ceaseless Torment guys come shake his hand, then we get to the gritty. Moonsorrow are in the upper echelons of their particular scene – one that has steadily & rightfully gained more traction in the United States over the past few years. "Epic Heathen Metal" best describes them, but I wouldn't hesitate to throw in terms like "*tribal*" or "*majestically blackened*" as well. For proof, do note that their last album was all but two tracks, and each of them clocked in over 30 minutes each...

"*The first time in Russia, that was really crazy – the whole audience was completely nuts. The security was completely nuts. This one guy almost killed me. I made the mistake of shaking hands with one girl & suddenly 10 hands grabbed me & I was crowd surfing. It was alright until one of the huge security guys – he was shaped like triangle, and nothing but muscles. He was piss drunk – he just saw someone surfing & didn't like that at all. I saw his face, eyes all red, and he grabbed me in this horizontal position, I thought my neck's gonna break. Then the audience, they kept punching his face – punching fists all over, and he wouldn't let go. And then the other guitar player, he grabbed my feet and got me back to the stage. Then I thought I really was gonna die. Russia is a very interesting country. You can have problems if you don't know what to do. You should have a Russian driver, because their is always fake cops and some need bribes. You need someone who speaks Russian so you don't lose too much money. Some stuff gets stolen on the trains, in sleeping compartments. I kind of like Russia otherwise – the people are great, great sense of humor. Its not so Soviet anymore."*

"Ever made it to Romania or Greece?"

"Romania has been interesting every time. The people are very good, organizers very good. But in Greece we had the worst show ever, this guy, he was this organizer that had run out of money. But he never canceled the whole thing. We were supposed to have a shuttle taking us from the airport far, far away to the festival. So we started calling people and they said '*there was a car accident,*' which was a lie because he didn't have money to buy gas. So we had to take taxis & a local bus because we didn't want to cancel the show – it was our first time in Greece. We could've gotten a hotel and went to the beach, but we said we're gonna do it no matter what. Once we got to the festival area, the guy refused to give us money for the busses & taxis because we didn't have any receipts. No toilets even in the Festival because he couldn't afford them."

"Were people shitting in holes in the ground?"

"Yeah they were. They were all sitting down on the ground – the festival was totally halted until they came. We were lucky enough to get a ride back to the hotel, but the guy never booked us a room, so we had to sleep on the floor. In the morning I found the guy and, '*hey, where have you been?*' Well, I've been sleeping. And you've been sleeping while all these bands are living on the floor? Its fucked up. And he starts telling me lies, shit about his mother, kept telling me lies. It was unbelievable. It turns out this guy paid the booking agency, but the next day he realized he couldn't pay the deposit, he went back to the bank & took it back. People like that destroy the whole festival scene."

"How have your USA tours gone?"

"I was really surprised by how strong the pagan/folk metal scene has become. In 2005 I thought we would never make it to America then we got an offer, and it was mind-blowing to see a lot of people coming to the shows. Actually I've enjoyed touring the USA much more then I've thought, compare to touring Europe where the venues are in fields or people's houses somewhere. The last tour we did with Finntroll, it was the best holiday I had & tour as well. Everyday I would just go to the city, be a normal tourist then get to the venue, play a show & have a party. It was very pleasant. I was impressed by Austin. Playing Hollywood is always fun… Canada is more like touring Europe…

"Moonsorrow is an overtly pagan band…"

"Paganism is strongly tied to nature, because nature is where all pagan belief systems go in every culture. For me its respecting traditions & history of my people, or any people, and that we are part of nature. Something I also wanted to point out about the pagan metal thing – so many people think that it's something that should be Nordic & also how so many right wing people use it, and that doesn't make any sense. There are pagans all over the world – Russia, South America, in Europe, Africa – if you are a fascist, or Nazi – these are the people that destroyed all this throughout history. They are destroying all this – it doesn't have anything to do with paganism…"

"What's the stupidest question you were ever asked by a journalist?"

"I think it was asked to Henri, somebody wondered about his pubic hair. Someone asked if they could have some of his pubic hair. He said yes."

"What is the Finnish nightlife like?"

"The first of May, there's a huge party – everybody are in the streets & people piss all over the place. Finnish people, they use all the excuses they have to drink, so they get piss drunk the first and just piss everywhere. The streets are just flowing, flooded with urine & passed out people everywhere…"

"How are the cops?"

"I think the police are quite fine here. The security guards think they're police but have no rights to beat up people… They don't eat so many donuts like they do in America. I think the funniest thing I saw in America – the stereotype of American police officers eating donuts. I saw 5 of them eating huge buckets of donuts. We don't have much police violence here. In Mexico they didn't have a fence, only a line of police officers. And the audience were smashing them up against the stage. I've never seen police officers so scared in their faces. They didn't have guns…"

"What was the Mexico tour like?"

"Times were crazy; we had to sign babies & everything. We almost got killed by some gangsters. We went to a park, late at night. During the day it was like a market square, people selling clothes. But at night it was run by some gang. We saw them playing football & we were drunk, just went here to have a good time. And they said *'hey gringos, wanna die?'* asking for money or something. Only thing that saved us was we were musicians, playing a show. They said *'ok, but if you ever show your face here again.'* We had experiences of getting shot at in America. In Seattle, somebody pulled a gun. There was a fight between some guys' sister & her boyfriend and then the boyfriend came in with a gun and shot..."

"Where were you playing?"

"El Corazon... In Houston there was a huge gang war during out show. There was a disco next to the venue – a couple hundred people came out & started shooting each other. At least one person died, others went to the hospital. The amount of shots were dozens of them, like serial fire, ****rrrrr-duhduhduhduhduh****. It was horrible to watch from the balcony. Then some 20 police cars, helicopters came in, firing warning shots... In 2005 we played a show in Lithuania for the first & last time. Many countries had just joined Schengen agreement so you didn't have to show passport at the border. Lithuania was not among those. A fact that Henri, our guitar player, found out at the port when we hopped on the ferry to Estonia. So there we are with only one guitar player, thinking of how to pull off the best show. We bought beers & started planning on the set list according to the fact that we had more simplistic sound & stage presence. Suddenly our singer Ville started to sound weird. He felt like his vocal cords were on fire & he could hardly speak anymore. He became completely mute. There was a shuttle bus taking us to the festival, which was a really pretty festival site in the woods. What caught my eye was a huge number of Hell's Angels or similar gang in the woods doing drugs & drinking. I stayed away from them as far as I could. Also lots of Baltic skinheads started to pour in. Ville still couldn't sing anything & we agreed that I start singing the first song & our drummer Marko will handle the rest. Ville, if possible, would sing whenever he could pinch something out his throat. The show time was at midnight and it became apparent that all the bikers & skinheads were actually there to see us. They pushed the other crowd out of their way & seemed really enthusiastic. I was sure that we will get beaten up for the one guitar/no vocals show. We started with song called 'Sankarihauta,' and after 5 seconds my guitar amp blew up. So no guitar at all... I started singing & after while Marko continued when I forgot the rest of the lyrics. The crowd was insane! Huge mosh pit of bikers & skinheads were spinning around the area & the rest of the more normal metal crowd were jumping further away. Someone gave me a new amp & I could go on playing. Then Ville's bass amp broke down, and so did my guitar's electronics. Much of the show was only handled by drums & keyboards & our drummer singing. He forgot the lyrics at some point and had to improvise. What came out of his mic was something like '*I chopped my cock with an axe, I put my fingers in a circle saw, now the boys are poking me with sticks!*' We couldn't but laugh onstage. After the show we tried to get away as fast as possible, but all the bikers wanted to carry our gear & get autographs. Some lower in the rank member got beaten up by the boss because he asked for an autograph from our keyboard player before he could. One guy had arrived all the way from Austria & told us how it was the best concert ever…"

** *"elävät pelossa varastettu penis"* **

Mitja Harvilahti dips out & two LAIBACHian soldiers stand at attention, with their own piecemeal army get ups & little fez hats. They are an industrial two piece called Grotesque Gallery that have crafted their own mock-dictatorship. They come from Dieselgrad, Kirkidia where *"an Austrian doctor known as Schicklgruber – a criminal hunted by interpol for his illegal tests with patients – formed his own land & country. According to the natives, the sun has never shined there…"*

"Things got violent in Israel – the Israelis tried to slaughter the Lebanese & spread combs which were able to shoot lasers through the head. The laser-beam melted the penis that pierced the body, went into the heart & killed a man. Schicklgruber demanded the blueprints for the robotcomb, the LCSCC [Laser-Controlled Surgical Cyborg Comb]… In the year 2004 Schicklgruber managed to jack the blueprints for LCSCC model RX-10. He built a robot-comb which was able to fly like a bird. He understood that he now could have his revenge against everyone who ever had doubts of his generosity again – and to conquer the whole world." If I'm correct, Grotesque Gallery works for him…

Gas L. Arsson [*aka Kristian Gustafsson*]: "Everyone talks of Finland as the promised land of heavy metal, but my view is quite the opposite. The bands are good, people can play – but if you have some band that plays like Metallica, you don't need another. One problem we have had is that there is another band similar to us – Turmion Kätilöt. They are widely know already. We sent our demo all over the world, and everyone said in Finland there's already Turmion Kätilöt, so… In Russia where we are going to focus our promotion, they accept better this music…"

"What's up with filming videos in Russian missile silos?"

"We did an exploration – we'd driven in our car through the Baltic countries, Poland, and visited abandoned soviet missile silos & abandoned cities and such. Our visual thing – collapsed shit."

Vesa Turunen: *"**Post-Soviet apocalypse…"*

"Is a lot of Russia collapsing?"

"I wouldn't say that Russia nowadays is collapsing, but some things they just leave– if they don't need it, they leave it. Factories, stuff like that…""

"Is Estonia all grey, dull & creepy?"

"The more South you went, the crappier it got."

"**Estonia was all white – like prison. When we got to Latvia, immediately after the border we saw this Soviet style block of flats."*

"What was Poland like?"

"We were supposed to go to The Wolf's Nest, the Nazi fortification… We were driving down the road – it needs to be somewhere here. It has to be grey… But they were selling tickets to the place. We call it 'theme park Hitler.' But this wasn't scary at all – it had like a bar, camping, people with cameras… We made videos, day by day & include our music. We do a full concept."

"About the uniforms…"

"When we walk around wearing these uniforms – all different kind of vibes, looks, how people react. It might mislead…"

"**Kirkidia is our own home-made dystopia, led by a dictator and sauron. It's a long story. The name of our coming album is a district in Kirkidia. And the place is totally post-Soviet…"*

"It's like a mixture of Nazi Germany & the Soviet Union, but we put this humorous twist on it, and that's a point people don't understand, at least in Finland because here you cannot have any humor in your metal because when your singing of your dragons & knights you have to be dead serious."

"**There is history on how this formed, and has to do with this Kirkidian owl which is a mechanical bird that kills people. They were sometimes afraid that it comes, it burns your penis off through your brain with a laser. These people really believe this owl comes, and are afraid, because their penis will disappear.. "*

*** "alkoholismi ei ole stereotypia" ***

From the files of Vanguard: *"Spawned into being at the turn of the millennia, Vanguard started it's musical refinement to create a coalition of raw power, massive momentum & beauty. Their victory in a band contest at Germany's Wacken Open Air festival earned them the chance to forge 'Succumbra,' the band's debut. Recorded & mixed in Hamburg at Tornado studios, mastered at Alex Krull's Mastersound studio, the first steps were taken to bring this force of nature into the world. After their debut, the band reformed its rhythm section & played gigs at TUSKA*

Open Air in Finland, Wacken Open Air in Germany & gigs here & there, including a couple of dominations in Russia. Soon after their reformation & live work, Vanguard parted with German label Armageddon Music after its split into two different companies. The band entered D-Studios in Finland to start working on their second album in the summer of 2007. No compromises were made & the follow-up 'Hydralchemy' was perfected in a year. The finishing touches were added by Minerva Pappi at the legendary Finnvox Studios. It was then released by Shadowworld Records in the beginning of 2009. At the start of 2010 Vanguard is back in the studio working on their third album, booking gigs between recording...

Meet Jori Grym, co-vocalist of Vanguard: "In Finland the scene is pretty small, everybody knows everybody. I'm a co-founder of imperiumi.net – one of the biggest metal media sites in Finland. Then I rolled into *Suomi Finland Perkele*, which was the first Finnish zine *[**not to be confused with the classic Impaled Nazarene album of the same name]*."

"What exactly does that name mean?"

"It's one of our national motto's from this book about the finish/Russian war. That was like our big fight – when Russia tried to invade us & couldn't. It mean, like, '*Finland Fuck Yeah!!*' so its to the point, and funny. And then Impaled Nazarene took it & it was a great punch line."

"So your band Vanguard..."

"Vanguard started around the millennia. As teenagers we hated – the metal scene started to go industrial. Tiamat & Moonspell, My Dying Bride all released these weird techno albums. We really wanted to do something else. So we had a piano, not a keyboard, male & female vocalist – cello & guitars, of course. The gothic metal scene, the dark metal scene or whatever you would call it – it was Theatre of Tragedy, Tristiania. We cut our first demo in 2003. Karmageddon Media heard it, invited us to this battle of the bands at Wacken. We won & got a record deal through that. But the same guys that ran it, it was a pretty new label, so our managers were Sabrina Klarrsen from Holy Moses & Lars from Metallium. But they split up, the company started fighting & broke into two. They only kept Blaze Bailey & Doro Pesch. They didn't have the money to invest... Then we started making our second album by ourselves. Finland's small, but we know everyone, so it's fairly inexpensive. I think we were of the last generation of bands that used to get plane ticket & money & '*come cut a record here.*' Now everybody does it themselves & sells their final product. But the first record, we were flown to Hamburg & lived there a month…"

"What was the result?"

"We got a lot of weird fan mail from around the world, but never got a major label. We jerked around quite a bit with EMI. And it was really annoying because the main A&R guy, he called us up & had us come for coffee to his office like 3 times. It was the main A&R guy, and he introduced us to a Finnish guy & set up some gigs for us & '*eh, maybe not.*' So we never got that big deal, but released our second album in 2005. We've started working on this third one, people started families, life changing moments, things like that… We weren't too hard, we weren't too heavy, we weren't too black metal for goth bands & we're too goth or pussy for Cradle of Filth fans. So we have to start doing Nightwishy stuff or something like that? Or start doing Dimmu Borgir-ey, Cradle Of Filth sort of stuff? And we decided we'd do more blastbeat stuff & dropped the lead cello melodies. The bass & the rhythm part is now real heavy, up-tempo, high-tempo stuff. We made half of [the new record] already, but we're still recording/mixing the string sections. This new record, it sounds like something nobody else has really done yet. We have this Dimmu Borgir/Cradle of Filth type stuff but with a female vocalist and catchy tunes – catchy melodies, clear leading melodies that are good, like mixing Sentenced-styled guitars but with a rock n' roll chorus. So we steer away from that Within Temptation, operatic – she sings, she doesn't howl. She's a rock n' roll singer. And there's this Finnish melodic metal – it's a brilliant fuckin' combo…"

"Tell me about the Finnish scene…"

"In Europe the Finnish scene, Scandinavia has this elite status. We have Children of Bodom, Nightwish, HIM – but we have this huge host of not-super-big but still touring bands. Norway has it's black metal, Sweden has its melodic metal. Finland, the thing is its really small & humble. Everybody's humped everybody… Everybody is kind of wanting to be a star, but we don't get into too many pissing fights. It's pretty tight."

"What are the stereotypes of Finland?"

"We are heavy drinkers – that is unquestionably the thing that all our jokes combine to. Not as bad as the Russians, cause they don't really have jobs… I think if you go to a bar in Germany & you order a shot its 2 centiliters. In Slovenia its 3. In Finland its 4, but in Russia it's a full liter, haha. All of our jokes, all of our depression things are linked to alcohol. Everyone has their stereotypical dad or grandfather that drank away their inheritance. Then, of course the cold, the dark, the depression. Metal, depression – it's our thing & it is really cold & really dark for really fucking long. We're not social in an open, huggable way – we speak usually pretty straight to the point. We don't look each other in the eye in public transport; it's considered rude actually… We have really strict medical laws, really strict food laws. In our fucking pharmacies where everything has to be prescribed – we can't even buy more then 10 aspirins at one time. And the whole service culture thing is pretty new here in Finland. And we don't tip – it's really hard for us, because we never know what to do. We don't even say '*hi*' when you go to a store, or to the bus driver… As a foreigner it might seem we're very closed, rude & unfriendly, unwelcoming because our culture is like… Klingon culture. Ha ha ha…"

"As far as metal in Finland goes…"

"We have youth cultures that are uniquely our own, and I think heavy metal is one thing that keeps us separated. Now the big Finnish media are starting to write about us. Sentenced, Stratovarius used to sell hundreds of thousands of albums – no one knew them in the mainstream media. Finland is a small country – if you sell 100,000 you're a superstar to them. And when you talk about Finnish exporting culture, the government supporting music, it was never heavy metal because it was considered fringe music. A couple of these big hits, like HIM, the media realized '*hey this is our music.*' These guys are selling millions. So now it's flip-flopped, invited into Independence Day meetings with the president. But then again, it still is a fringe culture even though it's much more massive. Here it's not weird if you have long hair. I used to manage a security company that did international logistic security, and no one thought it was weird that I had long hair & jewelry…"

"What about politics?"

"I follow a lot of American culture for fun. I watch *Colbert Report* everyday, *The Daily Show*, Bill Maher. I see Glenn Beck, and I know how crazy it is – this republican goes haywire. You got Michelle Bachman, this huge Muslim fear, this huge money in the presidential campaign. We don't have anything like that. We have really lame politics which nobody follows because everybody is the same. This year we have a little bit of a splash because the economic crisis brings a little more conservative. This last election, our congress, basically, got an almost majority vote on the 'True Finns party.' This real redneck, Christian…"

"Like the Tea Party in The States?"

"Pretty much, yeah, but as soon as they got into the government they do exactly what they've always done. So that's a part of the American culture that really drives the country, but in Finland its like me & 3 other guys that actually watch Colbert. We get the HBO, the fashions, the crappy music, but we don't get Glenn Becks, we don't get religious, we don't get anything like that in Scandinavia at all."

"Have you traveled all over Europe?"

"Russia is always weird – it's really close & a totally different culture. You jump on a train & two hours east suddenly the whole world changes, the color scheme changes. The Moonsorrow guys, when they went there they didn't have that much money, per se, but when they walked out the train there were mothers of the organizers bringing them pastries & stuff like that. They have ex-KGB guys armed at all times following them just in case. And they started mingling with the band. They were kind of like *'I don't know if I want a guy that drinks even more then a Finnish guy – train to kill & killed a lot – armed all the time'* with them. The bodyguards were *'let's sit down & start drinking.'* They were so drunk they couldn't even walk – they'd be really upset if we just got up to leave. The drummer, or something, stayed with them. when the bartender said, *'guys it's time to close'* they didn't threaten him or anything, but they showed their weapons & said, *'we're gonna stay here and drink all night.'* Ok. Locked up & left them with the bar. After that they went to the security guards' home where he had all these old medals he won in war, and he wanted to give it to them. And its really offensive if you don't take it. I don't want your war medals, you know? But he went home with them…"

"What is the message of Vanguard?"

"I write lyrics that are not too modern – I consider it poetry, I write it separately in poem form then fit it into the music. We don't have a message, per se, it is about human emotion & I try to write it in a more old fashioned, gothic way. There's a lot of despair; some love & sex, but I try to write not so obviously. People see a Rorschach thing. I'm a huge atheist & am trying to write a book about atheism – very anti-religious guy, and a pretty hard skeptic. Religion is something I don't tolerate at all…"

"How do you feel about the progression of metal journalism in particular?"

"The thing is I think most media has stopped being – at least in Finland, it wasn't professional. I know professional journalists but they never did heavy metal stuff, or never got paid for it. Right now only 3 are employed, and they are all editors at like 3 papers, run their own blog, and video blog & sell something as a PR worker. I think its changed into – the net, its easy to produce videos. Videos are the way – short snips, Youtube. Band websites don't exist anymore, except where you get your band press kit. I think people consume music media these days as Facebook links, Twitter links. I don't see a big thing going for music journalism, or written things – or even MTV styled programs. I think its going to be clips, bloggers. Books are a bit different – people still like books, so I think they still have a chance. My girlfriend is writing a book about Waltari for a big Finish publishing company. She gets paid a little, but not that much considering her work hours. If you condense it, she's probably making 10 cents an hour. But I bet some people will read that & she'll get some respect out of it. But magazines? When people say '*I heard this interview on so & so*,' I think its Twitter feed, links. Maybe 4 years ago I thought I'd start up journalism again & started emailing Brave Words & Bloody Knuckles. And they were interested in me writing from Finland, and I talked to Blabbermouth if their feed would release video. But I never got into it. I think 5 years later everyone's doing it & no ones getting paid. Bands are doing it themselves, so I don't think journalists are necessary anymore. I think record companies are no longer in the business of selling records, so they need to replace it with something else. So I think where it's heading, what it will be will be '*Journalistic PR.*' I don't know if it's that bad yet, but I bet its going that way…"

"What else would you like to talk about?"

"Finland is one of the most atheist countries, but they say they're Christian out of tradition. You know, our church law is actually written into our law, so we do not have this separation of church & state. It has a low influence, but it pissed me off. 'Let *the priests have their ways*' – that's how people think about it. But we should replace these ancient fucking barbaric, misogynist, weird, rape & kill things & just – don't we have anything more beautiful then god sending people to kill his child or open slavery or women abuse? Read the bible – it's so fucking bizarre. It's just the worst argument. Is this really what we want to put on the alter? A crucified fucking person and then get married? Don't wear a crucifix, wear the hammer of Thor…"

** "*rakas turisteja, voisitko lopettaa hymyillen*" **

Day III; back at PRKL Club, this time waiting on Ana from Anguished. Going to take my flight to Italy in the morning & miss out on TUSKA, but I'll be getting something unexpected in return. One of the guys from Fides Inversa [*the Italian black metal band from Under The Black Sun*] will be meeting me Downtown Milan & plans to interview me for some zine he writes for. Says it'll be worth my time, that he'll push me through to important Italian characters...

Last night I found my savior in a drunken Finn who said the only three good bands in all of musical history were Bathory, Morbid &

Nifelheim. I asked what he thought of Impaled Nazarene, who I said were one of the best Finnish metal bands ever & he laughed & called them "*totally gay.*" The next morning, he told me Mikka was his best friend & then called Impaled Nazarene & asked if they wanted to meet with me. Mikka was busy, but would do so if I made it to TUSKA. Well, it karmically counts, right?

To make it further a bizarre coincidence, this metal savior who discovered I was about to wander off into the night & instead offered me a crash spot, drinks & pizza, was also randomly the new guitarist for Anguished, who I am about to meet momentarily...

While this drunken pizza scene was going down, I had apparently been texted by Sami from Beherit, who was drinking down the street at his record shop with Nichjolas from Shingn & the guy from Dodheimsgard & they wanted to drink booze with me. *Metal City HELLsinki man, Metal City Helsinki...*

I swung by early on this last of my Finnish days & hung with Sami Tenetz for a bit, drinking Budweiser & listening to Ghost. The entire shop window was like as Beherit advertisement. Not that I'm blaming him or complaining – there should by Thy Serpent graffiti tags all over the building as far as I'm concerned...

The demented "*give it 5 years & she'll be Queen-Bee devastator*" arrives. With one good album & the right hands, Ana will one day own the world:
"What did you think of Texas?"

"Everyone had something to say about my tattoos & no one knew what Finland is."

"Ha! Figures..."

"When I started in black metal, it was two years ago. I just thought it would be nice to record an album, because you know the stereotype that women don't understand anything about music, and in black metal – nobody was really excited when I asked people to play. So I just play all day by myself. I've had a session drummer – recorded the album & published with Hammer of Hate [Records]. The vocals are very raw, the music is very primitive black metal. Like Darkthrone, Burzum – the old black metal from Norway. Its kind of simple, suicidal. The difference is the vocals – the songs are raw. There's also some melodies, but that's it..."

"Tell me about the black metal scene in Finland..."

"Finnish black metal is this thing where people play live, drink, have fun – but when they're at home they are very depressive & suicidal. We don't show it though. I think Finnish people – we are very suicidal &

depressive. I think everyone in Finland, its just wait for the weekend and get wasted."

"Ok, back to Texas. What were some aspects coming there, to Dallas, that you were shocked by?"

"I was always surprised by how friendly the people were & how they talk to you,. People, wherever I went, they were staring at me. Cause they're so much more Christian in The States. That was the thing – the looks…"

"The Wal-Mart thing – I know they tried in Europe but they all closed down…"

"I'd never been in such a big store. It was so huge when we went shopping I was exhausted the day after… Oh yeah – the gun thing. Everybody has a gun & you can buy one at any Wal-Mart. That was kind of shocking, when you are buying meals & some people are passing by with guns? What the fuck? Is this normal?

"Can you own a hunting rifle here, is that it?"

"Yeah."

"So did you go to Houston? Because Houston is like Dallas for real Texans. Dallas is where the Northerners move so they can wear their cowboy hats & pretend their from Texas. But Houston is like 4 times the size of Dallas & you have a Wal-Mart's 10 times the size of the Wal-Mart you went to, and the freeways are like 12 lanes – and named after George W. Bush – and the cops are like pit-bull Nazis and… I hate Texas. I passionately hate Texas…"

"I've never seen homeless people, so we went downtown. There was one black guy, 60 or something – he was wearing everything that he owns & carrying a bible. Screaming *'Jesus loves you, Jesus saves you.'* And when he saw us – *or me* – and my cross upside-down tattoos, he started to follow us. He was shouting after us – *'wait, Jesus wants to save you!'* He followed us like 8 blocks."

"About not seeing homeless people – does the Finnish government have projects for everyone? Cause I've seen no trace of what we'd call home bums…"

"Yeah. If you live in Finland, or Scandinavia or parts of Europe & try to live in some garbage place, there's gonna be social workers who will take you out of there, take you to the hospital, give you a home & food & everything like that. You can't live on the street in Finland."

"In the USA, it's more like 'fuck you go die.' Like in Seattle, they shut down all the mental institutions & just dumped everyone on the streets. They just decided not to pay for them anymore. So all over California too, it's full of crazy people everywhere on the streets."

"In Finland if you are sick & go to the hospital, you don't pay anything. Its like €20 a year. But when my sister birthed her son [in Texas], it was $15,000."

"Ok, ok, back to music – the essentials in black metal. Occult, Satanism, etc. What does it all mean to you?"

"Well you have to worship the devil if you're true black metal, hehe. That's just the way it is. It isn't black metal if there isn't any idealistic message… Its just a way to express your frustration, hate, anger – hate against Christians & every other religion. These days I hate very much the Islamic. Cause I live in a place where there is a lot of Muslims. They just fucking disgust me so much. And in the next album ,you're really gonna hear some of that shit."

"Extremism in black metal – do you have any cut off?"

"I'm a really suicidal person; I have these cuts all over my hands. At some point I have thought this is kind of too much. So last winter I was very drunk & took some drugs & was feeling miserable so I took a knife & stabbed my hand. It went straight through the arm [she shows me her huge scar gash]. I had to go to surgery & it didn't heal correct, so now I cant play guitar like I used to. I can't feel my fingers like – only half. When I think now, it wasn't necessary,. You can just cut yourself, get a tattoo. But sometimes I'm too extreme… [Show me her arm, which is all tore up] All of these are scars; it's not even a suicidal thing. It's just – physical pain… I like this body modification thing. This hand that looks like this [*she holds up her scabbed, sliced up hand*], it's not always that I'm feeling miserable that I cut myself. I just wanted it to look like this. It looks disgusting, weird or something…"

ITALIA

ITALIA

VIII. *"vi prego di scusare la mia merda in inglese"*

Mr. V & I enter *Il Duomo*, the Milanese apex of Catholic Soul. Where one would expect monuments to hope, we find mummified corpses of Cardinals. Preserved for morbid display, the waxy prunes of flesh rest in glass encasement...

Tonight is a celebration of awful ideas in the land of The Pope. How better to grace a first impression to God's holy land other then sip wine with a representative of Fides Inversa? VoidAD is the guitarist, the man who has brought me here to night for duel interviews. He's a brilliantly cocky bastard to be sure, enthusiastic & so very Italian, hiding behind thick aviator sunglasses...

Mr. V is the culprit who penned these words, describing the purpose of his nightmare machine: *"The musical & philosophical emanation of an intricate spiritual reflection, in order to self glorify the being through the inversion of the Judeao-Christian tradition & faith... The first opus 'Hanc Aciem Sola Retundit Virtus (The Algolagnia Divine),' is a revaluation of Christian Death, which, from a primeval punishment against the sinner, becomes an instrument of revenge towards Abraham's God. Through the first three stations, representing the main examples of malamorte, the concept reaches a final thought with an ode to the mighty Opposer, the flaming Rebel. Sin and Virtue become the instruments, for he who was born as a son, to reclaim his right to the Lord. Killing God in this sense, through Sin or our own Death, the individual will reborn in the glory of Cain's blood, not as a man, but as a God. The path undertaken by Fides Inversa needs, for the aim of his complete conceptual purity, total anonymity. Neither the minds behind the words, nor the arms behind the musical performance shall be revealed, in order to give not glory to men, but to our Lord..."*

"Are you happy living in Italy?"

"Is not so simple, because nowadays Italy is living this great decline. Young people have not so many possibilities to work. I always need to express myself in an artistic manner, but nowadays I think in Italy this is not so much possible... Black metal is a different approach in respect to other kinds of metal. For me its something really spiritual, you know? It's like a religion. I have a Christian background – my family is Catholic. And yeah, you know, here in Italy it's always very difficult for someone who wants to free themselves from such great oppression. You know, you have the Vatican. Maybe you in America cannot understand this problem because it is really great. We have a great censorship with every kind of art which does not respect Catholicism & Christianity in general. So it's been a great battle to spread these kinds of ideas.

"How did the band come together?"

"Fides Inversa is my personal project; the band was born just to bring this onstage. It follows my personal beliefs – not just an inversion of Christianity, but the inversion seen in a philosophical niche. It's a different approach then other black metal bands that only go onstage to make some noise. To me it's a ritual. I believe to go onstage is to build up my own alter to praise the inversion of the world conception of the universe. It's a universal concept because everything you watch nowadays is wrong. Everything is going wrong – politically, culturally. Everywhere. In Italy we suffer from the religious aspect because it pervades every aspect of our lives. You have to rebel from this sort of parody which is not the real truth, you know? My lyrics are to try and make everyone realize that everything must be inverted for the sake of truth. Because the truth is not what you see around you. The truth is inside – this is not probably the real world. The real world is probably what you see in your dreams. It's not so easy for me to explain this concept in English, but I'm sure you can understand"

"Are BM shows banned here because of the state?"

"If you go to the South of Italy it is not so possible to make some kind of shows. If you have a name like Impaled Nazarene you will never play in the South of Italy because there will be some fuckin' priest who will tell it to the mayor or the cardinal and they'll try to break up the show. It's fucking stupid, you know?"

"I was baptized catholic. I never went to catechism to be official, but if I went to the Vatican and demanded to legally be excommunicated on record will they help me?"

"Yeah, sure. If you send them a letter they will excommunicate you. My drummer was sent this piece of paper that said '*you are no more catholic.*' Heh heh… In Italy we suffer the same problem as you in the USA – pedophile priests, big time."

"Real big problem. When that was exposed something like 10,000 kids that came forward. And the pope knew what was going on, and they kept moving priests from parish to parish."

"Same as in Italy. We had school religion teachers – religion is a matter of science, you know. And I had this priest teaching religion & he tried to make some homosexual proposal to some guy at the school…

Christianity is all based on material reality, which is a shame, because Jesus Christ never talked about this. This is the great problem – Christianity does not have a great conception of spirituality. You are only going to a church Sunday morning, praying to god in front of a priest who does not care about you or about god. He makes his shit with the young."

"I had a friend in the USA whose parents were real Christian, and they actually brought in a priest to sprinkle holy water on him and exorcize the heavy metal demons out of him because he was really into Metallica at like age 12. Does this happen here much?"

"Heavy metal demons? Not in particular, but demons yeah. Exorcism is something concrete for priests here. I think it's a question of suggestion. We are just using 10% of our brains capabilities, and the other 90% is unknown to us. So I think this 90% could be also part of this shit, or telepathy, stuff like that. In Italy exorcisms are more everyday, maybe not in a big city like Milan. The real shame is people really believe in this shit. They give a lot of credit to water & stupid fuckin priests & it is no more then me or you. Maybe he's more sinner then me. It's really pagan from this side of views. Christians believe that every kind of damage you have in your life that's going wrong is due to a demon. There is an equilibrium between evil & good."

"Do you tip waiters & waitresses in Italy?"
"No."
"What countries to people tip in Europe?"
"Just United Kingdom. This is more Anglo-Saxon."
"In the United States they only give you…"
"Yeah, I know."
"Well they give you $2 dollars an hour and you live on tips"
"They receive more from the tips then their job?"
"Yeah, you are supposed to give them 15% of the check. That's the standard. And the government taxes those tips. You're supposed to declare at the end of your work day how much you made, and if you don't you go to prison. But it's an industry-wide thing for waitresses to declare they only made like 10% of what they actually did for the day. Everyone knows this goes on, but no one ever gets arrested. There's just no way to record it…"

"It's fucking strange. I've always had this vision of the United States as a country built on fake truth. Fake ideas. The American dream I think is a real catastrophe."

"My idea is the American dream means you can be a criminal and get away with it."

"America is this kind of background from the UK, which is not so great – the world mastery. Stuff like the Bank of America which is killing people. The crazy of the USA is clear to someone who has studied it. There is probably, you know better then me this side of American history, there is jus a few people who retain the real power. Who are surely not Barack Obama. The world has gone really mad. It's fucking sad, and for the people. I think Americans are a people with great potential. They are very strong, they built cities from nothing in the middle of the desert."

"Have you seen the videos of gay exorcism in the USA? Is that in Italy too?"

"Ha! Yes, I know in the United States there are these kind of Christian camps for homosexuals. You go there & you, haha, try to force vagina. Haha. It's fucking strange because Milan, here is full of homosexuals. This is the capitol of fashion and I have gay friends, you know? I really don't care – black or white, yellow, homosexual – we are all the same shit... I think that spirituality should be a great part of our life. it's quite sad that nowadays nobody cares about it. I do believe that I have my truth, you have your truth. If you believe that when you will die you go to hell or heaven, you will go there because it is a personal conception of your mind, if you want it..."

"How do you feel about dream states?"

"I think when we go to sleep, we are in a state where we don't think anymore, which is the state where you are living in total equilibrium with the universe, you know. Because you are part of the universe, a great body which is greater then you. Now, I do believe that state of mind can bring you some kind of truth... You know, I call myself a Satanist not because I kill gods, or babies. Everyone who calls themselves a Satanist is a solipsist in a metaphorical way. Because Satan – my personal tradition, which is the Christian one, tells me that the opposer – Satan, the rebel – so I cannot tell you I believe in Satan. I believe in myself, so I am Satan, you know? I saw you in that Berlin metal video, talking about how you were '*the real man in black.*' Haha. The satanic Johnny cash. Haha."

"Yeah, the Americana folk country thing..."

"I am curious how you would compare the black metal scene in the US to the black metal scene in Europe?"

"I would say that the US has more of a rock n roll background, where Europe has more of this epic, classical Wagner type background. In the USA we're so far away from everything,. Like black metal in particular – it was impossible to get this stuff in the late 90's. I came of age before Napster, Myspace, Facebook, so the only way to get it was to import it. I got into black metal because of the Gummo soundtrack... It

just seemed exotic & bizarre, but I'm more into Bathory, Impaled Nazarene – the ugly, satanic punk rock noisy stuff. The only thing that turns me away from the larger scene in general is the amount of closet racism, or closet Nazi sympathy. And people look the other way and don't speak up, mostly because they believe in freedom of expression, no matter what it is, and people want to avoid politics and just concentrate on the music. But, you know, if you had some satanic corpse painted band travel back in time and try to play Berlin in 1940, they'd be thrown into a concentration camp immediately. I don't see how it gels together."

"There is none – there is no connection."

"Yeah, Italian Fascism was deeply Catholic..."

"This is a great contradiction in black metal. I think it is due to the violent approach; I don't know. I really don't care about politics because the mother world is just wrong. I don't think that Communism or National Socialism or Fascism – I think we should see more and more behind this shit. In Italy it is written hat after the Second World War, the political ideas were dead. Just because in Italy after the second world war we had a strange situation where we tried to make by ourselves a natural state but it was not possible for the Americans, because the Americans were so – they had ignorance everywhere. During the cold war, you know. And Italy was a great danger for Americans because they were a great communist force. So they tried to move these forces away. So we have no more political ideas here in Italy. But they tried to bring the political ideas again but they have no more resource – it's fucking stupid to listen to listen to a guy like Berlusconi because he's not right wing. The right wing in Italy during the Fascists was a more socialist idea. Mussolini was a socialist before he formed the Fascist party."

"He became kind of an actor..."

"Yeah."

"I've read a great deal about this period. But growing up in the USA, you read the history books in public school, and I always had the impression as do most Americans that Mussolini was like a military dictator, like a Franco, and there was never any discussion about what he really created."

"Italian politics today are a great contradiction, because Berlusconi claims he is right wing, but he does not believe in these ideas. He is only attracted to vaginas and money. There is no reason to believe his words. He's stupid, just stupid. It's such a tragedy because if you go to the parliament you are the most intelligent one. We come from a generation who should have learned from these stories and to understand. Probably this is the real nihilistic period because nobody really cares about anything, nobody is really interested in anything,. I think Christians don't believe in what they are talking about. So probably Nietzsche is right because he predicted what we are living now."

"Every Italian I've met hates Bersculoni..."

"Italians do detest Bersculoni."

"What will it take for him to be voted out of power?

"Most Italians are induced to vote by the television, and he runs the television. And not just television – he is probably the owner of this bar we are at. He is the owner of everything in Milan because he comes from Milan. But you know nowadays he's gone crazy. He's not a politician, he is just a businessman. And he entered politics to preserve his great power. He tried to make rules for himself. Now he is the law. It's fucking strange."

"Do you think his reign is coming to an end?"

"There is a possibility. But I don't think so because everyone, me too, grew up during this period. So we need great years to go away from this shit. The great problem nowadays for people like me, for people that believe this is not the real Italy. Italians now are ancients, they are old. They are old and they try to preserve their own bank account. Young people have not a job, they starving. It's sad you know?"

"Your grandparents, what was their experience?"

"I have a couple of grandparents who are 96, 97, so they wee born during the First World War. No one knows outside Italy, but Italy is a country just since 50 years. We built this up after fascism. My grandparents, they are old and probably do not understand anything. One is in a wheelchair, the other is in a bed 24 hours a day. But I listen tot heir stories and they were fascists because everyone had to be a fascist. My grandpa was an officer of the army during the second world war. He saved a lot of Jews. He was probably a hero for risking his own life. if someone k new this shit during that period they would be executed for sure. Fascism had no reason o kill Jews. It was never part of it."

"They were forced by Hitler..."

"We had no possibility to fight a war – we had no money to build armaments. So we went to war, we lose in Greece, we lose in Africa – everywhere. It was not a great war for us. And during the last two years The Allies came to Italy. In Italy we had the partisans – the people against fascism, the rebels. And they came here and killed everyone in Milan, in Bologna. They kill women, children, because every Italian became an enemy. And Mussolini was joking that he was happy in his little Republic of Salo. We were just people trapped inside fake ideologies… Mussolini was Hitler's teacher, you know. But at one point Hitler had more concept of his power. Mussolini was just a great personality and was forced to sacrifice his personality. So there is a great speech in 1945 and it is a great example of his dialectics – but he was totally conscious that Italy had no possibilities to win this war. So he sacrificed millions of Italians just for saving his personality. And here in Milan he died..."

** *"colui che è tutt'uno con il sole non si lamenta mai"* **

Sweltering as it may be, I'm infatuated with this country. Life bleeds into the streets, bawdy & open... Milan is packed in peak tourist season. I've spent the morning investigating the thoroughfare where a capitol building resides in the distance, flags from all nations line the streets with sweat pouring through every crack...

Last night we'd a whirlwind excursion through Milan; Napoli pizza & hi-grade barley/hops, a rockabilly club then the reputed Milanese Square where fresh college grads celebrated through the night as if it were Barcelona. Trumpets & whistles pierced the air, foil hats & dancing... I soon parted from Mr. V, who led me to a crash spot near an empty, gated park. 'Twas a cement enclosure with a hasty anarchy sign spray painted red on the wall & the typically pissy smell of public urination...

Oh yeah, that magazine interview was for VICE. In a few months I'll be translated into 15 different languages in 27 countries, a one million distribution run of high-quality, glossy color pages FREE to all. Best part? It's a devastator of an Anti-Obama rant, chock full of Bohemian Grove rhetoric. To be the first all out attack in VICE against Barack?

Mr. V & I were supposed to hang with VICE staff, but they were unavailable. We ate pasta & soon made it to the only metal shop in Milan – the Sound-Cave, which is run by guys from Avant Garde Music. In terms of prog black metal labels, Avant Garde is among the top tier.

Says Roberto Mammarella: *"About the scene I can't say anything, probably I'm too old. Haha. The label, its existed since '94. It was called Obscure Plasma Records – we did some 7 inches, tapes, and one LP, the Mayhem Live In Leipzig album. We moved to something more professional & changed the name to Avant Garde Music. In '96 I joined forces with two other guys & opened the store. We have moved 3 or 4 times now."*

"Is it really difficult to run a metal store in Milan?"

"In 2011 it's more difficult to run a label then a store. It's a different volume of sales, people. But at least if you are a store you are the last ring of a chain & you just select what you want to sell. So people are generally coming to buy Morbid Angel CD's or an Electric Wizard t-shirt. You just select and choose. A record company is more difficult because you are choosing one band to release & you are hoping all stores will sell your release, which is very difficult today. Until a few years ago it was real easy to release any kind of band &sell quite a few 1000 copies without any kind of promoting. Today you still sell records but less copies."

"What are some albums you've put out you're proud of?"

"I would say in 2005, 2006 – almost all of them. In our history there's been over 130 releases. You cannot be naïve enough to think everything you've released is cool – some of them are shitty records &we are in crime from quite a few bad releases. Same as every label. I don't have any problem to admit 10 years ago, 15 years ago, sometimes you sign a band for a specific reason & it just doesn't work anymore. Then you end up getting a roster that sucks. You have to really be lucky to sign a band when they are giving their best, and we did quite a few times – Carpathian Forest. Taake & Keep of Kalessin, actually quite a few of them have had a career. I wouldn't say artistically they made their best records with our company – other times not. Evoken from the USA – they made some great albums & I don't like at all the ones they did with us. So there's always that. It's kind of the fortune & the condemnation of the great bands – when you have a career over so many years, its not so easy to make a great album anymore."

"What are some amusing stories of meeting these extreme metal personalities?"

"The most terrible band to spend some time together are Mayhem, because they're some bad guys. And Carpathian Forest to a certain extent. All the others I would say are nice guys – very polite and well educated…"

"Are there stereotypes you'd like to dispel about Italians?"

"Pizza? I'm very tired about that. Every time you say you are Italian it's '*Mafia & Pizza?*' But another is that they say we don't like to work, that we spend too much time playing the mandolin & singing love songs. This is a complete fake because our partners in this business, they don't work – we do. They're always taking holidays – Germany especially. Every two weeks '*we are closed for national holidays.*' Or when you are around places in Europe you hardly see record stores that are open on Saturdays or mornings. Finnish people, you cannot count on them from Thursday until Monday because it's their weekends. So I think we Italians are the hard workers, haha, not the German people. This is something that really annoys me really – to be considered the assholes of

Europe, because its not true. Workers in Italy have much tougher conditions… This is not good at all. I think we are all living well thanks to what our fathers & grandfathers did – everybody probably has a flat because our father gave it to us. I don't think this is going to happen it the next [generation]. My kids will not get much from me, you know. And I suppose this is a problem for the new Italy. I mean Italian people that worked from the 60's until the early 90's, they made the core fortune & richness of the country, but now it is fading away. I'm really worried for that. I don't see any perspective for change, you know. I don't see any kind of event – even for Greece. you can borrow billions of euros, but then? I don't think Europe will have the balls to collapse. You cannot afford to collapse. But its not that unlikely, because Italy was once a really nice place to be before the Europe — I would say that any family with an average salary could have everything – a house, two cars, holidays, whatever, even if you earned a very small amount, but now we are spending g as much as the Germans but with Italian salaries. But I think sooner then later we are reaching the bottom…"

"Do you think Berlusconi will be voted out?"

"For some reason I cannot imagine Berlusconi to ever get old. We are used to icons, growing up with them, but Berlusconi for some reason I cannot imagine…

** *"mentre il mondo diventa sempre più digitale, io diventerò più primitivo"* **

Riding the train through Italian pastures, gazing at grazing cows, the sun setting a glowingly cinematic amber en route to Venice... Let it be known that the Train Station in Milan was no joke, even if to admit so makes you recognize that Benito at least did one thing right... *€15 from Milan to Venice, €10 from Venice to Trieste, €10 from Trieste to LAIBACH; return voyage – €15 from Ljubljana to Venice, €15 then to Bologna, €10 then to Florence, €20 to Rome...*

I am amongst friendlies once again – power metal my friends; just pure, unrelenting, lead-frenzy, operatic & soaring metal claw to the sky worship of everything that rocks with epic grandeur...

BURNING BLACK – these duel guitar assassins & aficionados of grandiose duel guitar leads – are now feeding me pizza until my belly is to explode. They've abducted me from the train stop preceding Medieval Venice & lured me to a packed-yet-spacious restaurant with huge tables & huddled groups of belly laughing Italians eating massive pizza plates &

slugging Belgium beer. They feed me forever – a blizzard of thin crust mozzarella, pepperoni & basil, slopped in crispy rectangular shapes…

Intel file: BURNING BLACK *"live, love & play US Power Metal – no compromises, catering to the traditionalists as well as the Power Metal aficionados. The sharp-yet-smooth-style reminds you of West Coast Metal in its heyday: a perfect combination of aggressive riffing & those trademark vocals. BURNING BLACK songs consist of brilliantly arranged Power Metal with the necessary melodies – without being too kitschy. Stylistically, fast up-tempo songs sound like a mixture of Crimson Glory, Malice, Journey, Lion & Cinderella, and the catchy melody lines sail on the sharp riffs with gracious ease...*

"European tour with Circle II Circle & Manticora & another headliner tour hitting Italy, Austria, Slovakia & Hungary... The song 'Secrets To Hide' receives a nomination for 'Best Metal Song 2010' at the Hollywood Music in Media Awards, while RockGamer Studios have the song remixed to be included in the expansions of the 'Rock Band' videogame. "Purgatory Child" gets nominated at the USA Indie Music Fest & then again as "Best Metal Song 2011" at the Hollywood Music in Media Awards...")

"In November 2010 BURNING BLACK is confirmed as the opening act for the European tour of the Finnish monster rockers Lordi – the tour hits Italy, Switzerland, Germany, the Netherlands, France and Spain, giving the band a chance to play in front of sold out crowds in bigger venues than ever. In 2011 the band headlines various festivals in Italy, sharing the stage with renowned power metal acts such as Elvenking & Secret Sphere. Their third album will be released somewhere in 2012, together with the first USA tour...")

Enrico "Eric" Antonello: *"**You are from-a Detroit-a? We-a-know about Detroit-a because of the Robocop. Hahaha. Is it good to visit Detroit-a?"*

"If you want to see something you'd never believe, yeah. The thing is the music scene is amazing if you know where to go. And it is like Robocop. Have you ever seen 'John Carpenter's Escape From New York?' Or 'Mad Max?'"

*"**Of Course."*

"Think that for a 100 square miles. And if there are police, you don't want to see them. If you really wanna see Detroit, go on Youtube & look up 'Tour of Ghetto Detroit.' It's like empty fields, one house standing, and it looks like the 'Texas Chainsaw Massacre' house, all slooping down… It's a weird place. But even if you play a really good

show with like 5 great local bands, you'll still be playing for like 100 people. All of them die-hards though. Unless, of course, you play Harpo's Concert Theatre on a big package tour, and then it will be packed to the brim. But most likely you'll be playing for the same 100 guys that go to all the underground shows."

AJ Simons: "Here in Europe, we have the American dream to play in the USA. And I know in the USA, bands have the Europe dream to play here. Haha. So it is a problem."

"Yes, it's very interesting for me. What I've found I Europe..."

*"**Is it true you cannot drink alcohol in a car when someone else is driving?"*

"Yeah, and the driver – his alcohol limit varies from state to state. Mostly I think it's like two beers & you go over the limit. Maybe one beer in an hour is the limit."

"Yes, the same here."

*"**In Germany the limit is zero."*

"Artistically speaking, we feel we are a bit in the third world of Europe, because the best countries to do your career are Germany & Scandinavian countries. There have been some successful bands in Italy, like Lacuna Coil, but they started selling and moved."

"It seems everywhere I go, the European countries have their own history & culture, and that metal is this kind of fringe thing on the sidelines, whereas in America we're all indoctrinated into rock n' roll from a young age."

"Yes, we have achieved most of our success in the USA. So, we are feeling now that it is quite an important market for us. And maybe Japan. So the third album will be a little more American-oriented metal."

*"**A little bit of an 80's sheen, a little Sabbath..."*

"Is power metal one of the bigger forms of metal in Italy, because I know Manowar is gigantic here..."

"I think there was an almost power metal brand at the end of the 90's, where Italy was producing more & more power metal. Some of them were great, but a lot of them were just imitating each other. And in Italy there is a lot of boring classical-inspired power metal. I appreciate some of these bands, but we are trying to get a little bit out of this stuff. Our first album was very classical heavy metal – iron maiden, Judas priest. The second one we introduced a bit of keyboards, some more catchier riffs. But it was already more riff-oriented, more US inspired. I can tell you we have a great singer – a great energy onstage."

*"[The pizza comes] **Ah – 60 centimeters of pizza."*

"It will disappear in 10 minutes."

"What's your favorite city to hang out in Italy?"

"Good question – in our region, besides Venice, I would recommend Verona."

"As far as Malta goes, do Italians consider them to be racially Italian because it's so close? Or are they considered more Arabic, since it's also near Libya?"

"Not really. There are some islands in the Mediterranean, near Sicily, but geographically they are part of Africa. I've never been to Malta, but our relationships with Malta are not very good because they send us immigrants. The people that escape from Libya, sometimes the land in Malta. And the authorities, they pick them up and take them to our territorial waters. They won't tell you this, but sometimes, when they try to land on the border – the Sicilians, the Spanish – they shoot. We don't shoot, they do… Are you going to visit Rome?"

"I feel like I should, but there's a big price tag on it."

"If you can, at least go to Florence. You have to see Florence at least once in a lifetime. It's maybe one, two hours on a train. Florence is like the art capital of the world. Rome is like a big mess. In two days you can see Florence, but in two days you cannot see anything of Rome – it's too big. It's like 10 times bigger… I lived in Milan for 5 years, I went to the University. I studied law & economics. It's been tough for me – I lived in the countryside, so it was not easy for me… We have our rehearsal studio in the country side."

*"**I live in the middle of the fields, haha."*

"Tell me about the tour you did."

"We didn't really plan it, actually. We had only our first album out. We only played some shows in Italy and Switzerland and never thought we'd be able to do a full European tour having only one album out. It was at the beginning of early 2009 we were collaborating with a booking agency that told us there was a free slot for the Circle To Circle Tour, for the second leg which was mostly Eastern European countries. So we got a couple months warning... We were in a camper and traveled more then 8000km. We played in Budapest, Hungary, then Ljubljana, Vienna, Bucharest, Bulgaria, Athens, Serbia, Belgrade. If you go to Eastern Europe go to Greece and to Serbia – beautiful…"

"Tell me about these countries…"

"We were really surprised in Romania because not a lot of bands end up playing there, and you can say it's a very young country They joined the European Union only a few years ago. We thought the situation would be very difficult with logistical problems & so on. Instead we met many great people. We played in two of the most beautiful venues on the tour. The organization was perfect and people showed up, really. The first show was in Sarmizegetusa, the capitol of Transylvania. And then we played Bucharest which was in an old church. It was a gothic cathedral. After the show, the place turned itself into a disco party, because it was in front of the university. Our guitarist got really drunk, that night I think he puked 3 or 4 times. It was fun. Another nice surprise was Sofia, the capitol of Bulgaria, where we played our best show ever. I think it was the first time in our life that we signed a lot of autographs."

"No one really goes there though, so when they do it's a big deal, right?"

"It's very far, and the roads are in very bad condition. Bulgaria, it's at the border with Turkey…"

*"**I remember I drive-a the camper and in the morning I look at the landscapes, and there were dead dogs all over the streets…"*

"We got also stopped by the place in the middle of the night. They were only checking our documents, but I was shitting my pants. You want to get imprisoned by the Bulgarian police? I mean they became a democracy 10 years ago…"

*"**Haha… And in Macedonia, we did 4 hours at the customs…"*

"What about Belarus? Does anyone every play there? It's like the last dictatorship in Europe…"

"I don't think it's an open country. In ex-Soviet countries, there is even more piracy. There are some artists, U.D.O. for example, the singer from Accept – he plays in Russia, sells out cities, but there is so much piracy no one buys his albums.

*"**In record shops there, you will not find the actual CD, but only the copy."*

"They sell MP3's… Our ex-guitarist, he married a Russian girl and found our CD's pirated in shops… In Eastern countries it's easier to play in them because they are bit more influenced by the Western European underground. Also Poland which is influenced mostly by Germany – they have similar musical taste."

"What do you think are some stereotypes of the Italian people that are just not true?"

"Even though Italy is not a big country like the United states, the different parts are very different from each other. North of Italy is the most, you could say, 'European.' We have a way to talk & behave more similar to central European countries. South of Italy instead is a very different place. A lot of stereotypes come from Italians who emigrated to the US. Most of these people were from Southern Italy – so the Mafia, people eating pizza all day or playing the mandolin, or listening only to opera singers – it's more related to Southern Italians. There's always been a rivalry between the North and South – we joke about it a little. We don't hate each other…"

"Do you do any songs in Italian?"

"It's very hard for a singer to get a good accent in English, but, you know, we have to try anyway because English is the language abroad. In the late 90's there were many classically inspired Italian power metal bands with ridiculous accents. I could understand if some producers, labels & agents don't look at Italy like a country that could be useful. Everyday we have to demonstrate that we can challenge bands more important then us in their own style It's hard, but we feel that we grew up during these years & faced a little bit of racism, I think. I don't want to say bad things about anybody, but during last tour, we got on very well with Scandinavian people. The crew was from Germany. And sometimes – they never insulted us, or we never had really bad problems – but sometimes we heard some jokes, some things that made us think they see us as the third world of Europe. And in some way, I can understand them Our music underground doesn't work very well. Our audience is lazy, as I told you. But I think these people should remember that Italy created the art & music of the last 700 years. So maybe they should give us a little more-of-a-respect-a…"

** *"una terra di incanto e divorazione insetti"* **

To accept the fool's invitation of *Insect Leng T'che* is to experience the pain of parasitism by 1000 organic needles… No one told me Venice was a swamp. No one said, *"hey moron, don't do that idiot thing you're likely planning."* Maybe they figured I just plainly knew, same as everyone else in Europe…

When you are in a swamp, you don't sleep in the bushes. And when you are in a Mediterranean climate Swamp in muggy July peak, you don't get drunk & pass out in the raw like a slab of hapless cattle… My arms appear the victim of a hummingbird-girth mosquito locust. A blind man could read my flesh like Braille…

Too drunk to feel it, I re-emerge into the night. 3am; no security, shops, tour boats or *gondoliers*. Humid, sultry, sky a sharp violet from ocean proximity; green shrubs cut like twisting walls, mansion hotels with glowing, curtained windows. Venice is like an alien world. Walk up & down flights of stairways that ascend & descend without purpose – an impossible military outpost outdated by centuries & unable to be conquered…

Canal by canal, *ponte sul ponte*, it goes deeper into repetition. It is so beautifully designed that what would be a nightmare of absolute loss is obscured by the architectural beauty at every turn. One switch of the path leads to a new corridor leading to another seemingly secret pathway ripe with historic aura...

I walk for kilometers of circles & concrete twists; hours go by & the tourists which slowly fill the streets are nonexistent to my senses, for they are not part of the cobblestone tapestry but a virus of flesh cogging the purity of my vision... In silent morning I watch old men prepare the marketplace, gutting fish that bleed rivers into drains... I rest inside the empty crimson curtained church filled with burning white candles... Through art exhibits of barren landscape & cowboy honor slogans; past flat embankments & sparse rain, past backpackers slumbering in pairs upon moss covered cement... *With every shattered cocoon another gallows lurks foreboding...*

LAIBACH

IX. *"ploskve odebeli // zemljišča od Tito"*

Glistening Trieste, marvelous Trieste – with her Adriatic splendor, stunning rock cliff formations & sailboat escapism... I understand why TITO wanted it so badly; why the ex-dictator nearly threw us into WW4 over it's scrumptious borders...

You gaze at a marvel in a hurtling bullet train, zooming ever so closer to thousands of bikini tourists soaking up sun rays & smacking volleyballs on the beach. Past them laid out like a great archaeological discovery is a fabulous city ripe for tomfoolery... The second you hop off the temperature drops 20 degrees, the rain begins squirting as relentless typhoon...

Where I am going instead of Florence, instead of Rome, is directly into the heart of Slovenia for a one-on-one collision with LAIBACH. I am soon to embrace Ljubljana [** *phonetically spoken lib-eee-on-nah*], the capitol of Slovenia, which is an hour East of Italy's border & once only reached via perilous mountain trek...

This is where I clear everything up for you, since gibberish like the following will most likely maw your brain: *"LAIBACH excludes any evolution of the original idea; the original concept is not evolutionary but entelechical, and the presentation is only a link between this static and the changing determinant unit. We take the same stand towards the direct influence of the development of music on the LAIBACH concept; of course, this influence is a material necessity but it is of secondary importance and appears only as a historical musical foundation of the moment which, in its choice is unlimited. LAIBACH expresses its timelessness with the artifacts of the present and it is thus necessary that at the intersection of politics and industrial production (the culture of art, ideology, consciousness) it encounters the elements of both, although it wants to be both. This wide range allows LAIBACH to oscillate, creating the illusion of movement (development)..."*

** *"inteligence datoteke"* **

There are reasons why as an American you probably have never heard the name TITO outside of the Jackson 5. Here is the deal with LAIBACH & with TITO, because without this background it will be near impossible to process any of the conversations to follow...

We have omitted Josip Broz Marshall TITO from our government issued high school text books. It's not simply because of the state he presided over [*a communist scourge of the Eisenhower 50's*], but what he literally fought against as a guerrilla – that being the <u>USTASHA</u>. Historians worldwide have perpetually glossed over these atrocities...

Josip Broz Marshall Tito was for all purposes the dictator of Yugoslavia from 1945 until his death in 1980. Despite this autocratic business, he was extremely popular & remains venerated for a number of reasons. Mainly, because he created a generally fair system in a time of ruthless reactionary politics. While the Soviet nightmare armed & amassed itself at his borders – sending assassins, threatening war; butchering, beating, murdering their own people – TITO refused to become a monster like Stalin. He crossed his sword with Iron Joe & risked war to keep his people free of the neighboring evil. Stalin had no communist rival like TITO. For his people and the sake of history, TITO rebuked the beast...

Not that I'm apologizing for TITO, nor am I justifying anything bad he might've done. But TITO flourished in a singularly unique situation & I am simply remarking in terms of what *could've been.* When analyzing the reigns of Stalin & Mao, Josip Broz appears Saintly in comparison...

I shall explain TITO in *Americanese*: Born in Croatia in 1892, Josip Broz studied to be a metallurgist before being drafted in the Austria-Hungarian Empire to fight in WWI. Captured by the Russians in March 1915, he was a POW until working class rebels fighting against the Tzar's reign busted him out. Broz quickly joined the communist guerrillas & for the next three years kept getting arrested by the Tzar's forces, escaping, then going right back to fighting alongside the Bolsheviks...

By 1920 he returned to the Kingdom of Yugoslavia & joined the Communist Party, working mechanic positions while remaining an underground activist. By 1928 he was arrested in a government crackdown against commies & sent to prison for 5 years. After a full sentence he immediately went underground & began using the codename TITO [**the reasons why remain unclear*]. By 1937, he was leader of the [*still illegal*] Yugoslav Communist Party & had direct links to the Soviet power base...

April 1941 is when the chain of events began that eventually rendered TITO a living legend & major world leader. When Fascist & Nazi forces invaded, they soon took over nearly all Yugoslav territory. In need of a puppet dictatorship, Hitler propped up a Croatian terrorist group called the USTASHA to run everything for him in absentia.

The USTASHA were another in a long line of fascist political parties spread across Europe. Most Americans don't realize this, but Mussolini was once the most popular politician in the world. He was in power 11 years before Hitler was elected, and in that time he had many, many imitators...

Even if the *intelligentsia* found his public persona ludicrous, the fascist economy was taken seriously because it was the only one that actually defeated The Great Depression. This was not because of the flaunted "Corporate State," because that was never actually put into practice. Mussolini's success came from turning the entire country into a public works project. In rebuilding Italy from scratch, they employed nearly the entire nation & literally bought their way out of The Great Depression...

Since fascism was essentially state-based National Communism [*with a dangerous emphasis on imperialism*], there was a copycat fascist party in nearly every European country openly calling themselves "fascist" & trying to ape support. Mussolini had inadvertently spawned his own corporate franchises & condescendingly thought it was "*kinda cute,*" never dreaming a Hitler would materialize & call his hammy ass out...

All these fascist franchises were doing their own country-specific thing. The USTASHA were the Croatian variant, led by a man named Ante Pavelic. The Vatican was thrilled by their Catholic extremism & directly funded them; the Nazi's armed them to the teeth while the Italians gave them tanks. They were run by a man named Ante Pavelic, who remains a blurry figure to history. Little is known about him & only a handful of pictures remain. Unlike a freaky Hitler wannabe, Pavelic is indistinguishable, plain. He could pass for a high school janitor.

Under Pavelic's leadership, the USTASHA led a campaign to slaughter all non-Catholics. They were sent, by the grace of god, on a mission to "*expel a third, convert a third, or kill a third*" of the population. As a result, the atrocities were so ghastly & nightmarish that the USTASHA apparently scared the piss out of the SS who flatly refused to work with them whenever possible. I read one story of a Gestapo soldier finding a drifting, loosened rowboat that was filled with the decapitated heads of 70+ Serbian children...

USTASHA ideology was a blend of Clerical fascism, Nazism & fierce Croatian nationalism. They supported the creation of a "*Greater Croatia*" & the movement emphasized the need for a "*racially pure*" Croatia & promoted genocide against Serbs, Jews & Gypsies. The movement functioned as a terrorist organization before World War II, but by April 1941 they were appointed to rule Axis-occupied Yugoslavia as the Independent State of Croatia (NDH). Around 300,000 were killed by the NDH government's racial policies, which condemned all Serbs, Jews & Roma to death in the concentration camps, alongside Croat resistance members & political opponents...

The USTASHA aimed to create an ethnically *"pure"* Croatia, and saw the Serbs that lived in Croatia, Bosnia and Herzegovina as their biggest obstacle. Thus, USTASHA ministers declared in May 1941 that the goal of the new policy was an ethnically clean Croatia & they enacted race laws patterned after those of the Third Reich. Serbs, Jews, Roma and Croatian anti-fascists, including Communist Croats and dissident Croat Byzantine Catholic priests, were interned in concentration camps. The exact number of victims is not known, but estimates reach around 32,000 Jews, 40,000 Gypsies [*Yugoslav Roma*], and anywhere from 300,000-700,000 Serbs...

TITO emerged as the John Conner of Slav anti-fascism. It was TITO's prowess as a guerrilla commander that led to the defeat of this unspeakable brutality. Once the front lines of the Iron Curtain were drawn, TITO became the Soviet sanctioned leader & Field Marshall of the newly created Communist Yugoslavia, controlling the third largest army in the world...

Within 3 years, TITO essentially told Stalin to *"go fuck himself"* & broke apart from the USSR, thus creating a federation of six socialist countries [*Croatia, Serbia, Slovenia, Bosnia, Montenegro & Macedonia*]. TITO crafted a socialist democracy that was fully open to the west and started the Non-Aligned movement, which was basically a UN for all states not in the United Nations. It was the anti-west/anti-soviet block, and Yugoslavia was kingpin...

By 1980, TITO was an old man without a clear successor. After TITO's death at the age of 88, the Yugoslav Federation was a creeping train-wreck that finally shattered in 1990. This eventually led to the Bosnian massacres of the mid-90's, Kosovo, etc. As for Slovenia, the country I now travel to – they broke from TITO's Dead Federation after a 10 day succession war in 1990...

Now LAIBACH... It is erroneous to call LAIBACH a band, because they are more an entity. They also get pigeonholed into the industrial category. While it is true that they were among the first industrial bands in the genre's history, they have little in common with any music existing scene, per se, because they are their own surrealistic, literal nation-state...

LAIBACH are less a band & more a multi-faceted artistic project which includes every form of media. Again, *Americanese*... Imagine if in 1980 the nihilists from *The Big Lebowski* started an industrial project that had as its mission the vision to incorporate anyone working with them (*or simply watching them*) as part of a mass collective which existed to mimic a bureaucratic state. Something of a tongue-in-cheek empire that was anti-fascist to the core while intentionally appearing as fascistic as possible during the process...

The members of LAIBACH wear Nazi-like military uniforms as if they are part of a militant army [*with the black cross as their logo*]. They have released endless manifestos & perplexing interviews titanic in their scope which inevitably lead the reader in one head-scratching, gigantic circle. LAIBACH do not project anything but one big mirror in which you see only *what you choose to see* on an internal level...

They use your own mind against you, while operating in this vein of propaganda art. For instance, LAIBACH will take historical war posters & mix them with modern day corporate logos & imagery to make a hodge-podge of surrealist political art...

Their concerts were like bizarre art exhibitions colliding with abstract Nuremberg rallies from the get-go. They freaked out the authorities so badly that to even use the name LAIBACH in public was an arrestable offense. This is why they starting using the mentioned black cross logo to identify themselves [*taken from Russian Suprematist painter Malevich*]. Some of you may have noticed RAMMSTEIN using this symbol. This is intentional, because RAMMSTEIN were teen fanboys of 80's LAIBACH and by extension pay tribute to the LAIBACHIAN satiric direction...

LAIBACH derive their name from the occupation name the Germans would bestow upon Ljubljana [*capitol of Slovenia*] any time they invaded. So you can see why in 1980, right after the death of TITO & the entire Federation on edge, why people would react poorly to some crazy art collective with evil music, radical ideas & fascistic uniforms openly calling themselves Nazi city...

Their first TV performance led to the show host telling Slovenians to directly lynch them, which then led LAIBACH to go underground & tour under the auspice "THE OCCUPIED STATES OF EUROPE," setting up LAIBACHIAN cells all over the continent, city by city. By 1992, LAIBACH had formed NSK – a global state in time without borders or physical territory in which you can actually get a passport [*and apparently travel with*]...

If all of this sounds confusing, well, it's kind of supposed to be. The tale goes on endlessly, with controversy stacked effortlessly – including a failed car bomb assassination attempt outside a hotel...

** "nocoj smo pili za Oslo" **

Ljubljana, day two, still pouring rain. Today I scratch. The mosquitoes of Venice have left me mutated. I've been sitting here with ice packs melting bag after bag on my arms trying to get the swelling down. By the time LAIBACH shows, I'll be grisly...

Still, it's better then shrapnel. Had I followed my original plan, I just very well might've been in Oslo for the bombing of the maniac. The kettle of xenophobia boiling to climax... I've seen nothing of Ljubljana. Instead, I've been happily quarantined in METELKOVA, which is the Christiania equivalent of Slovenia. It was a lucky find, mentioned by local death act Dickless Tracy. I really had no clue such a thing existed, but the complex was 3 blocks from the bus station...

METELKOVA, just like KØPI, was a former commie military barracks – this time the Yugoslav National Army. It was squatted September 1993 & consists of seven buildings – 5 of which are music venues/workshops. The others are an invite only mega-squat. There is also an extremely cheap hostel with dirt-cheap internet café. I've been taking my cue all morning...

I walked through the gates with the red/black sheet-metal masthead & soon found dozens talking loudly and huddled in the yard. Very few mega-crust punks; these folks were dressed more low-key with lots of one color, basic shirts. Friendly people, smiles all around. I was soon chatting with members from melodic death band I Vs. I & the folk-punk Happy Ol' McWeasel...

** "celo v spanju še vedno divja vojna" **

"My family was from Bosnia & my father was a fireman in Northern Yugoslavia. When the war started, the big fear was... The politicians that were in jail, during the 70's when TITO was the president, those guys had gone out from the prisons & they made political parties & influenced many people. They turned the minds of the people to do anything with their lives. It was a very big propaganda. When my father died, the Croatian army was a legitimate army. But they wanted to attack the Yugoslavian army because they were still in the cities. It was a big problem for my family; they called us on the phone – 'they are coming

*from Kosovo.' My mom was very sick, she was in shock when my father
died – she get tuberculosis. My brother & me, we were put in a foster
family for 1½ years. My father, he died in Slovenia in the 10 days war,
and I had gone to class with other kids whose fathers died in the Croatian
war. My father was in the Yugoslavian army & died in the Slovenian war
and we were stressed in this elementary school all the time. You know, the
teacher said 'whose father died in the war? Stand up.' I stood also & they
said, 'Your father died in a hostile army – he was enemy." My father died
in a very – sometimes life is so weird... My father spent 25 years working
against fire – fire was his enemy. And he died in a truck where he was a
commandant, Chief Lieutenant to one Slovenian guy. The guy took a
bullet, he was injured, and Dad said, 'Go out & go surrender – you are 18
years old and I am old, I must drive this truck.' And my father was driving
the truck & he also took a bullet. And then this woman – they were
protesters. When my father took the bullet, he screamed – I heard this
story 1000 times – when he screamed for help, this one Slovenian guy who
was killed by the Yugoslavian army during this war – his wife come with
gasoline & burn my dad, you know? We identify him with the number of
the teeth... We lost everything. Really they wanted to kick us from the
apartment. It was a struggle everyday because we were in foster family.
My mom was abused, we were abused... This war was interesting in the
history of wars because you had three beliefs – like Muslims, orthodox &
Catholics – fighting each other in the lands where the people were
connected like 500 years. They were really good connected in Yugoslavia.
It was such a crisis man. I ask myself many times why so many young
people in Balkans are using drugs, going the wrong way. But if you see
what the world has done to all of these regions in our land, it will present
problems to many generations. I know people killing themselves because
they could not sleep anymore from the war in their head."*

Meet CJ, the fellow currently pacing around the hostel café. He's a 25 year
old Croatian visiting a friend freshly returned from Ethiopia. CJ doesn't
hang in Slovenia much, but he's seen a good share of The Balkans. He was
a roadie for Eyesburn, a reggae/metal hybrid from Serbia he claims is "*the
most original band in the Balkans.*" Their moment of glory was a
collaboration with Max Cavalera on Soulfly's *Prophecy* album [*the song
"Moses"*]. CJ is piping hot today, assailing into a grand rant…

He explains what led to the turbulence of the 90's: "Those people
who came into power after TITO died, they were in jail while TITO was
alive. There was no Croatia, no Serbia. Many of these presidents were all
in jail. History says Tito was a dictator – but TITO knew how to set up

one state with a big balance. He was a big friend of The United States & political partner of African states. It was not communism like in North Korea. Many people if you ask in all the lands how they lived, they will say it was awesome, you could buy a car. That was unbelievable in those days. You finish high school & have a great job; the factories worked full scale. In my town there was a factory making t-shirts, and many generations of the families were working there. They'd buy a house, car, and then when TITO died – those guys who were in jail – there is proof now that some of those people worked for spy intelligence outside Yugoslavia. For Russia, CIA – there are some theories that the CIA make this war in Yugoslavia. It is a theory, you know. But 1988, Milošević – he was the biggest dictator in Balkan lands. And he was the founder of the ID – you know, to make a big Serbia. And many many Serbs, it was like a big financial crisis. And then this guy came & said to Serbs, '*You want a big Serbia? I will give it to you.*' And then he said, like, '*we must attack Croatia.*' But in Croatia, at that time, 1988, '89, the founder of the big political party said, '*we must go into war with Serbia.*' And the war started in September 1991, from Belgrade there was like 20km of tanks going into Croatia. People in Serbia was celebrating against unarmed people. They collapsed whole cities – it was like hell, like Hiroshima…"

"What is your personal opinion of TITO?"

"I see TITO as a guy with some good & some bad. I know what my parents said to me, and my grandpa & my grandma. TITO was a guy to fix the problems of the small man, you know? He was the guy to give you a car, to give you apartment & education – nobody was hungry. Yugoslavia didn't have economical big problems, or wars. Many people liked TITO from African countries, even Hallie Selassie, the last emperor of Ethiopia. John F Kennedy was in TITO's home & TITO was also in the United States. TITO wanted to change something for the better on the view from the Second World War, because Yugoslavia was so damaged, many battles was here in the heart of Europe. He could have done things better, but I don't judge him. I think at that time he did the best possible things for Yugoslavian people."

"In the scale of what could have been, he was the best possible option?"

"Yes – especially when you look at every other communist dictator in the world. He told Stalin '*NO.*' Stalin wanted to finish Yugoslavia with his army & if he attacked Yugoslavia would be finished in 5 days. But he said '*NO.*' Later, Yugoslavia – in the 70's & 80's – was the third major military power in the world."

"I only learned about TITO from independent research because we aren't taught about him in our public schools in the USA. Especially not about the Ustasha, or Ante Pavilich – that the Vatican was directly involved in the ethnic & religious cleansing. Is that common knowledge here & how do the schools here confront that?"

"You know Croatia & Slovenia – we are very traditional lands. Croatia is very catholic. Is not good, because every healthy society must change with time. Croatia – most people don't want to change. That is our history. We have a land with a very sad history. We've always had unions with different countries – Austria, Hungary. We came here from one part of Russia in the 17th century. But the Second World War there are big black holes in Croatian history & very few people want to clear that up. I'm shocked how many young people are interested in ideology that spreads to Pavelic, who was like the worst guy in the Balkans after Hitler."

"It seems like there is no information about him – no books, no nothing in any language."

"No, not at all. What is real interesting is I read a lot of conspiracy books – this world is so clouded with people who are running the governments & running the people & they always get out. Hitler, there are many proofs that he run away – they didn't found his skull, the Red Army. Joseph Mengele, the 'Angel of Death' – he got out with American military support. And he would continue mind control in Brazil. There is one interesting interview, this woman wrote a book called '*Transformation of America* where she writes about Mengle and others, how they always get free. Milošević basically killed himself while the main architects of the war are not in jail – only a few people."

"Ok, the Hitler escape idea – what proof is offered about this escape to Argentina? Because I personally believe that he went down with the ship – he was just too physically sick & someone, somewhere would have identified him over time."

"I know the books from David Icke – all books from him. He's out there but I like his theories. I don't like that he's mixing new age shit with conspiracy theories. The Jewish Question, the universe, other galaxies, ancient histories, Annunaki, Nibiru. On the other side, he's putting the message to the people. You are infinite consciousness, you know? You do what you want – but isn't that the message from all the fucked up guru's from the East coming to the western world collecting money from the people? You give money to us & we'll do everything for you? It's very easy to manipulate somebody who is in fear…"

"Do you have a question for me about the United States?"

"Well, more a suggestion – I'm really surprised by how the United States is a very tolerant land. I like the mentality that you are not putting your nose in someone else's business. In European countries, it's a very usual thing to know everything about your neighbor. I can say that I was in trouble 2 or 3 months ago, and the Cavalera Family [**Max from Soulfly] sent me like 30 kilos of clothing. I was surprised, you know – the guy who sold 500 million CD's is sending me clothes because he knows that I am I trouble. And nobody from my neighborhood wanted to help me. What I think about the United States – as a land, with 300 million people – I think the economy is more problem then in Europe. Here, people are more without money but the economy is so stable that if 4 banks in Germany fell apart tomorrow there would still be money for the people because it's such a built up system. But if something goes down on Wall Street, then everything goes down. I think if you go in this direction, the world in the future will not be as David Icke says. We're gonna live in a world where people shoot people for 5 liters of gasoline, like in this movie *Mad Max*. The guy most powerful from gasoline is the new Stalin. Putin, you know? Vladimir Putin has more gas then all of Europe. We really must take our power back as a people & not listen to these crazy people on the top because what Barack Obama knows about your life – he probably knows nothing. When you see the speeches of them – every president, every guy on top of the system – he's talking not conclusions but something unspecified. I read many, many books & this paleontologist wrote two books about Obama. He say, '*I don't want to disturb you, but in the next 5 to 10 years will be the biggest catastrophe in all modern history. This guy say Putin is the New Stalin, because in KGB Putin was the most sick in the Eastern World.*' He said today's only difference is that so-sick people are controlling the world that 0.4% knows how sick they are. And if you have so sick people controlling billions of people... Look at Facebook – the most modern mind-control game. We must look into our mirrors. The mind control in these times is at the highest levels. I have one interesting book from this guy who explains the last book of the bible in scientific way – it's called *Hidden Secrets of The Bible*. He said that Jesus' last command was baptize all the people on the earth & if you see all the modern movies – *The Matrix* is the most biblical movie in the world. The spaceship is called the Nebuchadnezzar, the name of the Babylonian king. The woman is called trinity. And Neo comes back, the town Zion... This guy say the near future will be the most catastrophic in modern human history & what he said, I was so shocked, that 2011 will be the year of the war, that Barack Obama is the last elected president of the United States & that he will provoke Vladimir Putin to attack the United States & that by

2014 the United States will lose & collapse in 6 parts – one part to the Russians, one part to the European Union. After they lose war, the laws will be structured as in Communist China. You will not be permitted to have more then one child in a family, everything will be monitored... The European Union at that point will become something like a Third Reich. Because 12 stars, if you see everything, is so controlled. You cannot go in a gas station to go to toilet without having to pay money. The 12 stars, the sign is taken from occult books – that is the occult symbol. One religion, one army, one money – microchips in the skin, you know?"

** "brez nadaljnje zbogom" **

And finally... Dr. Bartek versus LAIBACH *and* SILENCE. Mr. Boris Benko & Primož Hladnik now sit before me, both slightly cringing at my horribly mutated appearance but still doing their best to pretend otherwise as much as possible...

SILENCE are extremely difficult to classify; they are a duo existing somewhere in the ambient/synth/prog universe. Characterized by: *"melancholy, experimental sounds & vocal arrangements as well as meticulous production,"* the band utilizes a variety of live instruments in their recordings ranging from the piano, to violin, viola, valiha, double bass, cello, etc. The duo are recognized for their vast involvement in Slovenian theater, creating music for a number of plays. Usually they tour with the cast performing their music live, if not performing with the cast as well as actors themselves...

SILENCE were the backing band & producers of LAIBACH'S *Volk*, which in October 2006 was released to universal critical acclaim. This powerhouse international best-seller featured remixes of 14 national anthems through a variety of media; many consider this to be one of LAIBACH's career defining moments...

SILENCE itself was founded in 1992 by Boris Benko, Matjaz Ferenc & Primož Hladnik. Their 1999 record *Unlike A Virgin* was voted Album of the Year in *Orkus*, which was like the German equivalent to Alternative Press in Mid-90's USA. Other feats include the soundtrack for *Midnight Meat Flight* [*a performance by the notorious 'Betontanc' dance theater*] & the plays *Maison Des Rendez-Vous & Peter Pan*, a play jointly produced by *Lutkovno gledalisce Ljubljana & Slovensko Mladinsko gledalisce*. *SILENCE* also wrote a soundtrack for *Winnie The Pooh*, a puppet shown produced by *Lutkovno gledalisce Ljubljana*. Their album *The Passion of the Cold* was released in 2008; a handmade book containing 2 CD's & 90 minutes of music from [*or inspired by*] Tomaz

Pandur's plays *Barroco* & *Kaligula*. Only 500 numbered/hand-signed copies exist, one of which Benko just popped into my hand – as well as a pint of Guinness...

"Boris Benko: We started as a band in the beginning, but then we went into composing theater, but also production to a certain degree. Mainly right now we're into theatre, music for movies, and from time to time we make records of our own..."

"What is it like working in theatre productions?"

"You're a composer on the market so whoever contacts you with good conditions, I mean, we accept nearly everything. We like diversity, so we're not really picky. We do everything from puppet plays to serious theatre. *[**Boris hands me their latest work 'Passion Of The Cold' – a CD inside a book of high-quality glossy pages, like a hardcover program guide for a full-tilt opera with quasi-BDSM imagery]*. This was interesting because it was the first opportunity we had to work with an orchestra. the first time was with *Volk* – we did 'Nippon' *[the Japanese national anthem]* with an orchestra but it was not an entirely symphonic experiment. So this is pretty rare nowadays, because the obvious economic restrictions. It is not a good situation now, economically. I don't know how it is in The States. In Europe it's…

"We're bankrupt. Depends on where you go, but it can be 40% unemployment."

"40%??"

"Yeah. The people they count, as far as statistics, are only those actually receiving money. And once you're off 'the dole,' they no longer count you. When you lose your job they'll give you unemployment for six months & then they no longer have to pay you – you just drop off the grid. Most Americans live off credit cards, so the average person is like $30 grand in debt. I'm one of the rare exceptions that have had a clean break. It took me about a year to save up for this, and I just barely work over minimum wage. I'm a chef."

<u>Primož Hladnik</u> *[the other half of SILENCE, who performed over 80 international shows with LAIBACH]*: *"You can do good living as a chef, no?"*

"Not really – no healthcare. But I don't have a mortgage, kids or a car, so… I'm curious the European economic conditions. You have a recession slowly creeping in – it's only been in the past year it's been catching up, right?"

"Here it's a little more complex. Ever since Slovenia seceded from Yugoslavia, there was this tendency of too much money invested into culture. There was too much socialist logic. It's been shrinking ever since, and this has all been an excuse to shrink it even more. I think the future is somewhat grim. We were used to big subsidies from the state, but I think this will be less & less the case."

"Has it gone from socialist to capitalist democracy?"

"It's somewhere in between, I think. There are still some remnants of socialist logic and also some hardcore, late 19th century capitalism going on – it's kind of a mixture."

"Let's talk about 'Volk' & the LAIBACH stuff. As far as the sound of the bees humming in the Chinese national anthem..."

"This was the LAIBACH guys' idea."

"What was it like collaborating with them?"

"We knew each other before *Volk* -- the main guy Ivan."

"The singer right?"

"No, Ivan does not appear onstage. He's kind of like the hidden mastermind. He does the concepts, the interviews ..."

"And no one has ever seen him on stage?"

"Rarely."

*"**In the 80's, the early 80's."*

"They're not a band in the classical sense. LAIBACH is a brand. They don't play any instruments, they hire musicians."

*"**When you work for LAIBACH you are LAIBACH. So it's a group idea actually."*

"They had these four figures – I think they were painters from the Nazi regime, and when you work for LAIBACH you become one of these four painters."

"All part of the totalitarian aesthetic?"

"Yeah, haha. Something like that"

"Have you met Irwin? Is there an NSK exhibit in Ljubljana?"

"You have some items in the modern gallery."

*"**In Maribor there was a big exhibition."*

"They have a lot of exhibitions but no permanent ones, except the modern gallery."

*"** In the future I think their interest is modern art..."*

"I know that NSK has won a high arts award in Slovenia. Are they regarded in Europe among the academic field as a serious form of art, or is NSK more a Slovenian or fringe thing?"

"They are quite famous in Europe. NSK were known mainly in Europe for their creation of a virtual state – they had passports & you could actually travel with this virtual, non-existent country. So from this and also music wise, they're pretty well known. I think now a little bit less because, how shall I say? Not the ultimate time for ideas like LAIBACH in the music industry. It's a little bit too radical, I think. It's a time when nothing is radical, yet everything is at the same time."

*"**Did you grow up in Slovenia?**"*

"**Yes."

"I moved around a lot because my father was a diplomat. We lived in Brazil as well."

*"**Slovenia is a fairly unknown country to the United States…**"*

"And Europe as well…"

*"**Are there any stereotypes about the Slovenian people?**"*

"Quite a lot, I think. A lot of the German mentality, I think. We're a pretty reserved people. There are a lot of suicides…"

"**I like the mixture in Ljubljana – you can feel the influence of Italy, but also the Balkans, the Germans,. It makes the city interesting."

*"**Do you think there's more of an Italian feel?**"*

"**It depends where you go. The east is more Hungarian, in the south it's more a Croatian influence…"

*"**The 'Ten Days War' – what was your experience?**"*

"That's a pretty surreal experience."

"**We were maybe too young to take it seriously – we were maybe 15. We went to the cinema the second day."

"You know, you always see the country – like The States, for instance – something you take for granted that does not change. Especially not overnight. These processes take decades, hundreds of years, but it actually comes incredibly fast. Once you experience that you get a sense of how volatile things are, actually. And now that we have this crisis in the European Union, I think we are a little more apprehensive then people who are in more traditionalist countries, like France. They're used to having France around from I don't know when. We have changed from about 5 countries in the past 80 years here. For the first time we have our own country with four different currencies in our lifetime. Nothing is permanent for us; everything is just a matter of time, I think."

*"**What areas in traveling Europe have surprised you?**"*

"Personally, I enjoy the most Portugal. A small village, we had a show there. But you can find a lot of diverse stuff in Europe, that's the best thing, because everything is so close & there is still so much difference between language & habits."

*"**When you went to the United States, what was the strongest impression that stayed with you?**"*

"We met a couple of homeless people in the street who were really extraordinarily talented. This was in LA. It really amazed me, these kind of people that had all this talent that were really good musicians & they could not find enough work to get by. This was shocking to me because here, you can be a pretty big loser & I think you will still get by somehow. It's not easy, it's getting harder, but still you can live…"

"Do you have any funny stories involving LAIBACH?"

"Well he did about 80 shows with LAIBACH [**points to Primož**] so he probably has better stories then me."

"**It's a problem because you stay in one city for a day…"**

"Actually rock n' roll life is not exactly as rock n roll as people think it is"

"**For me, I'm more interested in eastern Europe – just to see if there is some left of the socialistic time. You can feel it very much in Romania or Bulgaria."**

"I think if you're on tour, it's not a good way to experience different cultures. You see very little – it's a very isolated world. This is why I prefer working in theatre – you go to another country & have two or three weeks to experience the local culture. If you're on tour you don't experience much anything. It's…"

"**Like a circus – completely circus-like…"**

"Now LAIBACH – you can't exactly simplify it as simply a parody of fascism, because there's so much more going on there in terms of concept. In the United States, very few people know who LAIBACH is & if they do know who LAIBACH is, they've rarely ever heard of NSK. I'm curious the reactions in Eastern Europe with these countries that did actually live through communism, totalitarianism. Do you get protestors that misunderstand & label them as bizarre fascists? Or do people actually get what they are about & support them totally? In the USA, people could see their imagery, the uniforms, the singing in German & there is an instant knee-jerk reaction…"

"Not really – in the 80's they were seen as a step towards democratization. They were seen as liberators, not as fascists. They were never considered fascists. This is just iconography that they used. But the message is exactly, at least I see it this way – they are lefties. They are hardcore leftists. If you talk to Ivan, he's a friggin' communist. He's nostalgic as well, for old Yugoslavia. So they use this iconography because they know people will react to it. And also people tend to project their own conceptions of what it is. So when you see these guys in their Nazi-like uniforms onstage, people project what they want to see. This is actually what LAIBACH is – a giant mirror, I think. This is what attracted me to them the most. It's not about their message, because there is no message. The message, if there is, is very convoluted & very hard to get to. The people project their own visions into it. And they've lived with it, quite nicely, for the past 25 years."

"Have you ever heard of the Church of Subgenius?"

"No."

"It's similar. Like when you try to read about NSK, it almost leads you in an endless, bizarre circle. Subgenius is the closest I think we have to NSK & LAIBACHian rhetoric in The United States. The figurehead of this church is a floating head with a smoking pipe hanging out his mouth. He's smiling & his name is JR Bob Dobbs. He looks like a used car salesmen from th 1950's & is like this god-like figure propogating the 'Gospel of Slack.' But anyway, getting back to Slovenia & Yugoslavia. What is your impression of TITO? Are a lot of older people still sympathetic towards him?"

"I think a lot of younger people are sympathetic towards him through their parents. Every year you have this massive group of 13 year olds that go to this birthplace. And I think his persona is still very much alive. At this moment there is big disillusionment & now they turn backwards. They always do, you know? At the end of the 80's, everyone was rooting for independent Slovenia. Now I think people are nostalgic."

*"**It's always like you remember the best thing."*

"Is TITO a difficult person to judge?"

"I was really young at the time, but I remember that there was a – and this will sound a little naïve – but a bigger sense of brotherhood, a bigger sense of togetherness. But now these are very individualist times. Also – it's a paradox, but it's a nice one — the people united against Yugoslavia at the end. But now he's gone."

"In Europe, as I travel, there seems to be a greater movement towards the right wing. Is the anti-immigrant trend also here in Slovenia? Or is it generally left wing here, due to the historical background?"

"Slovenia is relatively moderate – there are no real hardcore extremists. We have a few nuts, you always do."

"Who is the famous writer from Slovenia?"

"For me it's Slavoj Žižek – he's a living legend. He's actually quite a joke here, which is unfair. He stated his political preferences that people didn't like. And he also openly claims to be a communist which is now here a big crime. I think that people here do not want to associate with communists. But he does it in the same way as LAIBACH, because reactions tell you as much about the person then it does Slavoj Žižek's supposed communism. And he's a very famous guy outside – probably one of the biggest living philosophers of the moment. But you know the story of prophets in their homeland – it's again the same story, I think."

"The guy that sings for LAIBACH, what's he like?"

"Milan [Fras], no one recognizes him when he's offstage. He's a completely different person. He has this wry, peculiar sense of humor. A semi-philosopher tendency – he's an interesting guy. And also it's really fun when you play with them. Onstage he's this God-like figure from below, and then during the concert he turns back to you & then he starts commenting on the babes in the front row & stuff like that, you know what I mean? Haha…

"In the United States a lot of people call RAMMSTEIN the "Poor Man's LAIBACH." Are they seen in Europe this way?"

"I think it's pretty obvious that they were heavily inspired. But I think the paradigm – they actually were just inspired by the musical aspect, they didn't incorporate the bigger part. LAIBACH isn't about the music; music is only one small facet."

*"**RAMMSTEIN is LAIBACH for kids…"*

"It is true though. If you look at LAIBACH only for music – I personally never listen to them, but I am a great fan. When we were approached, one of their thoughts was we could go as far as possible from their previous work. We didn't see ourselves in that sort of Nazi-rhythms… We wanted to see if it was possible to combine this totalitarian logic & put it with something that is very thorough, very direct through lyrics & idea, but also with music that is very complex. I think it was very necessary for them to do this album."

*"**It was actually the only way for their career, because doing all the time the same stuff. Now they are way more open…"*

"We were attracted to the album because of the ideas of doing national anthems. It's a very simple, very straight forward, and very, very powerful. It was surprising to us that no one came up with this concept before. It was very easy to work once you had a concept like that. You know, back in the 80's they couldn't advertise their concerts because they were banned. So they'd post these black posters, and everyone just knew it was a LAIBACH concert. And then they just said where & when & people came. I think it's a strong concept that is still relevant today, maybe even more so then it was in the 80's. It was easier for them to work in the 80's because the Iron Curtain. It was easier for them to market the idea – they were more interesting in The West. But their idea is more important now – we need to see ourselves in the mirror. It's really crucial to gather a little bit of objectivity…"

lange reis naar huis

X. *"vliegen hoog boven de zwarte vortex"*

The Hungarian Tank, be like The Hungarian Tank... *The Tank knows no fear, chugging forth relentlessly...* The cargo, the equipment, the sleeping musicians in the caravan – nothing will stonewall his mission... For 24 hours now, The Hungarian Tank has rammed us forward. *Without sleep. Without comment or complaint. Without the seeming blink of an eye...* Outflanking, outmaneuvering, out-pacing every rival on the highway...

The Tank is the ultimate tour driver. Tattooed, muscular, no-nonsense as a Bosnian mercenary – his thick, terrifying neck, his Rollins-esque nylon sport shorts. *Be like The Hungarian Tank.* The Tank does not care if you need to shit, because you do not have the authority to disturb these churning, brutal wheels like *Roadwarrior* Max & his dirt-filled mack truck. *Be like The Hungarian Tank...*

We are almost to Belgium, now, I think, en route to Amsterdam. The Tank has already pushed us through Milan, Switzerland, most of Germany in a near 24 hour burst... Plans kind of changed for me when I met Black Breath, the Seattle band exhaustedly slumbering in the rattling van. The Tank & I are the only conscience ones, but I don't bother him. I just remain in his shadow, trying to make sense of everything...

I was lost in Italy for 3 days before Black Breath saved me, wandering Bologna aimlessly. I couldn't make up my mind whether to head for Rome or for Barcelona. I could have made the Pisa/Florence/Rome string for extremely cheap, but Rome was now at peak tourist season. Expatriate Matt [*from London*] had sent a desperate dispatch: <u>*avoid Rome at all costs*</u>. It was a useless deathtrap good for nothing but €8 mayonnaise sandwiches, rampant pickpockets & elderly Catholics + the inevitable sweltering madness of an ancient labyrinth in Mediterranean August...

Barcelona seemed ripe but there was no cheap route. Rideshare was useless; English grows increasingly useless South of France. Hitchhiking wasn't a workable in Spain or Italy like it was in Germany, Czech or France. Sleazyjet was too expensive; if I were to pay the pretty penny it might as well be for Athens, Greece. I still pined for a ringside seat to the austerity protests which had engulfed the nation. If I were to reach Barcelona, it priced at $250. Then from Barcelona to Lisbon, another $175. From Lisbon to Brussels, another $150 at least. It was a shady mission sure to bankrupt me, leading to a definite 2 weeks wandering Belgium aimlessly...

** *"tragična komedija"* **

Back to Ljubljana... By the time LAIBACH/SILENCE had taken their leave, the rain had ceased pelting the Earth. The cold front lingered – it was like early Fall; you could see your breath. Ivan Capenac [*of death/grind act DICKLESS TRACY*] came to my aid, offering a warm place for the night & the drunken company of metal girls at a Communist housing remnant of the TITO era.

Ivan & his cohort Klemin [*of thrash band ERUPTION*] nabbed me from the hostel & we went straight for the Turkish Kebab's. Ivan was bemused by my rabid Francophobia. He chuckled heavy, then remarked: *"I read about 'The Paris Syndrome,' that most of the Japanese tourists that go there are so shocked about how different everything is from the 'Romantic Paris' that some people have to be hospitalized from the shock, haha. They portray it as this capitol of the arts, the everything, and then you come there & everyone acts like you are a cunt. Haha..."*

"Yeah, it's 'Phony Bologna' – that's what we call it in the US. I don't know what I hate more – Texas of France. Yesterday I woke up from a nightmare & it was just the outline of Texas but colored in with the Drapeau Tricolore..."

"When you mentioned Portland, do you know a band called Nekro Drunks?"

"Yeah."

"Those are some crazy guys – two guys playing old school thrash, drinking, doing mayhem all the time – crazy stuff."

"Portland's weird – it's this endless complex of tattooed people, and everyone is drunk all the time. Just drunk people being drunk everywhere to the point where you can't really make any real friends because everyone you meet is so hammered they barely remember you the next day. And we have this huge amount of suicides off the bridges, and we have 9 bridges, so it's almost like designer suicide because they are all different shapes, looks and sizes. You can choose your death like an interior decorator..."

"How much time did you spend in France?"

"Like 4 days, but it felt like a year. It was horrible..."

"Ha, ha, ha..."

"So anyway... Tell me who you are, the bands you work with, the scene in Slovenia..."

"There is one band for every scene – you only have a few quality death metal bands, a few quality black metal bands. 2 or 3 grindcore bands – sludge is coming up now, like 2 bands. A few in between are playing metalcore & deathcore. We don't have a metal magazine anymore. We have one alternative radio since 1969 – its called *Radio Student*. It was formed by the Yugoslav government at the time to settle down the tensions of the students at that time. But instead it became the tool of the student population. They are the first guys that played punk, extreme metal on the radio, and are still doing so to this day. We have many webzines, zillions of clubs. Billions of people who are into metal, punk rock, any kind of art from those areas. Since we are a part of the European Union *[**May 2004]* we have tons of gigs. Everybody comes here now. 6 years ago there wasn't many concerts, but now you stay home because you can't decide where to go."

"What is minimum wage here?"

"€400 & something Euros."

"So you do salary pay then?"

"Yeah – but when you take the taxes you lose about €100."

"Does the government subsidize your apartments?"

"It does it you're part of the student population or if you have evidence of, I don't know, being an endangered species in the population. Even my friend, he's working for the army, and they didn't give him an apartment for free but he only pays two-thirds the price. When you are a student you have these possibilities to be financed – cheaper accommodation, food stamps & medical expenses covered. But when you graduate & get your own job, then yeah, you have to pay everything."

"Are there any stereotypes to Slovenia?"

"They say that people here are really envious – if you're neighbor has a better car, you don't appreciate that someone has a better paying job. If someone sacrifices a lot for something, then it's, '*I hope you fail.*' This is the stereotype that I learned as a Croatian, but this is just a stereotype. I think every country has assholes. I think Slovenia is a little bit closed – when people move here they find a little evidence of xenophobia, but not a lot of the population."

"Is there an amazing Slovenian comedian no one knows?"

"No, most Slovenian comedians are like really bad. And the movies, all of them end with some weird murder or suicide. We are always making jokes that every Slovene comedy has to end with at least one person dying, and if not there will be a sequel that ends with someone dying. I mean, we are much more prone to watching Japanese horror movies or German porn or American catastrophe films. With Slovenians, it's always like a forced, '*is this thing on?*' sort of joke. The Slovene cultural scene is much more powerful when it comes to theater, poetry & prose. Actors, like Shakespeare or Slovene national epics, there are tons. All Slovenian art has this really depressive bent to it. All the Slovenian classics, the books you have to read – New York hardcore has nothing on them. He could have found a job, but for the next 300 pages he got drunk – beaten, stabbed, scorched, raped, whatever. But there's some great horror stories, warrior stories – but it always has that sad & bleak tone…"

** *"accettare il vuoto"* **

It's amazing how quickly scenery shifts; that within a few short days you can go from sleeping under a Slovenian awning & freezing in the pouring rain to… *well…* sweating profusely & sleeping under a shop widow in Bologna…

I had left Slovenia to tackle Trieste, but once I made the bus stop it was still freezing cold & raining. Back to Venice & the antiquated labyrinth? Straight to Rome? Florence? Or do I stab at Turin, the black magic capitol? *Fuck it – Bologna*. How could I go wrong? Work the element of surprise & get the Powerviolence Crew drunk as sailors on the eve of a fortnights leave…

I left the train station & meshed with the Bologna stream, nabbed a few brews & soon found myself at a public fountain/automobile roundabout near a fortress-like shopping center which has surely been the thoroughfare of commerce for at least 400 years. I dipped my aching feet in the bubbling water & cracked a dark ale, texting Lorenzo & e*veryone was out of town for 3 days*… No REPULSIONE, Brainwash or Cancer Spreading. Facebook pandering proved useless…

For three days I slept on the streets playing the tourist loner. Relaxed alcoholism, stretching out in the park, going basic yoga, enjoying the peacefulness of Italy. The first day was a vague matrix confined to a dull sulking over the rampant nature of absurdity. I'd grown beyond the ability to manifest a panic attack… Time had lost all meaning; homelessness had lost any semblance of terror. I did not yearn for a woman to be by my side; I did not care where I was. I was Straczynski's Lazarus & had obliquely slipped through the cracks. I was content with the void…

Following a deep sleep of dreams with zombies, I met the first interview – a guy named Marino from crust/speed band 2 Minuta Dreka. He was friendly & intelligent, but struggled to speak English. He'd get frustrated at his inability, tear out handfuls of grass & classically remark [*as all Italians do*]: "*please-a-excuse-a-my-shit-a-English.*" Marino took me to XM24, the huge communal anarcho-complex with a massive spray paint mural. The gate was locked, the building empty – no shows for a month...

I went back to the internet café, hitting up every metal & punk band I could from Bologna [*and Rome and Barcelona and Lisbon*] using Encyclopedia Metallum. I left messages over every Facebook profile I could locate, but no one was writing back or calling. Texts from my mobile were being repelled like gnats & Whitney [*from London*] was abandoning Rome in 2 days...

I accepted the void once again, purchasing a movie ticket to a poorly dubbed Italian version of current Hollywood summer movie "*Capitano Americano: Il Primo Vendicatore.*" Oddly fulfilled, I then marched off to another touristy area where I was soon sandwiched by bell towers in a cobblestone square. A public stage was erected with a massive projection screen behind it. It could've been anything – art show, a play, a movie – no clear idea. The city of Bologna had provided 500 fold out chairs in rows...

Soon a man in a brown, suede suit came on stage with a Hitler mustache. He was broadcast on the projection screen like a ludicrous Nuremburg, staring at us silently with crazy eyes for 5 minutes of silence. Soon he began making crazy noises like a cartoon character & the picture faded to *The Wizard of Oz*. Dorothy & Toto lit up the screen & the Hitlerian figure went into a seemingly coked out mega-rant, narrating every single line of the film as well as the sound effects & music in a jarringly bravado performance...

Day Three; waking again on the street, thinking Køpenhavn Korana was making coffee in a nearby kitchen. It was a slow process to realize I actually was in Italy. By 2pm I'd wrangled a power metal interview & Franco Nipoti now sat before me, munching on the hamburgers of Corporate Franchise XYZ...

Here to tell you of that very struggle power metal faces – that endless uphill battle of an art form which is not throwback to a lost period but rather something timeless & eternal – is Mr. Franco Nipoti of CRYING STEEL, which is the most power metal sounding name I've heard all year: "*Crying Steel was born in 1982 – first we start as hard rock band. So it was our kind of expression, at the beginning of the 80's, how I can say? We met Judas Priest's music, which was quite shocking for us. So this started to be our experiment. We had a singer like Halford so we mixed this sound...*"

Franco continues: "The first album was 1987; we played a lot cause our code was especially to play live. Of course it was not so easy in Italy because of the mentality of the people. In Italy it's very easy for bands that play melodic, easy listening, because of our culture. Not so easy for rock bands. Especially it was not so easy in the 80's. At the end of '88 we had a split in the band because two people were very frustrated by the lack of result. But they was frustrated about the lack of the result in the business. When we started playing this music we could not have the ability to become big stars. But when we played you see the result of people satisfied & screaming – these were very much our gigs. On the other hand you see the labels not caring too much about us. So you can understand someone being frustrated about the situation. And I'm talking about me – I was ready to go out. I can also understand that others do not understand this creation. The promoters like cover songs – they like a band to play Top 40, and ask for these figures... In the beginning of 2002, 2003, we found one more time the pleasure to play together & start writing something new. So we had this album in 2007 called *The Steel Is Back*. It was quite a good album, especially surprised from the reviewer end because people thought we would be some dinosaur."

"Back in the 80's, when Judas Priest would come do a concert, how many would come?"

"Well not so many people were following this kind of music. I remember Judas Priest playing. They did four concerts initially & the total was less then 20,000."

"What cities in Italy will you get a good response form? Which are the best?"

"Ah, I see you re a journalist – very good question, very, very good question. In Italy I think the best audience you can find for rock & metal is Milan. Milan is about 3 million people – Rome is 4 million, but you are talking numbers. But it is much more lower when you go South in Italy. You will find some of our very best fans in the South, because when they're a fan they are fan all his life. He is very loyal, you know, but it is very, very few. It is very difficult for them, especially in the 80's. It was difficulty for them to get the record because there were no shops."

"Have you played all over Europe?"

"Italy, Greece, the South of England. I love German people, they are-a-very strong, very oriented to metal. I know some people that played in France & it was a very terrible situation because France is, how I say – they think only good things come from France. Haha. So we would like to go touring in the eastern Europe – Ukraine, Slovenia. They are open people, very friendly."

"Tell me about the bad stereotypes of Italian people…"

"Most people think Italians are these stereotypes of the South. In the North is very different – it is 100% Europe. In the South you can see little villages, the old mother coming on the donkey, the vineyards – same as 50 or 60 years ago. I think maybe for the stereotype could be the music. I remember very well when we started a lot of people, the fanzines, they were surprised because they thought there'd be a violin or mandolin…

** *"l'eternità, sta ancora"* **

The slowness of Bologna crept drudgingly. A final band was to text me @ 3pm, this Nightwishy, Lacuna Coil thing. I sat in the park as the clock ticked in infinite gulfs… *The name?* ETERNITY STANDS STILL. Irony, you know? *Scomparso…*

After a 6 km haul I located crust venue ATLANTIDE, in an old military fortification. It was the last of government funded anarchist centers offered to the partisans following Mussolini's defeat. I caught some English on the front steps & was thrown into a dialogue with McAdams from Black Breath, a fellow Northwest inhabitant. Bologna was the last stop of their trek before heading back to Seattle. We knew a lot of the same characters back home…

The night was rad – Black Breath killed it with a blackened thrash punk meets Entombed sort of flavor. A dozen guys were there from the Obscene Extreme saga; Lorenzo & Matteo soon appeared. The local melodic death metal act Disease Illusion stopped by for a quickie interview; kind of a mix between At The Gates, Dark Tranquility & Trivium. It was the usual you'd expect in having a tape recorder spontaneously thrown in someone's face, but they were still totally pro. They stuck to the magic secret of journalism where no matter what question you're asked, you bend it to fit whatever you actually want to talk about [*thus, metal-centric as possible*]…

Most the night was spent chatting with Wizard from Black Breath & attempting to shake off a coked out prostitute. She just came at me from the street & started hanging off me, hitting booze from the crust mob on the steps. She kept tugging at my man sack, trying to drag me home with her dirty *shit-a-English.*

The Wizard offered a free ride to Amsterdam where Black Breath had flights. Considering my luck, I didn't see much success in a piping hot Spanish/Portuguese mission guaranteed to annihilate any remaining scraps in the bank account. *Gloriós Espanya, podem un dia junts la dansa…*

** *"ce pays pue comme un sous-sol"* **

When all is done, The Hungarian Tank will dump off the equipment in Belgium, depose of us in Holland, then drive back to Prague in one continual burst. He will then load the trailer full of an elderly woman's worldly possessions & drive her to Northern Germany, unload the truck & redecorate her new home. All without sleep, without rest, without complaint. *Be like The Hungarian Tank...*

Two hours from Amsterdam, The Hungarian Tank – the inhuman machine of a chauffeur – pulls into the parking lot of a Belgian hospital. Staring out the window, not addressing anyone in particular, he prosaically states: *"I have to take care of my stomach."* The Tank heads inside, leaving us to discern the conundrum...

Wizard & I get lost on a mission for beer in this strange land that smells like basement. It's a dark night; the buildings are ominous & no traffic hampers the road. Grass grows from the cracks of cement like a swamp suffocated by blacktop. Seemingly abandoned railroad tracks lay in the grass island between roads; children's play-sets are in fenced enclosures appearing untouched from years of neglect.

We find a convenience store where workers give us disturbing looks; shadowy figures lurk in the windowsills along dilapidated streets. A plastic container lay on the cement, covered in crimson clumps that Wizard seems convinced is human plasma... We try to backtrack, but we're completely lost; no hospital sign in the distance... A guy dressed off-key as Borat wanders up; he looks methed out & is wearing a windbreaker from the early 90's, these MC Hammer confetti pants & has a rat tail mullet going on. He points us towards the distance, disappears, and we are lost again...

Luck returns; Wizard & I find the parking lot with beer & chips. The other members of Black Breath are hurriedly ripping all their gear & backpacks from the caboose. The Hungarian Tank's *appendix exploded* while driving; had he avoided medical attention one hour further he would have died at the wheel, killing us all. To imagine the pain of this man must is unfathomable – and not the slightest grunt of dissatisfaction in his harrowing professionalism. *Be like the Hungarian Tank...*

The money man is long gone; Southern Lord isn't answering. If Black Breath miss their planes they lose out on nearly $5000; secondly, they do not have any money to book fresh return tickets. Without any other option, they clear out their bank accounts on €525 for a 2 hour taxi ride. Within 20 minutes the taxi-van rolls up, we furiously pack & burn up the Autobahn at 100km

_{8.1.11} KONINKRIJK VAN BELGIË _{8.8.11}

X. *"aucun gouvernement, mais beaucoup de bière"*

Santa Clause is black as night, frozen in eternal vigilance. Without pupils, without expression beyond a wide, untrustworthy grin, this monument to Saint Nick resides at the center of Rotterdam like a rancid Golem. But no one – not the sculptor nor city hall *let alone the denizens of Nederland –* could've precipitated the blatant architectural blunder.

Unless this actually was rigged as an inside joke by the sculptor himself knowing that the Dutch authorities would be forced to let it stand after having personally commissioned it. They wouldn't want to be in opposition to arts & humanities & general human progress – even if ignoring this blatant middle finger to everything decent about the country...

One can imagine the mayor of Rotterdam at a balloon-flanked spectacle, inaugurating the occasion. The Hollanders gathered around, huge sheet draped over the 10 foot high statue. The mayor shouts to the crew to unveil it while the trumpets of a marching band blare loudly to mark the occasion. The fabric drops & the citizens behold the sight which halts the band, alchemically causes their trumpets to rust, forcing the pitiful mayor into instant cardiac arrest...

What I'm talking about, my friends, is THE BIG BLACK SANTA. This statue of Santa is the pride of Rotterdam & the very flag they fly to rope in the tourist crowd. But the awful reality is that THE BIG BLACK SANTA is holding a miniature Christmas tree that looks <u>*exactly*</u> *like a* GIGANTIC rubber butt plug. And I mean levels of anal expansion as to set a world record in ass spelunking...

Sylvester says tourists come from all over Europe just to point and laugh at it. When families gather at the feet of Anal Clause [*Holland's nickname*], the cold-sweat, giggling parents have to hold it together as their children innocently ask: *"Mommy, what's that thing in Santa's hand?"*

This is the funniest god-damned thing I've seen all year – until you notice the glob of pigeon shit that hit perfectly on Santa's chin at just the right angle. Looks like Chris Cringle took a buckshot of jizz & it's slowly dripping down his grinning, spermy face...

It's a one-off for me here in Rotterdam, hanging with Sylvester from goregrind luminaries Fondlecorpse. They are ridiculously heavy on the 80's horror references. Their unofficial mascot is the fang-bared, porcupine alien from Critters & their imagery includes every similar tiny creature running amuck & eating half naked women or accompanying joining zombies in their Ghoulies/Gremlins/Boggles attempts of world conquest...

Sylvester calls himself "*The Misanthropic Hermit*" & this is the first time he's gone downtown in months. He rarely leaves his house working graphic design jobs & whenever he actually does get out just finds himself wandering aimlessly, wondering what happened to the glory days of the 90's. Like so many lost souls he doesn't know what to do following the mass closure of video rental stores. He was one of _us_ – that proud race of human whom spent years digging through VHS tapes, living the *MST3K* mystique...

Alas, we now live in the internet age. Red Box & Netflix have claimed dominion. Blue Ray hi-def makes everything looks like a BBC television show, removing the movie-ness of film. We stroll vacant Rotterdam on a sleepy Sunday, reminiscing about a world once packed with seedy metal clubs, chain-smoking coffee shops, luscious women in fishnets & knee-high leather army boots...

** "*le monarque misérable*" **

Bruxelles, I never thought I would reach you. With your world class brews & concrete swampland, your particular stench of moldy basement forever in the air... I'm at the DNA lounge, having been assimilated into the Be-Metal Webzine staff. One hour off the bus & the Belgian metal journalist Illuminati have already scheduled me a half-dozen interviews. I have both Catheline Fedurski & Gilles Desomberg to thank, who've graciously taken me into their home...

Catheline & Gilles have taken me directly to The DNA Lounge to meet the "*deathcore thrash*" band Blast Year Zero. DNA is a notable tiny venue that works as a coffee/alcohol bar & performance hub at once. Today's gig is with Steve Rawles, who is about to perform an acoustic set [**he's touring for the disc 'Bonus Room'**]. Rawles is a Canadian best known for his work in well-traveled punk act This Is A Stand Off...

As Rawles sets up to play, I make contact with Julien & fellow bandmate Thomas. Julien begins our exchange: "*So we are Blast Year Zero – a metal band. I'm not sure quite what style we are, haha. And yes, we are formed in 2000 and 8. We are rehearsing in this big building, every metal band in Brussels is rehearsing there. We go outside of Brussels to do the shows. The problem is not to get the show but to get the people to go there...*"

"I was told there are three separate sections to Belgium – the Flemish, French & the Walloon…"

"In the North there is the Flemish, French in the South and Dutch in the North [**Walloon]. There is a difference in mentality, money. There are many more metal bands in the North then in Brussels or the South…"

"What do you think of this Charleroi town? I hear it's the industrial wasteland of Belgium…

"That is the ugliest city in the world. It's like Pittsburgh, but even worse – haha. I know because Americans told me this. It's very ugly, it's an old mine city, but the people are nice. It's a very dangerous spot, but there are a lot of bands, yes. But it's not pleasant to walk."

"Do you have a question for me about the USA I can answer for you – something you never understood?"

"A LOT! We grew up, us Europeans, in an American way because of the movies, the music, everything. I've been only in New York – I fucking love it. But anywhere else, no. Americans told me that New York is not America…"

"Yeah, NYC is a whole other thing – it's like an alien planet & when you go outside of it you are in the real America."

"So how it is? You love your country?"

*"No. [**everyone busts out laughing]. You know, the average American doesn't really know what's happening because they aren't well read. And they have a short attention span – TV, radio, Facebook, video games. I've traveled all over the USA & now I've come to Europe. But just to listen to all of you, because I'm sick of talking, you know?... Is Naples the best place to get a pizza in Italy?"*

"Honestly, the worst pizza I ever ate was in Italy, actually."

"What do you think are some stereotypes about Belgian people?"

"The French people, they make the accents. Is not true, and then they joke about Belgium. Stupidity, and we don't care about things. But we have many good things – beer, chocolate. Haha…"

"Is Jean Claude Van Damme the biggest thing that ever came from Brussels?"

"For United States, yeah."

"What's the biggest thing that ever came from Brussels for Europeans?"

"I think it's Jean Claude Van Damme too, hahaha."

"Well, what kind of government does this country have?"

"Haha. I think you need more data, because this takes a lot of time to explain. It's, ah… hell here – a mess. We have, it's been… <u>We don't have a government</u>. Right now, it's been 1 year the struggle – the fight between the north & the south about Brussels. It's Flemish, it's French – we don't know. We have all these parties in such a small country with all different languages. We just fight about this. And at the same time people don't really care. I don't really care. But, you know, the country is still working. It's been one year, and we don't have a government."

"Wait… You have no government at all?"

"Yes."

"But you still have police? That's still going on?"

"Yeah, police, yes."

"So are the police the government now? Or the army? Is there even an army?"

"No – Belgium's army is just for the Independence Day show. And some logistics because they are in Afghanistan now."

*Thomas W: "**No, we have fighters in Libya…"*

"Like Special Ops?"

*"**No, we are famous for fighters – jet fighters. Other then that I don't know…"*

"We are in Afghanistan?"

*"**Yeah"*

"Really? I didn't know… And yeah, police is normal, I think."

"Is a government going to return to Belgium?"

"I hope… It's independent."

"What made it stop?"

"It's a conflict about the frontiers of Brussels. Brussels is in the Flemish region, but…"

*"**All of Belgium was speaking French, but then you have Flemish guys that have formed their own sense of identity. And they want all of Belgium to become Flemish."*

"Um… So, ok… The history of this country, because I'm a little uncertain. Has Belgium always existed or qas it new territory that came out of WWI?"

"1830 – it was part of Holland. It was always The French & Netherlands…"

"So they just kept shifting back & forth?"

"Yeah, and in 1830 they made an independent kingdom. So it's very new."

"When did the monarchy end?"

"It never did."

"You still have a king?"

"Yes, a monarchy."

"You have a king and no government?"

"Yes."

"Is he like Queen Elizabeth where he's just a figurehead?"

"He's a puppet, haha. He doesn't have any power."

"Is this the last king of Europe besides Britain & Sweden?"

"No, no – Spain has a king, Norway too. And Netherlands… The problems we had in government, the leaders of the political parties went to the king – doesn't change anything. But he's nice guy, you know? He's Belgian."

"Is he drunk all the time?"

"Yeah, pretty much, haha…"

"In Belgium, do you have free healthcare?"

"Yes."

"See, this is a lesson the United States needs to learn. You have no government and your healthcare still runs?"

"Yes."

"Without a problem? You still have police, you still have firemen, all these things. Now, say, your firemen – are they in danger of not getting paid because there is no government? Or does everything just keep moving along…"

"Everything keeps moving."

"And everyone is like: 'Fuck it, we've been doing this for so long, we know exactly what to do?"

"Yes."

"Is there any other country in Europe that is doing this?"

"No, no."

"Is this a trend or an idea that the Belgian people want to keep? Like we can be the only country in Europe that doesn't need, have or want a government?"

"Maybe, some people…"

"So are we technically in a state of anarchy? Does the common person here realize they now live in an anarchist state? Is it ever talked about as such?"

*"**We are really passive – compared to the French…"*

"If this were in France, there would be murders everywhere. We just say *'Aw, well, whatever…'*"

I leave scratching my head, feeling as if I survived a Monty Python skit… Belgium, it's like a civil war that refuses to bear arms. The fundamental state services are still there, rendering a sort of gentleman's anarchy. Perhaps this really is the solution humanity requires? Could the proof clearly exist in this pudding?

For clarification we head to Elektrocution, a record shop operated by Baldur Vilmundarson. He is vocalist of Arkangel, among the most important metallic hardcore bands in Belgian history: *"My name is Baldur Vilmundarson, I'm 42. I run a record shop called Elektrocution – it's a mix of rock music meets heavy metal, punk rock, hardcore music. I have also gothic/industrial music & neo-folk. I run this shop for 8 years now..."*

"Beyond the shop I'm playing in Arkangel; 10 years now I've played for them. We are on Good Life Recordings... I think the Belgium scene has always been very active with fanzines, labels. Like probably everywhere there is a high level of activity & then changing every few years. Maybe because people are influenced by other trends... If you think about the scene we create something very different then New York hardcore, for example. Always when I do a band I never thought we need to sound like New York."

"Are you happy living in Brussels?"

"Yeah, I think so."

"Do you think it's one of the better the European capitols?"

"I don't know if I can say that, but its always different when you are a tourist. I love to go to Poland – I think they are a very good culture. My friends over thee they have a very open mind. I think Brussels is a good situation if you look at working & everything."

"Has Arkangel toured a lot?"

"4 times in Japan, we tour a lot in Europe, but we've always been independent & never a big touring agency."

"What's it like touring Japan?"

"People are crazy there. The first time we played a fest – Independence Day fest – Misfits were playing, Heaven Shall Burn. We went back & did a tour of 12 shows. I love the culture.

"Tell me about being an independent music store owner."

"You know I try to run the shop in the shop & I sell nothing on the internet – I don't want to be a part of the internet system, like selling very high price record. My goal is that the spirit of the people coming & buying at the shop the record they've been looking or many records that's my idea. I'm near the biggest venue in Brussels, so I have people from TOOL coming here, Blur, a roadie from Motley Crue, Cradle of Filth. It's always funny to have guys from their bands and you say their taste in music."

""I'm just curious how you run an independent business in a country where there is no government..."

"I think I have no problem. There is no government – I think its big companies that have a problem with this situation."

"Well how do you – does the government tax you?"

"Yeah, I pay tax of course."

"So all the basic foundations are in place, there's just no governing body right?"

"I think it's typical for Belgium – we don't have a government because we have too many different parties. There is always people who want – there is small parts that want to be independent. I think the situation is very civil. They don't find a solution between 7 different parties. I don't live with this problem because I don't care. They don't listen to us, to the people. You vote for them but – you should have like one party & they are the winner but it's not like this. It's like football, yeah, you have playoffs. After season you have to make another small season & its crazy."

"Have you been to the USA?"

"In 2001 we play the HELLFEST in Syracuse. And then after that we went for a tour but got many problems because Arkangel was supposed to be – the guy who create Arkangel was hard-line vegan. And so when he left the band go on, but the band change the idea because they were very young – like 14 years, 15 years old. Then when you are 18 it is different – you have another opinion. But the tour was a catastrophe. The guy who organized it was not very experienced & we trusted him. After three shows we came back. Also, we got problem with people boycotting the band because all the vegan straightedge stuff. They said – its not all the people, just a few. Small groups, you know, who say, '*Arkangel you are sell outs.*' I was not vegan myself – I don't understand. It's human, you know. Some people don't think about the situation. Arkangel was very young kids doing a band & then after they try to destroy the band because they're not vegan any more & that's stupid. I never tried – I've been touring with many American bands but I never tried to be like them, you know? I'm from Brussels, and I show what's Brussels; I don't try to be New York hardcore. I think most problem of many bands from Europe is they try to act & be like them but they are not. That's the biggest problem for many bands in Europe..."

** *"le canular grande"* **

Day II; hot but not too hot, humid but not too roasting. I'm sipping beers with members of Sekhmet, inching closer to the perplexing truth of Belgian existence. Says Jérémy Laitem: *"We've chosen the name Sekhmet because our drummer always wanted to from a death metal band with Egyptian influences. We listen to Nile, Behemoth, bands like that – a new way to think riffs & music. We took this name which refers to Egyptian mythology…"*

"I know the country is divided with the Flemish population, etc. Do even you have a problem communicating with them, being from the French side?"

"The Flemish difficulties are more in politics. You have some people that are a little racist with this, but most of the people don't care that much. We speak the same metalhead language."

"What are best bands no one knows about from here?"

"You have to check out Dehuman – they are like a mix between Morbid Angel & Suffocation. And Age Of Torment."

"So this CD you just handed me, is this your…"

"First release, yes. [**points to cover*] This is the solar disc, which is very important to the Egyptian mythology. It's a symbol for the sun and Ra, the god of the sun. It's black to represent the dark side of our music. It's a story about a child that received the power of the sun & wants to hold it & raise a dark sun to put the old one in the shadows. It's better when I say it in French, hehe…"

"Do you have a question for me about the USA I can answer for you – something you never understood?"

"There are a lot of bands in America, or so it seems. Why is it that when you go on Myspace, on Facebook, you see a lot of them. But you only hear about the same few?"

"Because the entire media is basically controlled by the same umbrella corporation, which is called VIACOM. VIACOM own Clear Channel & Clear Channel owns something like 95% of all the FM radio stations in the United States & therefore dictates the set-list to be played on every station. The DJ's are handed one big jukebox list & told to pick from it. After 10pm those graveyard shift DJ's get to pick a few personal songs, but are still forced to play 90% of what they do off those same lists. Songs are like paid advertisements in the USA, and all the advertisements are for arena tours or large concert hall shows, because Clear Channel owns a vast majority of venues as well. Most of the big touring bands are on labels that are part of VIACOM, and Ticketmaster – which sells 90% of the concert tickets in the USA – is also in the VIACOM pyramid. It's like a big circle jerk where you can't win."

"You have a lot of metal played on the radio in the US, yes?"

"We have the usual, easily accepted hard rock bands like Ozzy, Judas Priest, Led Zepplin, AC/DC – all the stuff people are used to. When you hear something new, they'll slip in something like the bad Disturbed single, the lazy Rob Zombie single – that kind of shit, because

it's an advertisement for a corral where they can pack 20,000 people inside a sports arena & charge €8 per beer. And at least 80% of the time none of those songs they try to brainwash us into thnking are coll actually hold up. They just sort of disappear & the remaining 'kind-of-ok' 20% get attached to that big VIACOM approved 'it's ok to play this' jukebox list. And then at night, if you have a metal specialty show, sometimes you'll get a little Morbid Angel or Immortal played at like 1am. But it will only be a handful of songs because that's the award DJ's get from the bosses for working nightshift – let them get away with a few tunes. Now a college show you can get away with anything – they are all specialty shows run as independent programs through the school – but those DJ's are paying to go to college anyway, so it's like another perpetual scam..."

"Well, at least you have some classical rock broadcast. Here, in Belgium, we have *Classic 21* but it is nostalgic & they don't play much rock or metal except at night, and it is always bands like Helloween. It seems like extreme music, more underground music – it's something the radios are ashamed of..."

** *"la vengeance des médias"* **

Day III & lunch with the Belgian Heavy Metal Illuminati. I'm flanked by a barrage of journalists & promoters. One by one we head down the line. First up is Julien Masure, of concert organization umbrella Undercore Bruxelles: *"I am in charge of communications for a small organization who are organizing gigs in Brussels, but we are not yet legal – know what I mean? We don't have a real statement, we haven't yet put our names in the law, if you know what I mean. It's very underground, but one of our goals is to get known by the law & then we can ask money from the government. We pay the bands & the venue, all stuffs like that, with our own money. I think in Brussels there are a lot of hardcore bands & that's why we created this association, because we are not that into hardcore. We prefer to promote thrash metal, death metal, black metal. It is very new in Brussels, I think, to have real promoters. There are a lot of concerts but they are organized by one private person. I think it is a new step to have some organization."*

"Tell me about some bands you've worked with..."

"Dehuman is not enough famous band in Brussels, but they are the first death metal band to release one full album. There are a lot of EP, but they propose a full album. What can I say more? Enthroned, they are black metal & worldwide famous. In the 'ardcore scene you have Deviate which is worldwide famous, you 'ave Arkangel – those bands are famous but we aren't working with them. We work with Emptiness... There is a more important scene in the Flemish side of the country. It is a much easier scene because each band, they are receiving 100 euros by the Flemish government. Here in Brussels you are a band but you receive only what the promoter gives you. Flemish are well-organized but it is a government thing. In Belgium we are separated land... Undercore Brussels is my organization. Very much of the concerts in Belgium happen on the Flemish side so we are trying to relocate the metal place from Flemish to Brussels. I heard two days ago that the Minster of culture in Brussels was ok to create a house of hippie but not a house of metal. I'm really very tired that metal is not considered a real music. It maybe extreme but it as extreme as jazz or blues was a century ago."

"Tell me about Belgium..."

"What is said worldwide about Belgium is true. I think we are friendly guys – we like to eat, we like to drink something weird with our friends from the Netherlands & France. You know, French guys don't have this sense of humor. Belgium is known as a good compromise country."

"Do you have a question for me about the United States?"

"I'm not really interested in the United States... What I can say to you is that I would love to be a metalhead in America because all the cultures are mixed & it's quite – you can see very often black people, Hispanic people. I've been to Germany, France, Czech Republic and in Europe metal is a white guy music. In United States I think it's more multicultural. I'm disappointed as being considered a *'white metalhead.'*"

"They think this all over Europe?"

"It happens a lot, not to me, but I have seen guys wearing black t-shirt with Slayer or other thing, and people are telling them you are Satanist & Nazi, racist because you listen to metal... We don't have a European metal culture. In the general press, when you see metal, it is only to spit on it. How lucky we are that the crazy guy in Norway is not listening to metal. If he had listened to metal, he'd be Columbine. And this morning I saw on the news the killer was a gamer. And the government deleted from the market the game the guy was playing. They suppressed his game in the commerce, the market..."

**"I'm Saïd from FM Brussels. The show is called *Mental*. It started in 2000 – a two hour show on a Friday night. We go from very slow doom to the very fastest black metal. Metal – all genres, all origins. I'm running the show but I always have guests, like Pat Chouli here. We had Total Fucking Destruction in the studio a few months ago, with Rich Hoak…"

"Well, we are here in Brussels. If someone were to come here, what would they be most surprised by?"

"I think the people. There are a lot of different nationalities because of the European Union, because of NATO, because of a lot of factors we have diversity. Also I think people in Brussels are just kind in their own way. That is something that is to me the strength of the city. My father was from Iraq, came over in '68 to study to be a doctor. He met my mother & stayed. Thing is, when he arrived he studied in a city that was again a very complicated language – Flemish city with lots of French speaking people. But at one point in '68, people said Walloons get out. It was a very strange time for everybody. But my father, when he arrived, those were the people he met first. Of course he could only speak French. When my mother finished her studies they came to Brussels. My father as a foreigner decided, '*My children are going to go to a Flemish school instead of a French school.*' My mother is a French speaking Walloon – all about timing, languages, again. It was a language not easy to take, but it was a choice they made for my brother & me – that language. I'm French speaking from home, but working for a Flemish radio. I can speak Flemish like a Flemish guy"

"Do Flemish people generally know English well?"

"Yes, they are often better at English. That's also a question of media use. Everything people see on the Flemish side are seen with separators & that's the same with the French side. Which is a pity, because in knowing other people, cultures – for me it's a bummer to even identify people as French, and so on. But it comes with the French culture – the real France."

"With how the French are, everything has to be French – do they know they are going to be left in time & do not care? They seem to look backwards to their past and never to their future…"

"I could ask you the same question about America & The Tea Party."

"Well they're such a minority – they're all lunatics."

"But I mean when people are thinking in a way & they are sure it's the right way, I don't think they look at it as looking back. I think the French people, most of them, they are open minded & aware of things, they know the world. But of course there are people interested in nothing else but fancy clothes, stuff like that. I'm confident that the Belgian people are aware enough to see it."

"Have you ever been to Iraq?"

"I was 12, very young. I went on the eve of the Gulf Crisis."

"When Saddam invaded Kuwait?"

"Yeah – it was weird because the television was on all day and there was only one presenter with a big mustache. And he was always reading names – people that have to get ready for the front."

"The names of the soldiers for the frontline?"

"Yeah. And the thing is my father's brother, at that time, was just 3 months back from the Iraq-Iran war. So it was just 3 months back from there, staying 10 years in war with Iran. In Iraq, everybody had to go into military service. So he was there & had to go as well, but he didn't, because my father hadn't been in Iraq for 22 years. My uncle didn't want to leave because my father was there. So the thing is – in the city, where my family lived, all guys, all adults were shot from a rebellion in the city. So they came in with tanks & all guys disappeared. Nobody ever knew what happened. Only the women & the boys were left & I was told that they couldn't even go to the street to take their brother, father or uncle inside to bury them because otherwise they'd be shot as well..."

***"My name has been Pat Chouli since the 70's. I've wrote 18 years in the national region & broadcast on the French national radio. So I promote music I love – hardcore & heavy metal."

"How do you feel about the music scene here?"

"Brussels & Belgium in general? There's Channel Zero & the rest – Channel Zero is really the top. It's a good thing that they come back together; for Belgium, for metal in Belgium.

"What do you have to say about fife here?"

"Brussels, what can say? We 'eet good, we drink good. We 'ave a special appetite for french fries. Chocolate & beer. It's an open city for culture. And it's very interesting for us as metalheads. It's not far away to go to a good show. You 'ave a lot of fortune in going to Holland, Germany at times."

"You started one of the first pirate radio stations..."

"I write for the only rock magazine in Belgium at the time. It was the beginning of the 80's – pirate radio's are born here. All the cops were looking to find us, but at the university it was much more easy because only on specific days they could find it. These were my first real steps in radio shows. Normally it was from 10 to midnight, but normally we finish 6 or 7 in the morning. They were always looking for us all the nights."

"Ever met Blackie Lawless from W.A.S.P.?"

"Ah, Blackie Lawless! Very interesting person – crazy personage. It was something strange to do an interview with Blackie Lawless because he was so intelligent. There was a lot of stuff about social structure – it was heaven & hell. This was during that first tour for the first album, it was in Paris. He was really, really angry because that was their second day in Paris & there was no organization on the first day, as usual. When I said I come from Belgium he change his face. Since then I met Blackie nearly each album, so he becomes a friend, and sometimes it's difficult to speak with someone you are friends with – like Doro Pesch, for example. It becomes difficult to do an interview with them because I know her as I know him. But it's a lot of memories of course. Sometimes I meet people & they are funny, of course – really, really open – but they 'ave nothing to say. Same people are very pretentious, but you can become a star & stay human. Once you are a rock star, you still have a normal life. There are people who drink, who take drugs, you have people that are cretins – everything like in the normal world.

"What was your most memorable interview?"

"Probably Motorhead. It was not in the center of Brussels, but around the city. We could relate. It was for the pirate radio station, so not very important for the record company. But we ask for the interview & I meet Lemmy while he's waiting to go to the airport. He opens the fridge, takes all the drinks, put it in the car, haha, and take it back to the airport. It was first time for me with Motorhead and then in Belgium they become so regular…

"Who are your favorite bands of all time?"

"Motorhead. And I'm a lucky guy, cause I saw their first concert in Belgium. I've seen before Rolling Stones, Led Zepplin, Queen – saw a lot of bands but the shows with Motorhead it's solidly them, more then 25 years after they are still here, still playing rock n roll – and I'm still a Motorhead fan."

"Ever met Ozzy?

"Yeah, he was sober. He was very careful, open mind. Nothing to do with what we see on Mtv actually.

"Ever met Frank Zappa?

"Frank Zappa for me is a big mystery. I refuse to enter the Zappa world because the discography of Frank Zappa is so enormous that I'm afraid to take all the challenges. No – Zappa is a phenomenon & I refuse to go inside.

"How do you feel about not having a government here?"

"It is a very surrealistic situation & I need two hours to try & give you observations about how crazy is the situation. It's not only a political problem, it's not only a social problem or technical problem with little cities around Belgium – it's deep inside the heart. Since the Second World War, something has changed…"

** "*aucun être humain est illégalus*" **

They call it *Chateaus Bateau,* a squatted mansion on the outskirts of Gent – or at least what would pass for a mansion in crust circles. Imagine the Adams Family house deep in Flemish territory & obscured by fauna. The huge brushes & tree lines make it difficult to view from the nearby road, or even from the neighboring homes. It's a complex to itself, surrounded by a miniature forest of trailers, workshops, compost toilets & vegetable gardens…

It must've been four stories high, and despite the lack of water pressure, the electricity is still going strong. There is an inspiring ambiance; I could write 10 books in it's womb. Upstairs, in the the little room where I've created my overnight habitat, David & Leentje have crammed dozens of self-made instruments. Used for a noise project, they've created junkyard harps & electrified washboards glued together with fox skulls, raccoon femurs & stripped chicken bones. It's like the Sawyer Family jamboree…

David & Leentje live here – the duo which comprise doom act GURA. David begins: "We try to do a tour every year – it's difficult for us because… we're not slackers, but we're not really good at organizing."

Leentje: "**Especially things with the computer…"

"It goes a lot faster then before, because we don't have to telephone & write letters all the time…"

"**We always try to say we are 'Doom It Yourself,' so we always try to do everything ourselves…"

"It wasn't our first tour this year. We have certain contacts, but there's loads of places that think our music is too experimental – be it punk or metal or whatever kind of places… The front cover will be a picture we made at a small squatted village in the south of France. A lot of people do metal works there, sculptures. It will be a crane with a dinosaur skeleton hanging from it – so it's iconographically perfect."

"**A lot of the time it's with skulls, animal skulls…"

"Is there any big difference between the Flemish or Walloon communities?"

"**With GURA we play more on the French side & in France then we play in the Flemish side."

"It's definitely a cultural thing, because they are descending from Latin cultures & the French side is more from French culture."

"**Musically the French people are not so much inspired by American music…"

"Tell me about the bone instruments."

"That's a project we've been doing for 4 or 5 years now. We don't play too often but kind of noise made with self made instruments made out of skulls…"

"**We also have projections of films behind us.."

"It's not music or rhythmic – just noise"

"The doom scene in general – in the United States it's grown more popular. Is it still tiny in Europe?"

"It's still small & in the metal environment. Is growing but getting more dull – people just copying the original doom bands."

"Tell me about this place we're at…"

"It's a squat, kind of big. It's been squatted for 6 years now; we've lived here nearly 4."

"**In the beginning it was an entirely different crew that were into freak shows, stuff like that. But then they had a lot of fights, people ran out. It was almost empty. We were living in an abandoned factory near here for 4 years before this – there was no electricity, lots of a dirty fabric. So we were really happy to live her with a nice garden,"

"Of course there's electricity & water – that's luxury…"

"**There were a lot of bands rehearsing here & that was really good – we made a lot of good music."

"The inspiration is different, the vibes are different, people are more relaxed…"

"What are some of the weirder squats you've been to?"

"The village where we took the cover of our CD: La Villiet."

"**It's paradise…"

"The people have lived there now for 20 years, I think. They are rebuilding old ruins of houses with stones from other houses.."

"**They make sculptures & everything…"

"They make it look really nice – like there's no square windows, square doors & so on… And hen they have sculptures they built into the walls…"

"**They do concerts all year…"

"In the summer people move there to work in the garden & make food for the winter & in the winter lots of them leave again. Sometimes you can arrive there & there's 5 people & then in the summer they'll be 30. But they organize everything & don't spend any money because they don't have any but manage to live good."

"Is the anti-immigrant trend in Belgium as well?"

"Yeah, it's everywhere – Italy, Austria, Poland, gradually it's all of Europe. In Belgium we had the Flemish block – they had to change their name eventually. On one side, it's a very complicated story because parts of Europe have always been colonized. Like Belgium has been Spanish, French, German, knights, kings, blah blah. What remains now are two different parts & very little peace. There's always been xenophobia but even for ones neighbor. Right now the immigrants, the gypsies – there's always been lots of suspicion between different groups & the economic reality now is Europe is one big entity & there's outsiders popping in but that's the view people get when they get it fed & they believe it because its an easy way of rationalizing stuff. It's the '*others*' that come here and '*they're*' here to take your wealth & leave again. But it's always been like that – people passing through, living here a 100 years & off again so I don't know if the problem is that super big. I'm sure its happened over & over in history. Always in every country there will be an extremist nationalist party."

"You were talking about going to Texas for the Stoner Hands of Doom fest – what was your experience there…"

"It was absolutely, totally strange because it was two months after the 9/11 attacks & everybody was totally paranoid but also very friendly. And afterwards, I heard people are like that in Texas – friendly. Still the army & air force was… People were only talking about terrorists & Osama. Hardly anyone at the show & we came back penniless. Nobody got paid but everybody still smiled all the time…"

"Did the largeness of Texas freak you out?"

"Not freak me out, but I did get curious. I especially got the impression that the cities are so much bigger then I've ever seen. When I think Paris is big, I've never seen any big city in the United States. But the dimensions are different here definitely…"

"How do you feel about the King of Belgium? Does he have any power?"

"**[Laughs]*"

"I don't think about him."

"***Most people just laugh about him.*"

"He is an extremely old man…"

"***Most people don't take him serious…*"

"He has this veto right, but then they just discharge him for 3 days, make their law & that's it. He never mattered."

"Do the people here want him gone?"

"I think most people, yeah. They get so much money they do nothing with. Except for keeping their palaces clean & all their little travels to heads of state friends, giving expensive presents ..."

"Is there a problem with nationalist groups messing with squatters in Belgium like in Poland or Hungary?"

"Less. But before I started squatting, like 15 years ago, then every 3 weeks the fascist students would come to smash in some windows & run away. They gathered with a 100 to chant in front of our house & then run away. And some raids late at night where they'd come & ram in the door. Stuff like that happens, but I haven't heard about it for 10 years now. I think they changed their image when the fascist party changed their image. They got sued for being racist – you can't be racist in Belgium, its against the law. So they got tuxedos & ties & their street crews did the same – they got into different costumes. They tried to get what they wanted in a different way. They're quite organized & they have their philosophies."

"Are they like, 'Hitler was cool, the holocaust was good?'"

"They're more about these times. But they've all read *Mein Kampf*, of course. The Nazi's exist, of course, but the people that really cause problems are the well-educated fascist students. They know lawyers, they know judges, they know cops – they are all sons & daughters of cops & lawyers. They always find their way around the law. But it's not really that violent here like Eastern Europe..."

*** "anniversaire de mariage joyeuse" ***

Claude meets me at the Train Station, which seems large as an Airport Terminal. It's like the architectural centrum of the city, the one thing they are most proud of in a town eroding from age, where industrial smokestacks can be seen on the horizon...

I am now in Liège, in the French part of Belgium. Like Gent, it's filled with olden castles & gothic bridges & cobblestone streets. Everything bout Belgium has an old, debilitated feel. Even on the rickety Italian-style local train that went from Bruxelles to Gent, everything had bullet holes or some kind of moss. Everything vaguely smelled like a basement, the sky an industrialized yellow. The grass everywhere was brown, like the entire country got sprayed with Agent Orange. Not dead, just brown. In Detroit terms, Belgium was one big stretch of Melvindale, Ecorse & River Rouge...

My time in Gent was spent riding on bicycles with David & Leentje through drizzling rain while wearing my camouflage tarp with a slit cut for the head. We'd attended a crust punk show [** *with a few doom* *bands thrown in for good measure*] at an abandoned gas station turned venue. There was a Food Not Bombs vegan buffet in home-made oil drum furnaces. Above the pump shelter in huge red letters it was painted *"Aucun être humain est illégalus"* – a reference to the xenophobic politics of immigration in Fortress Europe. *Pizza slices & roasted stuffed peppers kept flying...*

As for Claude, he is happy to meet me, apparently having read about this book on news feeds all summer. Word has apparently been traveling – these chatterings over this mysterious Americano that just shows up out the blue & starts interviewing people.,,

Claude, his wife & I are at this fancy-pants restaurant inside the massive train station serving €12 hamburgers & €30 steaks; he is a former metal journalist that spent a significant time writing for Rockforce, the biggest metal zine in Spain from '88-'95. Bury Them All, the metal project in which Englebert plays bass, was started 4 years ago. He likens it to: *"if Amon Amarth was a deathcore band..."*

"When you start a new band in Liège you have to find a rehearsal space, and that is a nightmare. You have really only two places where you can rehearse – one is here behind the station. It used to be an apartment & the spaces are in the basement, so it's very wet. You get your gear & system totally crashed in just six months. There is another across the city, but it's pretty expensive – something like €350 a month for a small place. That place is mostly used for pop music & we are lucky to be one of the only 3 metal/hardcore metal bands there. You used to have 3 metal bars in the city – 2 just closed recently. The remaining places you can really play are a socialist union."

"Like a crust punk place?"

"Yeah – the far-left places. You really have to get connections with these people & you don't have a metal crowd & the local punks that come to that place – that's not really our audience. And the other place you can go is a pop place that sometimes has metal shows as a once-off, or some smaller festivals. It's very close to what's happening in France.

"Is Germany the easiest country to do these activities?"

"Yeah. Germany is pretty easy – we've been playing in Germany. No one complains about the volume or heavy metal bands playing. France used to be the place because they'd get sanctions from the government to welcome bands, whatever kind of music. Belgium is divided in two – in one part the decision was to back pop & classical music while the Flemish was more into rock & metal."

"Tell me about the band..."

"We do things seriously, but we don't take ourselves seriously We've been but here for four years & are recording our first full length. We try to bring a little gimmick. Since the band is called Bury Them All we want to play with zombies, because that's our singer's worst nightmare. So we had a music video we did playing as zombies. It's all about having fun. It's about movies; lyrics, as far as I can understand from the growling, it's mostly personal, private experience that some of us share. We've been touring over 4 years but we don't use all this imagery onstage because we don't have the opportunity to do so."

I heard Liège is an old industrial town ..."

"Exactly – I describe this place as being some kind of New Jersey together with the worst parts of Flint, Michigan. But what we can do well is eat & drink & we do it well..."

"So are industrial factories still here?"

"Yeah, we still have some steel industrial factories, but nothing compared to what the city used to be. I think in the 19th century this city used to be the third most powerful industrial city in the world. Today it's not even the first place in Belgium. I have a friend that lives in Flint & told me that Detroit is really, really down at the moment & it's really sad that you can buy houses..."

"For $1?"

"Yeah."

"You know, the amazing thing to me is that all these major corporations could buy up all that land & just make huge industrial factories in the middle of it for dirt cheap but they won't. Do you know how happy the population would be even if they were granted a solid minimum wage paycheck? It's depressing that that would be some lottery win at this point..."

"In this city, we are at about 25% unemployment.

"Do you think he EU is gong to buckle under?"

"We have to stay in one place because we don't have any other option. Portugal is a nightmare at the moment; it's impossible just to survive there... What a weird situation. The people here, I don't think they feel like they fit in with Greece or Portugal. We haven't had a government here for 3 years..."

"Yeah, it's such a surreal situation."

"People don't feel like they can do anything wrong, because no one is in charge."

"What do you think of the king of Belgium?"

"At the moment he's the one running the country & making the decisions. But he's not going to be the one finding a solution. I think he's quite tried of it. If I were him I would resign."

** *"frontières invisibles"* **

Claude rolls me across town to the crust venue; as we drive, I am struck by the classic look of Liège. Like most Old World architecture, the buildings are huddles together like cement congestion. The lines of shops are like a chain-link of one-story, flat faced buildings...

Claude drops me off a few blocks from the punk venue – enough to stay hidden for a few & enjoy a few beers to myself in the cement-floored park where little kids play soccer happily. The civilians, in usual European mode, do not fear each other. They communicate openly, randomly. They are just humans being human, not needing or yearning for the constant stimulation of hi-def blue screen TV's & X-Box counsels...

I soon meet my second interview of the day, Crustpunk Vince [aka "Vinnie Two-Pens"] – an extremely tall, dreaded & friendly chap with band patches sewn over every inch of his wardrobe. He speaks French normally with a heavy accent where I have to occasionally hone in desperately to realize what he is saying to me. He helps organize local shows here & plays in a band called Suit Side vs. Veda Plight which recently toured Brazil – and also an aptly dubbed punk group called Sux To Be You...

"I was at a gig & drunk & making stage diving. People didn't carry me so I jumped and they left me falling down. And then I broke my neck on the edge of the stage I was like oh fuck 'eeet urts. So I continue the parry, then after party, the day after I go to 'nother gig and it was very violent with people pogo dancing. Oh my neck 'urts. Maybe after one week, still hurts, I say, '*Ok maybe I go to hospital.*' So they made radiography of my neck and the seventh vertebrae was totally smashed. And they said, '*How is it possible that you are still walking with that? You should be paralyzed from the neck to the foot.*' So I said, '*Yeah, I don't know.*' So they put me in a brace, I had surgery – now I have a piece of metal in my neck. Like with a screw inside the 6th & 7th bones & they took a piece of the bones here [*points to hip*] and put it there [*points to neck*] and everything was smashed and they said you have osteo... os-tee..."

"Osteoporosis."

"Yes, I was only 19 at that time. So they say your bones are like a guy 60 years. So you have to take calcium & blah blah blah. So I took 4 months in the cast and after – stupidly I went to see GBH – I just removed and was like '*aaaah*' in ze front and I realized this was stupid because my bones were so fragile that I shouldn't have done that. but… Now these days I don't pogo dance anymore. I don't go stage-diving anymore."

"You got the surgery in Belgium right?"

"Yeah."

"What did the government make you pay? I'm just curious, as an American…"

"The hospital? Because I was still living at my parents house and I had health insurance – I don't know, I didn't pay by myself because I didn't have any money at that time. But I think that most of the cost were paid by the insurance. I think my parents paid 100 Euros. Everything was maybe €800 [$1,059 USD]…"

"Um… In the United States, they would charge us…"

"I don't know the price, but I know that in the USA the system of health insurance is not very working or not very good. I know is Belgium it is compulsory. And now as I'm an adult, so I pay something every 3 months, like €30. Something like €10 a month."

"€10 s a month & you have total health insurance?"

"Yes, covered in case of accident…"

"That's like $13 American dollars."

"Yeah, and…"

"Can I see your lighter…"

"Yeah, and because I'm poor here and don't make more then €9,000 a year, we have the right to special health insurance. So, I just pay €30 every three months, and if I go to the doctor or dentist, or anything, I just pay €1 Euro 50 Cent for that of my own money. But the insurance cover every health cost."

"A buck-fifty in Euro. For everything."

"Yeah."

"That's like $2 American."

"But that's only because…"

"You are poor."

"Yeah. But if you have a job, you pay more."

"Ok… That's… Fuck it, moving on… Is there anything you don't understand about my country I can illuminate for you?"

"It's strange for me, because I drink some alcohol thinking that you can't buy alcohol if you are less then 21. Not a question, just something – I can't really understand the drug laws. Maybe if you just smoke a joint you could go to jail. Here, it's not like that. If you got some pot on you and got arrested, if it's less then 5 grams you can keep it, or they take it and there is no charge against you. But the thing is – you can buy and drink alcohol if you are less then 21 but you can't have your driving license until 18. It seems really easy to buy a gun in the United States."

"Well, there's a waiting period. It's not hard to get a gun, but you have to wait somewhere between 3 days and a week. They just do that so you won't do something crazy in a fit of rage. I mean you can own hunting rifles in Europe?"

"Yes, if you can prove that you are making sport."

"But there's no way to get a concealed weapons permit?"

"You can't walk in the street holding a gun on you. Is stupid – if you go to a shop to buy a gun for sport, and get stopped on the way between your shop and your house, you can still be arrested."

"Even in the wrapping?"

"I've never tried to buy a gun, so I don't know…"

"So what about unemployment?"

"In Belgium it is really easy to get The Dole. I've been on The Dole since 8 years – I've never worked in my life. But not all the country in Europe. In France it's totally different – you must be 25 without doing anything. Otherwise you can go die, they don't give a fuck. Here when you are 18 you get out of the compulsory schools, like normal high schools, I suppose, and then you work or make some high studies for being a lawyer or doctor, or you can subscribe to The Dole. And you have a 9 month waiting period in which you are supposed to find work, and if you didn't find any work, you get The Dole. How much depends if you are living with some people or living alone. If you are living alone you get €750 a month [about $993.00 USD]. Every six months you have to go to an office and prove you are looking for work really intensively. But most of people here in the punk scene are on The Dole so maybe two weeks before they forge some fake letters to bring to their meeting. So you have to be active, but it's really easy. Maybe 5 years ago they change the system, make it stronger to get people out off The Dole – the parasites to do anything. If they think you didn't do enough to find the work, you get a contract you have to sign. And they said, *'Ok in 4 months we se you again,'* and you have to send at least 6 letters. You must go to the office, you must subscribe to seasonal work office, stuff like that. After this 4 months, if you did it well, ok you are free for 6 months again. If you didn't respect the contract, you are out of The Dole for 4 months. And you have another contract. After these 4 months, you can get it back. If you didn't make it right, you are out of The Dole forever."

"You've been dragging this out for 8 years?"

"Yeah, yeah, but there is no limitation. You can stay on The Dole all your life. Maybe the system is gonna change because there is problem between he south and the north – not civil war – but the politician from the north & the south can't get on together so thee is no government for more hen one year. No country in the world had that situation – even Iraq. So it is a surrealistic si9tuation. But for me I don't give a fuck, because I don't believe in any government, so I don't give a fuck. So for me, I just live about that,. I don't care about the nation or Belgium or being Belgian – I don't care I'm just human & I don't believe in any border, so fuck that. People, some people feel like '*Ah, I'm Belgian*' so they wear the Belgian flag and they are '*oooh we live in unity.*' For me, it is a joke. It's really easy to get The dole. Even if you are a stranger – male or female, it doesn't matter. Say, '*ok I want to take this guy under my charge.*' So you go to the office and say '*Ok, Mr. Blah Blah is on my charge.*' So you get €250 more Euro a month [$331 USD] because you are supposed o live with this person. And this person can't work, so it is a bit crazy, but it's real easy…"

"So you basically just fill a squat house with people and this financial foster care…"

"Yes. For example this squat down the street – all the people are registered as living there alone. They all get The Dole and don't pay rent – they pay electricity, water & gas. Really easy for that…"

** "*revenir à l'essentiel*" **

I wake up in *La Cité Des Enfants Perdus*, thinking that the whole of my American remembrances are derived from the lucid realms of fresh slumber… Since the squat was totally packed & few spoke English, it felt too strange to try & worm my way into their home. I was exhausted & needed sleep, so I wandered off towards the end of the show. My resting spot was at the edge of the cement field, hidden behind what looked like a garage…

When I lifted my eyes – again, somehow thinking I actually <u>was</u> French – all I could see were huge clusters of cobwebs, thick like the dregs of a cotton processing plant. I was in the crevice of a cement coated swamp, and this was a world of constant drizzle rain, moss, tarantulas, black widows & venomous snakes.. I took a walk on that early Sunday morning, my ragged shoes peeling apart. I felt great peace in vacant streets – every building I could envision bodies being thrown out from upper windows during the height of the Black Plague…

Hours later, amongst a plethora of bands raging technical death metal. It's a birthday party in a tiny underground venue that constantly makes me sneeze. The band Excavated brought me here after directing me to their practice space. We're now at coordinates halfway between Bruxelles & Liège at a venue we'd call a VFW Hall show in America...

The gig is a knock-out; the headliners are Excavated & Dehuman – even the generic punk band hits the spot. Despite the manic journey of my search & the high-fluting rhetorical garbage, this is what the metal scene is all about – a bunch of youthful minds 16-30 merrily rocking out to killer music. No assholes, no jocks, no tough-guys – no hillbillies with "FEAR GOD" hats aimlessly shouting at people with beat-red faces...

Dehuman go for the jugular with a Schuldiner approach to death metal – classic, authentic & vibrantly executed. Excavated have a similar sound but there is much more of a hooky, thrash element – and they easily take the crown as one of the best death metal bands I've seen all year...

Aubry André of Excavated is an unsung guitar hero of Belgian repute. Everyone in his country knows him that know metal – he was one of the original players in ENTHRONED (the most famous black metal band fro Belgium] & at his peak played in 7 bands at once. Right now he is drunk, philosophizing. He tells me the key to his existence in his trademark, heavily-accented way: *"I am not a lyrics writer, you know, I have nothing to say – I just have some emotion to translate by my guitar, but I don't have anything to say. I am not driven by politics – I am just a normal guy. Maybe it sounds stupid, but keep the planet clean. Everybody is doing anything, throwing cigarettes on the floor, or a sandwich – it's stupid. Nobody do that now. Everybody want to be on MTV, to be a star, 'you don't know who I am.' Yes, yes, I know you – you are a no one like me. Maybe I play in some band, maybe I tour Europe, but who am I? I'm just a guy who's playing music. You go from nothing to headliner in 3 years. What, so what? We are just guys playing music. Maybe you are unique, but do not be so stupid. So I am here to play music & I play music & I am enjoying that. But for me, in my life, this is only thing I want to do. If in one weeks I don't have rehearsals or concerts, I am lost I need that. For me it's very important because that is the soul..."*

** *"majestueux de l'eau brune"* **

It's like Jim Carrey reaching the edge of the sound-stage in Truman Show – the same feeling I had when reaching Hollywood for the first time. The cardboard, cut-out setting of it all falls to ruin when you recognize it's sham... We are now at Nieuwpoort, the finest of Belgian beaches. Where you can finally observe first hand the Atlantic ocean touching Europe. Thousands of years of pollution later, and the sea is completely brown like an oil spill of rust. Kids fly kites on white sand; I stare into the horizon of unlimited grime, the industrial refineries on the coast...

Blocks away we are attending a hardcore festival at a civic center on a sleepy Sunday. Unseasonably cold as it's been all year, yet the sun shines brightly. There are 6 local metallic hardcore/metalcore bands of generic stature filling the bill, with two high-grade headliners – the USA's sXe hardcore titan FIRST BLOOD & the most famous death metal band in Belgium ABORTED...

The audience are almost exclusively hardcore kids with the flat top/short-brim military hat. There are about 200 of them here, and everyone are spin-kicking like ninjas, crab-core slamming or *"picking up the change."* I've never actually seen a few of the moves I've been privy to – like the oe where two guys go into a standing 69, hold each others legs, then cartwheel across the pit in unison. There are so many people doing back-flips you'd think you walked into the rehearsal space of The Body Rock Crew...

It's getting close to show time for FIRST BLOOD. Bassist Joe Ellis is snug up against the brick wall outside the venue when I approach him. He's another Yank from The Bay Area, originally. In terms of metallic hardcore, this band really is among the upper echelons of similar acts like Hatebreed, Madball, Born From Pain – all the knuckle-dragging, beat-down stuff that clubs the solar-plexus like a no-nonsense Neanderthal...

"Belgium is hardcore central – do you agree?"

"Yeah, it's definitely one of the best areas in all of Europe for hardcore. We played here last year with Born From Pain. We toured with Napalm Death – we're doing Brutal Assault next Friday which is all metal bands. I think we & Hatebreed are the only two hardcore bands. Which is cool, we like to mix it up. A lot of people think that because we're in a hardcore band we hate death or black metal – not at all man. Dude, if you asked me & the singer, we'd probably tell you Cannibal Corpse, Death, you know, Decapitated, Sepultura are all some of our biggest influences. Personally, I love playing with bands like Aborted. We played with WATAIN at Full Force – it was awesome..."

"Have you had some bizarre moments on this tour?"

"We went to Bosnia, Bulgaria & Serbia for the first time, which was awesome. The kids were so stoked on hardcore & metal – it's not as easily accessible as it is here in Germany or Belgium."

"I heard if there are record shops in those countries, they are all counterfeit records..."

"Yeah, I went into a store & they sold bootleg Biohazards, Sepultura, Machine Head – anything bootleg you can think of, they had it. And it's still very expensive. Kids can't really afford that out there. I wouldn't pay €30 for a t-shirt either Other then that, the most bizarre thing is that it's been freezing all summer. You could've told me it was fall."

"I heard it was ridiculously hot in the USA..."

"Yeah, heat wave – a lot of adversaries saying *'don't go outside if you don't have to.'* In a sense, I'm kind of like, *'Am I really bummed that I missed hot weather to the point of not being able to be outside?'* Not really."

"Have you ever played the KØPI?"

"Yes, that's a good place. The festivals are the highlight of the summer; I think With Full Force was the best. We've done a handful of small fests. We played with Caliban, that was cool."

"What's the number one thing people ask about America?"

"Kids here are under the impression that the United States is like the best place ever for everything – shows, merchandise, for anything & I would say what they have here for hardcore shows – the kids in The States really take that shit for granted. There's a difference here – you might only see First Blood or Terror a couple times. It's not as easy – we can't just hop in our van & drive there, Kids in The States are spoiled in a sense. I love it there too, but the biggest misconception here is that every show has 600 kids in America & everyone loves each other – its just not the case."

"Do you do the artist visa thing in Europe?"

"When we started we'd just sort of come – fly separately, sneak our merch through the borders. Hide our instruments – *'we're just traveling college kids.'* Now we have an agency & we get visas, driver, all that stuff. It does make things less stressful. You never have to show up to the border & bullshit your way through."

"Have you ever gone into Russia"

"We really want to. I know that it's a harder country to do. First Blood's done Mexico, the US, Canada, Europe, Asia. I think we're gonna do South America. Anywhere we can, we'll go play."

"I haven't been in the USA all summer, so I was wondering if there has been any more discussion about Fukushima, if people are still freaked out..."

"Yeah, they are – we actually had a Japan festival right after this tour. We're not saying we'll never go – but right now it's just a little sketchy. It's really unfortunate because it's a great country. But it's a really – we don't really want to mess with it right now; it's just too soon with all the radioactive stuff. People are still freaked out but, you know man, in America, people are freaked about something new every week."

"Do you want to live in Europe?"

"I like my life in America, but I don't necessarily agree with the people in charge. Every country has its faults & things that are corrupt & you can go back & forth all day & compare Germany to the US, Belgium to the US, but it's really… Our singer lives in Sweden, but the rest of us are from America. None of us are from San Francisco at this point. I live in Iowa…"

"Where?"

"Des Moines. I started touring really young with a band called Too Pure To Die. That's actually how I met First Blood – they got me into what I do. Our singer prefers living in Europe to the States, but what's different? The foods different, I guess, the health care – but see you'll run into worse with the police officers in some of the far, far out European countries. They'll straight fuck with you for no reason because they don't have anything better to do. I guess it's really about finding out where you feel comfortable & where you feel safe, you know? It's hard to say…"

"Got a crazy story tour story for me?"

"Fuck man, we tour a lot & that's just how it goes. In another band I used to play for, we toured Mexico. And it was right in midst of all the super bad drug cartel stuff We played the capitol & we were just hanging out in the venue & they were shouting '*look out, the drug cartel is coming!*' and there were armed guards on the street & I'm like '*I can see the American border & I'm gonna die in Mexico*.' I guess this is what happens… Made it out OK only to get food poisoning 2 days later, pass out, wake up in Mexican hospital, they're trying to give me shots. I don't know what they're saying & I'm not gonna let them stick that needle in my arm. So I had to fly back into Vegas & it turns out I had this crazy infection in my liver. And I'm straight-edge, I don't drink. I almost died from that… At this point, when something wild happens, I don't even look twice."

"Yeah man, it's really gotta be something like Godzilla rising from the waters…"

"It would have to be a Godzilla at this point to be shocked…"

And I'm done… I can exhale now. The finish line has arrived & in the end it's just myself & a dozen hardcore kids a decade my junior… Just feeling old & out of place, wandering around like a nicotine zombie looking for a half-smoked cigarette butt on the ground…

When I return to the USA, that's going to be the first thing to go –
no more tobacco, bad food or exhaustion. I'm ready to move on, to repair
myself like Humpty Dumpty. Guys like Joe Ellis have at least one thing
right – strength is what counts. Authentic triumph is the self-willed power
for the great duration...

Cathline, Gilles & I drive off to Enochian Crescent's "Lyijysiipi,"
cruising through rural fields blanketed by the ever-increasing night. What
I need is <u>SLEEP</u> – *300 hours or more of it...*

RUIGOORD

8.12.11   8.15.11

XI. *"kinderen van de vlam // vallei van de zon"*

In life there are no epilogues – there is only continual flux. You can force
patterns into the chaos, you can link mad occurrences into a cosmic chain
of events, but understand one thing – even if futile, all of this is forgivable.
It is necessary perhaps, this longing for proof which validates our
existence, lest the human mind become its own self-destructive weapon of
confusion & volatility...

The important thing is that you do not struggle – *do not wage war
against the current.* You may choose your vessel of navigation; you may
perpetually renovate & upgrade it -- *but do not seek to control both*. This
is the fatal mistake. This is the ultimate heresy which no defibrillator can
resurrect...

** *"de geest van kerst toekomst"* **

Before leaving to Europe I read *Woodstock Nation* by Abbie Hoffman, a
classic revolt of 70's counterculture literature. That sort of genre prototype
with its message of unified radical freak politics – this was the sort of
muck-rack that distorted my ideology at a formative age...

Woodstock Nation, which I'd never read until May, was quietly
waiting at a quaint antique shop in Portland – beat up, dusty & marked for
$3. As I flipped it's pages, I vaguely comprehended the trip I was soon to
make...

All the literary greats of my hemisphere had taken a stab at *The
Great American Novel* & so did I. Yet time passes & here I was, about to
dive headlong into uncharted literary territory. Imagine *The Great
European Novel* – a bizarre feat to be acted upon in an equally bizarre

time & a mission statement which even most the author's I'm accused of plagiarizing never attempted themselves...

I analyzed my declaration in posthumous terms. What could be more relevant then a *Great European Novel* absurdly placed amidst a Worldwide Great Depression? I looked at it from the vantage point of a 1950's sci-fi writer. An Asimov type trying to envision some future shock commentary, but using the journalist as a device to reveal step by step the brutal nature of this distant, postmodern world. Absurdity was the key; *absurdity, gluttony, ignorance & vice...*

A Worldwide Great Depression in which there is no lack of food or goods in the nations paralyzed by its reign? A crushing depression with no shortage of housing or land? Absurdity is historic, staggering abundance brought to it's knees from rashes of suicides. Absurdity is record unemployment in the apex of record profit. Absurdity is blatant extraction by expert thieves protected by propaganda barons & bought congressmen. It's a man-made epidemic, a curb-job scam sodomizing the naïve which together feast upon the strength of its rancid weight...

If the shackles be freed our children will one day read the naked truth of our national abuse. Everything was phony about it, they will say. The Vampire Squid we've been sold as wrapping it's poisonous tentacles around our lifeline exists only on paper; it is nothing more then a figment of credit digits & empty bankers notes. This criminal enterprise was so lucid (*they will say*), so vast (*they shall claim*), that the blatant reality of it somehow rendered it transparently covert due to the sheer magnitude of its lie...

I ask you what has imperatively changed since the 60's, other then the fang-bared strength of their cunning evil? Has anything diverted from it's reality as an epic feast of hate & fear in which no one wins but the savage? How sick must a society be when it's puppet masters camp at Bohemian Grove, when VIACOM streamlines the pyramid of information, when occult symbols define the iconography of mass corporatism? When the final war is well underway, unreported & undeclared? *Just because it doesn't have a Chaplin 'stache don't mean it ain't fascism...*

We are the Internet Generation; with one click of a mouse we have the knowledge of god. Yet somehow we've been unable to flip the script; somehow we allow ourselves to be led by the heartless, corrupt stooges of a bygone era. They clog the echelons gluttonizing their trough as we collectively rot at the base of the foundations...

Woodstock Nation... There is a mention of one named John Sinclair – the same guy I'd randomly met in Amsterdam but didn't quite catch onto. I'm talking about the older gentleman from Ann Arbor. It dawned on me sometime in Berlin. One crack at Wikipedia & *yeah, of course* – it was him...

So he's here now & twisting a J. We're at 420 Café in Amsterdam – the last interview before I head to the biggest party of Ruigoord's calendar. It's the Summer Solstice gathering – 4 days long & what many consider might actually be the final mass gathering before the industrial titans gobble up the land.

Mr. Sinclair, the Ghost of my Christmas Future & proof of the invisible, spectral antennae – John is a notorious Detroit writer, 60's counterculture legend & former manager of the MC5 [*during their peak*]. He was also leader of the White Panther Party, which was a militantly anti-racist collective of white socialists backing the Panthers during their Civil Rights era peak...

As a journalist, Sinclair was central behind underground Detroit paper Fifth Estate, which is one of the longest continuously published alt zines in the USA. Sinclair was also contributor to the Detroit Artists Workshop Press, a jazz writer for Down Beat magazine from '64-'65 & one of the New Poets who read at the reputed Berkeley Poetry Conference in July 1965...

The MC5 thing, which he will constantly be asked about until kingdom come, can be summed up as thus: MC5 were one of the first punk bands, and Sinclair was their Tyler Durden equivalent, pushing them to get radically involved in the White Panther Party. He was managing the MC5 at the time of their free concert outside the 1968 Democratic National Convention in Chicago. The band was the only group to perform before baton-wielding police broke up the massive anti-Vietnam war rally, calling it a riot. Eventually, the MC5 split from him in 1969 due to his hardcore politics [*but they've remained friends*]...

Like many of the names in 60's counterculture, Sinclair did his stretch of time. After a series of convictions for marijuana possession, he was sentenced to 10 years for giving two to an undercover NARC. This predicament led John Lennon to record the song "John Sinclair" on *Some Time in New York City*...

This harsh sentencing inspired the landmark *John Sinclair Freedom Rally* in Ann Arbor [MI] in December 1971. The event brought together luminaries including John Lennon, Yoko Ono, David Peel, Stevie Wonder, Allen Ginsberg, Abbie Hoffman, Jerry Rubin & Bobby Seale, among others. Three days after the rally, Sinclair was released from prison when the Michigan Supreme Court ruled that the state's marijuana statutes were unconstitutional...

These events inspired the creation of HASH BASH, Michigan's annual pro-legalization marijuana rally [**an event which holds deep personal/historic meaning to Dr. Bartek] which led to the decriminalization of marijuana in the Ann Arbor city charter. Sinclair's case itself became a landmark Supreme Court decision that prohibited the government's use of electronic surveillance without a warrant...

Since the mid-90's Sinclair has performed & recorded his spoken word pieces with his band The Blues Scholars [**including members such as Wayne Kramer, Brock Avery, Charles Moore, Doug Lunn & Paul Ill]. He was also a long-running DJ for New Orleans' WWOZ Radio, the public jazz & heritage station. These days, he hides in Amsterdam, baked as a potato & typing infinitely in the cozy back-end of Café 420. We spark one up & hella chillax, yo...

"So is it easy to get a work visa, artist visa here?"

"I don't have any idea. I have no official standing with the government at all. I'm not using up any of their taxes. Any of the money I earned was done so in America. And when you get here, your money is worth maybe 68 cents on the dollar."

"This downgrading of the US to the AA+ standard – do you think this is the beginning of yet another financial crisis? Or just another benchmark in a perpetual crisis?"

"I think we're on a downward spiral and in total denial. And then you got these idiots from the so-called 'Republican Party' – they are using the government to prop up the insurance companies, manufacturers & the banks, and those are the people that really own America anyway. Prop them up, pay them off & hand them billions of dollars every 3 months. The rich people are just doing what you expect them to do. And the people, they are supposed to fight back, not just lie down... Unless you're from Detroit, then you're always prepared for the worst – hahaha..."

"When was the last time you were there?"

"Back in May."

"What was your impression leaving it? Same as before?"

"Yeah – it's fucked, it's a mess. Detroit, it's America at its very worst. Every horrible thing is in full bloom. It's the epicenter of American racism. Detroit, it's like a workshop on how far you can take this shit. You don't have any grocery stores – I mean what kind of shit is that? You buy food at the party store & pay three times as much. It makes me sick to my stomach..."

"Do you just sneak in & out when you go to Ann Arbor?"

"Anything I do today is so mild mannered..."

"How do you feel about Berlin?"

"I don't feel anything about it at all. They get bombed or something?"

"No man, I just thought it was a cool city. What are your favorite of the European capitols?"

"Amsterdam – I love Amsterdam. Place is the fucking greatest. For me, at least. I'm not looking for anything – I just want to be left alone, drink my coffee, smoke my cigarettes & do my writing. I go outside, I'm surrounded by beauty & classic architecture. And there's no work – I don't have to work, haha. I like to work, sure, but at my age I like not working a little better, haha."

"What other good writers are stationed here?"

"I don't know. I'm not really in a writers' community. I know 3 or 4 poets that I like, and I know a bunch of other ones that I like personally but I cant stand their work. I don't like the art here, I don't like the music – culturally, they don't have the African-American tradition here, it never reached…"

"What's your favorite city in the United States?"

"New Orleans. I was there 12 years, and you know, that's quite a long time. I was there right before I came to Amsterdam with like $200 dollars…"

"Did you ever meet Zappa?"

"Yeah, I met him, but he wasn't my kind of people – he didn't get high. I mean, what are we gonna talk about? Heh, heh. I like some of his music a lot. Of course you come here & you hear every note recorded. The owner [*of 420 Café*] has every vinyl, every 8 track – I appreciate that kind of compulsion. It's not a promotional or exploitative thing – he's nuts about his guys music… That's how I ended up here – I brought my band from New Orleans here in '98. We were playing the Cannabis Cup – I was the High Priest. The guy who owns this place said 'I own this coffee shop, be my guest.' Been here ever since…"

"What are you working on now?"

"I got a book coming out in New Orleans next month about John Coltrane… I had a book come out in England last year…"

"What do you think of Lew Welch?"

"I actually knew him."

"I found 'Ring of Bone' – think its one of the most underrated of the beats…"

"You know, Poetry – it was a lot more underground 50 years ago. In the underground, Lew Welch was a pretty well known guy. He went to college with Gary Snyder & Whalen. He was based in the Bay Area & good friends with Snyder."

"Did you spend a lot of time in San Fran in the 70's?"

"No. I was there a few times in the 60's, but just as a visitor. I always lived in Detroit, Ann Arbor. Then later New Orleans..."

"I always call New Orleans the 'Swamp Detroit.'"

"Well, the thing is New Orleans – they had a disaster & they rebuilt it. But in Detroit they didn't have a disaster – the disaster was just a white flight. They just abandoned it & they aren't coming back. But New Orleans has a real culture – it's the pinnacle of American civilization."

"You were in Chicago during the DNC riots – was there any belief that it would turn that violent going into it?"

"Ha! Sure – it was a police state..."

"Were you in Detroit when the riots happened?"

"Exhilarating – I thought this was gonna be the beginning of the end. I thought we were gonna win; that was my personal feeling. When they had an entire precinct pinned down by sniper fire I thought, '*this is a high point.*' You know, New Orleans, when they had the flood – you had almost 25,000 people in the fucking Superdome – that was the first time people had actually seen poor black people in reality on TV since the riots in the 60's. Americans couldn't believe those people still existed because they programmed them out of their world... I don't want to sound like a bad guy but I hate the United States government, I hate the banks, I hate the corporations, I hate the war, consumerism, idiocy of all sorts. I'm not happy with the world – its dominated by these tendencies..."

"How do you feel about Tim Leary? Did a lot of people despise him as a snitch?"

"There was a little bit of that for awhile... He seemed to rebound pretty well."

"What do you think of Gordon Lightfoot?"

"Too Canadian..."

"How do you feel about Celine?"

"I'm not his biggest fan, he was kind of a Nazi... Ezra Pound was my first bible of poetry – I got my whole basis of literary outlook from him..."

"Is there any book in particular that you think is lauded as being way better or more important...

"The Bible – ha ha ha... I think most the modern literary establishment is horseshit. The only modern writing I'm into are crime novels – I'm a fanatic."

"What do you think Elmore Leonard?"

"The King! Of the modern period, he started it. I like Raymond Chandler, James Lee Burke, but my favorite of all is Ross Macdonald. He introduced to the detective story the intricate plot…"

"What do you think of Billy Jack?"

"Who's Billy Jack?"

"Wow, I'm a little surprised. It's a movie, big 60's counterculture movie…"

"I'm not much of a movie person."

"It's all about the freedom school…"

"Freedom school, whats that? I've never seen Star Wars – that shows you how much I'm into movies…"

"Ever had any guy from the military come up to you claiming to be an MKULTRA survivor or with nutty alien conspiracy information? I've had some guys like that over time…"

"I'm not so paranoid, because its all transparent to me. You have rich people that will do anything to have more riches. So whatever they do, it doesn't shock me anymore. They'll do anything to keep going to Acapulco & playing golf for the weekend."

"What is the most LSD you've ever seen anyone consume & not go completely insane?"

"Oh I don't know, it's not a quantitative thing. You just need the tiniest amount to change your life in an 8 hour period. It just matters how much of an ass-kicking you can take…"

"What is the dumbest MC5 question anyone ever asked?"

"That's an interesting area… You know in some circles, they said that I was regarded as the guy who ruined the MC5… You know, if it wasn't for me you wouldn't even know they existed. Take your fucking guns off of me, you know? I was the one that was in prison, excuse me. Ha, ha…"

* * * * *

RUIGOORD, the final party. 2,000 in attendance – tents jammed like blood clots on the soil, eyes bugging out from Mali, so much purple, so many bells. Everyone knows this is The Finale. Together we've incinerated raver emptiness & evolved to Pagan Planet.

The drums are beating, the torches lit. The human snake wraps around the land with flute blowers, tambourine shakers, didgeridoo hummers. The adults play the host as children lead the march. It is a rite of passage – one generation to the next. The kids covered in mud play-act the elders – they carry the torches as we head to the pyramid of wood. It is a

Wicker Man of peaceful connotation, burning away the evils of Bilderberg's Moloch...

Where I come from, SWAT teams would raid this. They'd rush in with jackboots & AK-47's, throw the adults on the ground, beat them – arrest them, put them I jail for 20 to 30 years for child neglect. They would steal the children, throw them in foster care, into orphanages run by deranged disciplinarians & often child molesters. They would turn these pagan-hippie-raver-tribalists into monsters, smear their name and annihilate them.

No one here believes that sort of thing happens; they cannot comprehend it why any civilized government would do that to children for something as harmless, loving & pure as this. We are in the womb of tolerance. We are in the freak kingdom...

The children toss their torches into the stack; the blaze lights up to the heavens. The crowd roars, applauds, begin dancing. The Children, our newly crowned monarchs, giggle & play, sliding through the mud in bliss. Belgian Jesus tends the flame, pensive & crazed, poking it with a staff & curating the elements... All is beautiful. We sing & dance & laugh around our bonfire loving life. The ashes dim in twilight; the sun rises like the phoenix. There is no more horror, no more pain. We are in the Valley of the Sun.

viðauka // appendix // függelék

NEULAND

a mosiac of voices from uncharted territory

BRUTAL TRUTH // Rich Hoak (Drummer) // USA Grindcore // "I had a good time at the Obscene Extreme this year, I think it was on the same night we played that I ended up dancing with BRUJERIA at the end of their set. BRUTAL TRUTH played in 2007 & Total Fucking Destruction [**Hoak's other grind band*] played it in 99, 2000, something like that. It's a good festival – all grinding all the time, you know. There's really nothing else like it for that kind of music."

"During the Brutal Truth set you screamed 'fuck porno grind!'" "One thing I'll point out about Obscene Extreme.. it';s kind of hypocritical that you give all this respect to animals, totally vegan & all that, and if I tried to walk int here with a swastika or something I'd get put out right away – but you could walk int here with like a shirt that says like "rape women and hack up their bodies" that has a graphic depiction of that & they walk around like it ain't no thing. And it's not even like there's just a couple guys walking around with a porno grind shirt on, it's like 45% of the entire economy of Obscene Extreme fest is based on violent misogyny & demeaning women & animals & whatever else they can fucking think of to demean. I'm just saying it's a little hypocritical to be like *'we're doing it vegan & abide by all these rules'* but... I was about to go onstage & there's this guy with a hoodie that says in letters like 8 inches high "RAPE CREW" – that's where that line came from. And I had to plan what I was gonna say. That's usually where Kevin holds the mic up for me & I do the intro to 'Walking Corpse' but if you see the video I grabbed his hand & wouldn't let it go & started ranting into the microphone. I saw like half a dozen people that got it & jumped up like *'YAH!!'* Here's this guy wit RAPE CREW & he's standing around talking to two women & no one says anything. But if he wanted to eat a hamburger... *"I know BRUTAL TRUTH has played a lot of squatty venues – what are some of your experiences in this realm?"* "Most of my squat gigs were before BRUTAL TRUTH when TFD was still a sperm in my testicle. We played Ungdomshuset in Copenhagen [**The Youth House*] a bunch back in the day. I did a bunch of touring Europe between 87-90, whole tours that were squat tours. Those kind of places have mostly been put out of business. This place in Hamburg we partied, The Flora – that place is probably a condo now. Another was The Blitz, an occupied house in Oslo. There were tons of squats in Holland – and a lot of those people have been quote/unquote 'made legal' or are gone. There was one back in the day where these people had taken over an old WWII bunker with like submarine doors on it – a metal door you had to shut & lock it with the wheel, The room we stayed there was cold as ice because It was like a metal bunker, concrete bunker – this huge room with 4 clothesline & 10 cots where the bands slept. There was one in Der Haag that was part of the university where we stayed. It used to be a library but one of the rooms was actually a rotunda & it had ladders where you could go up a couple stories & go to all the different bookshelves... The real DIY cultures of people touring & putting on shows have differences in the United States vs Europe that are just sort of cultural differences, I guess. There never were really squats like Europe in The USA

because of our history of property rights within our legal system. Whereas in Europe there were more organized squats. You know, America is more of an individualistic society whereas Europe has more people getting together in small groups, organizing for themselves & collaborating at the youth center in a committee. Europe still has a lot of youth centers – they had this back in the day & still now. We don't really have stuff like   that in The States; you're sort of on your own. Like you can go rent a VFW hall. All that being said there are a lot of people that dress like squatters as there are a lot of people that dress like Grateful Dead hippies or like 70's disco people. There's that sort of fashion, you know? Just cause someone rolls up looking like that doesn't mean they are a DIY crew member putting on shows, hanging with bands, making music. They could, you know, just be a dirt bag in disguise..." *"What is your general comment on the situation in the USA with the Occupy movement, the upcoming election?"* "I think you'd really have to actively try to make things worse. And at the same time... I've extended the theory I have, my apocalyptic theory. When I was a kid, I thought that in 1984 Ronald Reagan was gonna start WW3 & we were all gonna blow up at once & the whole planet would be a cinder. Then I realized the end of the world was gonna take a long time. So while these current events might seem monumental, especially in these days of the 24 hour news cycle, I think that in the long term they won't be that monumental. I don't think any radical changes are going to happen fast or radically. Whether it be the culture, the government or society. You know, republicans have this fantasy that Obama is going to make America this socialist country. And democrats have this fantasy that republicans are going to make the United States a Nazi country or whatever, a fascist country. But I think to make such a radical change would nearly be impossible. I think the USA is stabilized as a very strange place. I'm trying to think of the word for it. Balanced? That's not right. It's... balanced on a tight rope, you know? Ha."
"When I asked Europeans in general if they had a question for me about the USA, it always seemed to be about health care or guns..." I've definitely found that they were anti-Bush & pro-Obama and the reasons for that are obvious. I hang out with metal guys & they don't really get into politics. It's not that they would ask me about the USA – more like *'so George bush is invading this country – is this something you agree with as an American?'* People were making a distinction between what America is or what America is doing versus what this guy who is an American is or is doing. Maybe that's a credit to the metal guys I was hanging out with. That was more the vibe." *"What was the weirdest place you ever woke up on tour?"* "With BRUTAL TRUTH this one particular time we'd been on tour playing like 300 shows a year for 4 years in a row & I was in some hotel room in the middle of tour somewhere. Everybody else woke up early & left. I woke up in the hotel by myself & I was like *'I gotta call somebody, I gotta do something'* & then I looked around & hey – I don't know where I am. I like looked out the window & the room didn't have a telephone book. I got kind of freaked out because I literally did not know where I was. So yeah, that was a pretty hairy situation." *"What's the weirdest venue you ever played?"* "A crazy show for TFD was a television studio in Paraguay. We drove in from Brazil, took

us 2 days to get there, but it was cool there were 4 or 500 people there, this TV studio with bleachers. People went ape-shit man, it was pretty fucking wild. I think the only other bands that played there besides locals were Napalm Death & a Sodom gig. Coming out of that gig at the border, we had to bribe the police. They popped us & wanted all our money. They put us in a room & two guys had machine guns to us & one guy sat at a desk with our passports & was like, 'you're going to jail, you're going to jail,' you know? Finally I just gave him like 40 dollars & he walked out the room, came back a couple minutes later with our passports, haha... A lot of crazy shit happened on that tour. I got a giant infection on my head, like a big blob bulge from sewage on the beach. We all got like stomach flu food poisoning. Just crazy driving & shit, a couple other different runs in with cops. A couple guys tried to mug me on the beach & I got hit over the head with a stick..."

AGATHOCLES // **Jan Frederickx (Guitarist)** // **Belgian Grindcore** // "We just came back from a tour in UK. Right now, we are working on some new releases like a new full studio album & plan to tour Mexico again in July 2012... We all need stick with our feet on the ground & live our lives in the real world. This underground scene is so little & restricted and I really don't think it's a good idea to make a parallel world next to the other one [since] there's just one reality with its good & bad things. To get this one world better for all people, things must change on a very large scale. An alternative parallel world would just lead to elitism. For a big change in real world, things have to be done in the real world, not in some little separate world that people with common musical preferences are creating. Does a homeless person freezing to death in the streets have any message to what some anarchist band is singing? I don't think so. Change must be made on a much higher level, not by creating a separate ideological scene... [*In terms of the Occupy Protests & The Arab Spring*] I am glad that it is finally happening. People all over the world have been shit on far too long. Banks ruling over governments, that's not a real democratic thing, is it? It's good to see that peoples eyes have been opened But there's still a long way to go to create global positive change for all people. The bubble of capitalism has exploded, but the rich are getting more rich everyday. There still is this capitalist elite which is untouchable... Europe is going an ultra liberal course. Ultra liberal over here means '*more privatizing of social security, privatizing of water, gas, electricity, public transport.*' It's going the wrong way & the rich get richer while the others just have to pay. Political parties are spreading fear because they wanna cover up their own hidden agenda which isn't a nice one for the working class. The aim of political parties, most of them, is to create diversion so they can do whatever they want... People in USA shouldn't be afraid of socialism; it seems like socialism is something "evil" in USA. I don't see anything 'evil' in solidarity between people or taxes based on income. Taxes should be used for good public services, not to create more prosperity for those who already have enough. I am not preaching for 'Total Communist Control,' but it would be a great thing if prices of water, oil, gas, electricity, rent would be affordable for everyone, no matter what income they have. And to keep these prices affordable for everyone, some things need be kept in the hands of a 'caring government,' not in private hands...

CORPUS CHRISTII // **Nocturnus Horrendus (Mastermind)** // **Portugese Black Metal** // "I am feeling the need to get out some of my ideas. *Luciferian Frequencies* took a lot of me, since I had something greater to do after *Rising*, but in fact it all came out very spontaneous – no pressure at all. I know of many bands that think way too much, that want to be different and so, but in the end Black Metal is all about being spontaneous and not giving a damn... Things in Portugal might seem a bit more open but in reality there are very few people in gigs and in fact sales went down drastically. There might be some more Media, shit loads of webzines & concert online promotion, but then again, it does not make a big impact. Even on TV the only Metal band who get any coverage is Moonspell. I wonder where are the 10.000 people that buy their records just in Portugal? Still they manage and they get what they worked for, but there is a huge gap between bands, really incredible that gap and I don't get it at all. In the old days we would get a show fully booked with just some flyers spread & word of mouth. Things worked somehow. Now there is so much information that people end up just going to a bar to drink. Also the money factor. Portugal is in a deep crisis, and people say they have no money, but still go out to have their drinks. There is a lot of hypocrisy in this scene. So I try to not care – I just do what I do & if anyone shows up, good. One is not in Black Metal for the money. People have to go back to the old ways and realize it is not about becoming famous. All over Europe, especially up north, you have all these bands that turned out so 'true' but in the end continue with their silliness for the money... Europe is not the paradise that it seems like. Germany yes, has amazing big fests and gigs everywhere, but then again it is always the same bands playing – and those get a big pay & the rest basically pay to play. I'd say that these days most people have heard the term Black Metal, which in my eyes is pretty sad since it was never meant to be that way, and certain bands are to blame. Many might say it is to spread the word, but do you really think some guy will change his lifestyle once he discovered Black Metal in his late 20's?! I used to believe it could be that way, but reality is that it is all just bullshit.... Well, most think Portugal is a sunny beach country. It can be a few months a year, but truth is that it is most of the time a pretty uncomfortable country, always rain, wind and cold. So when I get these reviews that Portugal is not meant to do Black Metal I just laugh. This is a country with a deep background on the esoteric & many dark arts. The religious factor is in fact not so strong. In Lisbon area where I live there are many so called Christians but truth is most don't give a damn. They embrace religion because it is part of culture, not because of their beliefs. In the end we are a pretty laid back country, with a huge diversity of areas, food, weather, sightseeing – a pretty complete country I'd say, even if very small... We all were 16 once you know, we all wanted to be different and change the world. The thing is that for me the world is all but normal. It is a complex manipulative mechanic worm in which we are entwined. And scene-wise in most cases it ends up to become what they hate so much – all so temporary & out of focus. A person has to realize that things are not black & white, there are tones that fade & cross by our own perception of things. The reality in which we feel & live is the same for all, because we all end up buying our groceries in the same place, we all have the same banks, we all have to pay taxes. All that shit, if one really wants to be different, out of normality, one has to get off all forms of imprisonment, and that is something people are just not willing to try out, because in most cases such 'alternative' people live in urban areas, where you are a rat stuck in a very well-designed labyrinth... In the end we are all part of the same thing, trying to reach the same goal. There is no need to think one is better than the other. We are all pigs, all scum anyway. When I joined Subcaos, a very old punk band, the punk crowd had issues with me having long hair and being from the Black Metal scene, so FUCK THEM! In fact FUCK all people who are so anti this anti that – all for freedom & then behave like Nazis. It is utterly ridiculous... Things are changing, people are being more aware of their surroundings. In a way people are waking up, realizing just how fucked they have been for all these years. We live in dictatorships disguised as democracy. In many ways what we live today is in fact way worse because things are done in front of your eyes & you don't realize it. And these days you cannot point the guilt at one single person. The so called NWO is so massive & entwined in world power that 'the people' just have no power whatsoever... If we are to make a difference, we need to use drastic measures. The politicians need to pay for what they are doing. Selling our souls to banks that make up money out of nothing and so on, no wonder everything is collapsing. This is something I carefully follow and care about, but it is a pretty well built complex system, where the ones who drown are ourselves... [**In terms of USA] The Patriotism, I just don´t get it. The US is from the so called Native people, not from the whites, so how can an American person be so Patriot while it was the Americans who killed native people and still today spit on them? Also the blind pride, being so oblivious to the rest of the world. All the security, the fear factor, the constant war for petrol and still the people don't figure it out. It is so clear for most people in Europe, why not Americans? We here know when our politicians are lying. Maybe we don´t do so much about it, but at least we are aware. Politicians in America are like rock stars. The whole Obama situation was unbearable & in the end he has been way worse than the disgusting Bush. Also in previous times so afraid of the Communists, but now America is giving China the whole power in the world. What is this about?!?! Not to mention the constant "help" for foreign countries like food and so on, but America has a growing alarming rate of people in the streets, of real poor people. The constant incoherence is just incredible. I believe America has fine people, open minded people, people who care deeply for their country and are not blinded by Democrats or Republicans bullshit. America is the awesome country of awesome Rock in general, Muscle Cars, Harley's and Indians and so on. People just have to stop fearing so much. They have to stop caring what they say on FOX news and so on. They have to block off their head each time Politicians come with the terrorist propaganda. I truly believe America is stuck ever since 9/11. Just move one with your lives. Try to work something out. Demand things from the government. Your government is a master at making people distract themselves from the real danger, the danger which is the government putting pressure on you. Things in Europe are somewhat getting close to how things work in US, and that really frightens me. Then again, who decides all this? Things used to work over here, not amazing but way better. It was due to globalization that things collapsed. Trying to get the same laws in different countries. That is just madness. Each country is a different culture. Gladly we Portuguese embrace a lot our culture. We are well rooted in small but deep things, things we will not throw away just because some 3 piece suits tell us to. But as you know TV is molding the people, and the kids of today are indeed less smart than previous generations. It is a fact. America needs to start focusing, stop with all that reality TV, stop trying to spread all over the world that your ways are the right ways, because it isn't. But we all are too weak to dismiss all that. Get a grip people, get a grip!"

Der Blutharsch // Albin S. Julius // Austrian Psychexperimental: "Besides heading on tour in 4 weeks we are currently working on a brand new album. We recorded most tracks but now have to add last bits & some vocals and mix. We are working on a collaboration with UK Band SKULLFLOWER which is great fun. Last but not least we are working on a collaboration with Josef Dvorak – a well known Austrian Satanist expert & psychologist (+*founding member of 'Wiener Aktionismus'*). He is doing the vocals with Austrian band FUCKHEAD... We have a really good underground scene in Austria. Many bands with various different styles as well a few metal bands, but I am not into them too much as most suck & metal in Austria is not really big anymore, with exceptions like Belphegor, Abigor & Amestigon (which is also the band of our guitar player. The only music I listen to which could be considered 'metal' in a wider sense is Stoner Rock. The really good thing in Austria, especially Vienna, is that we have really good venues & loads of bands passing by – as well as state youth radio stations which support independent music. We have a really good music TV station in Austria which promote a lot indie, underground & even metal music. .So i would say in general the music scene is very vivid & quite interesting... Living here is very nice & comfortable. People are quite open minded in their own narrow minded way. but in general I think the main theme is '*to live & let live too.*' It's a traditional society but not rednecks. Austria is a rich country & we have old traditions which people, even young people, adore. And here tradition for most is not negative. We have good food, nice countryside. we love to drink wine – especially in east Austria we have thousands of wine gardens. I love to live here, its one of the best places to be. 3 hours by train I am in Praha, in 2 hours Budapest. Bratislava takes 50 minutes, 4 hours to Italy, 4 hours to Munich... I give a shit about attitude. I fortunately can judge people quite easily & for me it always showed off very soon if someone is tough or a poser. So I always kept away form posers or people who talk talk talk... Most bore me who talk about themselves, or even more about what they do all the time. I am used to people who take action, people who do things instead of pretending to do things... I never gave a fuck about what other people think – we always did what we wanted, and expected that some of these people would try to boycott us. We always found a way to escape from them. In the end, I don't care about anything called 'underground' or 'mainstream' or whatever. I live in the woods & I have only a few friends – I do not need more & I live my life in the way I wanted & this is what I will do 'till I die. My only rule is 'no rules!' I never felt part of any scene, and I never will feel or be part of any scene... I have my own scene & people I let be part of it are doing so many different things & styles. This for me is the most important thing – i am very open, I listen all kinds of music... I know some people who do very conservative music who are much more punk than any punk can ever be. It's a lifestyle, not a term or label to feel part of something. I think most people are too narrow-minded to accept other scenes etc in their own life... There will always be corruption – there will always be power and counter-power. I do not think the world will ever be a 'fair' place, but so what? I do not care. I live my life in my own little way. It's good that people try to change things somehow, but will it be for a better? Time will judge... I never understood why American people in general are so puritan, like with drinking or sex. I never understood why the fuck they think they are the best country in the world. But they think whatever they want, I do not care. I went to the USA a couple of times and liked it a lot, but I do not care. I do not hate the American way of life, but its not my way of life..... Although we are always told we live in a democratic system, the people have not the power to change things. Maybe some buts here or there, but in the end its not even politics or politicians deciding – it's the multinational concerns. The only thing we can do is to boycott them a little bit. We won't change this system but at least we can try not to support it all the time..."

BATTLELORE // Jyri Vahvanen Battlelore // Finnish Fantasy Metal: "Finland is a true metal country. Nowadays the Finnish metal scene consists mostly the extreme edge of metal like 'true' black metal, rougher death metal, hc-punk, ambient metal... I want to make clear that all these answers are my personal opinions & the band Battlelore is 100% non-political & non-religious band, but... I honestly think that we are on a fast-lane to the inevitable end of our known world. Everything we do destroys our environment, morale & physical/mental health all the time faster & faster & there's nothing we can do to stop it. A lot of pretty words & campaigns are going on for the 'better future,' but the ones who have the real power to change things won't care a shit. As long there's something you can get profit from, you'll do anything to maximize it & even after that you still try to double it with any cost. We have had all the options to shape this world to anything we want & we have chosen the way of destruction... It is more than fair that human kind will destroy themselves & drown in their own shit. [**In terms of anarcho-punk & extreme metal uniting in any real sense*] Usually satanic bands are more on the right wing so it would be really hard to unite. The most fanatic supporters would probably raise a fight & extreme acts would happen, but maybe the music could be the glue between these two worlds . I don't know if it would be enough – this would be a really thin chance. I do not see a point why these two worlds need to get together. One united musical world won't happen. I might sound very pessimistic, but I believe that I'm only realistic.... I do not have anything against the, but USA's fanaticism for guns is just crazy. Because it is in your constitutional law is not a good reason to carry a gun. Also your highly sensitive patriotism is a bit weird. Once I asked a US citizen '*why do you keep your national flags out on poles?*' and he got very angry... The biggest problem here is in the European Union. We are paying hundreds of millions to € to cover up the debts of other countries who have totally fucked up their economy. There's a lot to take care of in our own country & all that money is needed, but we give it to other countries who's politicians have let the situation out of hands because of corruption. This really divides people. The real darkness behind the curtain is in exclusion & in decreasing mental health care. Every year they cut the money from social sector..."

BxSxRx // A Chat From Obscene Extreme 2011 // Norwegian Grindcore // "Just spreading the word of The Pig." ***"Who is Mr. Pig?"*** "He wrote all the lyrics, he is Mr. pig. But he's not here – he was born when the Norwegian government tried to make pigs out of people. This was the 1940's; in 1968 he started writing poetry. He got a lot of problems – he have a problem with the booze." "***He had problem with the booze, and then when he went into the well for a couple decades. And he came out & his lips were so beautiful. And when he talked he sounded really beautiful. Then he made music for us.*" "He make lyrics & music for us & we just use toilet. Everyone sing & everyone plays. In 1969 we released our first demo – the first demo of grindcore in Norway." ***"What does Mr. Pig think of the Buddha?"*** "He doesn't like it." ***"What does he think of the Church of Subgenius & JR Bob Dobbs?"*** **He don't know much of anything really – he just read the newspaper sometimes & drink beers & smoke cigars.*" "That is conspiracy, not the truth. He is Pig." ***"What does Mr. Pig think of the Norwegian government?"*** "***He want to vote for three parties. He borrow his votes from his sister & sister in law. To be sure he votes for the right & the left & in the middle.*" ***"Will he run for president himself?"*** "***Yes but he will never be in time for the election because he's so lazy.*" ***"What does Mr. Pig think of Pee Wee Herman?"*** "He likes-a-goldie-hawn-a movies. His biggest hero is Chevy chase in national lampoon movies." ***"What about 'Fletch?'"*** "He likes *Fletch* but has not seen #2 yet, because he wants to see both in one night. But every time he fall asleep because he smokes too much." ***"What's his favorite John Candy flick?"*** "***He likes most the movie Delirious where he write himself into a soap opera. But he don't like Home Alone – he-a-really hate it because it's so cold & he sees too much snow where he lives & he likes no snow except 'National Lampoon's Christmas Vacation.'*" ***"If McCauley Caulkin wanted to fight him in a boxing match for charity, would it happen?"*** "***I think he a lonely person who do a lot of drugs.*" "It's only one of his problems –

he has way too many habits." ***"What are his worst habits?"*** "Pissing in fjords & waking up with sexual ooze in his hair. Because someone tried to make him sausage hair."

PRIMORDIAL // Adam Nemtheanga (Vocalist) // Ireland's Premier Heathen/Pagan Prog BM Act // "Heavy metal continues whether the mainstream pays any attention or not. If you were to look at the 20 biggest music festivals in Europe during any given summer I'm sure you would find nearly half were metal fests. No one is really selling records anymore anyway – however we could say that metal as a subculture is more accepted as something you grow with & not out of in some countries in Europe, and especially in Scandinavia. Not in Ireland however... I don't think anything is entirely unique to any country. The fact though is most stereotypes are often grounded in some truth. For example in Ireland we do have a very definite problem with alcohol & violence – I see it every Saturday night walking through the city. So the drunken 'fighting Irish' has become a cliché, but you know what? There's a reason...We've run through every entire Spinal Tap cliché you could imagine – there's been sex, drugs & rock n' roll but there's also been sight seeing in towns bombed by the UN, armed border guards, fist fights, days spent in airports, drinking binges with famous scientologists... Well let's be honest – I'm the singer in a metal band (& a some time social/historical/political commentator) but I'm not a politician, a terrorist or a CEO of a large company or lobby group. What power do i really have to influence people? Of course the deeper you get into the forest the more people can't see wood for the trees. You have to see things in their relativity. I do personally view the art we make & very often my views as going against the grain & I could argue I've lived outside the confines of society for most of my life. At the same time someone else could argue I'm well within the confines, so we have to take things on individual merit & argument. Things are very often grey & not black or white... Traditionally metal was fantastical & escapist, and punk had a social conscience. These two things are somewhat impossible to reconcile, as punks often find metal too right wing or at least how they define that, while at the same time place themselves upon a very precarious moral ivory tower. Of course, in contrast, metal can often seem to glorify stupidity & every now & again i think it could do with a little more conscience and less escapism. That said, we can see the amount of punks gravitating towards metal musically in the last couple of years, this to me makes sense because ultimately punk is often musically redundant as anything other than socially driven protest music. As you grow older & want to expand on other themes you realize that metal has far more musical scope for doing so. Punks just bring their politics with them into the metal scene & expect to make the rules within a different scene fit theirs. This is where problems start – Antifa canceling extreme metal shows, etc. Whether black metal is on the right or not is not really the question, or whether i agree with them, but the fact remains that in a society which supposedly upholds freedom of speech you need both sides of left & right to create the social middle ground. Basically we need the clowns on both sides to put things into perspective.... Relating to my last answer I find it fascinating that, for example, The Tea Party in The States and The Occupy Movement basically oppose fundamentally the same thing – the failure of the current system. Don't forget the current corruption collapse & rebuilding that will happen has happened many times before in the 20th century. Only this time we have the details at our fingertips within seconds. The Arab Spring is very interesting & I wonder will the Arab nations cope with building democracies better than many African countries did after the end of colonialism? Democracy can take decades, even centuries, to build. Already people are back in the Egyptian capital demonstrating the lack of pace of change. Though do you hand over the running of a country to Facebook agitators? The power vacuum is being filled by extremists, which is not what anyone wants either... I've been to The USA now many times & always enjoyed traveling. I find the positive attitude people have really uplifting, sometimes considering the resigned gloom that seems to permeate Ireland. Of course the fact that most states are bigger than most European countries & a lot of people will never even leave the state and therefore have no interest in much of the rest of the world I find both fascinating & troubling. Also the connection between health care & communism i find odd. Bismarck was first to introduce that in Europe! The EU consists of 27 states, some within the monetary union & some waiting to join. Many people in Ireland would most definitely tell you we have a two tier health system & it's only a matter of time before full college fees are re-introduced. Unemployment right now is at about 15% & emigration is running at the thousands per month. Definitely in countries with even bigger problems like Hungary, Romania & most of Eastern Europe or even Spain with higher unemployment. And Italy with a higher debt to GDP ratio they would have worse tales to tell. The truth as i said before is often grey & not black and white.... The world better pray the EU doesn't dissolve because if you think the market crash after the fall of Lehman brothers was massive, this will be catastrophic. Imports into the EU will collapse – countries like Germany will have no export economy. It would spell economic ruin. The EU can handle peripheral countries like Ireland, Portugal or even Greece requiring bailouts but a lot depends on Italy, the 3rd biggest economy in Europe & a massive foreign bondholder sorting it's economy out. Recognizing the difficulties the notoriously crazy Italian political system has even been suspended to allow an unelected economist to run the country! Some countries might default like Greece & Europe will take the hit. But it won't dissolve, I don't think. However we can see now the absolute difficulties in trying to stream so many different economies running at different speeds..."

LIVSTID // Kristian (Vocalist) // Norwegian Grind/HC // "Bergen, our hometown, is really known for the black metal scene. A load of the bands that are really big are from Bergen. It's a really small town, a suburb. So actually its really strange because the role of black metal in that town has overtaken the role of everything to do with revolting against anything – its swallows up the whole thing. So a lot of the kids there, they've been sucked into the black metal scene &

you will not see anything like the bands playing here. If they're playing metal its either death or black, with the same references – its very, very homogenized & incestuous." *"Are you completely bored by it?"* "Completely fuckin' bored! Fuckin' hate it! Fuckin' ridiculous, stupid shit… I'll tell you one really nice story. We were in night club & we are drinking & there's a few guys from Gorgoroth there. We're bunched at the table, my friend has to take a piss, and one of the Gorgoroth guys he has to ask to move. He says, *'No, I won't move. I don't care – It's your problem.'* So my friend, he doesn't give a shit, he says, *'Well I will just step on your lap and go.'* So he does that, but then when he comes back the Gorgoroth guy says: *'That's good, that's good – you are a egotistical, uh, only care about yourself, don't care about other – good! That is a good way!'* What fucking bullshit man, this guy, what being an asshole, this guy. Stoo-pid idiot…" *"In the United States people generally feel Burzum is synonymous with white power. Is it the same in Norway?"* "In Norway nobodies gonna think its synonymous with a swastika. White power in Norway is really weak – it doesn't have a root. It's not a big group of people. You know, they killed someone in Norway, and that really puts the arrow through the balloon of white pride in Norway. They stabbed a black guy to death. He was a young guy, and it was a really big thing – and they really only killed him because of his color. And since that, the whole recruitment for that scene is really bad. These guys into this Norse mythology, they are more like history freaks, nature freaks that like to go camping & make brutal music…"

MINCING FURY AND GUTTURAL CLAMOUR OF QUEER DECAY & SPINELESS FUCKERS // Reef (Vox in MINCING/Drums in SPINELESS) // Czech Grindcore // "Extreme music is really hidden in the deep underground here in Europe, although if you want to come to see any brutal acts, it is very easy as there are many underground gigs every week. Many young bands are playing here now but they usually do not have their own face & style. Here in Czech Republic we have very strong world-wide known grind/death scene with many great bands – PIGSTY, INGROWING, GRIDE, POPPY SEED GRINDER, JIG-AI, FLESHLESS, GODLESS TRUTH, SPASM, MELANCHOLY PESSIMISM, DESPISE & many more. People here in Czech are really angry to the politics of today's situation – corruption everywhere, bad important decisions from the government, stupid people on high positions, etc. We had the opportunity to become leaders in Europe after 1989 when the communists were beaten. Instead we built a corrupted state with lazy people & now we are just 'in the middle' of The EU. On the other hand, we are still lucky people in comparing with some other states around… During our 3 European tours [*with MINCING FURY*] we had a lot of fun & crazy stories. Nightmares like crashing the van 1000 km from home, sleeping in the field during heavy rain, travelling almost 500 km for a cancelled gig, no beers/water on a well-known UK fest for £12 for 16 people for the food + promise that the rest of the money for gas will be sent later on via bank transfer… Here in the EU we do not understand why people from the USA think that only they have the right to 'save the world.'

Also, many internal US rules sounds quite strange for us, sometimes even funny. From many people I heard that in 'the most freedom country,' there is not so much freedom as it is announced. There are many more issues which US people shall take care about instead of 'saving the world,' like unemployment, the prison system. Besides, the unhealthy style of life makes USA the state of fat people, not like in a TV serials where only nice & slim people are there. Public health (non)system in USA is also very strange to us… I personally hate political shit – I do not care if anybody is on the left or on the right. It is still the same bullshit. In any case, extreme parties can be dangerous... I do no think EU will break, but this will be the best solution indeed. The idea about united EU is twisted...”

NAHEMAH // Pablo Egido (Vocalist) // Blackened Spanish Prog Metal // “At this moment we are taking a break to create our forthcoming album. The new album is going to be very important in our career as musicians & artists, so it will take us a big part of 2012. During this year we want to reach the perfection in our music & in our lives as well... Underground music in a country like Spain is almost non-existent. We love the underground movement but not in the Spanish way, and I think that sometimes is better to be out of that 'almost inexistent' Spanish underground movement, because there is a lot of stupidity in it. We feel better being independent & walking our own way. Musical culture in our country is really rich in general, but most people are focused on mainstream/Latin music. The labels & promoters don't support music like metal because that is not in the Spanish mentality & culture. So if you are an underground band in Spain you will feel alone. That's why we have more fans outside than inside our country, and we play more gigs around Europe than in Spain. It's hard to say that we feel more comfortable playing our music abroad, but it's true... Spain is a Mediterranean & warm country, and people are warm & passionate. We enjoy life because it is too short & so many people in other European countries think Spaniards are lazy, dancing Flamenco all the day & attending bullfights. But that's not true – we are a modern country with very good people & ideas, we work double the hours & we get half the salary than other European countries to remain in the 'Euro-business market level.' But we have a very bad politician class... We have always used our art & music to express ourselves with more transcendental codes. But not as an alienation. If you are alienated you are out of the reality and artists are part of the reality. Music is art and never has to be mixed with politics. We are artists, not politicians and if you mix art & politics you are mixing the most beautiful & sacred thing in the world together with the dirtiest. Music is to recreate the concepts of beauty & if some musician uses politics then it's because a not-so-good artist needs other ways to express his message. I think that it is good to be revolutionary, as it is the only way to change what we dislike. All the revolutions we have seen during the last year are good attempts to change the reality but that ways of revolution are obsolete & almost useless, in my opinion. They apparently have experienced success, but I think that if we really want to change our world we have to create new ways of making revolution adapted to the requirements of our time, not the old ones... Is too global to say that there exists a Pan-European movement towards right wing politics. Politics in Europe are very complex because every country has their own complex laws & ideologies. Everyone that has studied universal history knows that what is happening is the natural politic cycle, called 'particracy'. When there is a deep crisis or economical depression, the right wing politics become the governors. After that economical depressions have been overcome, the right parties are kicked off the government & the moderate/socialist parties become the governors and so on..."

Sakis Fragos // Editor-Publisher of Rock Hard Magazine in Greece // "I used to publish ROCK HARD magazine in Greece, but for the time being, I halted the release of the publication due to financial problems. I have launched www.RockHard.gr now... [In Greece] we have generally interesting bands in terms of music in the underground, but they do not seem to have the right attitude when it comes to playing live or recording. They are pretty much amateurs, while they pretend to be 100% professionals. But we have hundreds of bands, many of whom have potential... The biggest misconception is that ALL GREEKS are liars and thieves – and many people abroad believe that, too. They cannot understand that life in Greece is too expensive & we do not earn much money in general to get a decent life. Now with the austerity measures, life has become almost unbearable, as we have suffered a reduction of almost 40% in our salaries & pensions, whereas we have plenty of new taxes. Apart from unemployment that has officially reached around 25%, we have many poor people... [****In terms of underground culture**] I generally think that all edges are parts of a huge circle – in a way they tend to reach each other. As the extreme leftists & extreme right wings are almost the same in culture (even though they do not realize it), the same applies for music. In Greece there are demonstrations almost everyday about that. People believe (and they are right) that some politicians need to pay for the damage they've created to the country. Not a single one of them has been punished so far & we are on the verge of bankruptcy... Governments always need to create some 'fears' to make people afraid of something. Look what has happened in the last 10 years in the US with 'terrorists.'"

CRUADALACH // Jan Vrobel (Vocalist) // Czech Folk Metal // "I'm the proud member of the tribe of Cruadalach, which is basically a folk metal act. Our style can be described like that, however we try to do our best to simply do as great music as possible and we don't care about the genre. In 2012 we would like to perform as much as possible – our action radius is the whole of Central Europe including Germany, Poland, but also Slovenia & Croatia. In the past I was a member of one of the first Czech death metal bands ever, Nemesis, which was based even before the fall of communism, if I'm right. Unfortunately I dont know a lot about that since in that time I was a child & I played in Nemesis late phase, from 2005 on... From my point of view the European scene is generally more abstract, more 'fake' if you want me to use this word, however I dont use it in a bad connotation. Metal bands here sing about fairy tales, not their true lifestyle.

They establish a myth around themselves across the genres. In United States rock music tries to be far more authentic; people sing about their inner problems and struggle, where we prefer to create myths & stories which have nothing to do with us. American metal is far more direct... In Czech Republic metal surely is ignored by mainstream media, however the best-selling Czech band is a former speed metal group. That makes no change anyway, because if there is some rock music appreciated it is connected to our Communist 'heritage' and absence of good taste. We had some potentially good metal bands in the early 90's, like Masters Hammer or Root, but today you can find good music in totally unrelated genres, especially in alternative pop or funk. If something should represent Czech scene, I strongly recommend bands Tata Bojs, Sunshine, the last album of alternative pop singer Lenka Dusilova 'Baromantika' or the old prog rock band from the time of Communism, Flamengo and its 'Kure v hodinkach.' I appreciate Czech rap band Prago Union, but it probably cant have any good impression on anybody who doesnt speak Czech because it is especially about games with our language. I could give you plenty of tips on interesting acts, but they would be interesting for you probably only from point of view of student of music than music fan. Its Czech music for Czech people... When I started to travel more, I gained a bigger overview about our own Czech nature and I have to admit that stereotypes about us are generally more true than I was ready to admit myself. We are considered to be skeptical, problematic, smart-ass people. That is generally true. Also well known is our Anti-Gypsicism 'cause our country fails in dealing with some kind of ethnic problems. In other ways Czech people very generous; compared to Polish or Slovakian people we've a bigger sense for humour and are not that proud or serious. We are basically atheists; we have big tolerance to homosexuality which is not the example of every country in Eastern Europe. Czech people are basically rather depressed because we have lower life-standard in comparison to Germany or Austria cause of Communism, but in general we have pretty good level. Czech people in majority have also problem with being part of bigger pacts & alliances, because of the former influence of Soviet Union. From the same reason we are generally very Euro-skeptical, but also an unfortunately Anti-American nation. I believe people here should be more happy, less angry, more educated & less complaining and bullshitting around. On the other hand I admire our general tolerance... I dont care about 'scene' – only about music. Liking the sound of bagpipes isn't reason to pretend I worship Celtic Gods, you know. My mind is free, I listen to many music across the genres from 70s hard rock to dubstep. Recently I was listening to Gorillaz, the neo-folk Death In June & Rage Against The Machine. I'm interested in literature across genres as well & I can watch *Terminator* as well as *Stalker* from Andrej Tarkovskiy. When I faced, as you say, Czech anarcho-punk or black metal scene, it was always full of bullcrap. I don't want to generalize, but who are they to tell me how I have to live to be worthy to play 'their' music? Shut the fuck up, really. The most admirable bands are those which are individualist and really themselves, not trying to be part of some scene so hard... It is simple – European metalheads dont give a fuck about politics. Metal, in our minds, is connected to stories, emotions, myths, fairy-tales – not to social problems. Politics in Czech and Europe in general is just a tiny part of metal music and I'm glad it's like that. I care about politics but when I listen to music I want to have my soul in peace & not be poisoned by somebodies opinion... Man, I believe we have other problems that you simply can't imagine. What you call cheap or free college or healthcare is hardly free when its paid by money of every citizen & believe me our taxes are incredibly high. So 30-60% of everything you earn here goes to the state. I believe that historically your country didn't opress you (as Communism did here) so you have more fear from private sector & power of corporatons, whether in Czech Republic its perfectly opposite. I saw one documentary of Michael Moore & I could laugh my ass off when he sets his 'arguments' for having in The USA Czech-like healthcare. Man, dont believe this propaganda – every coin has two sides..."

SEITA // Michel Gambini // Amsterdam Death/Thrash (via Brazil) // "The culture is very different & in the beginning Amsterdam was difficult. Like you were talking about this right wing wave, in America as well as Europe. I think 10 years ago it was more welcome. We don't have that much a problem since we made friends & understand the society. The people are more laid back, more reserved & a little more serious. People are friendly when you meet them in social life, but to have a real connection – the culture is very individualistic. In Brazil you are sleeping & all of a sudden there is a friend kicking you in the back because my mother let him go inside. He kick me, we have a beer, that's how we wake up. But here you have to call, make an appointment, set the time & when & look at the agenda... The Brazilian people, even when things seem really unrealistic, they have this goal that they will still try to achieve – they don't have any shame. But, for example the Dutch people – they're not like this. They analyze, they are very rational, they see the chances that '*if this project will fail*' is a lot higher... The culture is very behaved. Everything has its place, its time. In Brazil you wake up & people are shouting at their kids, dogs barking, every street you go... In Spain we played a garage in one of these industrial areas. I look at this metal roof, so I think the sound will be shit. But then there came a lot of people, the place was packed. When we played, people were insane – I've never seen anything like this. We play & they force us to come back, we play everything we have, we tried to leave the stage & they wouldn't let us. The promoter said: '*you have to play something or their gonna start breaking stuff*.' The guy took the microphone & said '*you wanna hear the same songs again?*' so we played... The last time I did mushrooms was like 4 years ago. I did probably the most stupid thing you can do & that's go to the center of Amsterdam on New Years Eve. My ex-girlfriend got lost & did not recognize me anymore – she did not know who I was. And I also started to freak out. I grabbed one side of my face – '*ok, you need to take control; you have to take her and go home.*' So I grabbed her but then the streets were on fire – it was like a war zone. The paranoia was awful. Then I decided this was not for me..."

SOULSELLER RECORDS // Jorn Rap (Owner) // Extreme Metal Label (Holland) // "Well I started the label 15 years ago – I was still in high school. I released the first vinyl in 98... That's the good thing about metal people – they want to own things. Otherwise, I'd have gone bankrupt already. I have friends working at Universal & EMI, and they say the business market now is the e-market – everything is going down except for online... I'm not very familiar with Amsterdam – most metal people I know are from Southern Holland. The guys from a Swedish death metal band on my label, the first thing they asked when they arrived in my hometown was, '*where are the windmills?*' People will keep asking for the next 100 years to come. I'm not sure if I would recommend living here. I like living in Holland – when the weather is good, it's a good country, but it can rain for months & months. Not much to do, you get bored easily... I like Sweden, Stockholm a lot – remains me of Amsterdam. Norway is like the most expensive city in the world. If you want to hang out on a beach & do nothing, you go to Greece. In Spain, you take one of the islands. I've been to Crete only, but from what I remember the old buildings were really great. Millions of stones put together thousands of years ago, of old buildings & stuff.... A lot of those bands come out as an '*evil band*,' but these days it's a lot of black & roll. It's all about sucking the life out of people when playing live. I don't consider myself a Satanist at all – I'm into this for the music..."

MASTER // Paul Speckmann (Guitarist) // Classic USA Death/Thrash (via Czech Republic) // "These days I am only focusing on Master & it really takes up most of my time with the many tours/festivals we play throughout each year. The newest CD called *The New Elite* should hit the market in May on Pulverised Records & we'll continue to tour the world on this new album in 2012... Obviously I grew up in America & in all societies control is the key thing. People are often led to the slaughter; they truly believe what the governments tell them. The youth of today are brainwashed & it's really a sad state to be in. When I was young & growing up in Chicago, people were marching against authority & causing chaos across the country. Today, the youth just roll over & take it. Free thinking is a thing of the past in my eyes, anyway. It was once power to the people & now it's power _over_ the people! The biggest non-reality is that America is free. What is the biggest misconception of your country? I laugh when all these people are looking for 'The American Dream.' What dream is this? I suppose a shit economy, no jobs & nowhere to live are something to dream of. Thankfully I found my European Dream here. I began playing shows & working with my music two weeks after I stepped off the airplane for rehearsals, followed by my first trip to Japan. I have been playing my music ever since then. So many people are afraid to leave there own backyard & live and die in their parent's home. Let me tell you people – there is a big world out there, so don't sell yourself short & marry your first sexual experience. It's better to test the waters before settling down... At the Obscene Extreme in 2010 all walks of life were stage-diving during the Master set at 6:00 pm – the music brought us all together. I listened to bands like GBH, The Exploited & Discharge while growing up in Chicago and for me this is what Crust-Punk was, so I can relate to this music still today! Fuck the establishment! It's time for to revolt! The so-called organized governments are continually dictating the way we should all live. Rebellion is the only chance we the free people have at this time! Robots are coming to take over the world if we don't stand up. George Orwell's *1984* is quickly becoming a reality... Americans continually bully other countries into agreeing with them – the rest of the world is brainwashed into following the American ideal. You can find just about every American fast food joint here as well. The whole world is getting fatter & following the footsteps of American pigs... Americans forget that they are all immigrants. Stealing all the land from the Indians was the goal of the Europeans & they were successful. The Hispanics were swindled by the American armies & forced to give up the Southwest. I was an illegal alien in Europe for the first 5 years. I did radio & newspaper interviews & the police never came to my door. While touring with Krabathor in the USA the customs people were calling my old roommate in Arizona to check on the guys. The Krabathor guys had 10 year USA visas so this was simply uncalled for! Things were a bit more difficult for me when the borders were here. I had to lie to customs officers & say I was just traveling whenever questioned. Keeping calm when they spoke to me was the biggest challenge ... I pay about 50 dollars per month for health care services, but this covers everything. When I first tied the knot I had to look for work in order to get the free health care but as time went on I couldn't make the appointments anymore with more shows and tours & finally decided to just pay for services! Of course there are big dreary prisons all across Europe, but they are not filled & are not continually expanding! There is no perfect world – people die every day just the same here, but violence is more apt to come from the silly Nazi worship that continues here as people have still not figured out that Shitler is dead. There is still hope for humanity I believe, but opinions are like assholes and everyone has one! Let's face it there is not enough food or space on the planet for everyone. Education is needed. The rich would have to share the wealth, so to speak. I live in a unique situation over here in Czech. My father in law is a devout socialist, I am married to his happily free daughter & I work for an Eastern German company selling merchandise for bands or doing odd jobs on tours. My father in law says that when the Russians were here, families were fed the same food, had the same amount as their neighbors. Mother in law speaks of the long lines waiting for a loaf of bread & 1 banana. But interestingly my father in law said there were no homeless or drug addicts on the streets, as they were sent for reconditioning. Sounds like Orwell again, but interesting nevertheless! They had torture camps over here for if you didn't agree with the Russian ideology. I have been exposed to quite a bit here & realize I was blessed with freedom growing up in the USA. I am proud to be an American but I am not so sure about the ideology.

MANZER // Shaxul (Mastermind) // French Black Metal // "I work every day for my label LEGION OF DEATH Records, my full time job for 4 years now (the label existing for 11 years). My main band is MANZER; we are currently working on our first full length album & hope it will be available by the end of

2012. My first serious band was HIRILORN (formed 1994). It is mainly since this date that I became really involved in the underground. I've never been fond of the French underground because I always thought it was better in the past. There was the Heavy Metal movement (KILLERS, SORTILEGE, BLASPHEME, ADX, H-BOMB, STRATTSON), the Death/Thrash movement (AGRESSOR, LOUDBLAST, MERCYLESS, NOMED), the Black Metal movement (MÜTIILATION, VLAD TEPES, BELKETRE), but in the mid-90's it started to be very trendy & I got totally disinterested. I focused on underrated scenes in the world. But with time, it appeared to me that some valuable bands were fighting in the shadows, in various French regions. Paris is still the cradle of all trends in France, with very few valuable bands. With my label, I support the French bands that deserve it. You are right, Europe is always seen as a Metal paradise, but it's so wrong. Trends & commercial stuffs rule supreme. For example, since the creation of the HELLFEST in France (a kind of French WACKEN), it became even more difficult to organize underground gigs. People say they keep their money for this expensive & stupid fest. The situation was already awful in the past, as France has never had a strong Rock/Metal country. But now this is quite a disaster. Fortunately there are still people fighting but it's true that Metal people in France are divided in 2 parts – the underground maniacs & the "overground trendies." And I think it's great that underground metal is ignored by the establishment media & everyday culture as it's not meant to be among all the other pop shit for the masses. Some cunts want metal to be accepted by everyone but fuck those tolerant hippies... Most people think that Paris is beautiful and romantic. This is the exact contrary – it is ugly and dirty (*some museums are interesting but the rest stinks*) & people there are very arrogant & disrespectful. People from Paris think that *Paris = France* and the rest are uneducated peasants. It makes me puke, especially because I am really into the history & culture of my region Pictavia [*Poitou-Charentes-Vendée area, in French*]. Very few people abroad are aware that each region in France has its own history, culture, language, gastronomy, etc. For a very long time, French politicians tried to eradicate this & wanted to establish Parisian Supremacy, which means that everybody will be turned into the same soulless piece of waste flesh. It works very well as humans are stupid & get brainwashed. With MANZER, we have some songs in Parlanjhe [*the language in Pictavia*] as a symbol of our own resistance. Fuck religions & politics... Youngsters tend to see someone like me as a dork because I hate their shitty modern/Western way of life & because I am into traditional/ancestral stuff. Day by day politicians want to fuck with everyone & French people hate when someone wants to suppress their rights. Most of times French people are pretentious bastards. I've noticed that even abroad & I'm always ashamed when seeing a bunch of French people behave like assholes... I hate trends where religion & politics are involved. Most of the time I can ignore such stuff but of course it would be better without 'religious BM,' 'NSBM,' all this brainless crap. I don't live in an 'altered reality' world, I just feel like I found my own path. But of course you can't escape from living in this 'normal world' made of human sheep... I am interested in anarchy but not as everybody sees it, it is not left-wing or right-wing, it has nothing to do with politics as a whole. The kind of anarchy I imagine, which would lead to nihilism, can indeed be linked with metal, especially black & death. Needless to say that punk & metal have also influenced each other on a musical basis. But to create one entity? No way. To unify everything is rarely a good solution. Politics belong to the 'normal world', so bands into this are useless. There is no fucking hope on this planet so why trying to change the world with political lyrics? This is dumb. And this is the main aspect that separates punk from metal. They have their own respective trends & problems, so uniting them wouldn't change anything – it would be even worse. But collaboration is not excluded... I have many Arab friends (metal-heads) in countries where there's been this so-called 'Arab Spring.' So what's the situation now? Everything is ruled by military authorities & Islamists are beginning to take full control. The situation is worst than before. But the western world prefers to spread. Bullshit! We already live in Orwell's *1984*, you know. I'm definitely pessimistic. I may revolt when I hear or see things I hate but it won't change a damn thing. Not that I want to surrender – but I try to do the best for myself without caring too much about the rest, except people I respect. In the Western World, most people 'revolting' are middle-class people who live a peaceful life with their beloved money & some revolts are fake and made by hipsters. The whole system in which we live should be destroyed but it's impossible because even the protesters you're talking about don't believe in such a drastic way. We're all fucked & doomed man. I like to call my way of seeing things as 'satanism,' symbolic & not religious, of course, because I am against all established systems – religious, political, economic, etc. This is my individualist way to call the fact that I'm against all the idiotic things. This is atheistic satanism, I'm a 'Satanatheist,' hehe... [**In terms of immigrant xenophobia in Europe] Bullshit from Nazi's, who are a bunch of brainless scum. Actually immigrants are not responsible for the change, but the governments themselves. I told you that in France there is a specific culture, history & language in every region. I don't really feel French but more Pictavian, so I am far from feeling 'European.' Europe could become like the USA one day, as people tend to forget heritage. The problem with conservative politics is that they also believe in standardization. They think they are here to protect some kind of ancestral culture but not at all – it's all about clichés. [**Asked if he were given 'total control as an absolute dictator & could just remodel the world in his own twisted image] I have no faith in the human; I would think of my own future first. So the planet would be drowned in a total anarchy. Maybe you will find it a cartoon or non-serious answer, as sometimes people think you can't be serious if you refuse to discuss politics. When I say I hate them and I believe in individualism and in total nihilist anarchy, I am dead serious. Discussing existing politics & finding a solution to make a better world is pointless and shows how people are entirely manipulated by the system. Oh well, I hate dictators so I couldn't be one anyway. Once again, let the world burn. Future generations are doomed because of Man's idiocy; this is a simple fact & that's all..."

Guilty Parties

Brutal Truth, Rotting Christ, LAIBACH,
Wolfbrigade, Agathocles, Killing Joke,
Master, Funeral Winds, NAHEMAH,
Enochian Crescent, Moonsorrow, Defeated
Sanity, First Blood, Hello Bastards,
Abortion, Panthiest, GURA, Arkangel,
HATE, Repulsione, Dehuman, General
Surgery, Corpus Christii, Fides Inversa,
Excavated, Primordial, Splitter,
Cruadalach, Shit Comet, Solid Noise,
Pyramido, Black Breath, LIVSTID,
Ingurgitating Oblivion, Soulseller
Records, El Schlong, Melting Walkmen,
Weltbrand, BxSxRx, SEITA, Der
Blutharsch, Agantyr, Mincing Fury And
Guttural Clamour Of Queer Decay,
Metastazi, Crying Steel, Manzer, Burning
Black, Curby & Obscene Extreme, Jeroen
van Valkenberg, Sakis Fragos, Will
Carruthers & Mr. John Sinclair

**thank you all & anyone missed

Inspired by the legendary works of Henry Miller, Jack Kerouac and Hunter S. Thompson, Ryan Bartek traveled the USA to create his own heavy metal / punk rock road saga of extreme journalism. 1 year, 35 States, 600+ hours on Greyhounds later, "*The Big Shiny Prison*" was released – a unique travel book featuring hundreds of face-to-face interviews with legends in the metal/punk undergrounds, as well as other alternative & fringe cultures in America.

"FORTRESS EUROPE" (The Big Shiny Prison Vol. II)' chronicles the author backpacking Europe and his intense exploration of fringe and alternative culture. This genre-defying work features hundreds of face-to-face interviews with a number of legends in extreme metal, punk rock, industrial, experimental, rock, electronic, as well as many other alternative cultures in Europe today.

Less a music book and more a tribute to the Beat Generation, "*Fortress Europe*" combines the classic autobiographical road novel with current European Counterculture. The result is an odyssey of monumental scope that has amassed a cult following since its Free PDF release February 2012.

"*Fortress Europe (The Big Shiny Prison Vol. II)*" features appearances/interviews with members of Brutal Truth, Rotting Christ, LAIBACH, Wolfbrigade, Agathocles, Killing Joke, Master, Funeral Winds, NAHEMAH, Enochian Crescent, Moonsorrow, Defeated Sanity, First Blood, Hello Bastards, Abortion, Panthiest, Arkangel, HATE, Repulsione, Dehuman, General Surgery, Corpus Christii, Fides Inversa, Excavated, Primordial, Splitter, Pyramido, Black Breath, Ingurgitating Oblivion, El Schlong, Spacemen 3 & legendary Detroit writer Mr. John Sinclair + more.

**Ryan Bartek is a writer & musician from Detroit (MI) now living in Portland (OR). He is author of 6 books: "*Anticlimax Leviathan*," "*The Big Shiny Prison (Volume One)*," "*Fortress Europe (The Big Shiny Prison Vol. II)*," "*Return To Fortress Europe (BSP Vol. III)*," "*The Silent Burning*," and "*To Live & Die On Zug Island.*" Bartek is guitarist/vocalist of grindcore band VULTURE LOCUST, as well as the extreme metal act SKULLMASTER.

He also performs acoustic/antifolk as "The Real Man In Black" and spoken word performances as his regular old self. LURKING STRANGERS, his new multi-styled punk rock band, will be debuting 2018. Known for his journalism in the metal/punk undergrounds due to his long-term output for mass-market magazines, webzines & fanzines, R. Bartek is also the shadowy figure behind the press relations firm Anomie PR, servicing thousands of media outlets globally.

All albums & books have been released under Anomie INC / Anomie Press, as FREE digital downloads. Download Bartek's library/discography FREE @

WWW.BIGSHINYPRISON.COM

CPSIA information can be obtained
at www.ICGtesting.com
Printed in the USA
JSHW030516120922
30255JS00002B/154